STUDIES IN HISTORY, ECONOMICS AND
PUBLIC LAW

Edited by the
FACULTY OF POLITICAL SCIENCE
OF COLUMBIA UNIVERSITY

NUMBER 557

THE GERMAN SOCIAL DEMOCRATIC PARTY, 1914-1921

BY

ABRAHAM JOSEPH BERLAU

The German Social Democratic Party 1914 - 1921

BY

ABRAHAM JOSEPH BERLAU

1970

OCTAGON BOOKS

New York

TABLE OF CONTENTS

PREFACE

THE German revolution of 1918 and the Weimar Republic represented, seemingly, a radical break with the Wilhelminian Empire. The extent of this break may be indicated by pointing to the introduction of republican and responsible parliamentary governments in Germany and her member-states, the grant of a franchise as democratic and liberal as any in force in 1919, the extension and perfection of social, protective legislation, the relegation of the power and influence of militarism, and the markedly changed role assigned to Germany in post-1919 Europe.

Actually, however, the domestic and foreign policies pursued by the German republic do not bear out the assumption that—within the limitations imposed upon Germany by military defeat and the Treaty of Versailles—a radical break with the political traditions of the Empire had indeed taken place. In spite of the revolution and of the endeavors of many German statesmen, democratic ideals in internal affairs and pacific objectives in international relations failed to marshal growing public support. The democratic ideals embodied in the German constitution did not become firmly embedded in the hearts of the individual citizen and, consequently, the efficacy of German statutory changes was severely limited.

A large number of diverse factors combined to insure that many of the essential changes introduced in Germany after 1918 remained purely formal and sterile. Not the least among these owed their inception and effectiveness to the political parties in Germany and to their rivalries. The three parties in particular which, as it were, had acted as godfathers to the young republic, and had guided its destinies during its first year bequeathed to the republic a set of ideas and policies which largely determined the course of the republic in later years.

Among these political parties, the Social Democratic Party assumed a singular status. Alone among all other German parties it had not before 1918 exercised any dominant influence upon the course of Germany policies. Its elevation to the rank of one of the most influential political groups in Germany after 1918 assigned to the Social Democratic Party a crucial role: as the only new factor in the political constellation entrusted with the administration of republican Germany, it could claim the major share of credit for the resulting change—or lack of change. In fact, the policies of the Social Democratic Party during the years preceding the revolution, during the revolutionary period, and during the first years of the republic embody, because of the singular position of that party after 1918, the maximum of the changes which could be expected to result from the establishment of a republic. An examination of the doctrines of the Social Democratic Party during the years from about 1914 to about 1921 therefore reveals, in a large measure, the direction which the revolution and the newly established republic would probably follow.

While the contrast between the Reich that Bismarck founded and the Weimar Republic was all too often not very great, the contrast between the party which successfully defied Bismarck's attempted suppression and the party which contributed its crucial co-operation to the success of the Weimar Republic was extraordinary.

The Social Democratic Party (it was known as the Socialist Party of Germany from 1875 until 1891) represented, in theory, the embodiment of the economic ideas and political objectives of orthodox Marxism. Its program, clearly enunciated at Erfurt in 1891, reiterated in popular language the essential theses of 'scientific' socialism and provided, for a considerable period, the prototype for a Marxian program and a synopsis of Marxian thought. The program of 1891 committed the Social Democratic Party to the dogmas of the accumulation of capital, the concentration of economic power, the pauperization of the exploited proletariat, the inevitability of increasingly severe economic crises, the international solidarity of all workers, and the inevitability of economic and political

class-struggle. Hostility to state and nation were nourished
not only by the exhortations of Marx, but by the experiences
of the party between 1878 and 1891 as well. As its objectives,
the party program envisaged the overthrow of the then dominating economic and political groups, and looked forward to
the socialization of all means of production in order to solve
all social and economic ills.

The dominance of Marxism within the party in 1891 was
due to the particular circumstances prevailing in Germany up to
that time. Side by side with Marxism, the party, from its inception, carried forward the legacy of a different interpretation
of social and economic problems. This (Lassallean) heritage,
in spite of its eclipse during the last quarter of the nineteenth
century, showed surprising powers of resurgence. In fact,
after 1900, Lassallean ideas determined Social Democratic
policies in many important fields to the exclusion of Marxist
views.

The importance of this dual legacy of the Social Democratic
Party has made it advisable to include in the following study
two introductory chapters that examine in some detail the
origins of the party and the rival influences which helped shape
its future course.

This dualism, however, would not in itself be adequate to
account for the picture which the Social Democratic Party presented at the time of the German revolution. The eventual
dominance of Lassalleanism was due to the growing and successful criticism of Marxian postulates, the increasing stake of
the proletariat in existing social and political organizations, the
conservatism of the sprawling bureaucracy of the party, the opportunism bred by the growth of the party into the largest
single political group in Germany, the flowering of nationalism,
and the like, all of which helped whittle away the hopes and
confidence expressed by the Erfurt program. The program indeed never lost its effectiveness as propaganda, but its theories
eventually ceased to be considered as a realistic charter for the
party.

This slow process was precipitated by a number of events which forced the party to choose between various alternative policies, often deprived it of genuine choice so long as it wanted to retain its gains in popularity and voting strength, and finally caused the party to exchange its waning Marxist ideology for a rapproachment to the ideas of older, bourgeois parties. The outbreak of war in 1914, the October 1918 crisis, the revolution, the failure to win a popular majority in the elections to the National Assembly, and the need to differentiate itself sharply from Leninism and its growing inroads upon German socialism after 1917 were the main points of departure for this trend. Its consequences were, however, unfortunate for the German republic: by rejecting its socialist tradition in favor of non-socialist ideals at the very time of its elevation to power, the party obfuscated the thin line of differentiation between its new ideas and those of the older political groups, and the resurgent democratic and Lassallean tendencies of the party failed, therefore, to carry more conviction and influence than did the liberalism of those other parties which had been discredited by their impotence and lack of efficacy under the Empire.

Thus, at the time of the German revolution, the Social Democratic Party was in many ways quite different from what it had been in 1891. Gone were the belief in the theory of crisis, the theory of the pauperization of the masses, the theory of the imminence of a great social-economic catastrophe; gone were the belief in the concentration of capital, the need for violent class-struggle, and the efficacy of the socialization of the means of production. *All* political and economic groups were considered vital to the common weal by the Social Democratic Party in 1919; capitalism was no longer viewed as the bane of the proletariat; and the international solidarity of proletarian interests had given way to the pre-eminence of the national interests of the workers and to marked chauvinistic tendencies. The examination of the policies and objectives of the party during the years 1914-1921 leads to the main conclusion that, by 1921, the Social Democratic Party had, in all essentials, repudiated Marxism and embraced in its stead many of the liberal and democratic views of older, bourgeois parties.

The consequences of this change upon the fortunes of democratic government in Germany will be pointed out in due course. It remains here only to discuss whether or not the above conclusions regarding the Social Democratic Party and its radical departure from the program of 1891 may be accepted without qualifications in view of the fact that many of these departures were brought about under the tremendous pressure of the first World War, the German defeat, the revolution, the Peace Settlement of Paris, and the threat of Bolshevism, and that in many respects its freedom of choice and independence of action were severely limited by these and other conditions beyond the control of the party.

Indeed, in large areas of Social Democratic Party policy, due consideration to the needs of the situation facing Germany or to the necessity of compromise with other political parties restricts the validity of conclusions based on divergences between the policies of the party pursued in 1919 and the traditional, orthodox party program. It would, for example, be rash to conclude that the Social Democratic Party had undergone a far-reaching change of heart because the party in 1919 no longer opposed protective and revenue tariffs, or accepted the provisions of the imperial constitution regarding the duration of Reichstag sessions in disregard of the stipulation of the party program for biennial Reichstag elections, and the like. Such changes reflected only the pressure of outside events or the need to co-operate with other parties in a coalition government, and do not indicate any fundamental modifications of party doctrines. In view of the difficulty presented by these considerations, no conclusions could be based upon such detailed, but for the purposes of this monograph inconsequential, matters facing the Social Democratic governments after 1918, and they have therefore been left out of discussion.

There are, however, a number of areas where the compulsion of the particular situation or the need for compromise would not—or should not—suffice to sway a party as doctrinaire as the Social Democratic Party of 1891, unless the erstwhile doctrines have already lost their hold upon the councils of the party. There are a number of fundamental beliefs whose sacrifice by a doctrinaire party cannot be excused mainly—if at all—by the need for compromise or by external compulsion, and whose sacrifice, even if affected for the sake of compromise or under compulsion, would not restrict the validity of the conclusion that here party fundamentals have been abandoned.

Thus, a party professing a belief in the exclusive benefits and efficacy of the socialization of the means of production, and making socialization the very apex of its economic program, cannot point to its limited freedom of action in justifying its sudden rejection of the idea of socialization as impracticable and impossible. Similarly, due consideration of compelling circumstances or the needs for compromise and co-operation with other parties cannot qualify the conclusions which will be drawn if a party were to introduce, at its first opportunity, a political system radically different from its orthodox teachings, or initiate a foreign policy whose tenor contrasted sharply with its basic, erstwhile philosophy and traditions. In short, the rejection of the cardinal points of socialist and Marxist thought by a socialist party, even if brought about by circumstances or under disabilities inherently beyond the control of the party, can lead to no other conclusion but that essential socialist or Marxian ideas have been repudiated in favor of a different doctrine.

For these reasons, the examination of Social Democratic policy after the revolution has, in the following study, been limited to a discussion of the political ideals which the party strove to instill in the young German republic, and the steps taken by the party to effect these ideals; to the economic program advocated and initiated by the party; and to the field of foreign policy: all areas where no compelling circumstances

may be deemed sufficient to warrant a decisive reversal of
traditional, orthodox party views, and where the dogmatic
confession of a given set of ideas would have extremely restricted the potential scope of compromise and change. It was
hoped that by so doing, the conclusions presenting themselves
as a result of the following study would remain unaffected by
considerations regarding disabilities facing the Social Democratic Party after 1918, and could therefore be much more
firmly established. In fact, the author is grateful that the comparative richness of the sources encountered and their ready
availability have made it possible to concentrate on these fundamental aspects of Social Democratic policy without prejudice
to the adequacy of the sources available.[1]

Any interpretation of a narrowly defined historical subject,
being but a fragment of a much wider scene of historical hap-
penings, must fit readily into the general picture of historical
events and should contribute not only to an understanding of
the subject itself, but to the understanding of the general picture of the era as well. It is hoped that the present study will
fulfill this task and contribute not only to an understanding
of the Social Democratic Party, but to an understanding of
the later history of the Weimar Republic as well.

The author is deeply indebted to Professor John H.
Wuorinen for his encouragement and suggestions during the
writing of this study. Professor Wuorinen had kindly agreed
to read the manuscript and the proofs, and his patient, time-
consuming and detailed criticism constitute a contribution
which the author gladly acknowledges. Professor Ralph H.
Bowen kindly read the manuscript, and his suggestions have
guarded the author against many an error. Dr. John A. Davis
assisted in editing the manuscript, and several members of the

1 The bibliography appended to this volume lists, with but very few
exceptions, only those works which have been cited throughout the volume,
representing only about thirty percent of the works consulted. Both in the
bibliography and in documentation, adequacy, and not completeness, has
been the guiding principle.

Faculty of Political Science, Columbia University, have generously contributed their time and advice in discussing various aspects of this study. Needless to add, the author is solely responsible for the choice of the subjects treated, the sources consulted, the conclusions presented, the translations from foreign languages (unless credit is given in footnotes to other translators), and for all possible errors which may still be found in the text.

A. J. B.

CHAPTER I

THE ORIGINS OF THE GERMAN SOCIAL DEMOCRATIC PARTY

a. The Formation of the Lassallean Group

THE German Social Democratic Party represented the unification of various socialist organizations formed in the decade preceding the unification of Germany. The formation of these organizations had been stimulated by certain developments which left deep and lasting marks on the nascent socialist groups.[1]

Foremost among these developments was the accelerated industrialization of Germany. Limited as it was at the time to but a few regions (for example Saxony and the Wupper-Rhine district), it helped produce among certain sections of the population an atmosphere conducive to socialist objectives and organization. Germany presented only one example among many of the statement that socialist ideas and awareness of social ills tended to spread in proportion to the progress of industrialization.

Less important for the growth of socialism as such than for the growth of political groups and attitudes in general was the increasing pressure for the final unification of Germany. The Zollverein had gradually eliminated some of the commercial obstacles imposed by the existing political and economic system in Germany. Yet the industrial and commercial development made a uniform currency, uniform commercial laws, a uniform tariff system, and a uniform nation-state only the more imperative. The unification of Italy in 1860 made conditions within Germany appear only more disappointing, more galling, and more unbearable.

---

1 For socialist movements in the 1840's and 1850's see Georg Adler, *Die Geschichte der ersten sozialpolitischen Arbeiterbewegung in Deutschland,* Breslau, 1885; and Franz Mehring, *Geschichte der deutschen Sozialdemokratie,* 4 vols., Stuttgart, 1919.

It was a widely accepted belief that the unification of Germany would have to be brought about under Prussian leadership.[2] The liberal revolution of 1848 had failed, and, Prussia excepted, only Austria was strong enough to provide leadership towards unification. But Austria could not adopt a nationalistic program because the very existence of its Empire depended on the denial of nationalism. Thus Prussian leadership towards unification appeared to be a political necessity. In addition, Prussian leadership attracted many liberals in German industry and commerce whose fears of popular leadership towards national unity motivated their opposition to political radicalism.[3]

These hopes for the unification of Germany under Prussian leadership seemed to be endangered by the constitutional conflict raging in Prussia after 1862. Prussia at the time had an electoral set-up which allotted representation to the various electoral districts not on the basis of their population ratios but in proportion to their combined income tax payments. However, the 'Dreiklassenwahlrecht' had repeatedly failed to produce an assembly willing to support the King in his plans for the expansion and modernization of the Prussian army. Rather than yield to the recalcitrant assembly, the King called upon Otto von Bismarck who was willing to administer the state without a budget being voted for several years. In the constitutional struggle which had thus been precipitated, Bismarck had been pitted against the vast majority of liberals in the Prussian diet, and yet the liberal groups throughout Ger-

2 While Ferdinand Lassalle and his party advocated the exclusion of Austria, the 'Kleindeutsche' solution, Wilhelm Liebknecht and the men around him continued to insist on the inclusion of Austria, the 'Grossdeutsche' solution.

3 The fear of democratic institutions played a considerable role not only in the history of Germany at that period but in all of western Europe. As yet neither Disraeli's Reform Bill of 1867, nor the Norddeutscher Bund with its liberal franchise, nor Napoleon III's constitutional reforms had demonstrated that under a democratic franchise political and economic power would not rapidly pass to the fourth estate.

many continued to pin their hopes for the unification of
Germany on Bismarck's Prussian regime and to tone down
their opposition to Prussia. The liberals feared democracy more
than Bismarck's brand of constitutionalism, and Bismarck exploited this fear cleverly by flirting with Lassalle, by allowing
Liebknecht to return from exile to Berlin and by threatening
to grant equal, universal and secret suffrage by government
fiat.[4]

It was in this atmosphere that the socialist parties of
Germany had their beginnings. The early 1860's saw the
emergence of numerous small workingmen's organizations,
associations of small shopkeepers and artisans, and others.[5]
These groups were generally non-political at the time of their
organization, and their programs were restricted to the spreading of education and culture among their members. They
offered instruction in languages, especially German, and in
commercial arts, stenography, and the like.

Very soon, however, these groups were drawn into the
turbulent discussion about the political future of Germany.
They became critical of the contemporary course of German politics, but much less critical of Prussia than of the
German middle states whose particularism seemed to prevent
the long overdue unification of Germany. They reflected, in
general, the hopes of German liberals for the unification of

4 August Bebel, *Aus meinem Leben*, 3 vols., Stuttgart, 1910-14, I, 57 ff.
In the Reichstag debate of September 17, 1878, Bismarck admitted having
favored Lassalle's idea of state-subsidized producers' co-operatives, but
denied ever having considered the idea of a political deal with Lassalle
whose personality, he agreed, charmed him, but who had nothing whatsoever
to offer him politically. *Verhandlungen des Deutschen Reichstages*, XXXV,
40 ff., 66 ff.

5 This movement coincided with the growth of 'Turnvereine', of the
'Gesangvereine', and others. Toelcke, one of the successors of Lassalle in
the presidency of the 'Allgemeiner Deutscher Arbeiterverein', was so impressed with the possibilities of 'Gesangvereine' that he viewed them as the
perfect instrument for rapidly increasing the membership of that organization, thus assuring the early solution of all the social and economic ills
of Germany.

Germany under Prussian leadership, even though Prussia might, in the process, thwart their democratic aspirations.

One of those who under these circumstances actively entered the circle of these 'Arbeitervereine' was Ferdinand Lassalle. A brilliant but erratic character, diverted from the consistent pursuit of any political or other activities by his frequent 'affaires d'amour', he was afflicted with the impatience of the utopian socialists who demanded instant success for their various political or social schemes. He was convinced of his own great mission to an extent which only his utter sincerity prevented from seeming utterly ridiculous. Yet, on the whole, he avoided the unrealistic theories of the utopian socialists as well as the enmity of the powers-that-be. His romanticism vied with his aspirations as a 'scientific' socialist. He was an ardent German nationalist and a partisan of Prussia. During the Italian war against Austria he argued that "now is the moment, while the disintegration of Austria is in progress, to achieve the ascendancy of Prussia... Now is the moment to heal these heavily bleeding wounds... The sympathy for Schleswig-Holstein, the drive for a national attitude in the present crisis, the thirst for national grandeur as such, hate against Napoleon, the feverish desire for national unity, all these flames could combine into a fire feeding on the very obstacles in its path." [6]

In an address on April 12, 1862, later published under the title *Arbeiterprogramm*, Lassalle expressed his political and social ideas. He voiced the belief that revolutions furnished only the legal and formal sanction for changes which had already taken place in society. History was the struggle with nature, misery, poverty and the lack of freedom. Progress represented the gradual defeat of these; and it was the state alone and not the individual which could achieve such progress.

6 Quoted by F. Mehring, *Zur Geschichte der deutschen Sozialdemokratie,* Magdeburg, 1877, p. 8. Lassalle's nationalism presented a romantic brand of nationalism, akin to that of Mazzini, but lent itself later to an interpretation by SPD leaders which was essentially foreign to Lassalle.

" The state is the unit of all these individuals in a moral whole, a whole which multiplies a millionfold the powers available to each of them as individuals." The purpose of the state was, not to protect the individual, but to enable the individual to attain a cultural and moral level which he could never attain alone. Lassalle went on to say that the state could not fulfill this, its proper function, unless it passed into the control of the fourth estate by means of universal and direct manhood suffrage.[7]

Lassalle strongly opposed the Marxian view that the state was the product of class differences and that its function was the perpetuation of the existing distribution of power. While Marx believed that the state would disappear, together with class-differences, in a socialized world, Lassalle viewed the state as a separate power, independent of the nature of society, and indispensable for the realization of the socialist ideals.[8]

The Arbeiterprogramm received wide attention in Germany and, in 1863, Lassalle was asked for advice by a committee for the convocation of a General German Workers' Congress. Lassalle answered in March, 1863, in an open letter which developed his immediate program more fully.[9] " The working class must constitute itself as an independent political party and make universal, equal and direct suffrage the rallying cry and banner of that party. Only representation of the working class in the legislative bodies of Germany can satisfy its legitimate interests in politics." As for his economic views, Lassalle accepted the validity of Ricardo's Iron Law of Wages to which, he claimed, eighty-nine to ninety-six percent of all Prussians were subject. Hence individual thrift or the self-help of workers was destined to fail. He concluded that producers' co-operatives established with the financial aid of the state offered the

7 E. Bernstein (ed.), *F. Lassalles Reden und Schriften*, II, 9-50.

8 P. Weidmann, *Programme der sozialdemokratischen Partei Deutschlands von Gotha bis Goerlitz*, 1926, pp. 15-16.

9 *Offenes Antwortschreiben, Lassalles Reden und Schriften*, II, 409 ff.

only way to bring about the economic and moral improvement of the fourth estate.

Lassalle's interest in the conditions of the workers led, in May, 1863, to the founding of the ' Allgemeiner Deutscher Arbeiterverein' under his presidency. The only stated purpose of the organization was the peaceful and legal struggle for equal, universal and direct suffrage.[10] Lassalle expected the party to attract about 100,000 members within a year. His own works and those of Rodbertus, Becker, Moses Hess, and others provided the needed pamphlet material.

Under the leadership of Lassalle the party did not do quite as well as its founder had expected. The responsibility for this probably rested upon Lassalle himself. His vanity and impatience were not favorable to rapid growth. He became acutely aware of his failure to create a mass-movement, and his impatience and conceit persuaded him to attempt to influence Bismarck in direct conversations. Lassalle's attempts to realize his objectives by these means lent color to the opposition within the party and to the suspicions which he earned from many. When he died in a duel over a love-affair, the party had only 4,610 members and no detailed program.[11]

There is no need to go into the struggle within the party over the role of the Countess Hatzfeld, nor to examine in any detail the causes of the disintegration which only the growing apotheosis of Lassalle had prevented from becoming complete. Only after Jean Baptiste von Schweitzer had become president did the party become a little more stable and better organized.[12]

10 *Neue Zeit*, vol. IX, pt. 1, no. 21, pp. 681 ff.

11 For the discussion of the suffrage issue between Lassalle and Bismarck see Lassalle's letters to Bismarck of January 13 and 16, 1864; also *supra*, p. 19, note 4. It is highly probable that Bismarck engaged in these discussions to force the hands of the liberal groups by the threat of the universal franchise and to destroy the socialist group by discrediting its leader. In spite of Bebel's generous assumptions (*ibid.*), there is no evidence that Bismarck at this time was seriously planning to impose democratic reforms from above or that he was doing more than play with Lassalle.

12 At the fourth party congress in Erfurt, on December 27, 1866, Countess Hatzfeld left the Allgemeiner Deutscher Arbeiterverein and

As editor of the party organ *Der Sozialdemokrat,* von Schweitzer published on January 4, 1865, a program which postulated that the solidarity of economic interests in Europe must be accepted as a fact, that the unification of Germany— " das ganze, grosse Deutschland "—must be effected, and that the rule of capital must be replaced by the rule of labor. On December 30, 1866, the *Sozialdemokrat* summarized the immediate party objectives as follows: 1) the unification of Germany as a centralized state; 2) universal, equal and secret suffrage; 3) a parliament that would be more than an advisory body; and 4) the solution of the social problem in Germany with state aid.

The adoption of an official party program was delayed until the fifth party congress at Braunschweig, in May, 1867. The Braunschweig program advocated that all Germany was to be constituted as a unitary, democratic and free " People's State " (Volkstaat), that producers co-operatives were to be formed with state aid, and that the immediate party objectives were to be agitation on behalf of these points and the establishment of equal and universal suffrage.[13]

Von Schweitzer shared Lassalle's belief that Bismarck's aid could be obtained in support of a democratic franchise and of the Lassallean proposals for the improvement of the social and economic position of the workers in Germany. But Schweitzer supported Bismarck not only for these reasons. He regarded the policies of Bismarck as ' German ' policies and could

---

founded an unimportant party of her own. The role of von Schweitzer himself within the party and his own integrity were not free of suspicion. He was repeatedly accused of financial irregularities, and of diverting funds for his own purposes. Some evidence to support these charges was produced, but it was inconclusive and von Schweizer was exonerated. He was also frequently accused of immoral behavior, but these charges were never sustained in court. His prison record alone disposed of the wholly unsubstantiated accusations that he was a paid agent of Bismarck. The attacks along this line of Bebel (*op. cit.,* vol. II), were due to incomplete and misinterpreted evidence.

13 *Protokoll der Generalversammlung in Braunschweig 1867,* pp. 4 ff.

point out that even Lassalle had advocated a war with Austria
to solve the German problem.[14] Even though the liberals in
Prussia were deadlocked with Bismarck over the constitutional conflict, Schweitzer did not hesitate to attack the liberal
groups which, in his opinion, obstructed German unity and a
democratic franchise. In a series of five articles on the Bismarck ministry Schweitzer stated: " In the face of the evident
indefensible political constitution of Germany,... a Prussian
government... which resumes the policies of Frederick II
cannot stop after a minor victory; onward it must on the chosen
path, forward if need be with blood and iron. For to take up
the proudest traditions of a historically grown state and then
to shy like a coward away from decisive action means to kill
the innermost nerve of the life of such a state." [15]

Defeated in the run-off election to the constituent of the
Norddeutscher Bund, von Schweitzer threw his votes in Elber-
feld-Barmen to his conservative opponent, Bismarck. Elected
to the first Norddeutscher Reichstag in 1867, von Schweitzer
declared before that body on September 11, 1867, that, while
his social views were clear to everyone, he felt impelled to
emphasize that in a conflict with any foreign power he would
support the king and his government with all his might, for
the Prussian King represented the essence of national power
in Germany.[16]

14 *Supra*, p. 20. Liebknecht and the group around him, which had become
independent in 1867, opposed these views as serving only Prussian interests.

15 *Der Sozialdemokrat*, January 27, 1865, and following issues. These
articles appeared while Karl Marx and Wilhelm Liebknecht were still co-
editors of the paper. As a consequence of these articles they resigned their
editorship. Franz Mehring, *Geschichte der Sozialdemokratie*, III, 194-196,
argued that it was wrong to ascribe the arguments and sentiments expressed
in these articles to von Schweitzer, and that he only wrote with " a vivid-
ness which sometimes resembled adoration." But careful reading leads to the
conclusion that von Schweitzer indeed advocated these views as his own.

16 During the debate on conscription in the Norddeutscher Reichstag in
1867, von Schweitzer declared: " We have learned that the Prussian center
of power at long last has assigned to our German Fatherland, so long ill-
respected,... a place of honor and might... and it is far from us to deny

As president of the Allgemeiner Deutscher Arbeiterverein, von Schweitzer went so far as to offer a resolution to the party congress of 1867 to the effect that Prussia contained the promise of German unification and should not be criticized because of the Austrian war of 1866.

Because of attitudes like these, August Bebel, Wilhelm Lieb-knecht and others suspected that von Schweitzer was the paid agent of Bismarck entrusted with the task of destroying the German labor movement. There was, however, no evidence to support this opinion. The Prussian police were probably not subtle enough to jail their own paid agents in order to deflect suspicion, and von Schweitzer had spent much time in prison. On the other hand, the persecutions of labor leaders by the police, the limitations on the freedom of association, assembly and of speech, and the constant threat of exile perhaps made it necessary to over-emphasize a nationalistic attitude in order to enjoy even a limited amount of freedom of agitation.

Still, it should be pointed out that Lassalle and the many workingmen's organizations from which he created the Allgemeiner Deutscher Arbeiterverein revealed a determined romantic element. And this fostered strong romantic nationalism among the workers just as it did among the liberals and the broad masses in Germany. Evidence will be cited later to show that nationalism among German socialists was neither a transitional nor a superimposed factor. Suffice it here to state that even Engels defended the view that the demands of nation and class were not mutually exclusive, and that ' national ' duties had to be fulfilled before the obligations arising from class-consciousness. The worker was not only a member of a class, but a member of the state and of the nation as well; and both the nation and the class had an equal right to the allegiance of the worker.[17]

---

or criticize those qualities of Prussia which only last year even a hostile world acknowledged with awe. We are dissatisfied with the internal conditions and aspire to change them radically, but we support the nascent German Fatherland;" *Verhandlungen*, II, 470-71.

17 Ed. Bernstein (ed.), *Briefwechsel zwischen Engels und Marx*, IV, 318 ff., letter of August 15, 1870.

The Allgemeiner Deutscher Arbeiterverein had staked its hopes for the amelioration of the social and economic conditions of the workers upon a democratic franchise and on state subsidies for Producers' Co-operatives. The party therefore was hostile to trade-unionism. At the Congress of 1868 at Hamburg, the party resolved that while strikes might spread class-consciousness or ameliorate isolated instances of economic injustice, they did not improve radically the position of the workers.

However, trade-unionism was not to be impeded by the hostility of the Allgemeiner Deutscher Arbeiterverein, and as early as September, 1868, von Schweitzer felt it necessary to organize the 'Allgemeiner Deutscher Arbeiter-Unterstuetzungsverein,' an organization composed of a number of free unions and dedicated to the financial assistance of striking members. The membership of the group for the early years was as follows: [18] 1869, 35,232; 1870, 20,674; 1871, 4,257; 1872, 8,337.

The hostility of the Allgemeiner Deutscher Arbeiterverein towards trade-unionism was probably motivated by the consideration that in this eary stage of industrial development strikes would hurt the workers more than industry, not only financially, but especially because, at the time, strike leaders were liable to severe prison. sentences.

Another reason for this hostility towards trade-unionism was the fear that successful trade-union activities would create an economic and social interest in the preservation of existing social conditions and thus foster among the workers a conservatism which might impede the acquisition of political and economic power by the socialist parties. This view was illustrated by a resolution adopted on November 28, 1868, by the 'Lassalle'sche Allgemeiner Deutscher Arbeiterverein', the organization founded by the Countess Hatzfeld after she had

18 W. Schroeder (ed.), *Handbuch der sozialdemokratischen Parteitage, 1863-1909*, Muenchen, 1910, pp. 178 ff.

left the original party. The resolution stated that trade-unions could not improve the situation of the workers; strikes worsened the condition of workers and hurt them as much as industry. Unionism therefore ought to be viewed as a means of reaction.

The leadership of industrialists in the organization of the early German trade-unions, and their frequent restriction to co-operative insurance schemes no doubt gave some substance to the charge of reaction. As late as 1872, a congress of the Allgemeiner Deutscher Arbeiterverein held that " unions are a damaging product of the times, but can no longer be abolished."[19] Not until 1874, long after the rival socialist party of Bebel and Liebknecht had come out in favor of trade-unionism, did the Allgemeiner Deutscher Arbeiterverein concede that unions were needed to ease the pressure of industrialism. But it was held that a central organization of all unions was required for this, and the party suggested that the 'Arbeiter-Unterstuetzungsverein', founded by von Schweitzer in 1868, could best fill this need.

b. The Formation of the Eisenach Group

Not all of the numerous workingmen's organizations which had sprung up in the early 1860's had joined Lassalle's organization in 1863. Many of them had rejected the ideas of Lassalle which were rather radical for his time and remained independent. Others had joined in 1864 at Frankfurt am Main to form the 'Verband der Deutschen Arbeitervereine', whose first president was August Bebel.[20] And under the initiative of Wilhelm Liebknecht, still other groups had taken up the ideas of 'scientific socialism' after the publication of the first volume of Karl Marx' *Das Kapital*.

19 *Protokoll der Generalversammlung 1872*, p. 32.

20 Bebel, *op. cit.*, II, 98. At the time of its transformation into the Sozialdemokratische Arbeiterpartel in 1869, this organization numbered, according to Bebel, 109 local groups and 10,000 members.

As formulated by the congress of the International Workers' Association at Geneva in 1866, the Marxian program declared that the emancipation of the workers could be achieved only by themselves, and that the workers fought not for new privileges but for the abolition of all privileges. The economic dependency of the workers upon the owners of the means of production was viewed as the cause of all misery, bondage, and enslavement. The movement for the emancipation of the workers should utilize all means available. To achieve their emancipation, the workers of all countries were to act in unison, because the marked lack of co-operation had doomed all previous attempts to achieve this emancipation. Under the presidency of Bebel, the Verband der Deutschen Arbeitervereine adopted this program in 1868 and joined the international organization, although a large part of the membership preferred to leave the party.[21]

However, the program of the International Workers' Association of 1866 did not reflect an unadulterated Marxian doctrine, and Marx soon found himself at odds with this organization. In order to provide Germany with a socialist party incorporating Marxian thought in a purer form, Wilhelm Liebknecht, in August, 1869, founded the Social Democratic Party. The Verband der Deutschen Arbeitervereine happened to meet at the very same time and in the same city— Eisenach. Upon the motion of Bebel, its president, the latter party declared itself dissolved and joined Liebknecht's Social Democratic Party en masse.[22]

21 Lassalle, who was not an independent economic thinker, had adopted the economic views of the recognized authorities in his own program. When Marxism became a factor, the Allgemeiner Deutscher Arbeiterverein could no longer incorporate the newer Marxian theses. The residue of non-Marxian economic ideas could be detected in the programs of the later Social Democratic Party until 1891.

22 At the constituent congress at Eisenach in 1869, 1,930 localities and 155,486 members were represented. At the congress in 1870, the party mustered only 13,147 members; infra, p. 34.

The program adopted by this new group of Eisenach accepted the idea of unrestricted class-struggle. The function of the bourgeois state made it impossible to achieve social ideals with state aid. The party sought not political freedom but economic and social equality. Of the two ways leading to that objective—revolution or a legal evolutionary process—the party chose the latter, the way of equal, universal and secret suffrage aiming at a social democratic republic as the ultimate form of the state.[23]

The Eisenach program called for the establishment of a free " People's state " and declared that the injustice of existing political and social conditions should be opposed. " The struggle for the emancipation of the workers is not a struggle for [new] ... privileges but for equal rights and duties and for the abolition of all class rule ... The economic dependency of the worker upon the capitalists is the cause of all bondage." The present mode of production must be replaced by co-operative methods. Political freedom was the prerequisite for economic freedom. The solution of the social problem was therefore possible only in a democratic state. Since the emancipation of the workers was a problem common to all modern societies, " the Social Democratic Party considers itself a branch of the International Workers' Association in as far as the German laws of associations permit."

As its immediate objectives, the party advocated universal, equal and secret manhood suffrage for all citizens above twenty years of age. The program called for the introduction of legislation by plebiscites, the " abolition of all privileges of class, birth, religion and property, ... a militia system instead of standing armies, ...separation of Church from state and schools," compulsory free public education, the introduction of the jury system, of free legal aid, of public and oral court procedures, and the political independence of the courts. The program also demanded the " abolition of all press, association

23 Weidmann, *op cit.*, pp. 14-15.

and coalition restrictions, the grant of a normal working day, restrictions on women's labor and the ban of all child labor," the abolition of all excise taxes, the introduction of uniform, progressive and direct income and inheritance taxes, and the development of co-operatives with the aid of state subsidies and credits for producers' co-operatives.[24]

The theoretical part of the Eisenach program leaned on Marx, but it also professed the popular Lassallean faith in producers' co-operatives and in a free peoples' state. The latter presumably indicated that not only the government, but the administration and the civil service, too, should in some way be dependent upon democratically elected bodies and reflect in their composition the various social and economic classes. Many of the concrete demands of the program had to wait for their realization until 1919. Nor was adherence to the International a pronounced trait of the party. All through the nineteenth and well into the twentieth century, the international co-operation of this party and its successor party was limited to the dispatch of delegates to the congresses of the International and to the voting of resolutions. In fact, Wilhelm Liebknecht declared at Basel in 1869 that the Social Democratic Party was not bound by the resolutions of the International, and that it was free to determine its policy according to its own choice.[25]

The problem of trade-unionism provided the Eisenach group and its successor party with a controversial issue of major importance. In 1868, Liebknecht had indeed come out in favor of trade-unionism which should ultimately become the administrators of social insurance funds, but he had done so only because of his fears that state administration would provide the workers with too strong an interest in the existing state

24 Quoted in F. Salomon, *Die deutschen Parteiprogramme*, I, 129 ff.

25 Bebel, *op. cit.*, II, 102. Liebknecht's remarks were prompted by a resolution calling for the nationalization of land. In 1870, the party, however, adopted a concurring resolution.

and its conservation.[26] But in 1870 at its congress at Stuttgart, the Social Democratic Party resolved that political action and legislation were more effective means for the amelioration of the conditions of the workers than strikes, and that trade-unions should concentrate on political action rather than on strikes.

The Social Democratic Party faithfully adopted all the recommendations of the International Association regarding unionism, but no love was lost between the party and trade-unionists. The fight about the role of the unions continued long after the fusion of the German workers' parties in 1875. The problem was raised at almost every party congress, even after 1890. The hostility of the Social Democratic Party towards trade-unions was motivated by doubts regarding the usefulness of strikes, and union support for the party was often declined because of the stake which unions had acquired in existing society. At the Erfurt congress in 1891, the party rejected a resolution which sought to make trade-union membership mandatory for all party workers in their different trades. It was only in 1898 that a party congress resolved to bar the advertisements of struck firms from the party press.[27]

Another and more important struggle which was carried over into the twentieth century concerned the attitude of the party towards participation in parliamentary activites. After considerable wavering,[28] Liebknecht advocated complete passivity in the Reichstag. No attempt to influence legislation ought to be made, the only permissible participation consisting of protestations against proposed policies.

In a speech on May 31, 1869, later published as a pamphlet under the title *Die politische Stellung der sozialdemokrati-*

[26] *Cf. supra*, pp. 26 f. This fear was not unfounded; the conservatism of the trade-unions became one of the determinants of social democratic policy in the twentieh century; *infra, passim.*

[27] *Protokoll des Parteitags 1898*, p. 219.

[28] Bebel, *op. cit.*, II, 164. Liebknecht's failure to dominate the Reichstag may have influenced his views and the views of his party on parliamentarism.

schen Partei, Liebknecht summarized his opinions on parliamentarism as follows: The party as a social movement was purely revolutionary, but could not achieve success overnight. The realization of the program of the party depended upon the destruction of the existing state and the creation in its stead of a new state on a new basis. The fight in the Reichstag was only a sham fight; no co-operation was possible between the party and the other groups in the Reichstag because there was no common ground between the Socialists and the other parties. The dominance of certain classes and their views about socialism made socialism a conflict not of theories, but a struggle for power which could not be solved in the Reichstag but only in the streets. Speeches in the Reichstag were only a silly diversion without significant consequences.[29]

Bebel, however, advocated active participation in the debates of the Reichstag and the introduction of legislative proposals. He considered them a means of propaganda whose coverage by the daily press would aid the party. Bebel's point of view eventually won out and after 1890, the parliamentary activity of the party loomed very large indeed.

Liebknecht's views, however, continued to be reflected in the resolutions of the party. On June 6, 1870, the congress at Stuttgart resolved that the party participated in elections only for the sake of propaganda, and that elected members should not actively take part in parliamentary activities except in case of issues touching on the interests of workers. Liebknecht on this occasion declared: " The Reichstag does not make history but simply performs a comedy; the members do and say what the prompter suggests . . . And should we make this Reichstag the center of our activities? . . . If the Reichstag were not powerless and if the government did not control the elections, this might be possible." The party advocated participation in the Reichstag debates and in elections only because " the elec-

---

29 W. Liebknecht, *Die politische Stellung der sozialdemokratischen Partei,* London, 1889.

tions create a certain excitement which we must use for agitation." [30] And the congress of 1873 affirmed that the party considered the elections " only as a means of agitation." [31]

c. THE FUSION PARTY OF 1875

The relations between the Social Democratic Party and the Allgemeiner Deutscher Arbeiterverein were far from friendly and their animosity found full expression in the party press and in the statements of the party congresses. The Allgemeiner Deutscher Arbeiterverein actually passed resolutions in support of liberal candidates in preference to Marxian socialists. But the attitudes and views of the representatives of the two groups in the Reichstag showed no basic divergences. On the conscription bill before the Norddeutscher Reichstag on October 17, 1868, Schweitzer abstained from voting, whereas Bebel and Liebknecht voted against the measure; in 1870, Schweitzer and his fellow party members voted for war credits, while Liebknecht and Bebel abstained from voting.[32] But after the capture of Napoleon III at Sedan, both parties voted jointly against further war credits, and in 1874 the two groups in the Reichstag decided on uniform and coordinated action in legislative matters. Co-operation had become necessary for the effectiveness of the two minor groups in the Reichstag, and to

30 Schroeder, *op. cit.*, pp. 386 ff.

31 *Protokoll des Kongresses 1873*, p. 73. After 1870, agitation on behalf of a democratic franchise referred of course in general not to the German Reich, but to the member states, in particular Prussia, which retained the three class suffrage until 1918. In a new edition of his pamphlet in the 1880's, Liebknecht finally accepted Bebel's arguments regarding parliamentary activities and declared that they were of great value to the party and that his previous opposition to parliamentary activities was justified only in the period prior to the unification of Germany.

32 They declared in the Reichstag on July 19, 1870: "... Nor can we refuse the proposed credits, for this could be interpreted as acquiescing in the evil and criminal policies of Bonaparte." Bebel had this note inserted into the record, because the declaration of war and the first credits were voted without debate. *Verhandlungen*, vol. VI, pt. 2, p. 14.

prevent their being played off against each other by the other party groups.

After 1872, the increasing persecution of labor parties in Germany provided a potent stimulus to bring the two groups together. The problem of union was raised annually at the congresses of each party after 1870. In December, 1874, Hasenclever, President of the Allgemeiner Deutscher Arbeiterverein, and Eduard Bernstein made preparations for a union congress. In February, 1875, a joint committee of the two parties met at Gotha and drafted a program for the new 'Sozialistische Partei Deutschlands' (SPD) which was adopted with minor changes by the Congress of Gotha in May of the same year. Henceforth only one socialist party, only one political labor party existed in Germany.[33]

33 The development of both groups in membership up to 1875 was as follows:

Year	Members	Local Organizations	Delegates to Party Congresses
Allgemeiner Deutscher Arbeiterverein:			
1863	......	11	12
1864	......	31	19
1865	5,500	58	17
1866 June	9,422	34	12
1866 December ...	......	26	12
1867 June	2,508	41	18
1867 November ...	3,408	...	20
1868	7,274	83	36
1869	12,053	126	57
1870	8,062	...	39
1871	5,259	74	36
1872	8,264	145	44
1873	16,010	246	61
1874	17,316	...	...
1875	16,538	...	71
Sozialdemokratische Partei:			
1869	155,486	1,930	263
1870	13,147	113	66
1871	6,255	81	56
1872	......	...	51
1873	9,224	132	71
1874	8,767	142	52
1875	9,121	...	56

The program of Gotha stated the objectives for which the party fought and under which it later became the largest party in Germany. The program reflected the greater influence of the popular ideas of Lassalle. The writings of Marx were little read in Germany, whereas the works of Lassalle enjoyed great popularity among the workers. The shift of emphasis from Lassalle to Marx which occurred soon after the adoption of the Gotha program resulted mainly from the attempted suppression of the SPD after 1878.

The Gotha program opened with an exposition of socialist dogma. "Labor is the source of all wealth and culture, and because . . . labor is possible only in a social body, all proceeds of labor belong to society . . . In present society the means of production are monopolized by the class of capitalists," causing the dependence of the working classes, their misery and their bondage. "The emancipation of labor calls for the socialization of the means of production and the co-operative regulation of labor . . . The emancipation of labor is of necessity the task of the workers compared to whom all other classes form only a reactionary mass . . . By utilizing all legal means, the Socialist Workers' Party of Germany aspires to establish the free state and the socialist order, to destroy the Iron Law of Wages . . . to abolish all exploitation . . . and to eliminate all social and political inequalities." While restricting itself to the national scene, the SPD confirmed its international links. The

---

These figures did not represent actual membership but only the membership as represented at party congresses. Difficulty of travel, lack of funds, and police regulations kept many delegates at home and many members unrepresented. These figures are obviously too low, but they are more reliable than the extravagant statements of the party press. The voting strength of the parties was always considerably higher than the number of dues-paying members. Thus the Social Democratic Party elected two members to the Reichstag in 1871 with 113,048 votes or 2.91% of the total, and ten members in 1874 with 350,861 votes or 6.76% of the total. In the election of 1877, the first after the fusion of 1875, the new party elected twelve members with 493,258 votes or 9.13% of the total vote cast. A. Neumann-Hofer, *Entwicklung der sozialdemokratischen Partei bei den Wahlen zum deutschen Reichstag,* 1898, pp. 66 ff.

party demanded state-supported, democratically controlled socialist producers' co-operatives in industry and agriculture.

The political demands enumerated by the SPD included: universal, equal, secret, and compulsory elections which were to be held on national holidays; " direct legislation by the people, decisions on war and peace by the people; " universal military service (Allgemeine Wehrhaftigkeit), and a militia system; the abolition of all restrictions upon the press, upon assembly, upon associations and coalitions; " jurisdiction by the people; " free legal aid (Unentgeltliche Rechtspflege); universal, compulsory, free and equal state controlled education; and the declaration that religious beliefs were the private concern of each individual. The SPD also called for a single progressive income tax in place of existing excise taxes; " unlimited right of coalition; " a normal work day and the ban of Sunday work; " the ban of child labor and of all female labor detrimental to health and morals; " factory inspection; compensation laws; and the independent administration of social insurance funds.[34]

The common ground of both parties was provided by their view of the function of the state. Both parties in their previous programs had looked to the state for the realization of their objectives, while the Marxian doctrine of a stateless society had been rejected. As a result " the Socialist Party aimed at the . . . concentration of all economic power in the hands of the state, the utmost strengthening of the state." [35]

Yet the program did not represent any well integrated set of ideas, but was full of confusion. What " jurisdiction by the people " meant was not made clear, and the demand for universal military service scored the inequalities of the existing system and its preferences for certain social or educated classes rather than its lack of universality. The preference for a militia, common to all nineteenth century socialist parties, expressed

[34] Quoted in F. Salomon, *op. cit.*, II, 25-27.
[35] *Wahlaufruf der SPD*, October 27, 1881.

primarily the opposition of socialists to an army which had
been widely used as a mainstay of the status quo. Whether
direct legislation meant plebiscites, and whether " decisions on
war and peace by the people " meant something else than
action by a representative parliament, was not made quite
clear.[36]

Engels' criticism of the program showed how far short it
fell of the fully developed communist idea. In a letter to Bebel,
who at the time of the Gotha congress was in prison for a
political offense, Engels pointed out the error and the political
or tactical dangers of lumping all other classes together as reactionary. Such a Lassallean generalization left out of consideration agricultural workers, the class of artisans, and the
lower bourgeoisie whose attitudes towards socialism depended
not on their economic interests, but on socialist policy towards
them. The practical negation of internationalism and the
reiteration of the theory of wages as copied by Lassalle from
Ricardo were a repudiation of Marxian ideas on the subject.
The reliance on state aid and the neglect of trade-unionism
as a means of fostering class-consciousness were criticized

36 See Karl Marx' article " Zur Kritik des sozialdemokratischen Parteiprogrammes," written on May 5, 1875 and published in *Die Neue Zeit*, vol.
IX, pt. 1, no. 18, pp. 561 ff., (1890-91). Marx denied the validity of such
generalization as the 'present state' or 'present society', pointed out that
democratic ideals were already in effect in the United States or Switzerland,
that income taxes presupposed a capitalist state, and that socialists did not
want to free the state but to subject it. He objected to state-education, ridiculed the idea of 'free court procedures' which, he said, were always free in
criminal cases, and ought not to be charged to the people in civil cases which
most of the time dealt with property claims. He attacked the idea that the
proceeds of labor belonged to society including idlers, or that the undivided
proceeds could be distributed regardless of replacements, administrative expenses, public expenditures like schools, etc. Marx pointed out that if, as the
program claimed, labor was possible only in society and if its proceeds belonged to society, then each worker was entitled only to enough to sustain
present society which was in direct support of the existing economic distribution. For an able defense of the Gotha program see W. Liebknecht,
Was die Sozialdemokraten sind und was sie wollen, Chemnitz, 1894, originally published in the mid-1870's.

strongly. Living in England after the reform bills of 1832 and of 1867, Engels could point out in 1875 that the achievement of full political democracy did not automatically produce a change in social and economic relations. Engels emphasized that the sole function of the state in the socialized future was the suppression of reaction. Class differences, Engels pointed out, might be abolished, but the demands for the abolition of social inequalities were utopian, for social differences could never be abolished. Engels concluded his criticism by pointing out that the program itself was less important than the future action of the party, but he feared that a program like this would permanently prejudice later changes towards more orthodox Marxian views.[37]

On the surface Engels' fears did not seem to be borne out in fact; in 1880, during Bismarck's fight against the SPD, the phrase "by all legal means" was struck from the program while Lassallean ideas slowly receded in importance before orthodox Marxism. But these changes reflected less a new direction of policy than the necessity to survive under anti-socialist legislation. The unification of the two socialist parties in 1875 had not bridged the conflict between Lassalle and Marx, between national and international objectives, between democratic and class rule, between co-operation with and hostility for the state.

37 Letter reprinted in Bebel, *Leben*, II, 318 ff. Both Marx and Engels voiced their criticism to a draft program, but the actual program adopted at Gotha ignored their suggestions on almost every point. Bebel, being in prison, opposed the program and threatened to leave the party, if the program was adopted; *ibid.*, pp. 299 ff.; also *Protokoll des Parteitages 1891*, pp. 158 ff.

CHAPTER II

FROM THE ERFURT PROGRAM TO REVISIONISM

a. The Adoption of the Erfurt Program, 1891

ONE of the main causes of the fusion of the Allgemeiner Deutscher Arbeiterverein with the Social Democratic Party in 1875 had been the increasing hostility of the German government to socialism. This hostility had been fed by the example of the Paris Commune in 1871. Both the Allgemeiner Deutscher Arbeiterverein and the Social Democratic Party had openly expressed their sympathy with the Paris Commune.[1] Bismarck feared the occurrence of similar acts in Germany, and the attempts on the life of William I lent color to his fears. Wrongly attributing these attempts to socialist agitation, the government utilized them as pretext to enact measures of repression and control (the anti-socialist legislation of 1878).

The SPD suffered considerable inconvenience under the anti-socialist legislation, the strict regulation of the party press, the confiscation of a large number of newspapers, and the frequent arrests and imprisonment of party members and party leaders. The social legislation of the 1880's, the compensation laws, the national health insurance act, and the like presented an equal threat to the party. Yet in spite of Bismarck's attempts to deprive the SPD of its raison d'être and to fight the party by police measures, court actions, and similar measures, the SPD continued to grow in membership and voting strength. By 1884, the temporary set-back suffered during the first few years of the anti-socialist legislation had been re-

1 F. Mehring, *Geschichte der SPD*, IV, 20-21. Bebel's speech on the Paris Commune on March 10, 1876, reprinted in his *Leben*, II, 348-369, was one of the more noteworthy discussions of the Commune by a sympathetic commentator.

versed. In the election of 1893, the first after the lapse of the anti-socialist legislation, the SPD emerged as the strongest single political party in Germany.[2]

Restrictive legislation had thus failed in its purpose. After the dismissal of Bismarck, it was succeeded by the new policy of the 'personal government' of William II who had unbounded confidence in his ability to undermine the foundations of the SPD: the injustice of contemporary social and economic conditions. Indeed, Bismarck's social legislation had failed in this, but Bismarck's program had not been in force long enough to allow definite conclusions regarding its full effects upon the social and economic conditions from which the SPD drew its strength.

After the abandonment of the anti-socialist legislation in 1890, a restatement of the party objectives had become necessary because of the further development of Marxian theories through the publication of the final volume of *Das Kapital*. In addition, the rejection of Lassallean terminology during the anti-socialist struggle seemed to call for recognition in the party program. On the other hand, the lapse of the anti-socialist legislation gave rise to a tendency to arrest the increasing radicalism of the party and to return to Lassallean points of view. In 1890 and 1891, the opposition of the 'Young-Ones' (Opposition der Jungen) considerably embarrassed the party leadership by charging outright that the SPD had ceased to be a revolutionary party and had degenerated into a parlia-

2 The SPD votes cast in German national elections 1877-1893 were:

Year	SPD Votes	Percent of total votes cast	Mandates
1877	493,258	9.13	12
1878	437,158	7.59	9
1881	311,961	6.12	13
1884	549,990	9.71	25
1887	763,128	10.12	11
1890	1,427,298	19.75	36
1893	1,780,989	23.21	48

Neumann-Hofer, *op. cit.*, p. 66.

mentary group.[3] It was probably in support of the 'Young-Ones' that Engels in 1891 published the devastating critique of the Gotha program which Marx had written in 1875.[4]

The combination of these divergent factors seems to have been responsible for the Erfurt program of 1891. The materialistic conception of history formed its basis. The program asserted that the process of the pauperization of the masses could be reversed only through the transformation of privately owned capital into social capital. The struggle for this transformation was necessarily a political struggle. The criterion of the existing state was its class-character, and its purpose was the preservation of the existing distribution of wealth and power. The proletariat hence must gain control over the state and transform the state into a socialist society. The program did not reject the idea of the state: the state would continue to be needed for the supervision of the planned economic society.[5]

Although Bismarck had successfully launched the idea that reforms would ultimately harm the SPD, the SPD decided that it could not reject individual reforms.[6] Kautsky maintained in his commentary on the Erfurt program that state-socialism and piecemeal reforms could never complete the task to which the SPD was dedicated. The class-state would never allow state-interference to reach a point where it would seriously endanger the private ownership of the means of production. Furthermore, state-monopolies exerted even more pressure upon the workers than private monopolies. Hence there could be no objection to the inclusion in a socialist program of a considerable number of demands for individual reforms, even if they resembled state-socialism or liberalism.[7]

3 For example, *Protokoll des Parteitags Halle 1890*, pp. 80 ff.

4 *Neue Zeit*, vol. IX, pt. 1, no. 18, pp. 561 ff.; *cf. supra*, p. 37.

5 Weidmann, *op. cit.*, pp. 26 ff., 41 ff.

6 *Protokoll des Parteitags Erfurt 1891*, p. 162.

7 Kautsky and Schoenlank, *Grundsaetze und Forderungen der SPD*, 1899, pp. 17 ff.

Because of the importance of the Erfurt program in the discussions within the party, its main points deserve mention. Analyzing present society, the program stated the following:

> The economic development of bourgeois society leads inevitably to the ruin of small business ... and separates the worker from his means of production ... [which] become the monopoly of a relatively small number of capitalists.
>
> The replacement . . . of small enterprises by colossal, big industries ... and the gigantic increase in the productivity of human labor go hand in hand with this monopolization.... For the proletariat and the disappearing middle classes ... this spells increasing insecurity, ... misery ... and exploitation.
>
> The number of proletarians becomes increasingly larger, the army of excess workers increasingly bigger, the opposition between exploiters and exploited, increasingly sharp, and the class-struggle . . . which divides . . . society into two hostile camps, increasingly bitter.
>
> The gap between the haves and the have-nots is being widened through ... crises which become steadily more widespread and severe ... and prove that private ownership has become incompatible with the useful utilization and full development of the means of production.
>
> Only through the transformation of capitalist private ownership of the means of production ... into social property ... and through production by and on behalf of society may ... big industry and increasing production ... become a source of highest welfare and of universal harmonious perfection.
>
> These changes mean the emancipation ... of all humanity ... but [they] can only be the work of the laboring classes, because all other classes ... aim in common at the retention of the basis of present society.
>
> The struggle of the working classes is of necessity a political struggle ... [The working classes] cannot effect the transformation of the means of production into social ownership without gaining control of political power ...
>
> The interests of the working classes of all countries ... are the same.... The SPD ... feels and expresses its solidarity with the class-conscious workers of all other countries.

Hence the SPD does not fight for new class-privileges, but for the abolition of class-rule and of the classes themselves; ... it fights in present society ... against all exploitation and subjection, be it directed against a class, a party, a sex, or a race.

This analysis of capitalist society was followed by a set of concrete demands which included: 1) Equal, universal, secret and direct suffrage of men and women above twenty years of age, and proportional representation, legal redistribution of electoral districts after every census, biennial legislative periods and salaries for elected representatives; 2) direct legislation by the people through petition and plebiscite, responsibility and liability of civil servants, annual voting of taxes; 3) education towards universal military responsibility (Wehrhaftigkeit), decisions on war and peace through parliament, and the arbitration of international conflicts; 4) abolition of all restrictions on the freedom of speech, assembly, association, and the like; 5) full emancipation of women; 6) no public support to be granted to churches; 7) secularization of schools, " compulsory attendance in public schools, free instruction, educational aids and nutrition in public schools and in high schools for those ... capable of further training"; 8) "free legal procedures, [Rechtspflege] and legal aid," election of Judges, appeal in criminal cases, compensation for persons innocently arrested, indicted or convicted, abolition of the death penalty; 9) free medical aid, free funeral services, and the like; 10) progressive income, property, and inheritance taxes, and the abolition of all tariffs and excises " which sacrifice the interests of the public to the interests of a preferred minority."

For the protection of the workers, the SPD demanded a maximum eight hour day, a ban on the labor of children below fourteen years of age and restrictions on all night labor, a minimum weekly rest period of thirty-six hours, factory inspection, thorough industrial hygiene, legal equality for industrial, agricultural and domestic workers, the safeguarding of the right of unionization, and federal control of all social insurance funds.[8]

One of the striking features of the Erfurt program was the wide gap between its theoretical and its practical demands. A society in which every one of the concrete demands of the program had been carried out would still not be a socialist community. Bebel emphasized indeed that " simply to abrogate the first part of our program and instead to build further its second part ... [would mean] that we would cease to be the SPD."[9]

Kautsky, the author and official interpreter of the Erfurt program, probably succeeded best in analyzing the function of the list of concrete demands in the program. The grant of women's suffrage and the enfranchisement of all above twenty years of age instead of the existing requirement of twenty-five years was needed to counterbalance the lower life expectancy of industrial workers. Proportional representation would considerably increase SPD strength in the Reichstag.[10] To insure better popular control over the Reichstag and to provide more opportunities for SPD agitation, biennial legislative periods were advocated. Election day ought to fall on a legal holiday

8 Quoted in F. Salomon, *op. cit.*, pp. 67 ff. It is of interest that points 2, 3, 4, 7, 8, 9, 10, and some of the demands for the protection of workers were not enacted even after 1918. In 1891, the SPD changed its official name to the ' Sozialdemokratische Partei Deutschlands,' the Social Democratic Party.

9 *Protokoll des Parteitages Stuttgart 1898*, p. 93.

10 Kautsky and Schoenlank, *op. cit.*, pp. 29 ff. This volume is preferable to Kautsky's *Das Erfurter Programm* (1892) because the earlier volume was but a popular and polemical exposition of the theoretical part of the Erfurt program and of its Marxian views. In the election of 1898 the SPD received 2,111,073 votes or 27.23 percent of the total, but only 56 out of 397 seats in the Reichstag or 19.5%. The SPD on the average needed 37,733 voters to elect one member to the Reichstag, whereas the average number of voters represented by each representative was only 19,495. Proportional representation would have given the SPD 108 seats instead of 56 in the Reichstag's election of 1898.

so that workers would be able to vote.[11] The absence of salaries for members of the Reichstag was a serious hardship to
SPD representatives and the party treasury, because the SPD
was less able than any other party to support its representatives
in the Reichstag from the party treasury. Political rights
should not be abridged except after court action, and workers
on relief ought not to be disfranchised. Kautsky charged that
standing armies under the existing system and in present
society only protected the capitalist interests of the country.
A militia would be less expensive to support than the German
system of national defense which, between 1871 and 1893, had
consumed seventy-two percent of the total budgets. The educational demands of the program were aimed to benefit the
children of workers' families and to help them grow up healthy
and sound without being forced to work for their own support
from earliest youth.[12]

b. The Foreign Policies of the SPD

The Erfurt program recorded the eclipse of certain Lassallean ideas by Marxian views. This event had been prepared
by the fight of the SPD for survival during the years of anti-
socialist legislation. The Lassallean hopes for the co-operative
movement in particular had been attacked. In 1892, the congress at Berlin was told that co-operatives lacked the resources
necessary for successful business competition, and that they
could not train the personnel needed in the socialized state.
The congress resolved that the SPD opposed the formation of
co-operatives and deemed that they could not raise the standards of workers or replace the need for class-struggle.[13]

11 In 1898, only 7,758,745 out of 11,437,543 qualified voters went to the
polls. Incidentally, only 21.9 percent of the population in 1898 were en-
franchised.

12 Kautsky and Schoenlank, *op. cit.*, pp. 29-40.

13 *Protokoll des Parteitags Berlin 1892*, pp. 222 ff. Under the pressure of
revisionism these views were somewhat modified in 1904. It was then re-

But the program of Erfurt was even more the result of the opposition of the 'Young-Ones' who asserted that the party had lost its revolutionary character. The pronouncements of SPD leaders on foreign and colonial policies during the 1890's will reveal the causes which had motivated the opposition of the 'Young-Ones'.

The period between 1875 and 1900 was one of relative calm on the international scene. The SPD was primarily concerned with domestic policies, and statements on 'national' policies were few and far between. Yet they presented a pattern which was not always in accord with revolutionary beliefs.

On April 20, 1874, Motteler, a SPD member of the Reichstag, declared before that body: "We are opponents of the Reich to the degree to which the Reich represents certain institutions under which we suffer. But we are not opponents of the Reich as such, as a national, as a state unit." [14]

On March 12, 1880, Bebel declared in the Reichstag that "if any power were to try to conquer German territory, the SPD would oppose that enemy just as any other party." And in the same year he wrote: "In a struggle for the integrity of German soil it may be very hard for the SPD to help defend the infamous domestic system of government and the mortal enemy [of the SPD], but [the SPD] will not rid itself of these by foreign conquerors..." [15]

In 1907, Bebel reiterated before the party congress: "Now the term 'defense of the Fatherland' has been used... If indeed we should have to defend our Fatherland some day, we would defend it because it is our Fatherland, whose soil we live upon, whose language we speak, whose customs we

---

solved that the SPD was neutral to co-operatives which might be able to raise the standards of the workers or to educate them for independent administration, but which could never change existing wage controls.

14 *Verhandlungen*, XIX, 961 ff.; E. Bernstein, *Von der Sekte zur Partei*, 1911, p. 20.

15 *Der Sozialdemokrat*, 1880, no. 16.

possess, because we wish to make this, our Fatherland, a land unexcelled in this world for perfection and beauty." [16]

In his commentary to the Erfurt program Kautsky defended military training (Wehrhaftigkeit) in the following words: "The child must be inoculated with the belief that none deserves to be called free who knows not how to...die for freedom. Should there be need to keep a presumptuous enemy away from the home-land, the citizens trained since youth in physical skills and in the use of arms will defend their own hearths and the commonweal with flaming enthusiasm and high courage... The closed ranks of those who fight for their good cause will be ready to strike, and victory will be tied to their standards." [17]

Although the SPD viewed modern war only as the outgrowth of capitalist society, it considered the patriotic defense of one's own country a supreme duty: "Wars like revolutions are catastrophes which scourge present society from time to time with iron necessity and which will disappear only with it," but "the duty to protect one's own country from invasion is supreme." [18]

Even more interesting for the 'national' policy of the SPD were its pronouncements on colonial policy. Bernstein wrote in 1899 that while opposing the barbarianism and brutality of present colonial expansion, the SPD must recognize the civilizing role of colonialism. Expansion of markets, he held, was one of the mightiest levers of progress and largely responsible for the wealth of nations; the very chance of social progress depended on it.[19] At the time of the Turkish troubles in 1895, he wrote that not every revolt of native tribes deserved the moral or active support of the SPD, and that in spite of its

16 *Protokoll des Parteitags 1907*, pp. 254 ff.

17 Kautsky and Schoenlank, *ibid.*

18 *Neue Zeit*, vol. XXIII, pt. 2, no. 38, pp. 364 ff., and no. 37, pp. 343 ff.; articles by Kautsky on "Patriotismus, Krieg und Sozialdemokratie."

19 *Neue Zeit*, vol. XVI, pt. 2, no. 18, pp. 548 ff.

" sympathy for fighters for independence, the SPD must take into consideration the interests of general progress and of cultural evolution. Therefore the revolt of tribes who usurp the right of slave-trading, or of robber-tribes who make raids on neighboring agricultural tribes their permanent business, must leave the SPD cool, indeed even make it their enemies...We may be critical vis-à-vis our present civilization, but we acknowledge its relative merits and make this the criterion for our attitudes." [20]

Pronouncements like these showed the latitude SPD leaders accepted in colonial questions. Kautsky, to be sure, argued against the views of Bernstein saying that the necessity of colonial expansion in capitalist society did not require the SPD to support it.[21] But in 1904, the party congress turned down a resolution instructing all SPD members of the Reichstag to vote against the colonial demands of the government. And in 1907 Bebel stated: " The pursuit of colonial policies is not a crime per se. Colonial policies may in certain circumstances be a cultural problem; it all depends on how you pursue colonial policies." [22]

In the preamble to the resolution on the intervention in China the SPD made clear the reason for its opposition towards imperialism: " World or colonial policy, pursued in order to further capitalist exploitation and military glory... results from the avarice of the bourgeoisie for new opportunities to invest capital . . . and the need for markets . . . This policy consists in the forceful acquisition of foreign lands and their irresponsible exploitation... It also necessarily leads to the brutalization of the exploiting elements which seek to satisfy their hunger for spoils with the most damnable, even inhuman means... The policy of overseas conquests and pillage leads to jealousies and frictions between the rival powers

20 *Ibid.*, vol. XV, pt. 1, no. 4, pp. 108 ff., vol. XVI, pt. 1, no. 16, pp. 484 ff.

21 *Protokoll des Parteitags Dresden 1903*, pp. 388 ff.

22 *Protokoll des Parteitags Essen 1907*, pp. 271 ff.

and hence to unbearable armaments on land and sea; it harbors the seeds of dangerous international conflicts, ..."

Arguments like these were not specifically Marxian and therefore were subjected to scathing criticism by the 'Young-Ones' as early as 1890. The 'Young-Ones' were loath to tolerate the re-emergence of the conflict between Lassallean and Marxian ideas which had been held in abeyance during the anti-socialist legislation of Germany. They retained an uncompromising attitude in the face of the greater latitude which many prominent party leaders seemed to allow on 'national' issues. Their views were, with certain changes, ultimately taken up by the Spartacists during the First World War.

c. THE PROBLEMS OF AGRARIAN REFORMS AND PARLIAMENTARISM

After 1891, the major issue within the SPD involved not problems of foreign affairs and 'national' aspirations but disputes about the degree of emphasis to be placed on the different parts of the Erfurt program and about the steps necessary for their realization. The party operated within a constitutional system in which not even a majority in the Reichstag, much less a plurality, implied the attainment of governmental powers. Yet, the SPD could not evade the immediate problems raised by the abandonment of the anti-socialist legislation and by its own growth which indicated that large sections of the middle classes and of agricultural workers had become socialist voters.[23]

The early attempts of German socialists to grapple with the agrarian problem had, generally speaking, failed. In 1870, the party congress had declared in favor of rational agriculture, the progressive elimination of the small peasantry by large landed estates, and the nationalization of land. But such statements presented only lip-service. Under the leadership of Lieb-

[23] *Protokoll des Parteitags Breslau 1895*, p. 152.

knecht the party congress of 1874 had rejected an amendment to the Eisenach program stating that the private ownership of the land was one of the main props of exploitation and that expropriation of land (with full compensation) must be demanded. Liebknecht justified his stand by pointing out that " the SPD aims at the emancipation of human labor; once labor is free the soil also will be free." The agrarian question was shelved because, it was held, it did not constitute *the* social problem.[24]

The relative insignificance of the party before the 1880's had permitted this type of superficial treatment of the problem. But the protective policies of the Reich, the growth of the SPD in agricultural and South German districts, and the identification of the imperial regime with one of the groups in the agrarian controversy within the nation forced a more thorough discussion of the problem upon the SPD.

On the initiative of Georg von Vollmar, a South-German socialist of strong reformist inclinations, the problem was raised in 1894. "... The small peasantry, oppressed by conscription, taxes, mortgages, and personal debts... is disintegrating. Protective tariffs are for them only an empty gesture ... The peasant is being proletarianized... The next task of the party is to develop a special agrarian political program. The needs of peasants and agricultural workers must be satisfied by thorough reforms ..."[25]

The congress of 1894 set up a commission to examine the problem, and in 1895 a sweeping program of reform was offered for adoption to the party. A general program of agrarian reform was proposed for all of Germany, and special programs were recommended for North, Middle and South Germany and their particular conditions. The recommendations covered exhaustively many aspects of the agrarian problem: the organization of credit and insurance; the building of

24 *Protokoll des Parteitags 1874*, pp. 79 ff.

25 *Protokoll des Parteitags Frankfurt 1894*, p. 134.

roads; rights to commons, forests, hunting and fishing; co-operative irrigation; rents; expropriation; extensive experimental stations; free agricultural schools and colleges; veterinarians' services; sale of lands; and the like. The recommendations represented one of the most constructive proposals of the SPD up to that time. They were printed and widely circulated among the peasantry as propaganda material. But they were rejected by the party congress. The rejection was defended by the statement that "they promise to the peasantry an improvement in their conditions, that is, a strengthening of their private property; they identify the interests of agriculture ... with the interests of the proletariat..." Although continued investigation of the problem and the publication of the results were authorized, subsequent congresses failed to take any positive action on this important question.

What was most significant about the discussions of the congress of 1895 concerning agrarian reform was the fact that these proposals were made and discussed in disregard of party theory or doctrines. They were rejected, not as incompatible with party theories but as incompatible with the established policy of the party. They were discussed and judged solely on their relative merits for purposes of agitation, and they were rejected not because the party opposed them in principle, but because other conditions within the party, (for example preference for the industrial proletariat) demanded such a rejection.

Such tactical considerations also dominated the councils of the party when it was faced by the problem of parliamentary activities.

In the 1870's, the SPD had considered participation in the elections and in the debates of the Reichstag solely as a means of agitation. SPD congresses had consistently endorsed parliamentary activities only because of their value for SPD agitation. But already in 1890 it was pointed out that SPD voters had a right to expect SPD representatives in the Reichstag and in other legislative bodies to work actively on their behalf.

Constructive participation of the SPD in the affairs of the Reichstag was now viewed as necessary lest the SPD break faith with its voters and drive the trade-unions to the right by remaining only a party of protest.[26]

The extent and the nature of participation in legislative affairs proved, however, to be a baffling problem for the party, because not only had the Reichstag to be considered, but the legislatures of each of the individual German states where the SPD strength was often more decisive than in Berlin and where in some instances a larger share of parliamentary government had been introduced.

After 1890, SPD members in Southern states, especially in Baden, had begun to support the budgets in their legislatures. This was disconcerting to many in the party, and in 1894 a resolution condemning parliamentary support of budgets was offered. The resolution stated that it was the duty of all parliamentary delegates of the SPD to fight all injustice and evils inherent in the class-state dedicated to the preservation of the then dominating interest groups, and to use every available means to change these conditions. A vote for the budget in toto would represent a vote in support of an administration which was, in effect, engaged in fighting the SPD. The resolution therefore demanded that SPD members must not vote for the budgets. The resolution was, however, rejected by the congress, because, as von Vollmar argued, it would make impossible all practical success of the party. It would, for example, be embarrassing for the party to vote against social insurance funds. The SPD occasionally determined the parliamentary majority, and in such cases many items would be incorporated into a budget for no other reason but to please the SPD. Bernstein emphasized that voting on the budget was a most important means of propaganda and yielded immediate concrete gains.[27]

26 *Protokoll des Parteitags Dresden 1903*, pp. 397 ff.

27 *Protokoll des Parteitags Frankfurt 1894*, pp. 107 ff., 113.

The following year, too, a resolution to instruct SPD members in the legislatures to abstain from voting on the budgets of the states was unanimously rejected.[28]

In 1901, the party congress finally limited SPD support of the budget by instructing SPD members that "consent to the budget may be given only rarely, and for compelling reasons that arise from a particular situation."

Despite this limitation, the SPD blocs in Baden, Wuerttemberg and Bavaria continued to vote the budgets of their states. To defend their actions, the SPD members in these states pointed out the propaganda value of such actions. The SPD vote frequently decided between two budget proposals, and the failure to support the new budget could result in the prolongation of a previous budget much more unfavorable to the interests of the working classes.

Bebel condemned the action of the southern SPD: "We cannot reach our objectives through small concessions . . . We do everything possible to attain an amelioration of the conditions of the laboring classes . . . We do it to make the laboring classes stronger, abler for the struggle on behalf of our great aim . . . But this does not allow us . . . to meet the bourgeois administration halfway . . ." [29]

Yet even Bebel had been impelled to state rather early in the debate on the problem of parliamentarism: "We are not in a position to build the role of the working classes on the conquest of economic control . . . We must first conquer political power and then use it to achieve economic control . . . How do we get this power? There are a number of ways . . . agitation, . . . the press, . . . parliamentary activities. This [last] means was valued so highly by Lassalle that he did not present any other demands except . . . suffrage . . . From the moment this was granted there was never any doubt . . . about making the most extensive use of this means . . . The party

28 *Protokoll des Parteitags Breslau 1895*, p. 89.

29 *Protokoll des Parteitags Nuernberg 1908*, pp. 285 ff.

has to participate in the elections . . . and the representatives in the Reichstag . . . must use every means to achieve concessions in favor of the working classes . . . It would be folly if the party would not also discuss the daily need of the working class and would not strive to remove existing evils . . . and pressing conditions . . ." [30] And Liebknecht in 1897 agreed: " In the beginning . . . we went into the Reichstag . . . exclusively for the propagation of our ideas . . . But . . . the injustice of the prevailing social system means more than an opportunity to deliver beautiful orations . . . From the circle of the workers themselves we were asked to propose our own plans for the improvement of present conditions and laws every time that social legislation or other bills offered the opportunity. . ."

In the discussions of the parliamentary activities, too, the SPD had been guided not by ideological or theoretical considerations, but by tactics. Whether the SPD should only protest against pending legislation or whether it should constructively participate in committees and offer bills of its own, whether it should vote on certain legislation or not, whether it should support a budget not of its own making or reject it, all these questions were viewed not as questions of abstract ideas, of socialist views, or of party fundamentals, but as tactics. In its publications, the SPD itself labelled these discussions as ' Problems of Tactics ', ' Debate on Tactics ', and the like.[31] It was because of tactics that the congress of 1897 resolved that in run-off elections the SPD should not abstain from voting for non-socialist candidates but that " party members are exhorted to give their vote to that member of the bourgeois parties who obligates himself, if elected, to defend the existing suffrage laws and their extension, parliamentary control of the budget, freedom of assembly, and to oppose the

30 *Protokoll des Parteitags Erfurt 1891*, pp. 158 ff.

31 Bebel and Vollmar, *Taktik*, excerpts from the party protocol of the congress of 1903 regarding the Bebel-Vollmar debate on parliamentarism and revisionism.

re-introduction of anti-socialist legislation, the extension of tariffs, and the restriction of existing social legislation." [32]

d. The Emergence of Revisionism

Throughout the 1890's, the SPD unwaveringly insisted on the entire Erfurt program, its statements and views were clad in unimpeachable socialist terminology, and the latent radical opposition emanating from the ' Young-Ones ' of 1890 and 1891 remained relatively quiet. But in fact and in practice, radicalism within the SPD had been restricted to verbose statements and emasculated resolutions; in its every-day activities the party had become merely a party of reform. This development had been furthered by tactical considerations, by the growth of the SPD into a party that no longer included only proletarians, (by 1903, the SPD had become the largest single parliamentary group in Germany) by the fear of the defection of the trade-unions, and by the need to satisfy the everyday demands of the workers and to achieve token successes in the program of social improvements. This development exhibited a consistent nationalist flavor and a residue of Lassallean concepts. It had progressed farthest in respect to the question of parliamentarism where all other considerations had yielded to the problem of tactics. But co-operation with bourgeois parties was not only inspired by the need to relieve the social and economic conditions of the workers; a purely negative

---

32 *Protokoll des Parteitags Hamburg 1897*, p. 154. The policy of supporting some other candidate in run-off elections went back to the beginnings of the party. In the run-off elections in 1884, for example, the SPD and the National-Liberal party supported each other's candidates. Yet a SPD election leaflet at the time read: " The National-Liberal party, this party which lacks character [but possesses] political hypocrisy, is dead and has already begun to rot.... It is nothing but a lot of Bolognas.... Due to its pitiable cowardice and lack of character, reaction in Germany has grown strong. The laws [sickness and accident insurance passed with National-Liberal backing] which have hitherto been manufactured in the Reichstag are so bad as to evoke the pity of a dog. [... sind hundserbaermlich schlecht.] ... The whole... is the purest fraud." Mehring, *Geschichte der SPD*, IV, 249.

policy of waiting for the collapse of capitalist society gave the opponents of the SPD one of their most potent means of propaganda by picturing the SPD as hostile to social legislation and the like.[33]

This juxtaposition of theoretical Marxism with reformist practices within the SPD was disturbed by the emergence of revisionism. Although the anti-revisionist forces in the SPD saw in revisionism nothing but the systematization and theoretical justification of reformist attitudes, revisionism seems to have been a third factor independent of either of the two forces which had previously been active in the SPD. The confusion between the problem of tactics and the struggle over revisionism was of singular importance for the later history of the SPD.

In its most complete form, German revisionism had been developed by Eduard Bernstein. Exiled in the 1870's from Germany, he had finally settled in London whence he returned to Germany in 1901. He had become one of the more important socialist theoreticians. He was considered the heir of Engels, and he strongly influenced the opinions of the *Neue Zeit*, probably the most important socialist periodical at the end of the nineteenth century.

The thesis of revisionism was first presented in a series of rather groping articles in the *Neue Zeit*. The evolution of these first articles to the final and comprehensive statement of revisionism several years later showed the influence of the controversy raging about his views, of the confusion over his attitudes and those of other revisionists like Vollmar and Auer who never completely overcame their reformist beginnings, and of the personal bitterness which became evident in the attacks of Bebel and Kautsky.

Bernstein used the Marxian methods of inquiry and applied them with eminent skill. He turned to the examination of some

33 See Hans Blum, *Die Luegen unserer Sozialdemokratie*, 1891. The author made great political capital from the fact that the SPD had in the Reichstag voted against Bismarck's social legislation.

of the implications of Marxian thought, and to the economic interpretation of contemporary Europe by those claiming spiritual descent from Marx. Bernstein was able to discern that many of the industrial phenomena on which Marx based his conclusions represented only a transitional stage in the industrial development, that Marx had not observed capitalism in its 'normal' behavior-pattern, and that deductions derived from the interpretation of this transitional stage alone were not necessarily valid for later stages of industrial development.

In the first of a series of articles on ' The Problems of Socialism' in the *Neue Zeit,* in 1895 and 1896, Bernstein voiced the opinion that scientific theories would become utopian if they were considered as dogmas. If socialism was not merely a science but practical politics, the theories of class-struggle and of economic evolution left much undefined. Even if Marx and Engels could be cited in support of the thesis, the delay of all solutions of the social problem beyond ' the day of the final victory of socialism' was utopian. Society was not changing into socialism from one moment to the next; it was more correct to speak of society as growing into socialism.[34] He declined to accept the view that the trend was towards a completely collectivized society but asserted that a partially collectivized society was an immediate possibility.[35]

He examined the theory of the concentration of industry and found that while this concentration had taken place in Germany, the present stage fell far short of anything envisaged by Marx.[36]

Turning to the problem of agriculture, Bernstein concluded that the ownership of large estates did not seem to be conducive to large scale agricultural enterprises. He cited exten-

34 *Neue Zeit,* vol. XV, pt. 1, no. 6, pp. 164 ff.

35 *Ibid.,* no. 6, pp. 204 ff.

36 The share of large factories in German production varied from forty-seven to fifty-four percent in 1882 and from sixty percent to seventy percent in 1895; *ibid.,* no. 10, pp. 303 ff.

sive figures to show that even in England, which in the opinion of socialists was also the most advanced country agriculturally and most ready for the nationalization of its estates, the stage had not yet been reached when (according to Marxian theory) the socialization of the land would be practical or possible. He advised socialists to concentrate on objectives whose solution under the existing conditions had become possible.[37]

Bernstein scored the hostility evidenced by socialists against the use of the term ' state '. He agreed that, because of the problem of number and space, only few industries could be socialized by the state, but asserted that administration would continue to be necessary, and that dicipline in economic fields would not cease with socialism. A socialist community would make it easier to fulfill the demands of economic responsibility and discipline, but " the idea of the abolition of self-discipline is altogether anti-socialist. Its alternative must be either complete tyranny or the disintegration of all orderly society." [38]

Bernstein warned that conservatism was not the monopoly of reactionary groups, but that it was a danger to socialism, too. One must not refuse to see changing realities or to change one's view accordingly as did the opposition of the ' Young-Ones '.[39]

A critical examination of the data of the ' Preussische Gewerbezaehlung' of 1895 demonstrated to the satisfaction of Bernstein that neither the absolute nor the relative trend evidenced supported the belief in the rapid disappearance of small enterprise and the rapid increase of big industry. The progressive increase in the variety of industrial needs and growing trade allowed large and intermediary enterprises to co-exist in harmony. He rejected Marx' theory of economic crises and was not satisfied with Engels' remarks that modern transportation, communications, cartels, capital exports, expanding markets

37 *Ibid.*, no. 25, pp. 772 ff.

38 *Ibid.*, vol. XV, pt. 2, no. 30, pp. 100 ff.; no. 31, pp. 138 ff.

39 *Ibid.*, vol. XVI, pt. 1, no. 16, pp. 484 ff.

and the elasticity of credits alone could explain the failure of the predicted crises to materialize. If socialism, however, should come to power because of a sudden social and economic crisis, the existing decentralization (Zersplitterung) of industry would present to the SPD an insoluble task. Capitalism would still be needed to perform certain tasks, but it would be deprived of the needed feeling of security. Bernstein thought that such a difficulty would destroy the SPD. However, the simultaneous collapse of all branches of industry was becoming less likely, the more differentiation of each industrial branch progressed. A strictly communist society lay in the distant future, but the present generation might achieve some degree of socialism by the spread of democratic institutions, the socialization of some industries, and political economic responsibility. Socialism was a movement, a movement of social progress and of the organization of that progress; in its ultimate aims Bernstein professed not to be interested.[40]

Bernstein also asserted that socialism was an idealistic movement not only historically but in its very nature, (witness its emphasis upon recognition, and its interpretations and reforms) and that it would continue to be idealistic.[41] In fact, he went so far as to say that strict historical, Marxian determinism was incompatible with the purposes of a political socialist party.

Sharply differentiating himself from the attitude of the SPD, Bernstein rejected the notion that tactical, political, and party considerations were decisive. What was decisive was not the correlation of party activities to political considerations, propaganda value, party composition, and the like, but their correlation to economic realities, changing industrial conditions, and the modification of a theory conceived on too narrow a basis. Under the pressure of an anti-Bernstein agitation which attempted to picture his past activities on behalf of the party as

40 *Ibid.*, no. 18, pp. 548 ff.

41 *Ibid.*, vol. XVI, pt. 2, no. 34, pp. 225 ff.; no. 39, pp. 388 ff.

insignificant, his editorship of the *Neue Zeit* as purely honorary, and under the influence of the liberal bourgeois parties which professed to see in his ideas the dissolution of the SPD from within, Bernstein offered more concise statements of his views. Writing to the 1898 party-congress at Stuttgart from London, he stated: " I am objecting to the attitude that we face an early collapse of bourgeois society ... The deterioration of social conditions did not take place in the way predicted by the [Communist] Manifesto ... In all progressive countries the privileges of bourgeois capitalism recede ... before democratic innovations ... This trend is marked by factory legislation, democratization of municipalities and the extension of their jurisdiction, by the liberation of trade-unions and co-operatives from all legal restrictions and by consideration for organized labor in all projects initiated by public authorities ... The more the political institutions of modern nations are democratized, the more do the opportunities and necessities for a great political catastrophe diminish ... But does the conquest of political power by the proletariat mean only the conquest of that power by a political catastrophe?" [42] " The realization of socialist principles by way of piecemeal reforms is not only possible but is also the best and ... surest method for the socialist transformation of society." [43]

With constant reference to the text of the Erfurt program, Bernstein wrote: " The working class is the foremost political power which co-operates in the task of socialist transformation, but it is not the only one and will not remain the only one ... The 'natural necessity' [of the concentration of industry] ... cannot scientifically be determined ... It is doubtful ... that the army of surplus workers grows steadily more massive, and it is wrong [to say] that the class-struggle ... divides modern society into two opposing armed camps ... That crises are becoming ever larger and increasingly disastrous is not

42 *Protokoll des Parteitages Stuttgart 1898*, pp. 122 ff.

43 E. Bernstein, *Von der Sekte zur Partei*, p. 52.

impossible, but it has ... become doubtful ... Socialism will come not as the result of a great decisive battle, but as the result of a whole series of political and economic victories ... in the most diverse fields, ... not as a consequence of ever-increasing pressure, misery, abasement, ... but as the result of ... growing social influence and of ... relative improvements of economic, political and general social nature." [44]

Bernstein's criticism of the Marxian program consisted in the statement that neither the concentration of the means of production nor the accumulation of capital, neither the pauperization of the masses nor the cycle of crises had actually materialized. Marx had deduced these theories from hasty generalizations of incomplete data. The most obvious point of conflict between Bernstein and his orthodox Marxian opponents was the belief in the imminence of a great social-economic catastrophe, and that this should dictate the policies of the SPD. [45]

While Bernstein's revision of Marxian thought led to stronger emphasis upon practical reforms, this was incidental to the correction of the erroneous observations and faulty generalizations of Marx, and not the result of transitional political considerations or tactics.

Now it has been shown that the SPD during the 1890's had been divided on the question of reformist policies. All those involved in that discussion had defended the inviolability of the theses of the Erfurt program. But it was a generally accepted belief that tactics might justify a definite accentuation of such reformist, concrete, practical demands, even though it was recognized that tactical compromise on practical problems might endanger the party program.

Because of the prevalence of reformist tendencies within the SPD it happened that, except for their different motivation of the pre-eminence of reformist endeavors—theoretical versus

44 *Ibid.*, pp. 69 ff.

45 Weidmann, *op. cit.*, pp. 64-67.

practical considerations,—the views of Bernstein and the views
of sections of the SPD members in German legislatures approached rather closely. The SPD at large and the discussions
in the party congresses in general missed this not unimportant
difference: revisionism was viewed in the same light as the
reformist activities which had previously loomed so large in
the discussions within the SPD; it was viewed as a change of
tactics and it was condemned as bad tactics. Indeed, Kautsky
and others occasionally showed their awareness of the theoretical implications of Bernstein's conceptions,[46] and Kautsky
agreed that Bernstein's " emphasis on practical piecemeal economic work corresponds to a real need, his doubts regarding
... great and sudden ... political changes ... correspond to the
experience of recent years." [47] But Kautsky made it eminently
clear that for him revisionism was essentially a tactical problem: " Bernstein thinks that ... the proletariat gains continuously more political rights ... more economic power through
trade-unionism ... municipal administration, the formation of
co-operatives, and the like, so that socialist production will
slowly overgrow capitalist production ... This ... rests on
sound facts ... But it is our hard luck that these facts prevail
not in Germany but in England," and that the difference in
the conditions of the two countries imposed different tactical
procedures.[48] And again in 1903 Kautsky stated that revisionism originated in France (Jaurés and Millerand) and England
(Fabian Society), and that Germany was not ripe for it; " the
conquest of political power cannot take place piecemeal when
it is concentrated [as in Germany] ..." [49] It is surprising that

46 For example, Kautsky, *Bernstein und das sozialdemokratische Programm*, 1899. Kautsky-Bernstein debates in *Neue Zeit*, vol. XVII, pt. 1
and 2, *passim*.

47 Kautsky, *op. cit.*, p. 165.

48 *Protokoll des Parteitags Stuttgart 1898*, pp. 126 ff.

49 *Protokoll des Parteitags Dresden 1903*, pp. 380 ff. The example of
Millerand in France joining a non-socialist ministry had raised the question
of whether the German SPD should do likewise after the 1903 election. Ac-

Kautsky failed to perceive that this argument did not constitute a refutation of revisionism at all; Kautsky's statement
constituted an admission that revisionism was theoretically
sound in some countries, and that its rejection for Germany
was due to practical considerations. In fact, Kautsky's arguments implied a much greater modification of orthodox Marxism than Bernstein had ever suggested. If socialism could not
progress according to the same general principles in disregard
of the political differences in various countries, one of the most
basic tenets of socialism—its international character—would
be questioned.

Yet, Kautsky considered revisionism as a tactical problem
and this was decisive for the attitude of the SPD towards revisionism. Bernstein insisted in vain that revisionists did not
form a homogeneous group within the SPD. He pointed out
that he approved of the practical reformers within the party,
but that his main contention was the need of restating the
first six paragraphs of the Erfurt program whose economic
and political postulations had become subject to serious
doubt.[50] Auer, another prominent revisionist, protested vainly
against the SPD insinuation that revisionism desired to place
the party in a line with leftist bourgeois parties.[51] Auer stressed
that the work of Marx and Engels contained many glaring
contradictions, and that Marx and Engels were fully aware
that history had disregarded their predictions of 1848.[52] Peus,

---

cording to parliamentary tradition, the SPD was entitled, on the basis of
the election returns, to the presidency or vice-presidency of the Reichstag,
but the participation of SPD members in court life might provoke even
greater dissent than did the participation of some South-German SPD representatives in provincial court life. See G. v. Vollmar, *Lehren und Folgen
der letzten Reichstagswahlen,* and *Die Sozialpolitik in Frankreich und
Deutschland.* See also Scheidemann, *Memoiren eines Sozialdemokraten,* I,
203 ff., regarding the turmoil in the Reichstag when Scheidemann presided
as president pro tem for a few days.

50 *Protokoll des Parteitags Dresden 1903,* pp. 390 ff.

51 *Ibid.,* pp. 362 ff.

52 *Protokoll des Parteitags Hannover 1899,* pp. 206 ff.

another revisionist, pointed out in vain that beyond any set of final aims there must be further final aims, and that hence the movement, and not the final objectives, was of dominant importance.[53] And Dr. David stressed in vain that even Kautsky had admitted that working class misery was diminishing, that their standards were higher now than fifty years earlier, and that the real point of the argument was the theory of pauperization, which was in error.[54] The opposition to revisionism centered mainly on the problem of tactics.[55]

Bebel illustrated his insight into the problem of revisionism by choosing as his point of departure the coincidence that many revisionists were South-Germans or had lived there for a time. In a supposedly very clever vein he declared: " Munich is the Capua of the German SPD. In Munich none walks ... with impunity among beer mugs. In Munich even the proudest pillars of the party are broken ... Have a look at this Parvus; ... only recently everybody would have sworn that he was an uncorrupted radical. And this proud pillar having stood in Munich for some time, was broken and lies shattered ... A fine comrade, fast and true to his principles ... After a few years in Munich ... broken in spirit and soul ... If I should go to

53 *Protokoll des Parteitags Stuttgart 1898*, p. 98.

54 *Protokoll des Parteitags Hannover 1899*, pp. 127 ff.

55 *Cf. Protokoll des Parteitags Dresden 1903, passim.* Kolb, also a revisionist, made a very forceful statement regarding his position at the time. " The so-called revisionists maintain ... that the objective of our strivings will be the result of an organic evolution.... Kautsky maintains the same point of view, but thinks ... that the collapse must needs come. We on the other hand say that it need not come to that.... Have not all our leaders declared that we want to reach our objective by legal means? ... We may not say: it needs come to a collapse, for ... then the moment will come when force and not law will decide. I maintain ... that we have been in the center of the social revolution ... that it happens before our eyes.... Kautsky says ... we must conquer political power.... I maintain the very same point ... it only depends what we understand by the term ' to conquer.' If ... one of our comrades would be called into the governmment, then this is not a sneaking into political power ... for we would not get [the post], were not society forced to give it to us." *Ibid.*, pp. 348 ff.

Munich myself, I would be afraid for myself." In bitter irony
he referred to the revisionist view that the SPD was not ready
to take over the government all at once: " Of course, all political genius, all diplomatic aptitude . . . is in the camp of the
revisionists. Their . . . genius can be discerned one thousand
meters away, and their . . . aptitude can be smelled one hundred
meters away." [56] In a soberer vein, Bebel in the same speech
argued that the revisionists had no valid arguments on their
side, for he, Bebel himself, could point with pride to his own
parliamentary record. Citing examples of his own parliamentary endeavors, he declared that " we shall accept concessions
where we can get them," but while fighting for them, he did
not feel the need to vote for them in the Reichstag: laws which
had reached the voting stage would be passed anyway.

By considering revisionism as a problem of tactics, the SPD
agreed that Bernstein's ideas should be evaluated in the light
of tactics. Thus the SPD, by implication, discarded the
supremacy of any set of basic concepts in favor of considerations of tactics. By considering revisionism as a mere tactical
problem and by rejecting it as poor tactics, the SPD showed
that it could readily move to the right of Marxism, if tactical
considerations required it, and that the Lassallean influences
had never lost their firm hold on large sections of the party
membership.

The implications of the SPD attitude toward revisionism
indicated that the party was, under certain conditions, ready
to jettison not only the practice of political radicalism, but the
Marxian essence of its theory as well. All that was needed was
an impelling external stimulus, a sound need for a change in
tactics.[57] When under the stimulus of the first World

---

56 *Protokoll des Parteitags Dresden 1903*, pp. 299 ff.

57 For a very able discussion of revisionism and its implications in party
life within Germany see R. Brunhuber, *Die heutige SPD*, 1906, especially
pp. 208 ff. For a rebuttal of the views presented there see E. Bernstein,
Die heutige SPD in Theorie und Praxis, 1906.

War, nationalism and all its peculiar connotations for Germans posed a new tactical problem, when the change of party leadership after 1900 brought to the helm a group of men trained in parliamentarism, when the lucidity of the revisionist argument and the divergence between Marxian predictions and actual history became overwhelming, the majority of the SPD moved sharply to the right, producing the gap between the party of the Erfurt program and the party of Goerlitz. Most revisionists, however, refused to be guided by considerations of tactics. They were unwilling to compromise on their own deductive thinking and objectives. And seeing these objectives sacrificed by the shift in SPD policies during the war years, they aligned themselves, as did Bernstein and Kurt Eisner and Mehring and Parvus, with the 'Unabhaengige Sozialdemokratische Partei Deutschlands', the revolutionary USPD.

CHAPTER III

THE SPD AND THE OUTBREAK OF WAR

a. THE SPD IN 1914

Two major trends marked the history of the SPD from its beginnings until the first decade of the twentieth century: (1) nationalistic sentiments going back to Lassalle and von Schweitzer, and (2) the implied abandonment of purely Marxian doctrines which had become evident in the debates over revisionism.

During the war, SPD authors as well as opponents of the party produced an impressive array of statements and quotations to prove that the party had embraced the ideal of national defense at a very early date and that it had never, or only for a very short time, rejected the duties arising from citizenship.[1] But the attempts of both friends and foes of the SPD to demonstrate that the party had become a nationalistic group well before 1914 can no more be accepted than the judgment of those who saw in the war-time changes of the SPD only a sinister plot to deceive the governments and the good people of Germany in order more easily to carry on activities on behalf of an anti-national revolution.[2]

During the half-century before 1914, many factors within Germany helped shape SPD attitudes towards nationalism.

---

1 For example Ch. Andler, *La décomposition politique du socialisme allemand*, Paris, 1919, *passim*; K. Haenisch, *Die deutsche Sozialdemokratie in und nach dem Weltkrieg*, Berlin, 1919 (first edition 1916), pp. 73-94. Haenisch stressed the anti-national trend produced by utopian socialism and the hostility of government and industry towards the interests of the workers (pp. 95-101) in the face of the growing identification of the worker's interests with the interests of the state due to the expanding social legislation, better working conditions and the like (pp. 103-6). *Cf.* P. Lensch, *Die deutsche Sozialdemokratie und der Weltkrieg*, Berlin, 1915, pp. 46 ff., and E. David, *Die Sozialdemokratie im Weltkrieg*, Berlin, 1915, pp. 24-39.

2 For example W. Breithaupt, *Volksvergiftung 1914-1918*, Berlin, 1925, pp. 7-8.

From the time when the political unity of Germany was only a romantic dream, the utopian pioneers of socialism had favored anti-nationalist and internationalist attitudes. That the worker had no fatherland, that the proletarian had nothing to lose but his chains, had too long been not only the postulate of a strange new ideology but simply a statement of fact. As proof of this statement, German socialists pointed to the persecution of liberals and socialists after 1849, who, as exiles in France, England and the United States, enjoyed political and social liberties unknown in the autocratic German states. The repression of the socialist advocates of the unification of Germany, the distrust and hate accumulated under the anti-socialist legislation between 1878 and 1890, and the resumption of the anti-SPD struggle in the mid-1890's all tended to produce lasting and deep anti-nationalist sentiments among the rank and file of the workers.

On the other hand, nationalistic influences had also asserted themselves persistently during these fifty years.[3] The expansion of political rights and social legislation brought the worker closer to the state. Popular education, compulsory military service and universal suffrage in the Empire—which forced the political parties to appeal to the working class,—contributed to this development; Bismarck had succeeded in giving the workers something more valuable to lose by revolution than merely their chains. Trade-unions were among the first to appreciate this new trend in official policies. Germany was growing into a state of social utilitarianism in which the worker played not the least significant part.

The debates on revisionism indicated that the SPD might abandon its radicalism, and that reform was becoming the main aspiration of the party. The trade-unions in particular had acquired a considerable stake in existing society, and

3 Bebel's refusal to support Prussia in her war against France in 1870 was eventually misinterpreted as only a defense of the 'gross-deutsche' unification program; Haenisch, *op. cit.*, pp. 91-92.

therefore looked askance upon radical revolutionary experimentation. Yet, the party had formally rejected revisionism at the congress of Dresden in 1903, and the implications of the inter-party discussions on revisionism had remained only a potentiality. This rejection of revisionism pervaded official party pronouncements and motivated its continued hostility to the German Empire before 1914. Neither the attempts to trace back the 'class-treason' of the SPD into the pre-war years, nor the desire to cripple the pre-eminence of German socialism in international socialism, nor indeed the fervor of those desirous to erase from memory the embarrassing pre-war views of the party, can obscure this rejection of revisionism.[4] Among as large a group as the SPD, a respectable number of witnesses can always be quoted to support the view that by 1914 this or that attitude predominated. But, by 1914, none of these contradictory tendencies had triumphed. Any decision ultimately taken by the SPD in questions of nationalism, of the nature of the existing state and of reform was certain to have a long and consistent historical background; but no decision ultimately taken could claim to derive from the inherent compulsion of this historical development. The choice of the SPD between its rival historical antecedents depended on the introduction of a new, incisive factor. Such a factor was provided by the outbreak of war in 1914.

b. The SPD and the Outbreak of War

The outbreak of war occurred at a time when a decision by the SPD in favor of the national cause seemed rather unlikely. The antagonism between the SPD and the bourgeois parties had for years not been as keen as it was in 1914. Clashes in

4 For example E. Drahn and S. Leonhard, *Unterirdische Literatur im revolutionaeren Deutschland waehrend des Weltkrieges*, Berlin, 1920, p. 7. (A collection of Spartacist leaflets and the like.) E. Barth, *Aus der Werkstatt der deutschen Revolution*, Berlin, 1919, pp. 9 ff. Andler, *op. cit.*, accused the SPD of having abandoned its liberal, republican and socialist spirit before 1914. *Cf.* S. W. Halperin, *Germany tried Democracy*, New York, 1946, p. 19.

the Reichstag and in the Prussian diet exceeded all recent parliamentary records in acrimony. The government had announced that it would sponsor no further social legislation,
the after-effects of the Zabern affair were still rankling, and
the inter-party fights in the election of 1912 and in more recent
by-elections had done nothing to calm political tempers. After
the failure of electoral reforms in Prussia, promised by the
Emperor in 1908, the SPD had in 1914 seriously considered
calling a general strike to achieve reforms by force. The feeling
of bitterness and hostility towards the government had found
expression at the German Trade Union Congress in 1914.

For years, also, SPD policy had concentrated on the prevention of war. At the congresses of the second International
after the Morocco crisis, at Stuttgart in 1907, at Copenhagen
in 1910, at London in 1911, and at the Basel Peace Congress
in 1912, resolutions had recorded the determination of the
workers to oppose with all means at their disposal any declaration of war in their respective countries, and to utilize—
should war break out—the resulting economic and political
crises to hasten the abolition of class rule.[5]

It was in this atmosphere that the Serbian crisis took place.
The SPD feared from the outset that the threatening involvement of at least two major European powers would lead to a
general European catastrophe. As the crisis progressed, the
SPD therefore became dominated by the desire to prevent war.

The SPD press fought a losing battle to gain attention and
to shift public opinion away from war. After the publication
of the text of the Austrian ultimatum to Serbia, the party
press condemned practically unanimously the threatening war
and the criminal actions of German and Austrian war-mongers
as a threat growing out of capitalism, chauvinism, and militarism. On July 25, 1914, the *Vorwaerts* commented editorially:

5 Andler, *op. cit.*, pp. 28 ff., saw a far-reaching break with tradition in
the SPD refusal to favor a general strike as a means to prevent war in
Europe.

" They want war—the Austrian ultimatum makes it evident
. . . An insane crime [the assassination of the Austrian arch-
duke and his wife] shall be crowned by an even more insane
crime . . . This ultimatum is so shameless that a Serbian government that yields to it . . . must face . . . dismissal between
dinner and dessert." [6]

The SPD particularly feared German interference in favor
of the Dual Monarchy. The Pan-German press had exerted
its influence to utilize a situation so favorable to its objectives,
and it was not at all certain that it would not succeed. Allegedly, the Prussian minister of the Interior had warned the
SPD on July 26, 1914, that Germany would defend Austria
if Russia attacked and that the SPD should call off its protest
meetings against the war. This did little to allay the fears of
the party for an act of German aggression.[7] On July 28, 1914,
SPD mass meetings were held all over Germany, condemning
the Austrian action and calling for German neutrality.

These efforts of the SPD were coupled with attempts to
utilize the international socialist organization to preserve
peace. On July 29, 1914, the International Bureau of the International Socialist Party met in Brussels, and Haase
emphasized that " the German proletariat declares that Germany must not interfere, even if Russia does." [8] At Brussels,
too, it was decided to convene immediately at Paris the international congress originally scheduled to meet in Vienna in
September. The sole item on its agenda was to be the pre-

6 The editorial showed that the SPD was by no means pro-Serbian:
" Even if the Greater Serb movement is a part of the South Slav bourgeois
revolution and as such has all historical rights on its side . . . still socialism
cannot find much to commend . . . on the Serbian side. . . . It must certainly
set its face against an agitation which works with bombs and revolvers. . . .
The crime of the chauvinist press is that it goaded Germany's dear ally to
the utmost "; *Vorwaerts*, July 25, 1914.

7 According to Haase, at the Reichskonferenz der SPD, September 22,
1916; quoted by E. Bevan, *German Social Democracy during the War*,
London, 1918, pp. 7-8.

8 *Ibid.*, p. 9.

vention of war. But the handful of delegates who succeeded in reaching Paris met too late. Diplomatic and military events prevented them from taking any decisive action beyond an informal and unauthorized agreement that socialist parties should abstain from voting in favor of war credits in their respective parliaments.

The anti-war attitude of the SPD before August, 1914, rested on the assumption that, in the Austrio-Serbian war, Russia might interfere on the side of Serbia and that Germany, claiming to fulfill her treaty obligations under the Dual Alliance, would aid her ally and attack Russia. The SPD had not anticipated that Germany might become involved in the war by the seeming aggression of Russia. The judgment of later historians of the role of the Russian mobilization bears out the overwhelming impressions of German public opinion at the time. That Germany should seemingly find herself the victim of an attack took the SPD leaders unaware. " The cossacks had crossed the border of East Prussia; t h a t w a s t h e c a u s e o f t h e w a r ."[9]

The emergence of Russia as the main enemy placed the threatening war in a new light. Since the founding of the socialist parties, Russia had been viewed by socialists as the most reactionary state in Europe, and war against Tsarism had been preached with the fervor of a socialist crusade. From Marx and Engels onward, Russia had been depicted as the opponent of socialism and of progress par excellence.[10] With its anti-Russian conditioning of the masses, the SPD had pursued a program strangely in accord with the latent attitudes bred by the memory of the Holy Alliance and Olmuetz, and with those Pan-German ambitions whose realization were barred only by a strong Russian Empire.

---

9 Haenisch, *op. cit.*, p. 18; spacings in the original. Haenisch apparently used his inaccurate language to convey that Russia had attacked Germany.

10 *Ibid.*, pp. 22 ff., David, *op. cit.*, pp. 48 ff.

Nor had the SPD anticipated the unparalleled popular enthusiasm in favor of the national cause which swept through Germany in the early days of August. In the face of this overwhelmingly popular spirit, the SPD had to reconsider well what action it should take after the outbreak of hostilities. If the masses were convinced that their national existence was at stake, any minority which increased the external danger by raising difficulties from within would face destruction by popular wrath. Not only in Germany but in all countries, socialist minorities were compelled by this consideration to support the will of the great majority of the people.[11]

Noske, in a moment of blunt frankness, stated that the SPD supported the war credits on August 4, 1914, in order to avoid "being beaten to death in front of the Brandenburg Gate."[12] Koenig, writing on May 5, 1916, in the *Vossische Zeitung,* told that it was the wave of popular enthusiasm in Germany which caused him to support the war credits. He quoted Dittmann as saying that "the party could not act otherwise. It would arouse a storm of indignation...The socialist organization would be swept clear away by popular resentment." Even Andler, who admitted his hostility towards German socialism by opening his work with the words: "Ce livre est un livre de guerre," admitted that "the leaders of the party were...forced...to intone the same furious war-cry which carried away the masses and to maintain that this was a 'popular policy', a national policy, a democratic policy. The whole mystery of the attitude of the German party leaders consists in this obligation to make 'policy for the masses';... the dissatisfaction of the people with the socialist party would

---

11 David, *op. cit.*, pp. 40-41; Haenisch, *op. cit.*, pp. 24 ff. The fear of the repercussions of its policy and of repressive measures by the government was so strong that the SPD chairmanship ordered Ebert and some other SPD leaders to seek safety in Switzerland. See Scheidemann, *op. cit.*, I, 245.

12 *Verhandlungen*, CCCXIV, 6212 ff., October 10, 1918.

have been sudden and terrible if it had not ... satisfied the passions unleashed by war." [13]

If anything but fear of popular repudiation motivated the SPD in the very early August days, it was fear of possible government actions under the war-time state of siege (which was expected to dwarf Bismarck's anti-socialist legislation). In his declaration to the German people upon the outbreak of the war, the Emperor had proclaimed that he no longer knew any parties, that he now knew only Germans, but the cessation of internal party strife, the ' Burgfrieden ', depended of course on the SPD attitude.[14]

On August 2 and 3, 1914, an SPD party caucus deliberated on the declaration informing the Reichstag and Germany of the policy of the party during the war. Because of the pressure of public opinion, fear of possible government action, the seemingly unprovoked Russian attack upon Germany, and the traditional party policies towards Russia, no resolutions to vote against the war credits were offered by any SPD member of the Reichstag in the party caucus. A proposal to abstain from voting on the credits in line with the quasi-agreements of the international socialist party won the support of only fourteen SPD representatives. Because of party discipline, the dissenting minority bowed to the majority decision and voted to support the government and the war credits.[15] In the Reichstag on August 4, 1914, all of the SPD representatives therefore

13 Andler, *op. cit.*, p. 112. The argument that the SPD supported the war to evade popular ire and dissolution was also used to prove that the SPD had condoned such a turnabout in order to be the better able to spread its revolutionary propaganda; see Breithaupt, *op. cit.*, p. 7.

14 Could it be that William II plagiarized Poincaré's: "A cette heure il n'y a plus des partis, il y a la France éternelle!" ? *Messages, lettres, discours, etc. de M. R. Poincaré, 1914-1918*, Paris, 1919, Message of August 1, 1914.

15 See among others: *Verhandlungen*, CCCXIV, 6226, speech of Ledebour, October 24, 1918; Berger, *Fraktionsspaltung und Parteikrisis in der deutschen Sozialdemokratie*, Muenchen-Gladbach, 1916, pp. 5 ff.; *Protokoll des Parteitags Wuerzburg, 1917*, pp. 63-68, 316-339.

voted in favor of the war credits, including those who were soon to become the most outspoken opponents of the German war effort.[16] Haase, the chairman of the SPD bloc in the Reichstag and president of the party since Bebel's death, read the SPD declaration of policies to the assembled Reichstag amid general applause. " We need to secure the culture and the independence of our country ... We shall not abandon our Fatherland in its hour of peril ... As soon as the purpose of security is fulfilled and the enemy inclined to peace, the war shall be brought to an end by a peace which will make possible the amity of neighbouring peoples ... Guided by these principles we agree to the proposed loan." [17]

The SPD declaration of August 4, was in accord with the imperial pronouncement that Germany was not moved by desire for conquest. It also signified the consent of the SPD to the Burgfrieden and to the good-will extended by the government to the SPD in order to win the assistance of the party controlling the workers in German industries.

Indeed SPD opposition to the war effort could eventually have done much to destroy the morale of the people at home and at the front, and the failure to do so may not have been entirely free from utilitarian considerations. " When German

---

16 Eighteen months after the event, one SPD delegate, Kunert, declared that immediately before the vote was taken, he had left the floor and had not returned until after the vote had been taken, thus in effect abstaining from support of the war-effort. This claim was never contested by any of those who were on the floor of the Reichstag on August 4, but nobody there had in fact noticed Kunert's absence.

17 *Verhandlungen*, CCCVI, 8-9. Haase had recommended to the party in the caucus of August 2 and 3, that the group abstain from voting, but accepted the verdict of the majority. When the Reichstag convened on August 4, the invasion of Belgium had not yet become public knowledge. Censorship had kept this information from the German public until the chancellor, Bethmann-Hollweg, announced it to the assembled Reichstag. The Belgian invasion punctured the myth of national defense which had motivated the decisions of the SPD, but the SPD hurriedly decided to uphold its declaration even after the invasion of Belgium had been announced.

armies were pressing forward . . . in Belgium and northern France, when Hindenburg was dealing the Russians stunning blows, . . . our majority politicians felt no doubt about an overwhelming German victory . . . It was folly to resist . . . history for the sake of . . . theorizing . . . The fact of . . . victory . . . offered various chances which might be . . . turned to account . . . The more patriotic the working class had proven itself during the war . . . the easier it would be to effect . . . social and political demands." [18]

Under the Burgfrieden and the general elation caused by the rapid advance of German troops through Belgium, the SPD benefited by the termination of discriminatory practices, the dissolution of the ' Reichsverband zur Bekaempfung der SPD ', the admission of its publications to military establishments, the permission of troops to visit SPD pubs, the adjournment sine die of trials against trade-unions and their leaders, the sudden eligibility of SPD members to employment by the state-owned railways, and so on. These early results of the ' new course ' were followed by the cancellation of all strikes and wage disputes then in progress, aid in bringing in the harvest, and the prevention of the paralysis of the labor market due to inductions and the relocation of employment centers because of war production.[19]

These activities of the SPD on the domestic scene were paralleled by attempts to use its pre-eminence among European socialists in order to gain their support for the German

18 H. Stroebel in *Neue Zeit*, September 15, 1916, pp. 674 ff. Drahn and Leonhard, *op. cit.*, p. 7: " Opportunism and reformism is a process which by the protocols of the party congresses may be followed back through the last two decades." Fr. Stampfer, *Sozialdemokratie und Kriegskredite*, Berlin, 1915, p. 6, stated that if the SPD had refused the war credits, popular wrath would have swept away the SPD in the case of a German defeat, but in the case of a German victory, the SPD would also have lost.

19 Bevan, *op. cit.*, pp. 25 ff.; Haenisch, *op. cit.*, pp. 33 ff., rejected the notion that SPD support had been purchased by the government in return for political concessions. David, *op. cit.*, pp. 18-19.

cause. By sending emissaries into neutral countries and by spreading its own version of the causes and origins of the war and of its objectives, the SPD became in effect the handmaiden of the German foreign office and of the High Command.

c. THE SPD DEFENSE OF THE POLICY OF AUGUST 4

The SPD declaration of August 4 had enjoyed the public support of all sections and leaders of the parties. This unanimity was the result of the unforeseen conditions which faced the party during the early August days and of the pressure of events which precluded a full discussion of policies and prejudiced the decisions of the party caucus.

These conditions soon lost their hold on many sections of the party. In August 1914, no party member had advocated the rejection of the war credits, but already in December 1914, a few SPD representatives cast their votes against war credits on the floor of the Reichstag. This opposition to the declaration of August 4 and to the subsequent policies of the majority of the SPD increased steadily and eventually resulted in a formal division of the SPD. These developments and policies (which will be discussed in a separate chapter) added to the factors which forced the supporters of the declaration of August 4, too, to subject their policies to a searching analysis.

For SPD and trade-union participation in the solution of war problems on the local and national level, and their ready co-operation with other groups in planning the food supply, food distribution, the welfare of the troops and their dependents before state aid reached them [20] did in fact represent a radical departure from traditional Marxian policies. " From the sharpest conceivable internal political struggle against the government and against all other parties ... [the SPD] had to find its way within the whirlwind of wildest events and within a few hours into the common battlefront of the German

---

20 From August to September 1914, the SPD paid out of its treasury RM 16,000,000 in support of the families of inductees. *Ibid.*; *Verhandlungen,* CCCIX, 3049.

nation . . . The ink had not yet dried on the flaming calls for peace . . . when the terrible duty of the moment made it imperative . . . to call in no less flaming words for the struggle against . . . the invading hordes of Tsarism," [21] wrote Haenisch with some degree of poetic license.

Eduard David, from whom many later SPD writers have taken their cue, tried to minimize this fact by emphasizing that " sharp as the tactical turn executed on August 4, was, it was not a break with social democratic principles . . . Our joining the national front of defense was only a realization of what the trail blazers and the best qualified leaders of our movement had always emphasized . . . There may be individuals without a nation, and when they organize they may form a cosmopolitan sect. But a party wrestling for the soul of its people cannot uproot itself nationally. In fateful hours, when the nation fights for its endangered existence, there can be no passive standing aside." [22] David was supported by a host of other writers who asserted over and over again that the policies of the party after August, 1914, were only the logical continuation of pre-war policies.[23] If indeed the policy of August 4, 1914, were not such a radical departure from traditional party views, the nature of the arguments advanced in its defense constituted a radical reshuffling of the party and the sudden adoption of a heretofore ill-tolerated heresy as its new central doctrine.[24]

[21] Haenisch, *op. cit.*, pp. 19 ff., 93-94.

[22] David, *op. cit.*, pp. 5-6, 24-37.

[23] In addition to the authors cited in this chapter, the works of Zimmermann, Kuttner, Radloff, Keil, Erdmann, Kolb, Winnig, etc. seem to indicate, by their insistence in defending the war-time policy of the SPD, how little that policy could really be defended on the basis of pre-1914 party history.

[24] The literature under discussion was produced in 1915 and the early part of 1916; that is, at a time when the deterioration of the diplomatic and military situation of Germany had not yet initiated the stream of pro-war literature from bourgeois circles. There was as yet no need for ' morale builders' and this literature cannot be classified as such.

In the defense of that policy, the SPD pointed out that the vote for the war credits on August 4, had not been a vote in favor of war. Under the German constitution, it was the Emperor and not the Reichstag who declared war. The rejection of the credits by the SPD would therefore not have prevented the outbreak of war, it might only have weakened the war effort.[25]

The SPD stressed that the prevalence of the martial spirit in Germany during the August days restricted its freedom of choice. The actions of SPD members rushing to the colors, of SPD soldiers at the front, and of local party-chapters in solving the food-problem and aiding the dependents of inductees were interpreted as a sign of the mass-approval of the war-time policy of the SPD. " We did not deceive ourselves about the healthy sentiment of national solidarity which fills, too, the social democratic worker as a living part of the German body." [26]

Much attention was given in this defense to the question whether the SPD could have taken any effective measures to prevent the outbreak of the war or to check its progress. The SPD denied that sabotage or passive resistance could be effective in stopping the war. In its polemics with socialists in enemy countries, the SPD asked why the socialist parties of those countries had failed to take the very steps which the SPD was accused of not having taken in Germany. Regard-

25 David, *op. cit.*, pp. 43-47, p. 39; Stampfer, *op. cit.*, p. 5. Andler, *op. cit.*, pp. 47 ff., argued that if the SPD could not have prevented the outbreak of the war by refusing war credits, none could have accused it of prejudicing the war effort by the rejection of those credits. The importance or irrelevance of the SPD vote could not logically be affected by the nature of that vote.

26 David, *op. cit.*, pp. 17-19. The popular support for the SPD policy was of course no indication of the orthodox socialist content of that policy. If the war-time policy of the SPD lacked socialist content in any true sense, and yet enjoyed the enthusiastic support of the masses, it would only illustrate the degree of effectiveness of socialist propaganda within the ranks of the SPD.

ing the use of an international general strike, the SPD pointed
out that this could not be relied upon: the danger of the successful invasion of one's own country would have become too
great; what assurances were there that such strikes would
have been successful in any other country but one's own? [27]
It was doubted, in fact, whether the number of workers in
Germany ready to obey the call to a general strike, would
have exceeded 10,000,[28] if indeed a general strike would not
have been crushed in its very beginning by the military power
and by popular wrath. Such an action would not have prevented the war; it would only have insured the defeat of the
SPD and of Germany.[29]

But the central theme of the SPD in defense of its support
of the national cause consisted in the statement that Germany
had been the innocent victim of aggression.

According to one SPD author, the war was an imperialistic
conflict due to the ascendancy of Germany and the resulting
conflict of Anglo-German interests. These interests, he held,
clashed particularly in the Near East. The German attempts
at strengthening the Ottoman Empire provoked the opposition of Russia, while France, in return for a free hand in Morocco, agreed to British designs on Egypt. As a result of the
aggressive designs of these three powers, Germany had been
disregarded in the division of North Africa, even after Tan-
giers and Algeciras. The Young-Turk revolt in 1908 prevented
England and Russia from jointly carving up the Ottoman
Empire at once. But their ambitions were not becoming more
moderate. Russia in particular was willing to impose her will
upon the Near East and the Balkans even at the risk of war.

27 Stampfer, *op. cit.*, p. 7. David, *op. cit.*, pp. 41-42, 117-151.

28 *Ibid.*, p. 42.

29 *Ibid.*, pp. 24-37. Lensch, *op. cit.*, pp. 29 ff. Haenisch, *op. cit.*, pp. 73-94.
Andler, *op. cit.*, pp. 16 ff., 100 ff., etc. Haenisch, *op. cit.*, p. 112, pointed out
the error of socialists in overestimating their ability to prevent wars by
mass strikes in key industries; the example of 1914 showed that the workers
would support the war.

Germany had frustrated these Russian designs upon the Otto-man Empire time and again, and the second Balkan war had thwarted Russian attempts to use the Russian-inspired Balkan alliance against Turkey. Russia therefore considered Germany as the main stumbling block and was willing to utilize the first opportunity to attain her ends by war. That Russia was able to avoid internal and foreign financial bankruptcy, and to remain at peace until 1914, was due to her bumper crops of 1909-1912. But these had come to an end in 1913, leaving Russia with no other alternative but war.[30]

This 'Leitmotif' of Russian aggression was taken up by many other SPD authors. David, for example, related the origins of the war in similar terms. Russia with its " semi-Asiatic political-cultural character ", a product of oppression and exploitation, aimed to destroy Turkey and to weaken Ger-many. The German acquisition of Alsace-Lorraine and the re-strictions imposed upon Russian expansion at the Congress of Berlin in 1878 had brought Russia and France together in an alliance in which 'Realpolitik' dominated morality. The Austro-German Dual Alliance, effectively barring Russian expansion in the Balkans, made Russia an uncompromising enemy of Germany. The economic development of Germany after 1870 renewed English traditions of hostility towards a strong Germany. England, " the despot of the world markets ", initiated the policy of encirclement whose main instrument, the Triple Entente, was but " a syndicate for the division of the World." Austria did not possess any colonies at all, and German imperialism was but a babe as compared to England's. In view of the Anglo-Russian record of annexations since 1900, their claims to protect the world against German con-quest were but slanderous lies. " The aggressive policies aiming at political acquisitions by means of force were on the side of the Triple Entente; the policy of the two Central Powers fol-lowed in general the principle of the Open Door, of equal free-

30 Lensch, *op. cit.*, pp. 9-15.

dom of economic enterprise in the world." In no instance had Germany provoked the Entente powers by aggressive action.[31]

In the opinion of SPD spokesmen, the importance of the diplomatic relations in July, 1914, was greatly exaggerated. The Austrian ultimatum to Serbia admittedly was stupid. But if Austria wanted a little war with Serbia, this did not mean that she also wanted a European conflagration. None could deny that Germany had not tried hard to correct the early mistakes made in backing Austrian measures against Serbia. But Russia desired to spread the conflict between Austria and Serbia all over Europe, and Russia's mobilization paralyzed the German-Austrian peace moves. Even after Austria, Russia and Germany had become involved in war, Germany had done her utmost to keep France and England neutral. Yet France turned the Eastern European War into a general European war, and England turned the European War into a World War. Hence, the main responsibility for the outbreak of the World War rested, according to the SPD, with England and France. That Germany had adopted annexationism during the war proved nothing for the pre-war days; but that the Pan-Germans before the war had clearly been in the opposition, proved conclusively to the SPD that Germany before 1914 had not pursued imperialism.[32]

But regardless of such considerations, the SPD considered that the war was a defensive one for Germany, because, in August, 1914, Germany was the weaker of the two opposing groups. The alignment of powers during the first World War represented an unprecedented peril to Germany. In the opinion of the SPD, the discussions about the historical origin could not detract from the fact that the war was truly defensive for Germany and that everything else had to recede before the need to safeguard and to defend the Fatherland.[33]

31 David, *op. cit.*, pp. 48-62.

32 *Ibid.*, pp. 70-95. Compare this view of the origins of the war with Sidney B. Fay, *The Origins of the World War*, 2 vols.

33 David, *op. cit., passim*. Stampfer, *op. cit.*, p. 39. Lensch, *op. cit.*, p. 45.

The danger of bringing Central Europe under "semi-barbarian Russian rule" had been traditionally opposed by socialists throughout the nineteenth century, and the example of Russian actions in the occupied areas produced added terror.[34] This traditional fear of Russia sufficed to make a war with her appear like an immense peril.[35] But the combination of Russia plus the Western Powers made the danger of the war to Germany seem really terrifying. The Entente possessed superiority over German man-power and on the seas, and could apply a formidable blockade and effect the economic strangulation of Germany. The victory of this combination would have ended German territorial integrity, sovereignty and industry. The SPD could not accept such consequences;[36] it could not choose the victory of Tsarism in preference to voting war credits; it could not "pronounce the death sentence over Germany."[37] "We are convinced, today even more than at the beginning of the war, that this terrible struggle is a struggle for the political, economic and cultural fate of Germany; that it is a defensive war in the truest and most serious sense of the word. Hence it was our national privilege, our highest patriotic duty, to take it up resolutely and to see it through."[38]

34 David, *op. cit.*, pp. 97 ff. "We fight against Tsarism. With its bear's claws it will stamp out the culture of the whole of Western Europe and inveigle its barbarian population against our women and children.... The crowned hangman does not shy from putting the infamous murder of Sarajewo in the service of his criminal plans"; *Rheinische Zeitung*, August 5, 1914. (SPD paper.)

35 "Bonds of warmest sympathy united us deeply with the Russian revolutionaries, we strongly felt the sufferings of the unfortunate peoples panting under the rule of the whip of Nicholas II...and we placed high the influence...of Russia for the development of German literature; but economically, politically and culturally Russia continued to be for us the enemy.... Down with Russia!... This password...made the war so immensely popular throughout the whole couuntry. This it was which drove millions of social democrats...to the colors." Haenisch, *op. cit.*, p. 23.

36 David, *op. cit.*, pp. 11-12, 111-115.

37 Stampfer, *op. cit.*, pp. 4-5.

38 David, *op. cit.*, p. 116.

The SPD was satisfied that socialists in all countries except Russia and Serbia had also felt impelled to come to the defense of their nations. Emil Vandervelde had composed his differences with Monarchy and Church. The French socialists had concentrated their efforts on winning Italy over to their side, had endorsed the culture of anti-German hate, and had supported the sweeping war aims of Poincaré. In England, socialists had helped spread stories of German atrocities, had voted the war credits, and had supported the campaign of blockade and piracy on the high seas—though the SPD had to acknowledge that not all English socialists had been involved in this. The resolutions of the London conference of French and British socialists on February 14, 1915, had promised, according to the SPD, self-determination and hence the destruction of Germany and Austria. Yet the French had censured these resolutions as too moderate.[39] Therefore, if the SPD had betrayed its international obligations by its policy of national defense, so had all other socialists in Western Europe.

In fact, the SPD asserted that it had observed socialist maxims better than anybody else.[40] For in the controversy with its foreign and domestic critics about war-time SPD policies, most (except the unqualified supporters of Russian Bolshevism) agreed that in a clear-cut case of foreign aggression the policies under criticism would have been defensible.[41] And

[39] *Ibid.*, pp. 117-151. David was unable to comprehend that the liberation of European subject nationalities might not be motivated by the desire to destroy Germany and to acquire concealed annexations. See also, Haenisch, *op. cit.*, pp. 108-111.

[40] David, *op. cit.*, pp. 24-37. The author chided socialists for expecting anything else of the SPD but support of the war, and cited innumerable pronouncements by SPD leaders to prove that the SPD had always promised to come to the aid of the Fatherland in its hour of need, especially in election campaign speeches. David thus interpreted campaign promises made in the heat of anti-SPD electioneering as a valid indicator of party policy.

[41] *Cf.* Bevan, *op. cit.*, pp. 254-255. Haenisch, *op. cit.*, pp. 69 ff. Haenisch was one of the few participants in these polemics who did not lose his respect for the integrity and sincerity of his opponents.

with the causes of the war thus accounted for and the dangers threatening Germany thus itemized, the SPD was convinced that only Germany could claim to have been the victim of foreign aggression; a socialist therefore could not possibly have refused to support Germany on August 4, 1914.

But the SPD was not satisfied to rest its case merely on considerations such as these. It proceeded to make a virtue out of the necessities which it had faced at the beginning of the war. " The production and property systems which had been developed by German capitalism before the war [represented] a form of economic life essentially superior to the retarded labor and property conditions in England ... In a word, then, the war was ... a struggle of forward and upward surging forces, represented by Germany, against the powers of resistance and repression which we faced in the so-called democracies of the West." [42] The SPD began to consider Germany as the true inheritor of English liberalism, of the ideals of the French revolution, and of socialism; only a ' German ' victory could preserve this inheritance to Germany and to the SPD.[43]

The generally accepted notion that England rather than Germany was the homeland of liberalism did not quite fit into this picture, and that notion was therefore attacked. The SPD pointed out that nineteenth century English trade and colonial enslavement had led to the extinction of all native culture and economy. The exemplary political and social reforms of England—exemplary if compared to conditions prevailing on the continent—had been made possible only by the success of English monopolies in turning the whole world into either a source

42 Haenisch, *op. cit.*, from his introduction, pp. 1-8, which developed these ideas in full.

43 *Ibid.*, pp. 20 ff. The idea that a sweeping military victory was required to assure the continued well-being of the German working class, was exploited by the Pan-Germans and the government as well. See F. Behrens, *Was der deutsche Arbeiter vom Frieden erwartet*, 1917; and *Wirkungen der Kriegsziele unserer Gegner auf die Arbeitsloehne in Deutschland*, Berlin, Kriegspresseamt (probably in 1916).

of raw-materials or a market for British goods. " The much praised English ' freedom ' rested on the enslavement of the world." Because the progress of social and political conditions in England was impossible without English monopolies, English workers had a basic interest in preserving them. Hence their lack of international solidarity; hence their lack of class-consciousness in a country over-ripe for socialism; hence the dislocation of the struggle of the classes in England by the struggle for colonial possessions. But after 1870, the monopoly of England in industry and commerce had begun to collapse, and the results of that collapse had become evident at the turn of the century. Therefore, when war broke out, England embraced the opportunity to save its slipping monopolies, to crush a powerful competitor. " The participation in a world war was for the English bourgeoisie nothing but an escape from socialism. If any means existed for throwing back for decades the international struggle for the liberation of the proletariat from capitalism, it would be the collapse of the German Empire in this war against England." English socialism would then relapse to its position before 1880, and the German SPD would be crushed together with Germany. No party would thus lose more by an English victory than international social democracy.[44]

In regard to France, Germany and her soldiers felt, in the eyes of the SPD, nothing but deepest sympathy. Alsace-Lorraine had been a burning problem for France only because of the Russian campaign to make it so; in fact, France had entered the war only upon receiving her marching orders from Russia. A French victory, being tantamount to a Russian victory, was therefore incompatible with the advance of liberty. A combined French and Russian defeat would, however, remove all obstacles to Franco-German amity. For France, it would terminate all desires for ' revanche ', would terminate the need for heavy armaments, and would allow her to embark

44 Lensch, *op. cit.*, pp. 16-25.

on an extensive program of social legislation.[45] And just as the defeat of France in 1870 had brought the realization of the 'kleindeutsche' unification of Germany, so the defeat of Russia would now effect a new German unity, the unity of Germany and Austria-Hungary. The Russo-German war of 1914 was "the final act in the painful process of the development of the German people towards national unity." In addition, the defeat of Russia would end her aspirations in the Balkans and would force her to concentrate on internal problems, to solve the conflict between Tsarism and the people, and to break through the vicious circle of imperialist expansion and resulting social and economic unrest by means other than war. Russia's defeat, too, would therefore bring to realization more than one age-old socialist dream.[46]

A German victory, however, would not mean merely a boon to democratic and socialist aspirations. In some circles of the SPD the identification of Germany's cause with the interests of socialism went even further. The cultural advance of the common man, the extension of political rights, the broadening of the industrial base, and the resulting increment in

45 *Ibid.*, pp. 39-44. The author, however, agreed that this period of sweetness and light in Franco-German relations must be ushered in by a peace treaty which would not violate French honor but would leave her among the great powers.

46 *Ibid.*, pp. 29-38. Lensch ultimately concluded that the war was the long sought for revolution which had brought to a successful end the slow rise of Germany to a dominant position in world affairs. He strongly favored the culmination of that trend and endorsed protective tariffs and military aggressiveness as means in this advance. He wrote: "Nothing is more touching than the soft assertions of Germany's peacefulness by German politicians and professors. Certainly! One cannot doubt the subjective German peacefulness. But that does not prevent recognizing that, viewed objectively, we are and must be the disturbers of peace. . . . We must nolens volens break into pieces the existing balance of power, which is indeed only the hegemony of the Western powers, and create a new basis." He prided himself on being a Barbarian, since "only Barbarians are able to rejuvenate a world laboring in a comatic civilization." For him, the 'revolution' consisted of the eclipse of England by Germany; Lensch, *Drei Jahre Weltrevolution*, Berlin, 1918, pp. 60-64.

the share of each worker in the national economy, had helped produce a degree of national solidarity,[47] as a result of which the whole concept of the state could undergo a far-reaching change.

The state ceased to be considered as an instrument of class-struggle; the social and cultural advance of the workers now formed an integral part of its task. Only individual governments, in so far as they still opposed this new task, remained as legitimate objects of socialist criticism and attack.[48] The negation of the class-struggle imposed by the Burgfrieden became easily a virtue for the party which had long since ceased to be a one-class party, and which had come to include merchants, artisans and professional people.[49]

This trend was aided by the fact that the war had disappointed the anticipations and predictions of pre-war socialist writers. The ability of the capitalist system to withstand the upheavals of war without an immediate collapse and its success in staving off a sudden victory of the socialist revolution, caused the SPD to reconsider many of its pre-war theories.[50] This breakdown of Marxian tenets coincided with the political expediency of the declaration of August 4, 1914, and the long trend towards opportunism which has been traced above.[51] The ambition of Bismarck to tie the worker to the state by means of social legislation, political rights, and military service, had borne fruit. The objective of socialism was no longer the overthrow of the state from without, but its modification from within.[52] The emphasis on the international character of

---

47 David, *op. cit.*, pp. 173-185.

48 R. Calwer, *Das sozialdemokratische Programm*, Jena, 1914, pp. 87 ff.

49 Weidmann, *op. cit.*, pp. 83-84.

50 Haenisch, *op. cit.*, pp. 113-119. Andler, *op. cit.*, pp. 148 ff. *Protokoll des Parteitags Wuerzburg 1917*, pp. 145-163, speech of Cunow.

51 Andler, *op. cit.*, p. 86: " The last books of German socialism dealing with the question of right were those of Lassalle."

52 Haenisch, *op. cit.*, pp. 103-106.

the proletariat was argued away as the work of such anti-national foreigners as Radek, Pannekook, and Luxemburg, who lacked the sentiments of German nationality and were " consciously inimical to the state, especially without inner relationship to the German state and the German character." [53]

The idea of waiting for a catastrophe combining the features of the French Revolution with those of the Russian revolution of 1905 was rejected by the SPD after 1914 as erroneous. The war itself was accepted as the social revolution. Its revolutionary criteria were the change of the German army into a people's army, the mobilization of industry and its reorganization along socialist lines, and the rejection of the anarchy of private production and distribution in favor of social planning. The shortcomings of the war-time economy of Germany were attributed to the limited extent of this process. It was England that now presented a reactionary social-political organization, while Germany represented revolutionary progress. The dominance of the SPD in international socialism was viewed as but one indication of German leadership and an omen for the certainty of German victory.[54] If Germany in the past had lagged behind other countries in political democracy, it was because the country had faced war continuously after 1871. A German victory would remove this threat of war and the ensuing restrictions upon the unhampered cultural and democratic development of Germany. The destruction of Tsarism, the termination of the rivalry with France, and the final union with Austria would insure the full liberal and national growth of Germany and of Europe.[55]

53 *Ibid.*, pp. 101 ff. *Cf.* Fr. Thimme and Carl Legien (ed.), *Die Arbeitsgemeinschaft im neuen Deutschland*, Leipzig, 1915, for the statement of a postwar program of peaceful co-operation between the SPD and the bourgeoisie, presented by leading SPD and bourgeois politicians and statesmen. The Burgfrieden, it was hoped, could be extended into the post-war period.

54 Haenisch, *op. cit.*, pp. 120-26.

55 Lensch, *op. cit.*, pp. 56, 64.

SPD war-time policies were subjected to sharp criticism by French and British socialists and, ultimately, by dissident socialists within Germany.[56] In response to this criticism, the SPD attempted to tone down the impression created by these writings.[57] The adoption of chauvinist tendencies by some SPD members was termed regrettable but unavoidable.[58] The SPD had voted for war credits in 1914 " not in order to show its confidence in the government but to protect the German territory from invasion." [59] However, these attempts to counteract the often unfavorable reception of SPD arguments failed to check the growth of the Independent Socialists; they remained essentially unconvincing.[60]

The nature of the ex post facto defense of the policies to which the SPD committed itself on August 4, 1914, indicated a confession of the pre-eminence of national interests. In fact, some of the more prolific SPD partisans unreservedly accepted this pre-eminence of national interests. Other SPD writers were more hesitant about its adoption, but the new trend affected them none the less. The nature of the criticism of the SPD directed against the war-time governments and contemporary conditions in Germany revealed that this hesitancy did not result from the rejection of the war-time trend but was due to modesty.

56 See *infra*, Chapter 6.

57 For example Andler, *op. cit.*, p. 86; " When the egotistical interests of the German working class found themselves in agreement with the conquering action of a regime of force, then it was conquest and force which the social democracy preferred in the name of those strictly German interests."

58 Stampfer, *op. cit.*, p. 6. The SPD expelled those of its members who refused to support the policy of August 4, 1914, but it refused to expel the ' chauvinists' whom Stampfer chided.

59 *Neue Zeit*, vol. 33, pt. 2, no. 17, July 23, 1915, p. 532. *Protokoll des Parteitags Wuerzburg 1917*, p. 70.

60 Andler, *op. cit.*, pp. 75 ff., saw in the emergence of the Independent Socialists in 1915 and the SPD calls for peace on the basis of the status quo ante bellum nothing but an attitude dictated by the growing certainty of a military stalemate or defeat.

For the SPD had not ceased its criticism of the government during the war years. Before the war, however, the SPD had attacked the German government for concentrating on nationalistic policies at the expense of social endeavours. Now, SPD criticism of the government was increasingly directed against the failure of the German government fully to protect these nationalist interests against blunders and errors in the prosecution of the war.

CHAPTER IV

SPD CRITICISM OF GERMAN WAR-TIME POLICIES

SPD CRITICISM of the domestic policies of the German war-time government centered mainly on (1) the problem of food distribution and food supply, (2) military affairs, (3) the problem of ethnic minorities in Germany, (4) the state of siege, censorship, and related problems, and (5) the problem of the democratic reform of the German administration and of Prussia. The most incisive statements on these problems were offered in the Reichstag where the speakers enjoyed practically unlimited freedom of speech on questions admitted for general debate. In addition, critical statements made in the Reichstag could—in theory at least—be circulated as parts of the debates without interference by censorship. Thus, for the duration of the war, the Reichstags furnished the most important stage for inter-party play and changing party views.[1]

a. THE FOOD PROBLEM

After the beginning of the war, the trade-unions and the SPD proffered far-reaching recommendations regarding the administration and regulation of food production and food distribution. The official circles in Germany were, however, little inclined to accept suggestions regarding the organization of

---

1 One should keep in mind the way in which the German Reichstag transacted its business. The agenda of its sessions was usually determined ahead of time, and speakers for the various parties were designated in party caucuses and instructed what view to present. Thus each speaker always voiced official party views when speaking in the Reichstag. It was extremely rare that a party should have failed to name a speaker beforehand. In such a contingency, the person who usually represented the party on the particular subject would take the floor, and normally, further time for discussion would be demanded in order to find out the official views of the party. During the war years, it happened on only two occasions that SPD speakers spoke out of turn or without having their views previously approved in a party caucus.

the food supply. Even though the demands of the army had reduced the man-power required to insure top-yields of the major agricultural crops, it was hoped that increased imports from the Dual Monarchy would make up the food deficit. The cessation of food exports was also generally interpreted as favorable to the German war-time economy. But the major consideration for neglecting food-rationing at the very beginning of the war was the general belief that the war would last no longer than those of 1864, 1866 and 1870. In addition, the agricultural and industrial interests in Germany were close to the government and to the army and they successfully resisted the effective organization of food controls.[2] Indeed, the German food administrator was convinced that the search for chances to make a profit was the prime driving force of the war, and that instead of rationing, the government should purchase food in the open market for storage and allow prices to rise under the pressures of supply and demand until they were out of reach of most people, so that the utmost economy would automatically result.[3]

Even though imports of pork, butter, cheese, eggs, herring, and the like from Holland and Denmark rapidly increased far beyond 1914 levels,[4] the food situation in Germany began to deteriorate very soon after the outbreak of the war. The haphazard introduction of food rationing came too late to do much

2 The agricultural circles tried to prevent rigid food controls by the threat of a producers' strike and by the actual reduction of crop areas. This condition was illustrated by the publication, in 1915, of a letter by the Count Oldenburg-Januschau in which he revealed that he was reducing his agricultural production because of his resistance to the central control of prices and markets; see Scheidemann, *Memoiren*, I, 314-15. Michaelis, *Fuer Volk und Staat*, Berlin, 1922, p. 287, agreed that this type of sabotage existed. For a collection of the decrees and regulations issued in this connection, see J. Jastrow, *Im Kriegszustande*, Berlin, 1915.

3 Michaelis readily admitted this idea; *op. cit.*, pp. 276-7. Helfferich also thought that food prices should be high enough to encourage production and to discourage consumption; see *Der Weltkrieg*, II, 233 ff.

4 *Ibid.*, II, 215-21.

good, and the SPD recommendations regarding the production and distribution of potatoes and sugar, of fats, meat and coal were rejected.[5]

It is possible that, given the population, the size of the army, the needs, and the production of war-time Germany, no government could have prevented a serious shortage of food or errors in its distribution. It is highly probable that, given a more favorable progress of the war up to 1917, the people would have ignored hardships due to the food supply or its poor distribution. However, the progress of the war, especially in the winter of 1916-17, favored the growth of discontent. The government had consistently failed to give evidence of serious efforts to alleviate the situation or to heed the constant and voluble criticism offered. Wealth could still purchase all the food desired, while the workers, more than any other economic group, felt the full measure of war-time deprivations. The rightist parties, the army, censorship, and the government all too often condemned the criticism of these conditions as prolonging the war and giving aid and comfort to the enemy. But it was difficult to substantiate such an accusation in a situation that tolerated black markets, food speculation by army officers at the expense of the troops, provocative menus in officers' mess-halls, use of grain as livestock feed instead of as food, excessive punishment of food rioters in cities which for days had been without bread, and military inefficiency in shipping and storing food against the advice of food experts so that it spoiled.[6]

5 Haenisch, *op. cit.*, pp. 36 ff. The SPD had begun to present petitions favoring rationing as early as August 13, 1914. *Cf.* Gradnauer and Schmidt, *Die deutsche Volkswirtschaft*, Berlin, 1921; P. Eltzbacher, ed., *Die deutsche Volksernaehrung und der englische Aushungerungsplan*, Braunschweig, 1914; A. Skalweit, *Die deutsche Kriegsernaehrungswirtschaft*, Stuttgart, 1927; and F. Aereboe, *Der Einfluss des Krieges auf die lanwirtschaftliche Produktion in Deutschland*, Stuttgart, 1927.

6 *Verhandlungen*, CCCIX, 3049 ff.; CCCX, debates of May 10 to 12, 1917, and pp. 3491-3621; CCCXI, 3972, 4498 ff., etc. These points were brought out by the spokesmen of all parties, and the government repre-

The attempts of the government to ignore the true food situation met with little success.[7] The bare food shelves in the stores, the black markets, and speculation told the civilian population of the failure of the government to create the best possible system of food production and distribution, or to overcome those factors which prevented such a solution. It may be doubted whether speculation, black marketing or profiteering really deprived the population of a significant amount of food, but it cannot be doubted that they deprived the government of the confidence of the public.

---

sentative could usually defend himself only by asking that they be considered as unavoidable errors not indicative of general policy. By mid-1918, over twelve thousand food ersatz products had appeared on the market without being subject to control, testing, etc. Under rationing, the food value had been reduced to one thousand calories per diem. There was a lack of physicians, hospitals, qualified factory inspectors, etc. Protective legislation for female and child labor had been suspended. Medical papers dealing with these conditions had been barred by censorship in the hope of keeping the enemy ignorant of them. The resulting deterioration of health had produced a mortality rate of thirty-three percent among infants of one year of age, and a corresponding increase in tuberculosis, lung-ailments, etc.; *ibid.*, CCCXII, 5361, 5363 ff. The government, however, consoled itself that health conditions would deteriorate in any war, and that there was no cause for alarm; *ibid.*, pp. 5369-5371. *Cf.* F. Bumm, *Deutschlands Gesundheitsverhaeltnisse unter dem Einfluss des Weltkrieges*, 2 vols., Stuttgart, 1928.

7 On July 17, 1915, the discussion of problems of oil and fats was barred from the press; on November 25, 1915, the press was instructed to paint a rosy picture of the food situation and to emphasize that Germany's difficulties consisted exclusively of problems of distribution and not of production. Even though on March 23, 1917, the government admitted to the press (but not for publication) that the 1916 harvest had fallen short of expectations by a million tons, or admitted on March 15, 1918, that the hopes of bread from the Ukraine were illusionary, these regulations were never withdrawn; see Muehsam, *Wie wir belogen wurden*, Munich, 1918, pp. 64-125. Michaelis, *op. cit.*, pp. 270 ff., talked of an intentional waste of food, of a true orgy of cake baking in the winter of 1914, in order to impress England and to bluff regarding the effects of the blockade. Michaelis, however, declared that he objected to this waste. See also Professor A. Penck, *Wie wir im Kriege leben*, Stuttgart, 1916, being a letter addressed to the Rockefeller Foundation and trying to show that the food situation was on the whole satisfactory; if there were shortages, they occurred in the field of table luxuries which should better be done without in any case.

By the middle of 1915, the first detailed criticism of the food situation was offered in the Reichstag. Particularly under attack was the rise in the cost of living, the hoarding of food stuffs by farmers in the hope of an advance in maximum prices, and the failure of the government to prevent rises in the price of commodities such as sugar, an adequate supply of which should have been assured by the cessation of their exports.[8] In granting the war credits on behalf of the SPD, on December 21, 1915, Ebert called for rigid price controls in order to counteract the spread of popular discontent caused by speculation and profiteering.[9]

With the prolongation of the war, this criticism became general. By the middle of 1916, all parties had joined in attacking the lack of government action, the spread of black markets, the profiteering of farmers and dairy associations, the refusal to market produce through regular channels or to surrender it to the government, and the refusal to extend hunting privileges to the common folks, so that crops and fields could be protected against the ravages of game whose increasing abundance went unchecked because of the induction of hunters.[10]

On October 27, 1916, Ebert again qualified the SPD support of the war credits by calling for the reduction of prices on necessary consumers' goods and for a more efficient organization of food distribution.[11] But in spite of the unanimity of all parties regarding the need for an improved food supply, no action was taken.

The food crisis in Germany became grave during the winter of 1916-1917. Coupled with the failure of the peace offensive in December, 1916, and the participation of the United States

8 *Verhandlungen*, CCCVI, 188-194, speech of Wurm, May 29, 1915.

9 *Ibid.*, pp. 506-507. Not until 1918 was an attempt made to control the prices and profits in war production; *ibid.*, CCCXI, 4498 ff.

10 *Ibid.*, CCCVIII, 1593-1634; debate of June 7, 1916.

11 *Ibid.*, p. 1852.

of America in the war, it exposed the government to sharp criticism by all parties. " In social policy a completely wrong way has been chosen. The psychological excitement of the war and the undernourishment of the people create the danger that the productive power of the people may be undermined before its time. Hence it should have been the task of a far-sighted social policy particularly in this time of war to correlate workers' protective legislation with the conditions." [12] " The undisguised fact is . . . that because of the war very grave conditions prevail . . . This must not free us from the duty to watch over these events very carefully and to strive to do everything in our power to ameliorate these sorry conditions." [13]

The sharpest words on the food situation, spoken up to the time in the Reichstag, were uttered on March 22, 1917, by Dittmann, one of the Independent Socialists : " It appears as if neither the House nor the . . . government knows the conditions prevailing . . . in the country. It appears not to be known, or they pretend not to know, . . . that workers collapse at their work because of hunger . . . Although censorship bars much of what happens in the country from publication, . . . it is known well enough . . . Gentlemen, don't try to deny it, but use your efforts to overcome famine as soon as possible." Even less passionate speakers had to agree that one could indeed talk about a famine in view of the great need for adequate supplies of proteins, fats, and carbohydrates.

These facts could not be denied, but they were countered with the statement that " speeches like the one just held here

12 *Ibid.*, CCCIX, 2545 ff.; speech of Hoch, March 20, 1917.

13 *Ibid.*, pp. 2634 f., speech of Hoch, March 22, 1917. Also, *ibid.*, pp. 2671 ff. This criticism coincided with the vehement condemnation of the breakdown of transportation and the " idiotic " dispositions made by " asinine bureaucrats ", which Dr. Stresemann, then still a Pan-German and an ardent supporter of the war, offered on March 20, 1917; *ibid.*, pp. 2548 ff.

... will only prolong the war." [14] How easy it was to refute such a charge was shown by the spirited reply hurled by Ledebour against such an accusation: "We must present these grievances here, because there is no improvement, and this way we serve the best interests of Germany. *Not* those who cause such evil, not those who hide or embellish it, but those who through public criticism work towards an improvement are the best friends of our Fatherland ... Gentlemen, we must present these grievances, we must criticize, because the Reichstag is the only forum where one may express openly what exists and what must be demanded." [15]

The failure of the government to act in a constructive manner or to accept the proffered recommendations eventually caused a notable reduction in the efficiency of workers and soldiers, growing discontent, increasing support of the radical opposition, and demonstration strikes such as those of April 16 and 17, 1917, which, as the reporter for the Reichstag's committee investigating them admitted, had been caused solely by the announcement of further reductions in the bread ration.[16]

When these protest strikes of April, 1917, took place, the SPD utilized its influence among the trade-unions and the workers to end the strikes and to return the strikers to their shops. And in January, 1918, the SPD once more came to the aid of the government and helped terminate a strike which

14 *Ibid.*, pp. 2635 ff., debate of Dittmann, Kunert, and Dr. Bumm who, as President of the Reichsgesundheitsamt, was unable to refute the facts that Dittmann referred to, although he condemned his conclusions about famine. It was a practice of the German Reichstag that the government representative concerned would rise immediately after any criticism of its activities to challenge, if possible, the facts cited by the party spokesmen.

15 *Ibid.*, CCCX, 3398 ff., debate of May 15, 1917. Ledebour was one of the leading Independents, and one of the sharpest critics of the government and of SPD war-time policies.

16 *Ibid.*, CCCIX, 3045 ff., debate of May 4, 1917. Altogether about 300,000 workers were involved, mainly in ammunition factories in Berlin and Leipzig.

had been called in protest against conditions which the SPD itself had repeatedly criticized in strongest terms. Indeed the actions of the SPD in January, 1918, were the more significant because, in 1918, the major strike issue had been provided not by questions of food, but by the government's nullification of its promises in regard to a non-annexationist peace with Russia.[17]

The SPD motivated its criticism of the food situation by emphasizing that it was a supreme patriotic duty to point out harmful conditions within the country. The SPD spokesmen stressed that the relief of the strained food situation would provide an important means for preventing the further growth of discontent, and for preserving the morale and the physical ability of German workers and troops for a better fight on the battlefronts. But the criticism of the SPD never developed into an attempt to force concessions from the government by withholding SPD support. For the SPD, the temporary harm done to the German war machine by the withdrawal of its support or by successful food strikes seemed to have become more objectionable than the permanent damage resulting from the continuation of existing conditions in regard to nutrition.

Yet, the SPD faced an even greater difficulty in the attempts to translate its criticism into constructive legislation. During the war, the civilian government of Germany had steadily lost in influence, and the Supreme Army Command gradually became the maker of political decisions, until, ultimately, a military dictatorship ruled in war-time Germany. And the SPD had succumbed to the national aversion towards criticizing those who had successfully led the German defense. In criticizing war-time conditions, the prime objective was to improve the economic and military power of Germany. Because victory was the main objective, the policies of the Supreme Army Command had to be supported as long as the Supreme Army Command could sustain the hopes of victory. The Supreme

17 See *infra*, pp. 111-112, 161-162.

Army Command could not be singled out as responsible for the policies which the SPD had attacked and, until the German armistice offer, the SPD directed its criticism against underlings in the army or influential circles, even though the responsibility of the Supreme Command for the policies criticized had been plainly evident. The reluctance to criticize the real powers in Germany deprived the objections of the SPD of most of their effectiveness; it subjected the SPD to the accusation that its opposition to the powers-that-be and to their objectives was changing into criticism of their inability of achieving them.

b. SOCIAL CONDITIONS IN THE ARMY

Post-war appraisals by German historians confirmed substantially the SPD war-time indictment of social conditions in the imperial army. A wide gulf separated officers and men according to the social, economic and educational cleavages in the country. No attempt was made to relax the resulting discrimination during the war, even though the daily sacrifices and the patriotism of the non-professional citizens' army belied the monopolistic claim that the officers' corps was the foremost and best servant of the Fatherland. " Dass Dein aermster Sohn auch Dein getreuester war—denk es, oh Deutschland! " was more than just the pious utterance of SPD propagandists.

Due to the unfavorable progress of the war, the improvement of the lot of the common soldier became a factor of prime importance in the struggle to preserve the sinking morale of the troops. The government spokesmen in the Reichstag probably were not entirely wrong in rejecting much of the criticism as the unavoidable complaints of the eternally dissatisfied elements among the soldiers. But in spite of the efforts of the army to prevent it, a swelling stream of complaints reached the members of the Reichstag, and a growing number among them began to contend that the army was not doing its best for its troops. Mal-distribution of honors and decorations, failure to grant furloughs in some instances even after two years of continuous front line service, differences in food supplies for officers and men, and political considerations in appointments to higher ranks are probably endemic in any large army, and the degree to which they are tolerated by the troops is inversely proportional to the reverses suffered in combat. What made these conditions so destructive to the morale of German troops was their widespread prevalence, creating the impression that they were typical and normal occurrences within the army. Officers would keep numerous orderlies who never served at the front and yet received furloughs for frequent trips into Germany laden with food for their masters' families. Officers sometimes purchased the entire food stocks destined for the canteens of men. The vile language, the arrogance, and the insults with which officers were accustomed to address their troops might be taken in stride by peace-time inductees who never tasted personal or economic independence and responsibility; men who had made good in civilian life and enjoyed the respect and dignity commensurate with their social standing and success could not but resent it. Discrimination against Jews, socialists, and ethnic minorities within the army had been rife for years. The lowest commissioned officer received pay twenty times as high as that of the common soldier who frequently could not meet his expenses on furloughs because of black market prices. Troops taken back from the front for rest periods were often drilled until exhausted. Severe and ignominious punishments were inflicted for minor breaches of military discipline. It was rare indeed that a soldier would choose the cumbersome and dangerous path of filing a complaint against his superior officer; the execution of punishments was not delayed by such appeals, and trivial complaints or errors in filing the complaints were punishable in themselves. Nothing testified to the extent of these intolerable conditions better than the fact that the Prussian Minister of War, General von Stein, himself had asked for the discontinuation of the practice of punishing soldiers for daring to complain.[18]

It is difficult to resist the conclusion that as a result of these conditions " the army created the most decisive enemy of the state: the indignant soldier." The longer the resentful yoke of command had to be borne, the more violent the final reaction. And the smaller the prospects of a successful defense against the enemy, the smaller the justification for them or the willingness to tolerate them. Indeed, the German " system of defense had been ruined by its own operational faults." [19]

18 *Verhandlungen*, CCCIX, 3047 ff. *Cf. Das Werk des Untersuchungsausschusses; Ursachen des deutschen Zusammenbruches* (hereafter cited as *Ursachen* ...), vol. XI, pt. 1 and 2.

19 Hobohm, *ibid.*, vol. XI, pt. 1, pp. 80-255, 277-375. Volkmann, *ibid.*, vol. XI, pt. 2, thought that the post-1914 army was not representative of the ideal of the Prussian military spirit; too many who had never gone through peace-time training served in it, and there was an acute lack of trained officers. It should, however, be remembered that as late as 1912, the army resisted training all men available in order to avoid expanding the officers' corps beyond the narrow social groups hitherto admitted to it; Moser, *Das militaerische und politisch Wichtigste vom Weltkrieg, passim*; F. L. Neumann, *Behemoth*, pp. 6, 383; and Volkmann, *Ursachen* ..., vol. XI, pt. 1, pp. 34 ff., who lamented that up to October 18, 1918, only 82 men of the Prussian army and 135 of the Bavarian army had been advanced to officers from the ranks on the field. But Volkmann thought it was not permissible to criticize a class of such merit as the officers' corps; *ibid.*, pp. 99 ff. Ritter, *Kritik am Weltkrieg*, pp. 40-42; Maercker, *Vom Kaiserheer zur Reichswehr*, Leipzig, 1921, pp. 43 ff., agreed that some of these conditions prevailed, and made proper arrangements to prevent their recurrence in the Reichswehr; but most German authors were unable to perceive that they were responsible for the success of the leftist propaganda which was so heavily indicted for its role in destroying the morale, and which consisted almost exclusively of attacks on conditions like these. Some authors therefore assumed a priori that revolutions were not due to conditions prevailing at the time of their occurrence, but were due solely to revolutionary leadership; *cf.* A. Niemann, *Revolution von Oben—Umsturz von Unten*, Berlin, 1928, pp. 9-11. Others ignored completely the existence of these conditions in their discussion of the effects of revolutionary propaganda; *cf.* Professor Cossmann, in the ' Dolchstosshefte' of *Sueddeutsche Monatshefte*, April and May, 1924. For SPD attempts to ameliorate these conditions, see *infra*, p. 103. Also Mueller-Brandenburg, *Von der Marne bis zur Marne*, Berlin, 1919, *passim*.

Beginning in 1917, the stream of complaints about these conditions from all parties grew steadily. The enumeration of dozens of fully documented individual instances formed a constant feature in the numerous Reichstag debates on the subject.[20] The SPD spokemen in one of these debates pointed out how destructive this treatment of soldiers was for their morale and warned that it would eventually undermine their ability to stand up at the front.[21] Yet no action was taken to remedy these conditions. The temptation was too great to consider the discussion of these conditions, rather than their prevalence, as destructive of morale, and censorship was called upon to cope with the discussion.[22]

In trying to improve these conditions, the SPD was motivated by the desire to assure the success of the German cause; its warning voice had been raised only in order to forestall dangers which might threaten the German cause because of a breakdown of morale among the troops. But the criticism of the SPD in these fields went hand in hand with its undiminished support of the government; in the field of military conditions, too, the SPD was criticizing not the objectives but the faulty methods of the regime.

c. THE PROBLEM OF ETHNIC MINORITIES IN GERMANY

If the treatment of the troops by army authorities proved to be a constant source of vexation to the members of the

20 *Verhandlungen,* CCCIX, 2340 ff., 3049 ff.; CCCX, 3107 ff., 3453 ff., 3604 ff.; CCCXII, 5383 ff.; CCCXIII, 5411-5526, 5791 ff.; etc.

21 *Ibid.,* CCCIX, 3049 ff., May 4, 1917, speech of Schoepflin. Also CCCX, 3453 ff., May 16, 1917, speech of Stuecklen.

22 *Ibid.,* CCCIX, 3066 ff., reply of Colonel von Wrisberg, the government spokesman, to these charges. The apparent success of the military system of Germany, enabling it to fight on foreign soil and to knock Russia out of the war, was held sufficient justification for the hardships which such a system imposed. That the minister of war should agree to those charges carried no weight. In Germany, the minister of war was always inferior in rank to commanding generals and could give no military orders. Any field commander could override both the civilian government and the minister of war. See *ibid.,* CCCX, 3474 ff.

Reichstag, the treatment of the ethnic minorities in Germany and of the populations in the occupied countries proved to be even more vexing.

The treatment of the French, Polish, Danish and Belgian minorities presented Germany with a real dilemma. Enough precedent and good sense could be marshalled to argue that an enlightened and liberal treatment of these groups would have fostered the growth of anti-German national forces among them, and entailed the dangers which restive alien nationalities might harbor in war-time. On the other hand, military repression and forceful Germanization of these groups, strikingly illustrated by the Zabern affair in 1913, might preclude their peaceful adjustment and produce instead a pronounced desire for separation from Germany. No matter what policy Germany might have chosen for the treatment of her minorities, the policy chosen might have proven harmful to her own national interests.

As it was, the illiberal and repressive pre-war policy was only intensified during the war and the results of this exposed the government to severe and scathing criticism.

At the outbreak of the war, many of the minority populations had been deported to different parts of the country, the use of their language in public had been forbidden, and other repressive measures had been instituted. As early as March 20, 1915, Ledebour, on behalf of the SPD, condemned these measures as stirring up discontent and enmity at home. " Gentlemen, you are always looking for traitors in Germany; the worst traitors in Germany are those who drive the French speaking population of Alsace-Lorraine into the arms of the French, . . . the Poles . . . into enmity against Germany." [23]

23 *Ibid.*, CCCVI, 108-113. Ledebour then proceeded to criticize the Supreme Command for the retaliatory burning of Russian villages in the occupied areas in the East. His criticism of the High Command was condemned by all parties, and Scheidemann rose to declare that Ledebour represented the SPD only on the language question and not in his attacks upon the army authorities; *ibid.*, p. 115.

These words contained the substance of the growing stream of criticism in which, eventually, all other parties except the extreme right joined.[24] But the criticism offered by the SPD and the other parties was futile; and the causes for criticizing the "military reign of absolutism and terror in Alsace-Lorraine" and in other German minority districts increased steadily.[25]

The untoward consequences of this policy were revealed most completely in Alsace-Lorraine. On June 7, 1918, an SPD spokesman pointed out that as a result of the arrests, deportations, the ban on the French language, non-enforcement of the legal protection of the people, and the like, the German administration of Alsace-Lorraine had lost the confidence of the populace and had contributed to the spread of hostility and discontent. Before the war, eighty percent of the population would have favored Germany in a plebiscite, argued the SPD spokesman, whereas now, the overwhelming majority would undoubtedly vote in favor of France. And this had come about not because of love for France, but because of the resentment and discontent caused by the German policies after July 31, 1914.[26]

24 For example in the debate of February 23, 1917, *ibid.*, CCCIX, 2345 ff. Under the state of siege many arrests for protective custody had occurred. In order to establish legal ways to handle them, the Reichstag had, on December 4, 1916, passed certain laws. The three army commanders in Alsace-Lorraine, however, refused to abide by their provisions. All parties joined in calls for disciplinary action, except Count Westarp, who, talking for the conservative party, declared: "The Reichstag has no right to know what happens to a military commander who refuses to obey orders"; *ibid.*, p. 2353. This curious immunity of the military commanders led to the Reichstag resolution of May 16, 1917, which asked the government to see to it that orders of field commanders in conflict with the law be revoked; ibid., CCCX, 3498.

25 SPD representative Wendel, on May 15, 1917, *ibid.*, pp. 3420-21. This remark was made when, in violation of the agenda, the general discussion of Alsace-Lorraine on the floor of the Reichstag had been barred. *Cf. ibid.*, CCCIX, 2429 ff.

26 *Ibid.*, CCCXII, 5264 ff. Other party spokesmen regretted this SPD statement but agreed that sentiments in Alsace-Lorraine had changed and

Criticism of the treatment of the civilian populations in occupied regions started more slowly, because much of what occurred in these areas could be excused as unavoidable in enemy or combat areas, or could more readily be obscured by censorship. Yet, by 1917, denunciations were hurled at the policy of exploitation in these territories which forced them "first ... to satisfy the needs of the German army, secondly ... to provide for the German inland," and allowed them to retain for themselves only what little may still have remained.[27]

After the practical termination of hostilities on large sectors on the Eastern front in 1917, criticism of German policies of occupation began to flow more freely. Although the civilian government had repeatedly accepted national self-determination as the guiding principle, the military commanders in the occupied regions rejected it. The Baltic provinces contained about seven to ten percent Germans, yet local diets with German majorities were created by the armies of occupation, and these diets were prompted to ask for rulers chosen from among the German princes, or for direct annexation. Non-German schools were closed and non-German languages banned; agrarian reforms, for example, effected by the Kerensky regime after February, 1917, were revoked over the opposition of the peasantry, and German militarism was given free reign. The net result of these policies was the alienation of the people and the necessity of keeping over a million troops in these areas, enough to nullify most if not all of the military advantages of the Eastern peace treaties of 1918.

Here is how David, speaking for the SPD, summed up the situation in June, 1918: There was no peace in the East, German blood still flowed there. The hopes of the Ukrainian peace treaty had been disappointed because of the military methods

that the military authorities were responsible for the growth of discontent and anti-German feelings.

27 *Ibid.*, CCCX, 3480 ff., May 16, 1917. Also CCCXI, 3848 ff.; CCCXIII, 5554 ff., 5612 ff., etc.

applied. Threats and bayonets had created ill will, and so did the revocation of agrarian reform by German militarists and the expelled landlords. " If you view the whole Eastern territory, you see that the German government is everywhere doing its best to instill hate against Germany among the broad masses ...Instead of liberation, ... the population feels a new enslavement, an enslavement which is felt as tougher than the Tsarist one, ... which shackles their political, intellectual, and economic life ... It is a ... policy of greatest harm to German interests ... It results in inciting all the Eastern peoples and forging them together against the new German tyranny." [28]

In view of this character of German policies, it was not surprising that, as soon as Germany sued for an armistice in October, 1918, the Reichstag representatives from Alsace-Lorraine, Schleswig, and Posen asked for separation from Germany.[29]

The criticism of the SPD had foreshadowed these consequences. But the SPD joined in condemning the demands of the minorities of Germany for separation. Noske viewed them as the most sordid statements made during the war; they threatened, he held, the dismemberment of Germany. Landsberg revealed that he listened to them with " bleeding heart ". Even Ledebour who, by 1918, had become one of the most outspoken of the Independent Socialists, stated that love of one's country was not incompatible with socialism and that he would oppose all Polish attempts to annex West Prussia or to separate East Prussia.[30]

28 Speech of June 24, 1918, *ibid.*, CCCXIII, 5617 ff. Also *ibid.*, pp. 5755 ff., regarding the illegal war on the Soviet Union in spite of the peace treaty just signed, etc.

29 Debate of October 23, 1918, *ibid.*, CCCXIV, 6183 ff.; and debate of October 25, 1918, pp. 6253 ff.

30 *Ibid.*, pp. 6212, 6290, 6226 ff. Ledebour, who more than anybody else had criticized the German government for its minority policies, asked that the Poles should allow either history or language to determine the limits of their aspiration, and should therefore cede their claims either to Danzig or to Silesia; *ibid.*, pp. 6226 ff.

Although Germany violated the principle of self-determination and disregarded the elementary political rights of nationalities, the SPD was apparently less concerned with these aspects of the problem than with the prevention of their consequences: the growth of separatism. The separation of any territory under German control had to be circumvented, and provocations and blunders committed by the government made this difficult. The soundness of any claims for separation did not matter to the SPD; in the eyes of the SPD, self-determination and nationalism had become privileges to be enjoyed only when they served German interests.

d. PROBLEMS OF STATE OF SIEGE AND OF CENSORSHIP

Many of the policies under attack during the war stemmed from the establishment of a state of siege throughout Germany at the outbreak of the war. The Russian invasion of East Prussia and the uncertain success of the German advance through Belgium had seemed to require it. The proclamation of the state of siege had been accompanied by the promise that it would be rescinded as soon as the danger of foreign invasion had passed. Its legality rested on Prussian laws dating back to the first half of the nineteenth century; in the expectation of a short war, the government had passed no new and comprehensive legislation regarding its administration and jurisdiction, the protection of civil rights, and the like.

The administration and the enforcement of the state of siege had been entrusted to the commanding generals of the military districts in Germany. This factor alone fostered rather than alleviated internal dissent. Believing itself to be infallible, the army tolerated no criticism of its policies and actions. Neither troops appealing the decisions of their officers, nor political groups appealing the rulings of army censors had much of a chance of finding an officer willing to override his fellow officers. In some instances, the ministry of war did indeed grant permission for meetings which had initially been prohibited, but unfortunately for the political groups concerned, this permission frequently came long after the date of the meeting had passed.

After the Western front had become stabilized towards the end of 1914, inter-party discussion in Germany tended to resume its pre-war character. The restrictions on civil and political liberties, the state of siege and censorship, the prohibitions of meetings and assemblies, and the establishment of protective custody for persons allegedly holding undesirable political opinions became burdensome and objectionable to all parties concerned. Already on December 2, 1914, the SPD declaration supporting war credits protested that the restrictions on the freedom of the press were contrary to the interests of efficiency and public confidence.[31]

In the following years, a steady flow of detailed criticism of these conditions came from all German parties. The documented individual cases cited in the Reichstag ran into the thousands. There were the usual complaints which occur whenever restrictions upon political meetings and personal liberties are imposed by the exigencies of war. Stupidities in the application of censorship probably belong to the normal operation of any such system, and to them war-time Germany contributed her share.

In at least one instance, a person accused of treason and freed by the Supreme Court upon the motion of the prosecuting attorney, was at once re-arrested by army authorities in the court room, and placed under protective custody. According to a report from a Reichstag committee meeting, Vice-Chancellor Helfferich had indicated the principle behind such actions: "It is better that M. Mehring is in protective custody than that he remains free and commits a punishable offense."[32]

31 *Ibid.*, CCCVI, 20-21, declaration of Haase.
32 *Ibid.*, CCCVIII, 1859-85; CCCIX, 2429-41.

But of all the results of the military administration of the state of siege none were resented more universally than the point of view that certain parties and certain opinions were destructive of the objectives of the state. The Burgfrieden had indeed been proclaimed by the Emperor, but the army did not feel bound by it; traditional hostility to certain parties continued to be the criterion for the application of censorship and of the state of siege. The idea that some parties were less patriotic than others sowed dissension at home and in the army. The administration of the state of siege and censorship, prohibitions of assemblies and newspapers, and protective custody decreed on a partisan basis incited the protests of all parties all through the war.[33]

This partisanship produced its most untoward results by interference in the discussion of German war aims. The army preceded in the belief that public spirit and morale could best be maintained by stressing annexationist dreams and the idea of conquest. Although it was the idea of national defense which had aroused the nation in the August days of 1914, the army held that the idea of defense was insufficient to maintain the morale of Germany.[34] The most vociferous antagonists of

33 On annexationism, see *Ursachen* . . . , vol. XII, and *infra*, pp. 125 ff., SPD criticism of these conditions will be found in *Verhandlungen*, CCCVI, 97-106; CCCVIII, 1859-60, 1875-83; CCCX, 3714-3805, 3858 ff.; CCCXII, 5170 ff., etc. For the criticism of other parties, see *ibid*., CCCX, 3729-3806, 3868 ff.; CCCXII, 5166-5259, etc. Most of the nearly 400 questions submitted to the government by the Reichstag during the war dealt with instances of discriminatory application of the state of siege.

34 See Muehsam, *op. cit., passim*, in regard to censorship regulations, instructions to the press, and official press releases. Muehsam concluded that had it not been for censorship which had kept Germany in the dark about all military setbacks, the armistice offer in October, 1918, would not have produced the revolution. The Marne battle of 1918, for example, proved to be so completely lost, according to Muehsam, that not a word of it appeared in print during the war; *cf. ibid*., pp. 64 ff., press releases of September 16, 22, and 23, 1914, regarding the Marne battle which officially was referred to as a minor engagement on the banks of the Ourcq. The name 'Marneschlacht' was banned in Germany all through the war; von

annexationism eventually were silenced by a blanket prohibition of all their writings and meetings. Nothing testified to the extent of these conditions better than the fact that Bethmann-Hollweg, as Chancellor, had to take the floor of the Reichstag on June 5, 1916, to protest against the harmful character of pro-annexationist views and writings.[35]

Dissatisfaction with this fettering of undesired opinions regarding army policies and the brazen flouting of the July, 1917, peace objectives in the negotiations at Brest-Litovsk finally vented itself in the January, 1918, protest strikes.

The SPD had not taken part in the preparation and organization of these strikes. The party, however, soon joined the strikers in order to moderate their demands and to lead them back to work. But the military ban on assemblies and the general prohibition of calling strike meetings made it impossible to do so, contributing instead to ill-will among the strikers and prolonging the duration of the strikes.[36]

Hausen, the German Commander of the Third Army at the Marne felt constrained to write his memoirs in order to inform the German public that indeed such a battle had taken place and had been lost. Falkenhayn, incidentally, was one of the few to realize the importance of the battle and to advocate that as a result Germany should seek the earliest possible opportunity to terminate the war, and that the government ought to inform the public of the seriousness of the situation. See Falkenhayn, *Die Oberste Heeresleitung*, Berlin, 1920, pp. 8-10, 20-21, 241-46.

35 *Verhandlungen*, CCCVII, 1509-12.

36 The SPD party council resolved to join the strikers in order to terminate the strikes without damage to public interests and in order to keep the strikes in orderly channels. The number of strikers was estimated at 180,000 by the Secretary of the Interior, at 400,000 by some strike leaders, and at 1,000,000 in Spartacist pamphlets. Coming at a time when the negotiations at Brest-Litovsk had broken down because of the German demands for territorial cessions by Russia, the government accused the strikers of being in the pay of enemy powers. The strikes had originally been called for three days, but the arrest of strike leaders and the inability to hold meetings made it impossible to terminate them on schedule. They did probably not damage German production, because the winter of 1917-18 was one of work-stoppages and lay-offs caused by the lack of coal for industrial production. A three-day week had been observed in most struck plants before the strike, and in fact, the temporary cessation of all production allowed

Such flagrant instances of the stupidity of censorship, the arrests of members of the Reichstag without defensible charges, the interference with the mail of representatives, the inability to combat official lies, the prohibition of circulating copies of the *Verhandlungen,* the drafting of men for their political opinions, and the attempts to fetter political thought formed the main SPD grievances.[37]

Eventually even the bourgeois parties concluded that the civilian government was powerless against the Supreme Army Command, and a change in the laws of the state of siege was enacted, setting up a civilian body of censorship and review. These changes came too late, however, and did not produce the effects desired.[38]

e. The Problem of Democratic Reform

In its criticism of the policies of the government in regard to the problems of food, social conditions within the army, minorities, and of the state of siege and censorship, the SPD to a large degree was in agreement with the bourgeois parties. In fact, their joint criticism and scathing analysis of war-time

---

many plants to build up a meager supply of raw-materials for the resumption of capacity operations for the first time in many months. In view of the censorship, the workers had chosen the strike to express their dissatisfaction. As approved by the SPD, the strikers demanded better food supply, effective control of production, lifting of the state of siege and of military censorship, immediate grant of Prussian reforms which had been made a mockery of in the Prussian diet, and a peace treaty free of all concealed annexations. Only in Berlin, where the government refused to negotiate with the strikers, had there been any excesses. The Bavarian government, for example, expressed its official thanks to the SPD for taking over the leadership of the strikes and thus making them an abortive movement. See *Verhandlungen,* CCCXI, 4154-4216; *infra,* pp. 161-62. The texts of the leaflets regarding the agitation prior to and during the strikes may be found among others in Drahn and Leonard, *op. cit.,* pp. 99-103, and E. Meyer, *Spartakus im Kriege,* Berlin, 1927, pp. 183-194.

37 In addition to previously cited references, see *Verhandlungen,* CCCVI, 174-8; CCCVII, 842-60; CCCVIII, 1898-1976; CCCIX, 2345 ff.; CCCX, 3453 ff., 3681 ff.; CCCXI, 3883 ff., 3958 ff.; etc. and CCCXII, 5166 ff.

38 *Ibid.,* debate of June 4, 5, and 6, 1918, also CCCXII, 5166-5259.

conditions indicated the extent of the provocations offered. Yet, the SPD continued to support the war effort. It defended German policies abroad, it helped to end and to prevent strikes, it rejected the class-struggle as a means for obtaining its objectives, and it justified its criticism by concern for the reputation of Germany abroad and the danger of discontent within the country. Added to the war-time relationship between the SPD and the German governments, the nature of SPD criticism indicated that the SPD considered the success of the German cause as the most important objective: 'National' interests were beginning to override all other considerations of SPD policy.

In the problem of democratic reform of German political institutions, too, the SPD motivation revealed the same emphasis. However, the struggle for democratic rights during the war had ceased to be a purely domestic affair or a mere conflict of rival political systems; it had become a burning issue of international relations and of the propaganda campaign carried on between the belligerents. Each step forward in democratic reform meant the repudiation of Entente claims and peace objectives, every advance in democratic rights meant the rejection of Entente assertions that Germany was a military dictatorship obedient only to the whims of East-Prussian Junkers. In its struggle for democratic reforms during the war, the SPD tried to wrest from the hands of the Entente a powerful propaganda weapon and, at the same time, safeguard Germany against the stupidities and blunders so sharply criticized during the war. The struggle of the SPD for democratic reforms was a struggle for a system better able to protect the ideas to which the existing system was dedicated.

The SPD had taken great pride in the spontaneous response of the masses to the call to arms in 1914. This response had invalidated many of the arguments previously advanced in defense of the German political system, and had made it difficult to obstruct the just demand that those who shed their blood for their country must no longer be politically ostracized.

SPD support of the war credits, its co-operation with the government, its abandonment of the half-century long hostility towards the existing class state, the symbolic significance ascribed to the fact that the first member of the German Reichstag to shed his blood for the Emperor was an SPD representative, were all interpreted as proof that the SPD had been true to its country. " A policy of mistrust towards one's own people can no longer be tolerated in the German Empire," was the SPD conclusion.[39]

This heartening response of the German people in the August days was held to result from the broadened national appeal of the imperial government and its parties, growing out of the extension of the democratic and economic basis of the Bismarck empire. The further ascendancy of the German Empire could be continued into the future only by the extension of democracy, argued the SPD writers.[40] Yet, except for casual and inconsequential hints in favor of the democratization of Germany, the SPD had long delayed bringing the matter up for discussion either in public or in the Reichstag.[41]

There was general agreement among the leftist and center parties that democratic reforms must include free, equal, universal and secret suffrage in Prussia, the introduction of proportional representation at least in the larger electoral districts of Germany, a redistribution of election districts according to population, and closer co-operation between the government and the Reichstag. Not even the SPD insisted from the beginning of the war on full parliamentarization, women's suffrage or general proportional representation. All of these reforms, however, had been repeatedly discussed in Germany long before the war and the need for them had been widely acknowledged.

39 David, *op. cit.*, p. 23.

40 For example, Lensch, *op. cit.*, pp. 52-55.

41 For example, *Verhandlungen*, CCCVI, 171-72; CCCVII, 857 ff.

The German government in 1914 had indeed recognized the need for reform. It had recognized that it was impossible to continue holding in political tutelage a people which had so strikingly demonstrated its fervor and spirit in August 1914 and it had promised political reforms which were to take effect after the war.

At the time, this promise was quite satisfactory to all concerned but none had foreseen a war lasting four long years. Nor had anyone foreseen that changing the political character of the German Empire was to become one of the war aims of the Entente. As a result, the three class suffrage, the restrictions of civil rights under the state of siege and the arbitrary suspension of constitutional guaranties regarding free elections and election meetings became increasingly intolerable to the SPD and to other parties.[42]

The ensuing discontent had been nourished by the apparent inability of the government to pass and enforce laws which would ease the food crisis, the inability of German diplomacy to prevent the participation of Italy and of the United States in the war on the side of the Entente, the failure to anticipate the effects of the British blockade, the revelation of the ' Zimmermann-note ' and its naive assumptions, the publication of the ' Willy-Nicky ' correspondence, and the failure to estimate correctly the effects of submarine warfare. This led to a state of mind which prompted the German government to temper the news of the democratic revolution in Russia by some political concessions. On March 14, 1917, in a speech before the Prussian diet—the Reichstag being in recess—Bethmann-Hollweg promised definite political reforms for Prussia to take effect after the war.

---

42 *Ibid.*, CCCIX, 2345 ff., February 27, 1917. In spite of severe restrictions placed on SPD meetings during the war-time by-elections, the SPD voted in favor of strengthening the machinery to enforce the state of siege. On the problem of democratic reforms, the SPD lagged behind non-socialist parties who had called for parliamentarization sooner and in stronger terms than the SPD; *ibid.*, CCCIX, 2481 ff.

Bethmann-Hollweg's speech failed to avert the anticipated effect of the news of the Russian revolution upon the public and the Reichstag. Loud calls for immediate democratic reforms were raised, and they were inhibited neither by doubts about the constitutionality of federal action in this respect, nor by the vehement opposition of the Prussian diet to the proposals of Bethmann-Hollweg. Pan-Germans argued interestingly that Prussian reforms were unpatriotic and would undermine the source of German strength, even after the Emperor and Prussian King (in his Easter message of 1917 and in his imperial rescript of July 11, 1917,) had endorsed Prussian reforms and had asked that a bill incorporating equal suffrage be brought before the Prussian diet.

On March 29, 1917, these problems came up for discussion in the Reichstag, and the position of the SPD taken there revealed the reasons for the SPD demands of democratic reform: " It is possible . . . to say regarding the effect of certain speeches in the Prussian diet and . . . the House of Peers recently, that they provoked extreme pleasure among the enemies of Germany. The main argument of the Western enemies. . . creating sentiments hostile to our people . . . is the German lack of freedom . . . This is why the world is prejudiced against Germany . . . The moral factors working against Germany are not . . . of smaller importance . . . Even with the most ill-will, it is increasingly difficult for the reactionaries to preserve the existing system of government, when Germany is surrounded by democracies not only in the West, North and South, but, as we hope, will for all times have a democracy as its neighbor in the East." The proposed political reforms could not be as far-reaching as the economic changes imposed by the war, and there was therefore no reason to delay them till after the war.[43]

In response to these debates of March, 1917, a committee to recommend democratic reforms was appointed, with

43 *Ibid.*, CCCIX, 2835 ff., speech of Noske. *Cf.* Scheidemann, in *Vorwaerts*, June 24, 1917.

Scheidemann as chairman. In a report on July 6, 1917, it recommended re-drawing the large electoral districts and the introduction of proportional representation.[44]

However, the hopes raised by the report of this committee and by the imperial rescript of July 11, 1917, remained essentially unfulfilled. Bethmann-Hollweg, who had promised to consider the report favorably and who had secured the assent of the Emperor to reforms, was removed from his office by his opponents a few days after the publication of the imperial rescript.[45]

He was succeeded by Michaelis who did not even consult the leaders of the Reichstag majority before assuming office.[46] Michaelis was unable to remain as Chancellor for more than a few months. His successor,[47] the Bavarian Centrist Prime

44 *Ibid.*, CCCX, 3507, 3508. The committee did not discuss Prussian reforms, which were adjudged to be matters for the Prussian diet; it had refused to make the chancellor responsible to the Reichstag, or to grant the Reichstag the right to declare war or conclude peace; in general it had stressed its unwillingness to decrease the privileges of the crown. *Cf.* Haase's revealing comments on the committee, *ibid.*, pp. 3444 ff.

45 Bethmann-Hollweg, *Betrachtungen zum Weltkrieg*, II, *passim*. Helfferich, *op. cit.*, III, 102-136. Payer, *Von Bethmann-Hollweg bis Ebert*, pp. 25-38. Erzberger, *Erlebnisse im Weltkrieg*, pp. 287 ff. Scheidemann, *ibid.*, II, 34-41.

46 Michaelis, *op. cit.*, p. 324. Bethmann-Hollweg, *op. cit.*, II, 215 ff. At a reception given to the political leaders of the Reichstag after his appointment, Michaelis told them that he knew little or nothing about politics or policy, that heretofore he had been strictly on the sidelines; ("er sei neben dem Rad der Geschichte einhergelaufen.") Erzberger, *ibid.*; Payer, *ibid.* At an audience given by William II, on July 20, 1917, the Emperor commented on the hopes for democratization by remarking that "where the guard appears, there is no democracy any more;" Erzberger, *ibid.*, p. 52; Payer, *ibid.*, p. 48. Scheidemann, *ibid.*, pp. 117-18. This was the audience where William termed a peace of conciliation (Frieden des Ausgleichs) one where "Germany took from the Entente money, cotton, oil, minette." Erzberger terms this audience as the "tiefste Spatenstich zum Sturze des bisherigen Regimes," *ibid.*, p. 53.

47 Michaelis fell in consequence of an SPD interpellation regarding Pan-German propaganda in the army, which led to a heated debate in the Reichstag on October 6, 1917. In the course of this debate, the 1917 naval

Minister Count Hertling, felt constrained to consult the leaders of the majority before assuming office, and to agree to the peace formula of the Reichstag resolution and to further a program of internal reforms.

But the guarded reception of Hertling on the floor of the Reichstag indicated that few trusted him to introduce democratic reforms.[48] Scheidemann utilized the introduction of Hertling to the Reichstag to reiterate the demands for Prussian reforms, higher pay for the troops, termination of the state of siege, and removal of the constitutional bars for members of the Reichstag to join a cabinet.

Demands like these indicated the degree of the change effected.[49] In fact, the proposals under discussion in the Prussian diet only attempted to replace three class suffrage by a six-class plural suffrage bill. Yet, although the SPD realized that the lack of progress in regard to democratic reforms especially in Prussia was a major contributory cause for the January, 1918, strikes, the party did not show any undue concern over the consequences of the slowness of reform. " Only under the pressure of Tsarism could a movement develop which seems intent on dissolving the immense empire into its smallest atoms." [50]

mutinies were revealed, and the government declared repeatedly that it considered its culprits, the extreme leftist parties, to be outside the pale of political respect. But because the evidence on which the government based this indictment of the left was inadequate, and because of past experiences like the Kulturkampf or the anti-socialist legislation, the majority parties decided to fell Michaelis. See *Verhandlungen*, CCCX, 3714-2805; and *infra*, pp. 162 ff.

48 Hertling, *Ein Jahr in der Reichskanzlei*, pp. 25-45. As a monarchist and an "absolute opponent" of parliamentarism, Hertling reassured the Prussian diet as early as December 6, 1917, that his nomination did not signify the introduction of parliamentarism.

49 *Verhandlungen*, CCCXI, 3948 ff. For Conservative criticism of this matter, see *ibid.*, pp. 3953 ff.

50 *Ibid.*, pp. 4233 ff., speech of Landsberg, February 28, 1918. The SPD reception of the February revolution was favorable but it condemned the October revolution and its results. Scheidemann blamed the Bolsheviki for

An entire year elapsed before the first bill incorporating certain minor democratic reforms was introduced into the Reichstag. On March 12, 1918, the constitutional committee formed in 1917 recommended legislation providing for the introduction of proportional representation in the twenty-six electoral districts which had more than 200,000 voters. The SPD decided in favor of this bill because it fulfilled "the demands of the time in giving large cities with dense populations an increased number of representatives ... although it will also make provisions so that this new representation will benefit the workers as little as possible... In these districts, the minorities shall be protected, while the minorities in all other election districts shall be muzzled." [51]

Until October, 1918, the SPD exerted no further pressure upon the government to augment this bill in conformity with its belief that "in critical times, that state has the best hope of maintaining itself, which is firmly attached to the hearts of its citizens, whose citizens feel themselves as one with the state. But the prerequisite for civic-mindedness is the influence of every citizen upon the formation of the policies of his state. And such an influence can be exercised only where all elements necessary for the maintainance of the state possess the franchise and only where the franchise knows no privileges of individual classes and no artificial delimitations." [52]

---

the decay of the Russian army and the growing disruption of the empire. According to him, the Bolshevik recipe did not work well enough to be recommended to Germany, and Brest-Litovsk was the inevitable result of the October revolution; *ibid.*, pp. 4162 ff., February 26, 1918. These sentiments were widely shared by other SPD leaders.

51 *Ibid.*, pp. 4323 ff., speech of Gradnauer. It is noteworthy that for instance in Saxony, in the 1903 elections, the SPD gained twenty-two out of twenty-three seats with a popular vote of only fifty-eight and eight-tenths percent. *Cf. ibid.*, CCCX, 3508 ff. Gradnauer attacked the fact that proportional representation, which was to be introduced in the large districts only, would benefit the non-socialist minorities in them, while the socialist minorities in the smaller (rural) districts would continue to be unrepresented.

52 *Ibid.*, CCCXIII, 5912 ff., speech of Landsberg, July 8, 1918.

CHAPTER V

THE SPD AND GERMAN WAR AIMS

a. Formulation of SPD Peace Aims

Foremost in all SPD discussions regarding peace objectives were the concepts which had led the party to adopt the policy of August 4, 1914: "In defending our country we protect the vital interests of the German worker."[1] "As long as the enemy powers persist in their plans of destruction, as long as the enemy powers fail to show their desire for peace, we will support our people in the defense of our country."[2]

The SPD thus accepted the statement of the government that no desire for conquest had driven Germany into the war. Germany fought to preserve her culture and independence, and, in the opinion of the SPD, the peace terms were to be such as to make possible harmonious relations between neighboring people.

These generalities revealed the inability to discern what further objectives the progress of the war might bring within the realm of the possible; they soon gave way to more precise statements.

The SPD never rejected the principle that the war should end without territorial acquisitions. But this did not prevent the SPD from endorsing the ambitions of certain Flemish émigrés for an independent Flemish state; and in this the SPD, during the early war years, found itself in complete agreement with the Pan-German interests. The SPD also favored the desires of the non-Prussian and non-Austrian Poles for independent statehood.

1 *Verhandlungen*, CCCVII, 857-61, speech of Ebert. As quoted by Bevan, *op. cit.*, p. 124, he stated that the ruin of Germany would substitute for the temporary distress of the German working class, due to the war, its permanent misery, due to an Allied victory.

2 *Verhandlungen*, CCCVII, 857-61, speech of Ebert, April 5, 1916. *Cf. ibid.*, CCCVI, 506-07; CCCVIII, 1852; CCCIX, 2899 ff.; CCCX, 3390 ff.; CCCXI, 3972 ff.; Stampfer, *op. cit.*, p. 9, and Bevan, *op. cit.*, p. 137.

The SPD refused to be bound by the settlements of dead diplomats; a peace settlement at the end of the war without some rectification of borders was not desirable.[3] " It is impossible to end this war without changing border markers ... That a village changes hands, or here and there a boundary is moved by one or two kilometers, need not mean annexations." [4] In fact, some members of the SPD advocated sweeping territorial acquisitions in the West and East, but their demands were promptly toned down to a more moderate level.[5]

This approval of " rectifications " of borders in Germany's favor at a time when the progress of the war still favored Germany was complemented by the acceptance of the principle of indemnifications. On March 1, 1917, Keil, an SPD member of the Reichstag, declared in a speech before that body that " it is a risky thing to depend entirely on war reparations ... The total war costs of the states participating in the war grow with the continuation of the war in proportion to the inability of any of the two parties to transfer its entire war costs to the other "; but " we all hope ... we shall receive substantial war reparations." In the debate over this speech, Scheidemann refuted the claim that he was opposed to reparations. He was opposed only to those who considered reparations as an adequate cause for prolonging the war.[6] As late as July, 1918, Noske defended the imposition of reparations on Rumania by the treaty of Bucharest.[7]

In principle, however, the SPD adhered closely to the letter of its declaration of August 4, 1914, and was careful to deny

3 *Verhandlungen*, CCCVI, 174-178; CCCVII, 889-896, speech of Scheidemann, April 6, 1916.

4 *Ibid.*, CCCX, 3390 ff. *Cf.* speech of Scheidemann at the Reichskonferenz der SPD, September 21 to 23, 1916, quoted by Bevan, *op. cit.*, pp. 131 ff.

5 Haenisch in *Vorwaerts*, September 5, 1916, and the answer to this article by Stampfer, *ibid.*, September 7, 1916. Also *ibid.*, September 9, 1916.

6 *Verhandlungen*, CCCIX, 2454 ff. *Vorwaerts*, March 9, 1917.

7 *Verhandlungen*, CCCXIII, 5750 ff.

that its minor digressions from the principle of peace without annexations was inconsistent with its original declaration of peace objectives. This was in fact not always easy to do. Thus, after the SPD had endorsed the objectives embodied in the peace moves initiated by Bethmann-Hollweg in December, 1915, and in December, 1916,[8] the SPD found it difficult to demonstrate that Bethmann-Hollweg had accepted the principle of 'no annexations' and had rejected Pan-German demands for French-Belgian ore and coal fields and for the Polish-Baltic region.[9]

However, the opposition of the Independent Socialists, the evident harm caused by annexationist propaganda, and the deteriorating progress of the war allowed the SPD no other course but progressively stricter adherence to its original principles. "It is important to note that the contraction of the demands of the Majority Socialists were not due to an inner principle, but to the course of outside events which made the chance of Germany's getting more seem small." [10]

8 *Ibid.*, CCCVII, 889-96; CCCIX, 2386 ff.

9 Scheidemann's speech at Breslau, June 20, 1916, printed under the title *Die deutsche Sozialdemokratie und der Weltkrieg*, Breslau, 1916. Bethmann-Hollweg's disavowal of the Pan-Germans as harmful to the German war effort lend credence to Scheidemann's defense of his war aims; *Verhandlungen*, CCCVII, 1509-12, June 5; 1916. In the condemnation of Pan-German objectives, Bethmann-Hollweg cited the pamphlets of Wolfgang Kapp as particularly harmful. However, while rejecting the annexation of the areas claimed by the Pan-Germans, Bethmann-Hollweg had advocated that they should be constituted as German satellites; *Ursachen...*, vol. XII, pt. 1, pp. 47 ff., 175 ff. The SPD was not the only political group in Germany which rationalized concealed annexations as consistent with a peace without annexations. On March 2, 1917, the Conservative Schiele told the Reichstag that "the Center, the National-Liberal Party, and a part of the Progressive Party... want to keep Belgium economically, militarily, and politically in our hand; this is what we have so far demanded. If you would view this as annexationism, you would exaggerate beyond all factual basis." *Verhandlungen*, CCCIX, 2494 ff. *Cf. infra*, pp. 125 ff. on annexationism.

10 Bevan, *op. cit.*, p. 99. *Cf. Leipziger Volksstimme*, September 25, 1917, thus motivating the vaccillations of Bethmann-Hollweg and Michaelis in their peace aims.

While the SPD was quite ready to deviate from its position regarding annexations or indemnifications, it never wavered in its insistence that all German territories, as they existed before 1914, must remain inviolate.

The re-acquisition of Alsace-Lorraine was one of the main French objectives of the war. And traditionally the SPD had not approved the German acquisition of these provinces, nor indeed the manner of their administration. But during the war, the SPD opposed rigidly any concession in regard to these provinces. The principles of peace, drawn up by the SPD bloc in the Reichstag, made this attitude clear.[11] The SPD party congress at Wuerzburg, in October, 1917, re-affirmed the opposition of the SPD to any concession towards France in regard to Alsace-Lorraine. If France were to insist on the return of these provinces, the war would continue forever, because nobody in Germany would seriously consider ceding of the ' Reichsland.' [12] The results of the last pre-war elections in Alsace-Lorraine were, in fact, considered as the equivalent of a plebiscite in favor of Germany.[13]

The SPD was equally intransigent in regard to possible concessions in other German borderlands. And as late as October 24, 1918, the SPD viewed the loss of German colonies as incompatible with a just peace.[14]

11 *Vorwaerts*, August 24, 1915. According to W. Heine, the bloc had split eighty-one to fourteen on this problem; *Berliner Tageblatt*, January 11, 1916. Among the other principles which these resolutions called for were the grant of the Open Door for Germany's commercial development, and the grant to Germany of most-favored-nation status, the integrity of Turkey and of the Dual Monarchy, the establishment of an international court of arbitration, the freedom of the seas, and the renunciation by Germany of claims for ' foreign ' territories as weakening the ' national ' state of Germany and her foreign relations. It also called for the restoration of Belgium, but an amendment promising Belgium unlimited internal and external, political and economic freedom was rejected. K. Kautsky in *Neue Zeit*, vol. XXXIV, pt. 2, no. 24, September 14, 1917, pp. 553 ff.

12 *Verhandlungen*, CCCX, 3813 ff., speech by Gradnauer, October 9, 1917. Also *ibid.*, CCCIX, 2899 ff.; *Protokoll des Parteitags 1917*, pp. 39-44.

13 *Verhandlungen*, CCCXIII, 5617 ff., June 24, 1918, speech by David.

14 *Ibid.*, CCCXIV, 6212, speech of Noske.

The SPD rigidly opposed any contraction of German territories or of German economic and commercial interests. As the official spokesman of his party, Scheidemann made it clear time and again that "the territorial integrity of our state, its political independence, and its free economic development must be safeguarded." [15] According to the SPD, even the principle of self-determination for all nationalities, which the SPD had traditionally advocated, must not be applied to the detriment of Germany or Austria-Hungary.[16]

An attitude like this was presumably part and parcel of the idea of national defense; that Germany should forego all annexations was only the counterpart of this attitude. Under the swelling tide of victory in the early war years, the SPD had not always insisted upon the unqualified adherence to its original war aims, but the SPD did not deviate from that policy for very long. Growing opposition within Germany to an imperialist war and the waning chances of a decisive victory prompted the SPD to return to the principles of August 4, 1914. However, a main factor for this return to its original principles was provided by its analysis of Pan-German annexationism and its consequences upon the duration of the war, the reputation of Germany abroad, and the possible strength of Germany in future diplomatic discussions regarding the termination of the war.

15 *Ibid.*, CCCX, 3390 ff., May 5, 1917, and pp. 3419 ff., same date. Also Stampfer, *op. cit.*, p. 9. The SPD had presented a petition signed by 899,149 persons which called for a peace leaving Germany intact; *Protokoll des Parteitags 1917*, p. 34.

16 At the SPD party congress at Wuerzburg, Hermann Mueller warned that self-determination would destroy the Dual Monarchy. At the Stockholm conference in 1917, where the SPD leaders experienced a rude shock at the contact with views and attitudes outside Germany, the SPD had favored the following peace aims: the freedom of Ireland, Egypt, India, Poland, Finland, Tripoli, Korea; the termination of British control over Gibraltar and Suez, and of American control over Panama. But self-determination was not to apply to Alsace-Lorraine or to the Polish provinces of Prussia; *ibid.*, pp. 39-44.

b. The SPD and Annexationism

The first half of 1917 had brought a whole series of setbacks to Germany's war-effort. The peace-offensive of December, 1916, had proven abortive, the United States had entered the war, the high hopes placed on the unrestricted U-boat campaign had been disappointed, the food situation had become worse than ever, and the Russian revolution had given encouragement to the extreme socialists and to their agitation. The April, 1917, strikes had shown that the ensuing discontent could no longer be moderated by mere promises of political reforms. In order to defend the Supreme Command and its policies against criticism and in order to forestall defeatism, an annexationist campaign had been launched which enjoyed the support of Michaelis and Hertling and of the Supreme Command under Hindenburg and Ludendorff. Its chief argument was that Germany had been the victim of a base enemy attack, and that victory and peace must make the repetition of such an attack impossible by the acquisition of adequate territory in Europe. Its claims ranged from the moderate digressions of the SPD from its strict no-annexation dogma to demands for the acquisition of the entire region lying between the Boulogne-Belfort line and the Lake Peipus-Dnieper line. There was a flood of pamphlets, articles, speeches and books claiming one or more of these objectives, and they left no doubt about the ability of Germany to acquire all of these regions; to be satisfied with less were to deprive Germany of the fruits of victory.[17]

17 The basic discussions of annexationism were: *Ursachen...*, vol. XII, pts. 1 and 2, the 'Gutachten' of Volkmann and Hobohm; M. Hobohm, *Die Alldeutschen* (vol. II of his *Chauvinismus und der Weltkrieg*); S. Grumbach, *Das annexionistische Deutschland*, 2 vols. Lausanne, 1917. Of course most authors writing on this period touched on the problem of annexationism. No complete bibliography of annexationist literature exists; however, some publishers restricted themselves almost completely to publications of this nature. The list of titles presented, for example, by J. F. Lehmann, Munich; Politik Verlagsanstalt und Buchdruckerei GmbH., Berlin; Hugo Bruckmann

The pro-annexationist campaign was backed by almost the entire German press, except for social-democratic publications and a few democratic papers. It was backed by educational institutes, associations of teachers, physicians and many other professional groups. Members of the German Parliaments supported it and local governments and their officials gave it generous assistance. Members of the civil service contributed to it, though sometimes under pressure. Soldiers were indoctrinated in its tenets; the publications of the Kriegspresseamt reflected its views; and its private and official backers viewed anyone who disagreed with the program as a potential traitor, even if exception to the program was taken on strictly patriotic grounds. Indeed, if the success of propaganda were determined chiefly by persistency and quality of effort, coverage of the population, diversity of approach, frequency of exposure to it, character and range of its advocates, egotistic appeal, or any of the factors subject to control by the propagandists, this campaign would have been overwhelmingly successful.[18]

Verlag, Munich; Haas und Grabherr, Augsburg; Alexander Duncker Verlag, Berlin; Vaterlaendischer Schriftenverband; C. A. Schwetschke und Sohn, Berlin; Theodor Weicher, Leipzig; Konservative Schriftenvertriebsstelle GmbH., Berlin; "Das groessere Deutschland" GmbH., Dresden; George Stilke, Berlin; S. Hirzel, Leipzig; Hermann Kalkoff, Berlin, each exceeded several hundred publications, many of which enjoyed circulations exceeding one hundred thousand.

18 The annexationists violated so flagrantly the shibboleths of nationalism, substituting in their stead a crude imperialism, that rightists too eventually repudiated it. For example Volkmann, *Ursachen...*, vol. XII, pt. 1, *passim.* See also Conrad Haussmann ed., *Geheimbericht Nummer 7 von Februar 1917*, Berlin 1921. This document had been received and privately circulated in Berlin in April 1917. It allegedly was a report by the chiefs of the French propaganda units during the war, and argued that annexationism and its opposition to the moderate views of the German government would produce so much internal discord in Germany, that the war effort of the Entente would be considerably strengthened thereby. The Pan-Germans were referred to as allies of France who effectively deprived Germany of the support of public opinion throughout the world and aided in keeping the morale of the Entente countries high. The 'Unabhaengiger Ausschuss fuer einen deutschen Frieden,' the 'Alldeutscher Verband' and the 'Vaterlandspartei'

To further annexationism was the chosen task of the 'Vater-landspartei' which had been founded in 1917 under the sponsorship of Admiral Tirpitz and others. Cutting across traditional party lines, this group enjoyed the particular sponsorship of the High Command. Many officers compelled their soldiers to enroll in the new party, although political activities by men in active service were unconstitutional; lecturers indoctrinated the troops with the ideas of the Fatherland Party, or attacked viciously the Reichstag, holding it responsible for the lack of U-boats and arms; government buildings were at its disposal for meetings, which took place without the required registration with the boards of censorship; army generals, city-officials and government employees furthered its cause with speeches and official funds; indeed, work on behalf of the group was accepted by the army in lieu of the requirements of the German 'Auxiliary Service Law.'

Due to an SPD interpellation, Pan-German propaganda in the army and the one-sided application of the laws of the state of siege became, on October 6, 1917, the subject of a vehement Reichstag debate. Except for the extreme right, all parties agreed to the substance of the charges and condemned prevailing conditions in sharpest terms. Landsberg bitterly complained about the impertinence of the Fatherland Party which pretended, with official sanction, that it alone represented patriotic interests, while all parties had, in fact, equally shared

---

were the chief organized exponents of annexationism. The main annexationist statements were contained in *Denkschrift der sechs wirtschaftlichen Verbaende*; Heinrich Class, *Zum deutschen Kriegsziel*; Dr. Wolfang Kapp, *Die Maidenkschrift aus dem Jahre 1916*. Gustav Stresemann's *Michel Horch, der Seewind pfeift!* deserves attention because of the later history of its author. The regular periodicals of the annexationists were the *Alldeutsche Blaetter* and the weekly *Zur Deutschlands Erneuerung*. Perhaps Friedrich Oels' *An meine lieben Deutsche. Allen Heervolk und Heimligen im Deutschen Heimbereich*, ein Sendschreiben Lutheri wider Peter Peterlein, Diesdorf (1917) may be cited as an oddity advocating Pan-German objectives in their most extreme form by using the inimitable language of Luther's 'Tafelreden'. In its extreme form, the annexationist movement showed anti-semitic and 'voelkisch' tendencies.

the sacrifices and deprivations of war. The SPD charged that the economic interests which benefitted most from the war were now trying to prolong their source of profits. The damage to the reputation of Germany abroad was bitterly lamented.[19]

But rankling as the self-righteousness of the Fatherland Party was, the SPD rejected sweeping war aims primarily because they only strengthened the determination of the enemy to fight. Annexationism gave substance to the accusation that Germany was the aggressor in the war. Annexationism, in the opinion of the SPD, stimulated resistance in the Entente countries in the same way as the rejection of the December, 1916, German peace offer and the war aims then projected by Entente leaders had done in Germany.[20] " Through the Pan-German bull-in-the-china-shop policy we have come under the really silly suspicion of being ... a nationally organized band of robbers of seventy millions ... Among the most detestable elements ... of the Pan-German propaganda is the persistent ... involvement of the person of the Kaiser ... These world conquerors seem to place themselves protectively before the Kaiser, but in truth they misuse his name ... They are responsible for the fact that abroad the Kaiser is now held to account for the Pan-German war insanity and for the outbreak of the war." [21] " We think that ... we must ... keep in mind ... the broad masses in the countries engaged with us in war, that it must be our tactics

---

19 *Verhandlungen*, CCCX, 3714 ff.

20 *Ibid.*, CCCIX, 2386 ff., speech of Scheidemann, February 27, 1917.

21 *Ibid.*, CCCX, 3390 ff., speech of Scheidemann, May 15, 1917. He continued by defending the war aims which the Pan-Germans mocked as a peace of abnegation: " We reject the continuation of the war, we reject hundreds of thousands of dead and maimed, we reject the continued devastation of Europe, but we sacrifice no piece of German soil ... or possessions, we sacrifice what we do not own, we sacrifice the illusion that the war may bring us profit to which we have no claim, for which we have to bring further stupendous sacrifices, and which we could not achieve anyway."

to assist the tendencies towards peace in our enemy countries from below. This ... can be achieved only if we allow no doubt abroad that Germany does not harbor plans of conquests or of the dismemberment of foreign countries."

The SPD hoped that the acceptance by Germany of a peace without annexation would split the Entente world and break the morale of its populations.[22] " The truth is that we can no more end this war with military means than our opponents can. For three years, we have waged war against an enemy whose overwhelming power, due to a—shall I say—incomprehensible policy, still keeps on increasing ... If certain people had saved themselves the ridiculous talk of conquest and had not acted as if they wanted to devour the whole world ... we would today have had fewer enemies, perhaps we would already have peace." [23]

The SPD demanded that Germany must not be endangered by the quest for Belgian coal or French ore or Russian territory. The history of the German empire from 1871 to 1914 proved that Germany did not need them. Foreign, non-German populations in Germany had proven indigestible; they presented a danger since " we lack the talent for moral conquests." The SPD questioned Germany's ability to dictate peace to the whole world,[24] for, in order to realize annexationist dreams, Germany would have to crush the Western powers as decisively as Russia, and even then the result would not be peace, but the transformation of the whole world into an armed camp.[25] And above all, argued the SPD, the record of Louis XIV's annex-

---

22 *Ibid.*, pp. 3408 ff., speech of Dr. E. David, May 15, 1917. These two speeches were held in support of an SPD resolution to inquire into the government policy in the face of Russian acceptance of the principle of ' no annexations ' after the February, 1917, revolution.

23 *Ibid.*, pp. 3575 ff., speech of Scheidemann, July 19, 1917, during the debate of the Reichstag peace resolution.

24 *Ibid.*, pp. 3714 ff., speech of Landsberg, October 6, 1917.

25 *Ibid.*, CCCXI, 4162 ff., Scheidemann, February 26, 1918.

ations should conclusively prove the folly of incorporating foreign territories and then expecting a lasting peace.[26]

Nor did the SPD agree that the military security of Germany necessitated the conquest of large territories in the East and West. The Russian invasion in 1914 supported demands for protection of this nature; the SPD, however, emphasized that "military security through the acquisitions of land or some other military position which is enforced at the cost of a political understanding, which will be paid for with the permanent hostility of the neighboring people, is a caricature of true military security ... The genuine and best military security consists in political conditions which render a coalition against us more difficult if not impossible ... What the Gentlemen [of the right] want to attain as military security represents the greatest danger to our future tranquillity and peace." [27]

In this controversy raging between the groups representing these divergent views, the army spokesman and the rightist parties charged that the criticism of the center and leftist parties stiffened enemy resistance and enemy hopes for the internal collapse of Germany. The center parties and the SPD argued that annexationism hardened the decision of the enemy to fight to the bitter end. But the sincerity and patriotism of the criticism emanating from the SPD impressed the bourgeois parties. With the unfavorable progress of the war, they increasingly adopted these views and made them their own. By the middle of 1917, the parties of the center had in general endorsed SPD criticism of annexationist war and peace aims.

c. THE SPD, THE PEACE RESOLUTION AND THE TREATY OF

BREST-LITOVSK

The treatment of ethnic minorities in Germany, the policies applied in the occupied countries, the problems of parliamentary reform and the like had all been criticized by the SPD as

26 *Ibid.*, pp. 4233 ff., speech of Landsberg, February 28, 1918.
27 *Ibid.*, pp. 4431 ff., speech of Dr. David, March 18, 1918.

failures in the field of foreign relations, and the SPD had viewed with alarm the effects of these policies in the enemy countries. The submarine campaign and the Eastern peace treaties in particular provided the SPD with ample opportunities for criticizing pro-annexationist meddling in German politics and to document the damage which the influential advocates of annexationism had caused.

As late as April 6, 1916, Scheidemann had still defended submarine warfare in the Reichstag.[28] But by the middle of 1917, the miscalculations regarding the effects of the submarine campaign had become obvious. England proved able to recoup her shipping losses by drawing on the merchant ships of practically the entire world.[29] The hopes fostered by the advocates of the submarine warfare had been disappointed, and the participation of the United States in the war could no longer be discounted as inconsequential.[30]

28 *Ibid.*, CCCVII, 884-95.

29 In regard to these calculations, see among others Erzberger, *op. cit.*, pp. 208 ff.; Bethmann-Hollweg, *op. cit.*, II, 1114 ff.; Helfferich, *op. cit.*, II, 300 ff., 380 ff. The failure to assess accurately the potential effects of the submarine was probably best illustrated by the proposal of von Holtzendorff, the German naval chief of operations, to blockade the coast of the United States with *two* submarines; Hertling, *op. cit.*, pp. 115 ff. Holtzendorff had at one time proposed to end the war in the following manner: Germany was to annex the Belgian coast, France was to renounce all aspirations in Alsace-Lorraine and to be compensated for this by the acquisition of the remaining part of Belgium, and King Albert was to be compensated by becoming King of the French.

30 For the hopes privately expressed by German military leaders, see the references quoted in the preceding footnote. Among the publications of the Kriegspresseamt which publicly propagated these hopes, the following are of most interest: *Wirkungen und Aussichten des Ubootkrieges*, Berlin, 1917; *Zum Jahrestage unseres Friedensangebots*, Berlin, 1907; and *Vortrag des Major Hosse im Generalstab, Oktober, 1917: Das Eingreifen der Vereinigten Staaten in den Weltkrieg und seine Bedeutung fuer die militaerische Lage*, Berlin, 1917, which promised that because of the submarine campaign and the American obligations regarding armament production for France and England, "America in 1918 cannot and will not interfere effectively" in the war. Of the privately printed literature advocating submarine warfare, the most important titles are W. Bacmeister, *Der U-bootkrieg als Weg zum Endziel*, and E. Pistor, *Die entscheidende Wirkung des U-bootkrieges*.

The submarine campaign had been foisted upon the German public and the Reichstag not only as the quickest way to end the war successfully, but as the only remaining way to end the war victoriously.[31] However, on July 6 and 7, 1917, Erzberger presented some devastating revelations to a committee of the Reichstag regarding the failure of the submarine campaign. And these revelations left meager hopes that the war would end victoriously. In this situation, a majority of the political parties of the Reichstag thought it advisable to proclaim that Germany would be willing to conclude peace at any time without insisting on annexations or indemnifications. It was believed that the military situation no longer justified the continuation of the war, if peace could be concluded on the basis of the status quo ante bellum. These sentiments were recorded in the Reichstag peace resolution of July 19, 1917, which was adopted with the support of all parties from the SPD to the Catholic Center. The Reichstag thus endorsed the peace objectives which the SPD had officially advocated more or less consistently since August, 1914.[32]

The failure to clarify German aspirations in regard to Belgium, the Eastern peace treaties, and Michaelis' qualifi-

31 On October 16, 1916, the Reichstag resolved to support the submarine campaign provided that the Supreme Command declared it necessary in view of the military situation. There is general agreement among German authors that the unrestricted submarine campaign was declared to relieve the West front. From numerous references, the following may be cited in this connection: Bethmann-Hollweg, *op. cit.*, II, 128 ff.; Helfferich, *op. cit.*, II, 385 ff.; Ritter, *Kritik am Weltkrieg*, Leipzig, 1921, p. 184.

32 *Verhandlungen*, CCCX, 3569 ff. furnished the debates of the Reichstag in regard to the resolution. In this connection, see also *Ursachen* ..., vol. VIII, 'Gutachten' by Dr. Bredt; Bethmann-Hollweg, *op. cit.*, vol. II, *passim*; Helfferich, *op. cit.*, pp. 102-41; Erzberger, *op. cit.*, *passim*; Scheidemann, *Memoiren*, II, 34-50; Payer, *op. cit.*, pp. 25-48; Conrad Haussmann, *Schlaglichter*, Frankfurt, 1919, pp. 95-143; Hertling, *op. cit.*, pp. 13-14; Michaelis, *op. cit.*, pp. 320 ff. In regard to previous SPD declarations, see *Vorwaerts*, August 25, 1915, SPD declaration of peace aims, August 11, 1916; *Verhandlungen*, CCCVIII, 1852 ff.; CCCIX, 2899 ff.; CCCX, 3384 ff., 3575 ff.; CCCXI, 4536 ff.; etc.

cation of his acceptance of the peace resolution by the words
" wie ich sie auffasse " indicated that before October, 1918,
no German government had unequivocally endorsed the peace
resolution. However, the military necessities which had persuaded the Reichstag to formulate the peace resolution could
not be ignored. The German public seemed unwilling to tolerate
a continuation of the war for the sake of annexations. After
July 19, 1917, all chancellors recognized these facts by repeatedly giving lip-service to the peace resolution of the
Reichstag. Scheidemann, in fact, was convinced that "if the
peoples of the Entente could influence their governments to
declare their readiness to accept a peace on the basis of mutual
integrity, it would become evident within the hour that the
annexationists enjoyed the support of only a small minority." [33]

However, neither the parliamentary majority nor the civilian government controlled German policy during the war.
German policy was controlled by the Supreme Army Command whose ideas had been revealed by the treaties of Brest-
Litovsk and Bucharest.

Already on February 26, 1918, Scheidemann had warned
that the separation of the border states from Russia would
not serve the German cause. It would only produce feelings of
revenge in Russia. The newly created states, too, would oppose the new relationship to Germany imposed upon them.
" We are convinced that we are the best patriots in Germany
when we warn of thinking solely in military and not in political terms. No state ... can permanently live without friends,"
and the German system had proven its inability to win or hold
friends either abroad or at home.[34]

On February 28, 1918, Landsberg warned that the support
given to the July peace resolution must not depend on the
momentary military situation. The violation of its principles,
and the repudiation of the German answer to the Papal peace

33 *Ibid.*, CCCXIII, 6145, July 13, 1918.

34 *Ibid.*, CCCXI, 4162 ff.

move of 1917, would strengthen the Western powers in their war against an annexationist Germany. "Regardless of how little the majority of the Russian people stand behind the present government, the humiliation of the Bolshevist regime will be felt as their own humiliation. We want to conclude peace not with the Bolshevist government alone, but with the Russian people ... We see the best military security in a peaceful foreign policy and a liberal domestic policy." [35]

On March 18, 1918, Dr. David compared the Russian capitulation at Brest-Litovsk to the Prussian capitulation at Tilsit. At Brest-Litovsk, German diplomats had surrendered to militarism. The German government should have trusted democratic self-determination to achieve its objective in the East. If the loss of the border states had not been dictated by Prussian officers, the Bolsheviks would have accepted it without protest. But now, the Western powers could successfully use the treaty of Brest-Litovsk to undermine confidence in the trustworthiness of the professed German peace aims. The Bolshevik regime in Russia would soon be succeeded by a different regime, and this treaty would then furnish a pretext for the revival of an anti-German East-West alliance. Even if the enemies in the West could be forced to submit to a similar treaty, their enmity towards Germany, and Russian hostility, would continue. Because of the treaty of Brest-Litovsk, an honest policy of understanding between Germany and her enemies had become impossible. The net result had only been the eradication of all sympathy for Germany. [36]

The SPD belabored the treaty of Brest-Litovsk not because it took advantage of the Russian government, nor because it violated the democratic principle of self determination; the SPD attacked the treaty of Brest-Litovsk because it was detrimental to German interests, prolonged the war, and prejudiced Germany by the destruction of pro-German sym-

35 *Ibid.*, pp. 4233 ff.
36 *Ibid.*, pp. 4431 ff.

pathies among the Western powers. " It is time that a different political method is chosen in the East," and that, by strict adherence to the principle of self-determination, of no annexations, and the like, an anti-German weapon be wrested from the hands of Entente warmongers and placed in the hands of those among the Entente who worked for peace, concluded the SPD leadership.[37]

d. Conclusions: The SPD During the War

The SPD had represented the fusion of two rival groups, the Lassallean socialists and the Eisenach (Marxian) socialists. The necessity of surviving under the anti-socialist legislation from 1878 to 1890 gave the party a semblance of unity and integration and emphasized its radical character. But after the repeal of the anti-socialist legislation, its dual character was again revealed. While still officially committed to Marxism, the growing criticism of Marxian ideas, the failure of Marxian predictions to materialize, the changing character of the state, and the growth of the economic interests of the working class in society, made the retention of an exclusively Marxian program ever more difficult. The remarkable growth of the party by itself tended to relegate radicalism to the background. A decisive shift away from radical Marxism towards a humanitarian liberalism had been made possible by the conservatism of the trade-unions and their stake in existing society in the form of tangible legislation, contracts, and organization. This possibility had been furthered by the consistent nationalism of Lassalle, and by the revisionist inroads, the very rejection of which implied a further shift to the right.

When war broke out in 1914, the SPD supported the national cause. The attitude chosen by the party on August 4, 1914, was dictated by the pressure of public opinion, by the fear of government retaliation, and by a sincere belief that Germany was faced by a case of foreign aggression.

37 *Ibid.*, CCCXIII, 5617, Dr. E. David, June 24, 1918.

However, in its subsequent defense of its original declaration, in its attempts to justify its co-operation with the government on many war-time problems, and in its controversies
with foreign and domestic critics and with the Independent
Socialists, the party came to extol the policy of August 4 as
a virtue and a privilege. The SPD discovered that the interests of the workers were closely intertwined with the interests
of Germany and her imperialistic ambitions. It repudiated that
part of its history which was in conflict with its war-time policies, and adopted the official ' German ' version of the origins
of the war as its own.

Although the party did not cease its criticism of the government during the war, the purposes of the criticism revealed a marked change. The party was concerned lest the
continued toleration of conditions subject to criticism might
interfere with the successful termination of the war and the
prosperity of the German Empire. The claims of German nationalism were now accepted by the party to a degree which restricted most other traditional SPD principles, socialist, democratic or humanitarian.[38]

Thus, in demanding democratic reforms in Germany during
the war, the SPD was motivated by the desire to make Germany a better national state, to silence domestic and foreign
critics, and to invalidate the moral pretensions of the enemies
of Germany. The relative merits of democratic and other
political systems were decided not on the basis of principle but
by pragmatic methods; nationalistic interests rather than the
interests of the people or of the workers or any other interests
became the test for the choice. To strengthen the state in its
internal and foreign relations was the basis of SPD advocacy
of democratic reforms.

---

[38] W. Heine, writing on May 1, 1916, in the Bremer *Buerger Zeitung*,
stated that "even if the present government bore the sole guilt of the war
...with the purpose of subjecting Europe...we could still not act in a
manner different from that in which we have." This indicated the direction
in which the SPD had moved.

The demand that self-determination be extended to other peoples—excluding the subject peoples of Germany—was no longer the consequence of a theory which failed to differentiate between Russian Poles and Prussian Poles, but was motivated solely by considerations of German national interests. In rejecting imperialist aspirations and annexationism, neither the thought of defensive purposes already achieved, nor the idea of equal justice, was the decisive factor; the decisive factor was that imperialism and annexations were harmful to German interests, their realization impossible, and their propagation indefensible from a nationalistic point of view.

After a brief pause following the outbreak of the war, the SPD slipped back, to a marked degree, into opposition to the government. However, the essence of the renewed criticism of the government was the statement that the policies of the government were self-defeating, and not that their purposes were objectionable.

But not only were principles rejected in favor of opportunism and socialism in favor of nationalism: the class-struggle too was rejected by the SPD as the means to attain these new nationalist objectives. Class-struggle, with its violent methods and ultimate objectives, its assumption of an unabridgeable conflict of interests, its uncompromising antithesis of class structure and cross purposes could not serve the nationalist objectives of SPD war-time criticism. For SPD criticism during the war was motivated by opposition to the means employed by the powers-that-be and not their objectives, by a different interpretation of the needs for the same purposes and not their rejection, by the acceptance of the supremacy of national interests, not by their relegation to a rank lower than domestic interests and social progress. That the SPD was able to form a majority coalition with parties as far right as the Center party on domestic and foreign policies only indicated how narrow the gulf which still separated them had become.[39]

39 Ed. Bernstein, *Die deutsche Revolution*, Berlin, 1921, p. 65. For the interpretation of the SPD shift in its relation to the Minority Socialists, see *infra*, pp. 146, 168 ff.

CHAPTER VI

THE SPD AND THE INDEPENDENT SOCIAL DEMOCRATIC PARTY

a. GENESIS OF THE PARTY

THE previous three chapters have indicated the nature of the changes within the SPD during the years 1914-1918. However, not all leaders of the party approved of these changes. Opposition to official party policies appeared as soon as SPD attitudes towards the war had become a subject of discussion and debate.

Traditional hostility towards the government, suspicion of the official version regarding the causes of the war, refusal to act under the impulse of the moment, reluctance to abandon all semblance of international solidarity, rejection of the Burg-frieden and the ensuing cessation of class-struggle, and the inability to brush aside the entire social platform of the party motivated this early opposition. There was no talk about voting against the war credits in the party caucus of August 2 and 3, 1914. But Haase and Ledebour earnestly exhorted their party comrades to abstain from supporting the war credits which they considered to be incompatible with socialist traditions and teachings. Out of 110 SPD members in the Reichstag, fourteen proposed to abstain from voting. Only party discipline led all of them to abide by the majority decision.

During the first few months of the war, the opposition comprised only a small group of SPD intellectuals. It was carried on unnoticed by outsiders, and its strength in party committees was negligible.

However, the German retreat from the Marne and the Russian successes in Poland and Galicia dissipated the hopes for a short war. The mere lapse of time allowed many members of the party to reconsider the decisions of August 4, 1914, and permitted party traditions to assert themselves in opposition to official SPD war-time policies. On November 4, 1914, the ' Landesvorstand der SPD ' in Wuerttemberg, took over the oppositionist *Schwaebische Tageswacht,* providing the first hint to the public that all was not well within the party.

On December 2, 1914, war credits again came up for a vote in the Reichstag. The opposition bowed once more to the majority decision of the SPD to support the war credits. But in the party caucus the opposition now counted seventeen members, and Karl Liebknecht voted against the credits on the floor of the Reichstag. The statement of his motives for doing so was denied a place in the records of the Reichstag, but it was circulated widely as a pamphlet and helped usher in the pamphlet warfare which raged in Germany from 1914 until 1918. Liebknecht defended his rejection of the war credits by arguing that the war was a preventive, imperialist war. It was not wanted by any of the peoples involved and it did not serve the interests of any of them. The war would benefit only the semi-absolutism of Germany and would help crush the labor movement. He refused to support a war which had been caused by capitalist policies. He protested against the violation of Belgian neutrality, the annexationist war aims, the state of siege and its military ' dictatorship ', and the social and political irresponsibility of the German government.[1]

But the majority of the SPD was convinced of the good cause of Germany and of the needs for unified party action on matters of basic policy. Nor could the majority of the SPD rely upon the international proletariat; faith in effective co-operative action by the international proletariat had been dealt too severe a blow by the nationalist response of all Western European socialist parties at the outbreak of the war. The SPD therefore violently attacked Liebknecht as a dreamer who failed in his duties both to the party and to his country. And by January, 1915, Liebknecht referred to the SPD as "a party

---

[1] Karl Liebknecht, *Reden und Aufsaetze*, Hamburg, 1921, pp. 133-36.

which has revealed its lack of resistance against mass-psychosis, against the howling mob of the street, against over-clever demagogy from the government, against a piece of paper and printer's ink proclaiming the state of siege; a party which honors its name of 'revolutionary party' only by revolution-izing its own principles . . . Such a party deserves neither con-fidence nor respect." [2] For Karl Liebknecht, security consisted of the economic and cultural solidarity of the people; he con-sidered all other concepts of security to be outside the pale of socialist thought.[3]

A small but active group soon gathered around Liebknecht. Rosa Luxemburg, Franz Mehring, Ruehle, and Borchardt were most prominent among these opponents of the government and official SPD policies. The attempts to stifle the group by cen-sorship, arrests, and the like, forced them to work largely underground. As a result, the violence of the growing conflict was only intensified. The SPD enjoyed the protection of the government in its attacks upon the Liebknecht group while the latter was able to exploit the role of socialist martyrdom.

The vulnerablity of SPD policies, in terms of orthodox socialist thought, and of the German policies during the war, gave ample opportunities for attacks. The SPD had rejected the class-struggle during the war as destructive of national solidarity, and international solidarity of the proletariat as applicable only in peace time, stated Rosa Luxemburg. That would be permissible only if the laws of historical class-struggle and of social evolution in war-time were not identical with those applicable in peace. But in fact, the causes of class-struggle were only intensified during war-time. Luxemburg emphasized that either class-struggle was the dominant factor in history and could not be suspended during a period of war,

2 Speech of Liebknecht, circulated as a pamphlet; quoted by Drahn and Leonhard, op. cit., pp. 16 ff.

3 Ibid.

or class-struggle was a criminal violation of national interests in peace time no less than in war-time.[4]

This appeal to the orthodox socialist creed could not fail of some success. About one thousand party functionaries attached their signature to the so-called *Unterschriften-Flugblatt* in July, 1915, which protested against pro-annexationist trade-union demonstrations.

The entry of Italy into the war in 1915 provided another major occasion for a sweeping attack by the group around Liebknecht. " The causes and purposes of the world war ... have become clear even to the German people. The craze of holy war aims has receded step by step, enthusiasm in favor of war has vanished ... Italy's entry into the war is expected ... to kindle a new ecstasy of national hate, to stifle the will to peace, to efface the traces of ... own guilt ... Who is responsible ... for the continuation of this horrible war, who for Italy's intervention? Who else but the irresponsible ones in [our] own country ... The main enemy of the German people stands in Germany: German imperialism, the German war-party, German secret diplomacy. The German people must fight against this enemy in [our] own country ... How much longer shall the gamblers of imperialism abuse the patience of the people?... Down with the war-mongers on this side as well as on the other side of the border! " [5]

The pamphlet, *Die Krise der Sozialdemokratie,* brought out by Liebknecht, Luxemburg, and Mehring (the Junius pamphlet), argued that the war was a well-planned and well-prepared war of conquest by German-Austrian imperialists and that the SPD must at once begin to oppose it. For the Euro-

4 Rosa Luxemburg in *Internationale*, April, 1915, quoted *ibid.*, pp. 18-20. This was the only number of this paper to appear. It has already been shown that the SPD accepted this argument as valid; this is but one instance of the involuntary acceptance of consequences by the SPD because of the need to defend a position against the attempt to lead it ad absurdum.

5 May, 1915. Liebknecht, *op. cit.*, pp. 140-44. This appeal was entitled: *Der Hauptfeind steht im eigenem Land.*

pean proletariat, victory or defeat in this war was as meaning-less as the status quo ante bellum which had never been the result of self-determination. The creation of new states, dis-armament, the abolition of secret diplomacy, and the like were utopian, because they did not reach the roots of the present conflicts, the capitalistic class-state. Until the workers of all nations fraternized regardless of the wishes of the imperialists, there would be no peace.[6]

In reply to the statement of SPD principles for the con-clusion of peace formulated in August, 1915, this group pub-lished a scathing critique and a statement of its own principles under the title *Krieg und Proletariat*. It argued that no pos-sible justification existed for the continued retention of Alsace-Lorraine by Germany, or for the perpetuation of the Dual Monarchy, or for the SPD advocacy of these objectives. The present war was not a national, defensive war and it could be terminated only by the initiative of the working classes. The war had not interrupted the class-struggle; nor had it created a conflict between the proletarians of the different belligerents.[7]

These statements revealed the cardinal arguments of the Liebknecht group: the war was not defensive but pursued only imperialist class interests; class-struggle as a social force could not be suspended during war-time; and the national rivalries of class-states could not efface the international solidarity of the workers. The group around Liebknecht, known by the name 'Internationale', and two other splinter groups, the 'Internationale Sozialisten Deutschlands' and the 'Bremer Linksradikale', had thus retained many old SPD principles. They had completely separated themselves from the war-time SPD and the ideals which the latter had embraced.

6 Haenisch, *op. cit.*, pp. 56 ff., criticized the Junius pamphlet because it assumed that the power of party and proletariat could be translated into revolutionary action at a single stroke.

7 Quoted by Meyer, *op. cit.*, pp. 57-65.

Their uncompromising insistence upon international proletarian solidarity and internal class-struggle placed them to
the extreme left.[8]

However, the 'Internationale' was not the major source
of dissent within the SPD. On August 4, and on December 2,
1914, the war credits had been presented to the Reichstag as
special emergency measures. In March, 1915, the government
again asked for war credits, but this time they formed an
integral part of the regular budget. Many members of the SPD
found it difficult to ignore the long and sacred tradition of the
SPD and to vote for the budget. In the party caucus thirty
members voted against an approval of the budget. On the
floor of the Reichstag, Liebknecht was joined by Ruehle in
voting against it, and thirty-one SPD members abstained from
voting. In December, 1915, forty-three members voted against
the war credits in party caucuses, and twenty opposed the war
credits on the floor of the Reichstag. The declaration of this
'group of twenty' in support of their action attacked annexationism, which, it was claimed, made an early peace impossible. They argued that the war had progressed favorably for
Germany and that it was now the duty of Germany to initiate
peace negotiations. But instead, the policies of the government
tended to prolong the miseries of war. The group therefore
felt compelled to oppose the war credits.[9]

8 The group 'Internationale' eventually changed into the 'Spartakus-
bund' and then into the Communist Party of Germany (KPD). The main
periodicals of these groups were: *Internationale*, only one issue in April,
1915; the *Spartacus Letters*, September, 1916-November, 1918; the *Politische
Briefe*, January, 1916–December, 1916; the *Lichtstrahlen*, under the editorship of J. Borchardt; the *Bremer Buergerzeitung*; *Bremer Arbeiterpolitik*;
and the *Braunschweiger Volksfreund*, edited by Radek. To counteract these
periodicals and the steadily increasing flow of anti-SPD literature from the
left, the SPD founded the 'Verlag der Internationalen Korrespondenz',
which edited, among others, the series *Kriegsprobleme der Arbeiterklasse*
and the *Sozialistische Dokumente des Weltkrieges*.

9 Statement by Geyer, *Verhandlungen*, CCCVI, 507 ff. Geyer stated that
he represented nineteen SPD members of the Reichstag; Drahn and
Leonhard, *op. cit.*, p. 28, talked of twenty-one; Haenisch, *op. cit.*, pp. 51-52,

The group of twenty rejected the suggestion that it should not publicize its opposition to official party views by a vote in the Reichstag. It charged instead that the SPD had been trying to gag it, and that although they had been allowed to take the floor of the Reichstag about as often as the supporters of the August 4, 1914, policy, they had been restricted to non-controversial matters such as the criticism of the food situation, or censorship; when the minority views differed from the majority, the practices of the majority in determining who should speak had tended to silence them.

The SPD party executive condemned the action of the twenty as a breach of party discipline, and as obstructing national defense in time of war.[10] The individual reactions of SPD leaders towards the group of twenty are of interest. Dr. David charged them with consistent Marxian action, accused them of considering the proletarian to be without a fatherland and of sabotaging the war effort.[11] " The twenty dissidents put their convictions above party discipline. This is an event which, since the fusion of 1875, has never occurred in the SPD." [12] The *Chemnitzer Zeitung* offered the following criticism: " The independent action of the twenty tends to prolong the war. A reliable source from Switzerland quotes the French minister of war as saying that the solidarity of German labor

talked of twenty; so did Berger, *op. cit.*, p. 5, and the SPD resolution of January 7 and 8, 1916, condemning their action. There was no roll call for this vote on the floor of the Reichstag. But since the SPD party executive committee accepted twenty as the number of persons involved, this appears to be the correct number.

10 Resolutions of January 7 and 8, 1916; *Vorwaerts*, January 9, 1916. These resolutions also stated that the *Vorwaerts*, by supporting the action of the twenty editorially, had become unfit to be the official party organ.

11 *Frankfurter Zeitung*, January 9, 1916. Dr. David apparently believed that the SPD should take a stand which was not a consistent Marxian action.

12 The *Dresdener Volkszeitung*, to whom this charge was attributed by the *Niederrheinische Arbeiterzeitung*, December 29, 1915, could not condone, apparently, the seriousness of such an indictment.

... would force France to terminate the war, but that there are indications that the split of German Labor will allow a successful conclusion of the war." [13] The paper warned that a party divided on the defense of the Fatherland must be considered as impotent in all future political campaigns.[14]

However, technically the party had not yet split in December, 1915. The final break came as the result of a tumultuous Reichstag session on March 24, 1916, when the emergency budget was being debated. Haase opposed the budget. He motivated this by pointing to the state of siege, the food situation, and annexationism. He accused the government of being unable and unwilling to end the war. He denied that Germany would win a victory, or that the war would produce anything but losers. The continuation of the war benefitted only imperialism, he charged. Amidst shouts of "we don't want to hear you!" Haase stated: "You won't deny that [many] capitalists ... in all countries agree ... that the war was a miscalculation." Yet, he charged, Germany was becoming more and more annexationist.[15] In a party caucus immediately following this tumultuous scene, Haase and his friends were read out of the party.[16]

In order to protect their rights to sit in committees of the Reichstag, this group organized the 'Sozialdemokratische Ar-

13 Quoted *ibid.*, December 30, 1915. This argument was repeated by the Dortmunder *Arbeiterzeitung*, December 27, 1915, and others.

14 *Ibid.*; also, *Frankfurter Zeitung*, December 31, 1915, January 7, 1916.

15 Haase was repeatedly interrupted and was finally prevented from continuing his speech; *Verhandlungen*, CCCVII, 842-844. Bernstein later on declared that the SPD caucus had previously ruled that Haase should not take the floor that day; *Neue Zeit*, vol. XXXIV, pt. 2, no. 1, April 7, 1916, pp. 1 ff., article "Die Spaltung der Reichstagsfraktion." Scheidemann rose immediately after Haase's speech to declare that the SPD would not abandon the Fatherland in its hour of need; and David accused Haase of acting like an agent of the enemy. Cf. *Protokoll des Parteitags Wuerzburg 1917*, pp. 126-130, 316-339.

16 *Vorwaerts*, March 25, 1916; *Frankfurter Zeitung*, March 26, 1916.

beitsgemeinschaft'. (Social-Democratic Co-operative Group.) In 1917, they formed the Independent Socialist Party, the USPD.[17]

This division of the SPD did not correspond fully to any previous division or controversial alignments within the party. Many who had been the most radical proponents of Marxism before 1914, supported the policy of August 4, 1914, and became its foremost advocates. Lensch and Cunow belonged in this group. Former revisionists, who had come to revisionism with a reformist opportunistic background, remained within the SPD, such as Vollmar, David, and Kolb. But a surprisingly large number of revisionists now found themselves within the USPD. Bernstein, Eisner, and Erdmann may serve as examples. Former anti-revisionists now joined their former antagonists within the USPD; Karl Kautsky probably was foremost among these. And many regular members of the SPD who could not follow the radical shift executed by the party during the war went over to the USPD; for instance, Haase. But it appears that those who had in the past consistently refused to allow the SPD to become a party of tactical maneuvers, who had rejected opportunism, and who had preferred idealism to political pragmatism, seceded from the SPD; whereas those, who considered tactics as dominant in political actions and a realistic opportunism as superior to strict doctrine, and those who refused to form public opinion and rather submitted to it, remained within the SPD.

The USPD was able to acquire control over a number of influential SPD publications, for example, the *Neue Zeit*, the *Kampf*, and the *Vorbote*, while the SPD eventually wrested

17 The USPD included some members of the Spartacists who joined because Liebknecht and other prominent leaders of their group were either under prison sentences or under protective custody. The initials USPD will be used to denote both the 'Sozialdemokratische Arbeitsgemeinschaft' and the party founded in 1917.

the *Vorwaerts* from its USPD editors, though only after a violent struggle and only with government aid.[18]

The USPD had gained the support of the majority of the workers in Berlin and other large cities, in Saxony, Thuringia, and the lower Rhineland. The attitude of the local party press rather than the influence of the representatives from these districts determined the character of SPD constituencies. Ebert was not the only SPD representative whose district was a stronghold of the USPD after 1916. Women and youth augmented the strength of the USPD. But the new party never gained control over the large miners' or textile workers' unions. It is interesting to note that USPD strength was concentrated in roughly the same areas as SPD strength in the 1860's and 1870's.

There are no accurate ways of measuring the strength of the USPD or its influence upon the membership of the SPD. The continuous decline of SPD membership during the war was due to the fact that the SPD had lost seventy-five percent of its male members to the armed forces, and active members of the armed forces could not belong to political parties.[19] Nor

---

18 Berger, *op. cit.*, pp. 66-78. Bevan, *op. cit.*, pp. 138-139. Ledebour's statement in the Reichstag, *Verhandlungen*, CCCX, 3398 ff., May 15, 1917. The SPD had retained control over *Sozialistische Monatshefte*, the *Korrespondenzblatt der Gewerkschaften*, the *Glocke*, and the *Internationale Korrespondenz*, and regained, late in 1917, the *Neue Zeit*.

19 SPD membership during the war declined as follows:

March 31, 1914	1,085,905	members
March 31, 1915	585,898	"
March 31, 1916	432,618	"
March 31, 1917	243,061	"

Party press subscriptions did not decline as radically:

March 31, 1914	1,488,345
March 31, 1915	1,060,891
March 31, 1916	900,731
March 31, 1917	762,752

Trade-union membership, which had declined from 2,482,046 at the beginning of the war to 934,784 in December 1916, rose to 1,201,770 by September,

did the by-elections of 1917 furnish accurate indications, because the government openly administered the laws of the state of siege and censorship to favor the SPD at the expense of the USPD.[20]

In September, 1916, a 'Reichskonferenz der SPD' had been called to iron out the differences between the two divergent groups. 445 delegates had been elected who alligned themselves in the following manner:

	SPD	USPD
Number of delegates	276	169
Number of party members in their districts	524,797	516,079

But none of the districts had voted unanimously in favor of one group or the other. The USPD was stronger in large districts where the minorities, too, were more numerous than in smaller districts. An appraisal of party allignment in individual districts on the basis of the votes of their representatives at the Reichskonferenz would therefore favor the USPD. It may hence be concluded that, by 1917, the USPD had not gained a majority of the workers, and that SPD policies continued to enjoy the support of the majority of the party members.

b.   USPD CRITICISM OF WAR-TIME POLICIES

Like the SPD, the group of twenty placed increasing emphasis upon its original views regarding the war. At first, they desired only to modify SPD policies without producing a

1917; *Protokoll des Parteitags Wuerzburg 1917*, p. 10; *Neue Zeit*, vol. XXXVI, pt. 1, no. 16, January 18, 1918, pp. 361 ff. The membership of women both in the SPD and in trade-unions declined similarly, from 174,754 to 66,608.

20 In the by-election of March 14, 1917, in Berlin, between an SPD candidate and F. Mehring, the SPD received 16,881 votes and Mehring 5,010. The government influenced this and other elections by prohibiting newspapers and meetings, arresting scheduled speakers, and facilitating the campaign of the groups which it favored most by corresponding applications of censorship.

rift among the leaders of the party. The war had changed into a reprehensible war of conquest, warned Bernstein, Haase and Kautsky in *Das Gebot der Stunde,* and the SPD should therefore repudiate the policies of August, 1914.

This suggestion had been discussed and rejected by a SPD party committee, which met from June 30 to July 1, 1917. And in August, 1915, the party committee together with the SPD bloc in the Reichstag adopted a set of principles for the conclusion of peace which again ignored the views of Bernstein. This steady disregard of the views of the minority led Kautsky to ask for independent parliamentary action by the minority. It was no longer enough merely to abstain from supporting the war credits, as the minority had been doing since March, 1915; it was now necessary to act.[21]

The USPD firmly believed in the co-responsibility of the German government for the outbreak of war. The accumulating evidence piled up by the revelations of diplomats and foreign governments, and a study of published documents regarding the outbreak of war led, it was held, to no other conclusion. " The war ... is a consequence of a policy of continuous armaments ... sponsored in particular by the government of the Reich ... It was the government of the Reich which had opposed more stubbornly ... than any other big European power the attempts to implement the system of international courts of arbitration, ... aroused mistrust towards Germany among the democracies of the entire world and ... played into the hands of imperialist politicians ... This mistrust has been accentuated to an extraordinarily high degree by measures ... which stand in sharpest conflict with the rules of international law and by the manner of conducting unrestricted submarine warfare ... The ... number of enemies of

21 Karl Kautsky, in *Neue Zeit,* vol. XXXIV, pt. 1, nos. 5 and 6, pp. 129 ff., 161 ff., October 29, 1915, November 5, 1915. The following month, the group of twenty took Kautsky's advice and voted against the demands for additional war credits.

Germany has been increased ... Even in countries ... which are still neutral ... dissatisfaction with Germany has reached a degree hardly capable of intensification ... The spirit of militarism ... acts like poison on all attempts of arriving at an understanding with the nations." [22]

In the discussions preceding the peace resolution of July, 1917, Haase declared that the policies of the Conservatives, which Michaelis would undoubtedly continue, would deliver Germany to the mercy of her enemies. He pointed at the false claims made for U-boat warfare, and held its failure responsible for the decline in the morale of the people. Yet, he also attacked the peace resolution itself. Until recently, its supporters had themselves been annexationists, and the resolution repudiated neither reparations nor ambitions in Belgium or in the Baltic regions. He noted that the resolution failed to endorse self-determination and disarmament, and warned against illusions regarding the possible effects of the resolution abroad.[23]

On October 10, 1917, the German policy in the Baltic region was attacked by the USPD. In Riga, the largest German center in the area, only sixteen percent of the population were Germans. Yet the German military commanders treated Riga as well as the entire region as German, thus laying the basis for the permanent hostility of their populations towards Germany.[24]

After the breakdown of the peace negotiations at Brest-Litovsk, Haase assailed the German ultimatum to Russia in

22 *Verhandlungen*, CCCIX, 2824 ff., March 29, 1917, one of the rare speeches of Bernstein in the Reichstag. This statement appears especially scathing if one bears in mind that Bernstein did not view international law as deduced from some transcendental concept of justice, but as the empirical result gained from the observation of actual relations between sovereign governments. See E. Bernstein, *Voelkerrecht und Voelkerpolitik*, Berlin, 1918, Chapter I; *Die Wahrheit ueber die Einkreisung*, Berlin, 1919.

23 *Verhandlungen*, CCCX, 3585 ff., July 19, 1917.

24 *Ibid.*, pp. 3848 ff., speech of Ledebour; also CCCXI, 3958 ff., speech of Haase, November 29, 1917.

the following terms: "The German ultimatum will go down in history as a document of an exorbitant policy of power and conquest." Those who still argued that the government wanted a peace of understanding, could no longer do so in good faith. The ultimatum did not correspond to the July peace resolution or to the answer to the Papal note, he stated. The claim that the German advance against the non-defending Russians had been caused by Red atrocities was as spurious as all other atrocity tales spread by Germany since the fairly tale of the attack by French aircraft before the outbreak of the war. If the Polish border were to be fixed in accordance with German military needs, the result would be rampant annexationism. The German actions in the East only underscored the fear of the Western powers that the July resolution had been a trap.[25]

Ledebour, on March 22, 1918, declared that the three majority parties seemed to be dissatisfied with the treaty of Brest-Litovsk, and the annexationists seemed well contented. He asked the Reichstag to reject the treaty and to force the government to present a new one. "We maintain ... that this peace treaty ... contains the gravest dangers for world peace, for the German Empire, and particularly for the German people." He condemned the military authorities in the East who made opposition to German officials and laws punishable by death, hanging all Bolshevist troops upon capture.[26] " The German people will ultimately have to pay the costs ... if other peoples feel themselves violated by such a treaty ... And if we ... protest against such a violation of other peoples by this treaty, we prove ourselves to be better friends of Germany than you, Gentlemen, who agree to this violation. You, who advance and support such annexationist plans, help in the formation of permanent emnity [Verfeindung] towards Ger-

25 *Ibid.*, CCCXI, 4208 ff., February 27, 1918. Also p. 4283, March 1, 1918, speech by Vogtherr.

26 *Ibid.*, pp. 4473 ff. Also pp. 4540 ff., March 22, 1917, speech of Haase.

many among all foreign peoples and prove yourselves to be the worst enemies of Germany and of the German people." [27]

The peace treaty with Rumania gave Ledebour a chance for a long oration in the Reichstag on June 21, 1918. He criticized the treaty because it provided for annexations. He held that territories should not be shifted except by plebiscites, because the creation of irredenta was dangerous to future peace. The treaty contained the promise of religious toleration in Rumania, but Ledebour attacked it because the treaty, by enumeration, restricted the religions which should be tolerated. The treaty also provided for the protection of the language of the German minorities in Rumania. Ledebour emphasized that if Germany forced Rumania to protect alien minorities, then Germany herself should also protect the rights of the alien minorities living within her borders. " Recently, I received the information that in the occupied Baltic region, the local German administration has abolished the Estonian schools—nine-tenths of the population are Estonians—and, because of the craze of Germanization, has introduced German as the language of instruction ... How impudent of the military commanders and their handymen, the civil authorities, to permit themselves ... to rob the population of these territories of their language ..." Referring to an earlier attack by the Conservative and National-Liberal parties on the Rumanian dynasty, Ledebour declared: " It released in me a feeling of satisfaction and joy that our view about the need of abolishing dynasties which have been of utmost harm and which have demonstrably injured the public weal, has received support even from Count Westarp ... But why stop with Rumania? Dynasties commit evil all over ... Yes, in the German Reichstag, we shall ... some day hold court against all people whose harmful policies drove their own people to ruin ... Even the so-called monarchists do not propose retaining monarchies or dynasties unconditionally in control without any interference. The two

27 *Ibid.*, pp. 4559 ff., speech of Ledebour.

gentlemen, Count Westarp and Dr. Stresemann have directly or indirectly ... asked the Rumanians to set aside the dynasty. I do not object to this. It is always a good example. You start with a Hohenzollern in Rumania, and this can have its effects in other countries ... Whether this should be extended to other Hohenzollerns? Yes, I merely draw the consequences of your initiative. Yes. Yes. Well, Gentlemen, if members of dynasties can be proven to have committed a grave crime against the public welfare by inciting wars, by prolonging wars, or by other actions damaging the people, they must of course be put aside ..." Ledebour concluded with the warning that punishing Rumanian war criminals would justify a similar demand of the Entente.[28]

The USPD never doubted the soundness of its criticism. Haase quite openly asked that the German peace aims be openly avowed and that Ludendorff be appointed chancellor. For him, the belief that Germany must rule the world was the misfortune of Germany. The crux of the war was imperialistic ambitions, not ideological conflicts. In sharp terms he condemned the German ambitions in France and Belgium and the German attempts to overthrow the very regime with which peace had been concluded in Russia. " There is need to take up not only the battle of words in parliament ... but the masses of the people who want peace must at last throw their entire weight on the scales." [29] The USPD did not agree that the

28 *Ibid.*, CCCXIII, 5554 ff. The latter part of the speech was delivered amidst general uproar in the House. The government's spokesman insisted that German had not been introduced as the language of teaching, but as a language to be taught in all schools. Under the treaty of Brest-Litovsk, Estonia had remained part of Russia, to be occupied temporarily by German police forces. That the Kaiser should abdicate, if this demand were the alternative to continuing the war, was first demanded by Dr. Cohn, *ibid.*, pp. 5505, June 14, 1918. The USPD rejection of the treaty of Bucharest was motivated by Dr. Cohn with the remarks that peace could not come until German militarism, which knew no peace, had been conquered. *Ibid.*, p. 5755.

29 *Ibid.*, pp. 5660 ff., June 25, 1918.

sweeping war aims of the Entente justified even more sweeping
German demands in retaliation.

It was of course out of the question that the USPD should
support war credits. The USPD bloc " cannot grant a vote of
confidence to the government of an imperialistic state whose
nature just now is sharply revealed in the erection of a military
dictatorship, the enrichment of large capitalist enterprises, the
peace of violation with Russia, the hacking down with sabres
of the revolution in the Ukraine and Finland, the bloody oppression of the masses in Riga, Kurland, Latvia, and Estonia
in favor of a small privileged class." [30] " The war was never
a war of defense. It was and is a war of conquest with imperialistic objectives. The Imperial government covers up and
favors the drives of the annexationists ... Upon Russia and
Rumania they forced a peace of violation ... Peoples, whose
liberation had been promised in big words, are being enslaved
and exploited. The right to self-determination is ... being
mocked .. The reputation of the German Reich, the confidence
in the sincerity of the promises made by the government is
being destroyed ... A state of siege and censorship gags the
free word and deceives regarding the true attitudes of the
people ... We reject the credits ... Down with the war ! " [31]

Yet, in spite of the vehemence of its language and the uncompromising character of its views, the USPD denied that
its attitudes prejudiced the true national cause. For unlike the
groups around Liebknecht and Borchardt, the USPD did not
reject the principle of national defense in toto; it rejected only
the idea that the present war was a war of national defense.

" A duty to support war credits ... would give any government, whatever policies it may pursue, the power to ruin
the German state and the German people ... It must be rejected
as the unqualified statement of government absolutism." [32]

30 *Ibid.*, CCCXI, 4424, March 18, 1918, declaration of Haase.

31 *Ibid.*, CCCXIII, 6145 ff., July 13, 1918, declaration of Geyer.

32 *Ibid.*, CCCIX, 2369, February 23, 1917, speech of Ledebour.

" The deeds of the German government, the wrong measures, act unfavorably on the foreign countries. But their criticism may correct those evils, and hence acts in the interests of our German Fatherland." [33] We serve our country best by insisting that at long last domestic as well as foreign policies follow different paths." [34] " You believe ... that you can further peace by concealing everything, by deceiving ourselves and others. Experience taught us that peace can only be attained by clarifying the facts." [35]

Much of this criticism was eventually echoed by the SPD and the civilian governments of Germany. And seemingly, the USPD attacks and SPD criticism differed mainly in degree, choice of expressions, implications of urgency. Yet an examination of USPD war aims and of the means chosen to translate them into fact shows that the difference was more basic.

The USPD rejected the proposition that the Austrian or Ottoman Empires should be preserved intact. The demands of self-determination prohibited the preservation of these strongholds of semi-absolutism and reaction, and the USPD was willing to see them pass away. Alsace-Lorraine should be returned to France. Under no circumstances should Germany refuse a plebiscite in the provinces. To refuse a plebiscite would mean to admit that the Reichsland was not as German in sentiment and desire as had been claimed by Germany. The treatment of non-German areas within the empire was such that the USPD could not condone the acquisition of additional territories with alien populations. In fact, the USPD thought that the loss of present German possessions with minority groups would rather strengthen the national character of the German empire. By losing her alien populations and areas, Germany would remove most causes of friction, armaments

33 *Ibid.*, CCCX, 3134 ff., statement by Ledebour.
34 *Ibid.*, pp. 3398 ff., May 15, 1917, speech of Ledebour.
35 *Ibid.*, CCCXI, 3958 ff., November 29, 1917, speech by Haase.

and high taxation and would contribute significantly to the permanent pacification of Europe.

The USPD had adopted the peace aims of the dissenting group at the Stockholm conference in 1917. In order to evade the ban on their publication in Germany, Haase read them into the records of the Reichstag. These peace aims consisted of the following main points: universal disarmament; freedom of international migration; international treaties for the protection of workers; equal rights for the inhabitants of a country regardless of citizenship; and the abolition of secret treaties. The peace treaty should contain neither annexations nor indemnities, and should be drawn up on the basis of the rights of national self-determination. Serbia, Poland, and Belgium should be restored without qualifications, and Alsace-Lorraine should be returned to France. No further colonial conquests ought to be made. The international proletariat would be able to establish a supra-national body to enforce such peace terms.[36]

The territorial objectives of the USPD were narrowly limited by common language, common historical background, common cultural components, or their equivalents. In its peace program and war-time criticism, the USPD did not therefore sacrifice any legitimate German national aspirations which might fall within this classification. On the other hand, the SPD—within the limits of the German power to effect them—advocated peace aims which condoned German domination over alien regions. Faith in the excellency of one's own nationality sufficed—in the eyes of the SPD—as a reason for disregarding the national demands of others and advocating nationalistic peace aims.

The rejection of such nationalistic peace aims by the USPD found, however, little sympathy in Germany. There was no

---

36 *Ibid.*, CCCX, 3585 ff., July 19, 1917, speech of Haase who offered these proposals as an alternative to the peace resolution then under discussion.

hope that the USPD would be able to *persuade* Germany to give up its nationalistic ambitions in the war. To thwart nationalistic peace aims and to forestall an unnecessary prolongation of the war because of such ambitions, the USPD had to resort to more effective measures than the mere rejection of war credits or blasts in the Reichstag. It was this active struggle for the realization of its program that differentiated the USPD from the SPD and marked it as the inheritor of the revolutionary antecedents of the SPD.

c. PROPAGANDA, STRIKES, AND REVOLUTION

In order to prevent the realization of the imperialistic aspirations, which in the opinion of the USPD had become characteristic of all parties to its right, and in order to effect its own program of a just peace, the USPD resorted to the traditional means of political class-struggle. It produced a vast output of literature striving to spread its own gospel and to revile its opponents in the most condemning terms; it prepared strikes whose purposes were purely political; and it undertook the preparation of violent revolution.[37]

The early pamphlets and leaflets, distributed in 1915 and 1916, sharply attacked the SPD peace aims. *Krieg und Pro-*

---

37 The Spartacists, who had begun their own campaign of pamphlets and leaflets in 1914, had remained rather cool towards the group of twenty which on December 21, 1915, had rejected the war credits, and which, in March, 1916, had formed the 'Sozialdemokratische Arbeitsgemeinschaft'. In the first of the *Politische Briefe* of January 27, 1916, and in the third letter of April, 1916, Liebknecht and Luxemburg had attacked this group as being disunited within itself, and without hope of ever taking serious revolutionary action; men, who for years had tolerated the domination of the SPD, had not overnight become lions; quoted by Drahn and Leonhard, *op. cit.*, pp. 29-33, 38-42; E. Meyer, *op. cit.*, pp. 112-116. The arrests of the leaders of the Spartacists and the need to fuse the different splinter groups of radical socialists in the face of government opposition led to a measure of cooperation in 1917 and 1918. The illegal pamphlets showed every conceivable variation of socialist doctrine, but their purpose in furthering the class-struggle gave them a degree of unity which was emphasized by their common hostility towards the SPD.

letariat, written by Karski in 1915, *Der Annexionswahnsinn* by H. Duncker and distributed in 1915, *Entweder-Oder,* written by Luxemburg and distributed in the summer of 1916, serve as examples.[38]

After the arrest of Karl Liebknecht during the May-day demonstration in 1916, Rosa Luxemburg wrote: " High treason! High treason! May festival is high treason! Criticism of the war loan—high treason! International solidarity—high treason! Rejection of the budget—high treason! Strikes to raise starvation wages—high treason! Public discussion of food profiteering—high treason! The plaints of hungry women in front of shops—high treason! What has been said a thousand times in social democratic newspapers, in social democratic election meetings, in social democratic speeches in the Reichstag, is high treason today ... David-Landsberg-Scheidemann have excelled all district attorneys, shamed all police presidents ... If these fellows had to administer Bismarck's anti-socialist laws, they would have sent to prison all social democratic representatives and editors, would have brought our August Bebel, our old Liebknecht to the gallows ... A dog who licks the boots of rulers who for decades have dealt him only kicks. A dog, who, muzzled by the state of siege, wags his tail gently and looks into the eyes of the military dictatorship whining for grace ... David, Landsberg and their followers are and remain dogs." [39]

The internal conditions in Germany and the excesses in the state of siege and arrests for protective custody provided the USPD with more than enough material for the most scathing denunciations.

A pamphlet by Karski under the title *Deutschland-ein fertiges Zuchthaus,* summed up the situation in the summer of

38 Their authorship is doubtful and ascribed to different persons. The judgment of E. Meyer, *op. cit.,* has generally been followed here, because his volume was published later (1927) than any of the others and presumably assigned authorship after due examination of rival claims.

39 Quoted from *Hundepolitik,* by Berger, *op. cit.,* pp. 82 ff.

1916 as follows: " Instead of raising [workers'] benefits—withdrawal of benefits; instead of raising wages—lowering of wages; instead of extension of popular rights—abolition of the freedom of movement and of the right to strike, after the freedom of coalitions, assemblies, and of press have long since been torn to shreds; instead of freedom—serfdom; instead of reforms—renewal of feudal oppression of the people; instead of bread—hunger and prison; instead of lifting the stage of siege —general prison . . . There is no help, not against the old, not against the new misery, except the self-aid of the proletariat." [40]

Under such titles as *Hunger,* and *Weniger Brot, keine Rechte, neue Steuern,* the attacks upon the internal conditions in Germany were continued. In 1917, a leaflet entitled *Preussen der Welt voran* attacked the proposals for Prussian reforms, because "only as the fruit of a revolutionary struggle for power against the ruling classes . . . do reforms have real meaning, because [only] then will they be filled with revolutionary meaning by the working classes, and utilized only as a step in the struggle for the complete abolition of capitalist exploitation." [41]

The discussion of the origins of the war and of the war aims loomed large in this illegal literature, and some of the best of the pamphlets dealt with them. *Die Ursachen des Weltkrieges,* August 1914, *Wer hat die Schuld am Kriege?* and *Krieg und Proletariat,* both written by Karski in the summer of 1915, and *Eine Petition gegen den Frieden,* Autumn 1916, were the most notable among them.

The steady denunciation of the havoc and devastation of war assured the success of these pamphlets among a war-weary nation; it predominated among their subject matter. During the winter of 1914-15, Auslaender wrote under the title *Die Welt speit Blut!* : " The mass of dead that the Strangler War has felled in the East and West has already grown to more than a

40 Quoted by Meyer, *op. cit.,* pp. 153-156.
41 *Ibid.,* pp. 195-198.

million, the number of wounded to thrice that much. In vain does reason seek to comprehend the abundance of misery which is described by such numbers ... That war spares the peaceful citizen has become a laughable phrase, on land as well as at sea ... Out of the fog of blood and ashes rises ever heavier the cloud of hate ... Every day of war enlarges the bill which peace, that is, the creative work of the people, will have to pay off." [42] This theme was further exploited in the following war years; Liebknecht's appeal *Auf zur Maifeier* in 1916 achieved a sort of climax in this respect.

This literature was marked by the general absence of all ideological or Marxian discussions. Instead, it exploited the state of siege, the food situation, and the heavy sacrifices of the war in order to win support for the idea that the war should be ended at once. The success of this literature was therefore due not to acceptance of USPD ideology, but to the ever-growing war-weariness which prepared the people to respond to the appeals of any group promising to terminate the war at once. " It is not true that the masses are torn asunder by profound disagreements ... The masses ... have no knowledge of theoretical disagreements ... The party controversy is carried on almost completely by the leaders ... What the masses want is peace ... What brings adherents to the USPD is the general embitterment." [43]

After the arrest of Karl Liebknecht in May, 1916, various leaflets called for demonstration strikes, and some short strikes occurred in Braunschweig, Stuttgart and Berlin. But the USPD was not ready to assume leadership of the strike movement until after the strikes in April, 1917, which had been called as a protest against a reduction in bread rations. A leaflet bearing the title *Die Lehren des grossen Massenstreiks* analyzed their failure and concluded that rations before the

42 Quoted *ibid.*, pp. 36-38.

43 K. Wendemuth, " Parteistreit und Masse" in *Neue Zeit*, vol. XXXVI, pt. 1, no. 6, pp. 138 ff., November 9, 1917.

recent reductions had already been near starvation level; they could be increased only by the indiscriminate slaughter of cattle and the consumption of seed potatoes. Not even the bumper crops in 1914 and 1915 had been sufficient to provide adequate food. Only an immediate peace could ease the food situation because one could not distribute foods better unless adequate food supplies were available at all. Future strikes must therefore carry a clear political message; they must also be kept free of trade-union interference.

The preparation of fresh strikes began rather early. In September, 1917, a leaflet called for a new demonstration strike, because " for the sake of the greedy moneysacks the world has been turned into a gruesome blood bath. For three years our fathers and brothers have been carried to slaughter under the deceiving mirage of the defense of the Fatherland. In destitution, misery, and sufferings, they must shed their blood against their own interests for the sake of a murderous group of pharisees. While our own people are close to death from hunger, the rulers behind the scenes celebrate the profitable mass-murder in festive orgies. The demand for peace, the cry for freedom and bread is being answered . . . by a hypocritical deluge of words." [44]

The call for the January, 1918, strikes was issued under the slogan *Am Montag, dem 28. Januar beginnt der Massenstreik.* The call followed a wave of successful strikes in Austria, news of which had spread in spite of censorship. The political character of the strikes was emphasized by a series of leaflets, distributed in January, 1918, such as *Arbeiter und Arbeiterinnen, Hoch der Massenstreik, auf zum Kampf, Der Kampf dauert fort,* and others. All demanded lifting the state of siege, of censorship and of protective custody, complete freedom of speech, press, assembly and associations, and the abolition of the compulsory labor laws. In some pamphlets, demands for a political

---

[44] Quoted by Drahn and Leonhard, *op. cit.,* pp. 87 ff.

amnesty and the organization of workers' councils to enforce the acceptance of an early peace were included.[45]

In order to bring the workers out of the factories, these pamphlets attacked the domestic disintegration of war-time Germany: the breakdown of the food situation, the mockery of Prussian reforms in the Prussian diet, and the breakdown of the peace negotiations at Brest-Litovsk because of German demands for annexations. The USPD agreed with most German parties on the substance of this criticism and on the need for improvements, but it opposed sharply the contention of all other parties including the SPD that improvements were of secondary importance if they conflicted with the war effort. The USPD considered the continuation of these objectionable conditions to be more intolerable than the sacrifice of the objectives for which the war was still being fought.

The strikes of January, 1918, ended in complete failure. The SPD had utilized its influence to keep the strike demands as moderate as possible; the police disbanded the workers' councils which had been formed; many of the strike leaders were drafted into the army; and eventually the workers were forced to return to work. After the breakdown of the strike movement, the USPD had to look for other means with the aid of which to pursue its policies. The pamphlets *Aushalten um jeden Preis* and *Der erste deutsche Massenstreik* outlined the way for the renewed endeavors of the USPD. Germany, it was argued, had now succeeded Russia as the most reactionary European regime. The only remaining way to save Germany was the way chosen by the Russian proletariat in 1917. In Germany, there existed now an acute need of 'talking Russian', and of preparing an armed proletarian revolution.[46]

In the opinion of several USPD authors, of several members of the Michaelis government, and of a large number of Ger-

---

45 The texts of these and other strike leaflets are quoted by E. Meyer, *op. cit.*, pp. 183-93, and Drahn and Leonhard, *op. cit.*, pp. 98-102.

46 Quoted by Meyer, *op. cit.*, pp. 195-96; Drahn and Leonhard, *op. cit.*, pp. 102-03.

man historians, the naval mutinies of the summer of 1917
were the first result of USPD efforts to prepare an armed
revolution in Germany. These mutinies began in June and
ultimately affected fifteen units of the German fleet. Sailors
refused their food or threw it down the drain, and many over-
stayed their shore-leaves. But no overt act was committed
against the ships or the officers, and the sailors voluntarily returned to their stations within a few hours. A series of courts-
martial condemned five sailors to death, but only two were
executed. Admiral Scheer, in his order of June 10, 1917, attributed the mutinies to the food situation which had been
aggravated by a reduction in the rations of the sailors without
a corresponding reduction of the rations of the officers. Admiral Scheer also assigned some of the responsibility to the
length of the war and suggested remedies on the basis of considerations like these.[47]

Some of the sailors involved in these mutinies were members of the USPD. They had collected signatures in favor of
a peace without annexations, which were to be used at the
Stockholm conference. Some of the mutinous sailors had
visited the offices of USPD representatives and received
propaganda material from them. But the 1917 mutinies have
been free of political causes and purposes, although the knowledge of the Russian revolution and the role of the fleet at
Kronstadt may have been a factor in providing an example on
how to voice grievances which had been consistently ignored.

The USPD (and other parties) was informed in confidence
by the government about the mutinies and the steps taken to
suppress them. When, however, in October, 1917, an SPD
interpellation regarding Pan-German activities in the armed
forces was being discussed in the Reichstag, USPD representatives accused the government of having executed and im-

---

47 The best treatment of the mutinies is Ch. Vidil, *Les mutineries de la
marine allemande 1917-1918*, Paris, 1931, pp. 113-36, 193-202.

prisoned several sailors solely because they had favored a peace without annexations.[48]

In accordance with his duty as government spokesman, the minister of the navy, Admiral von Capelle, thereupon rose to reject the notion that sailors had been condemned to death for nothing worse than spreading anti-annexationist propaganda. True, sailors had been condemned and executed, but they were agents of the Bolsheviki, who had been caught trying to organize mutiny in the imperial fleet. They had been in contact with certain USPD representatives in the Reichstag who had had fore-knowledge of their plans and had approved them. But the further statements of the government showed that the matter was several months old, and the failure to press charges of treason at once could be explained only by the absence of even the flimsiest evidence to support von Capelle. When the government presented to the Reichstag its most incriminating evidence against the representatives accused, it became clear to everybody that there was no justification for the charges: even the rightist spokesman had to admit that, in view of the evidence, the accused USPD members would quite probably be freed in a court of law.[49] And in 1917, the Department of

48 *Verhandlungen*, CCCX, 3765 ff.

49 *Ibid.*, pp. 3773-3805. Vidil, *op. cit.*, *passim*, attributed the search for political motives of the mutinies solely to the desire to substantiate the Dolchstoss theory. Noske later on frequently proclaimed that if the government in 1917 had had sufficient material to indict Dittmann and the others accused of complicity, it deserved even now to be spat upon its face for its failure to do so; see Beckmann, *Der Dolchstossprozess in Muenchen*, pp. 94-98. See also W. Dittmann, *Die Marine-Justizmorde von 1917 und die Admirals-Rebellion von 1918*, Berlin, 1926. On the basis of the court records of the courts-martial of 1917, Dittmann concluded that the mutinies were due solely to inherent factors rampant among the sailors. See Lothar Popp and Karl Artelt, *Ursprung und Entwicklung der November Revolution, 1918*, Berlin, 1918. The authors, two of the most active agitators of the fleet, claimed that the mutinies were due solely to their own propaganda and fomentation of discontent, and that they were motivated predominantly by political factors. Cf. *Der "Dolchstoss", warum das deutsche Heer zusammenbrach*, pp. 17 ff.; the Dolchstosshefte of *Sueddeutsche Monatshefte*, April

Justice (Reichsanwaltschaft) ruled that sufficient evidence to indict the USPD or any of its members for participation in the mutinies did not exist.

Although one section of the German public continued to blame the USPD for the mutinies, and although the USPD later eagerly claimed credit for the mutinies, it must be concluded that the USPD did not contribute a major share to the mutinies and that the attempt to attribue the mutinies primarily to USPD propaganda was motivated solely by political considerations.

While the USPD cannot thus be held responsible for preparing the mutinies, some of its members, however, embarked upon a different program of active revolutionary mobilization immediately after the strikes of January, 1918. This preparation for the day of the revolution was carried on by speeches and pamphlets, by open street demonstrations and by secret meetings. Emil Barth was especially active in this activity. He organized and trained a group of revolutionary foremen in Berlin's industrial plants and secured a few cases of small arms.[50]

---

and May, 1924; the testimony of Admirals Trotha, Roeder, Heinrichs, and Levetzov at the Dolchstoss trial, Beckmann, *op. cit., passim*; *Ursachen...,* vols. IX and X; and H. Herkeler, " Wie kam es zum Zusammenbruch unserer Marine? " in *Sozialistische Monatshefte*, January 20, 1919, pp. 30-33.

50 The following quotation from an obviously reconstructed speech of Barth (it had been delivered without preparation and had not been taken down in shorthand) illustrated his most effective line of argument: " In this ... struggle of humanity against the cruelest beast, the beast man, only the most reckless lack of consideration may lead to victory.... You will have to eradicate from your hearts all patriotic sentiments. For this most devilish poison spreads not only hate and rivalry... but also murder and famine, ruin and rapine.... Patriotism has fertilized Europe with human blood and corpses; with its breath of plague it has poisoned the souls, the breath of men, of mountains, of valleys, of fields, of forests; it is covetiveness and cruelty....It is our task to commence the struggle against ... the infidel leaders of socialism." E. Barth, *op. cit.*, pp. 24-25, speech of February 9, 1918, made to some of his friends at the start of their revolutionary preparations.

This sort of activity appealed not only to the permanent nucleus of the eternally dissatisfied which may be found in any social group. It appealed also to those who were dissatisfied with prevailing war-time conditions and the inability of the government to solve the problems of the war. The USPD was an opposition group and its appraisal of the political situation was hence free of the prejudices and inhibitions that restricted the government and the majority parties. The USPD had frequently displayed sounder judgment in the analysis of political conditions than other parties. The other political parties and the government frequently lagged behind the USPD in pointing out critical conditions within Germany. Many therefore succumbed to the temptation to assume that the party which diagnosed the existing situation best, was also, in many respects, best able to provide the needed remedies.

However, neither the importance of the activities of Barth nor the growing public support of the USPD sufficed to influence decisively the course of events in Germany. The USPD did not foresee the change in the military position of Germany which occurred between February and November, 1918. Nor did it have any control over the factors which caused the rapid deterioration of the seemingly impregnable position of Germany at the beginning of 1918. The consequences of the German armistice offer cannot therefore be ascribed to USPD preparations which had been undertaken before the armistice offer could be anticipated. The chronological sequence of revolutionary preparation and the event of the revolution is not identical with causality. No causal relation can in fact exist where the actual revolution took place under certain crucial conditions which were outside the control of the groups carrying on the revolutionary activity, and which could not have been foreseen by them.

The record of the USPD during the week preceding the German revolution demonstrated the lack of correlation between USPD preparations and the actual revolution. Although these preparations were eventually given sole credit for the revolution, it should be noted that the most fanatical defender of that thesis, Barth himself, lamented that the well prepared and anticipated "revolution had been strangled" by the Kiel mutiny and its political consequences. As late as November 2, 1918, Dittmann and Haase told the revolutionary committee in Berlin that they were convinced of the ultimate failure of their plans, and Karl Liebknecht strongly advised against the use of arms and proposed only peaceful demonstrations. By a vote of 21 to 19, this committee ultimately voted to stage a revolution on November 11, 1918. On the day of the revolution in Berlin, November 9, the USPD played a secondary role. Haase was absent from Berlin on that day, and Ledebour stayed in bed till noon. After the revolution had been successful in Berlin, the USPD refused to take over the government alone and, because of its avowed weakness, hesitated long before joining in a coalition with the SPD.[51]

This behaviour can be explained only by pointing out that the revolution did not result from USPD preparation. The revolution conquered Berlin, where it had been prepared, only after it had been victorious all through Germany where no

51 *Ibid.*, pp. 126-127; because of mass-psychosis, "the mighty army which in a struggle about socialism would certainly have stood on the side of the socialist traitors [the SPD] imposed...the cessation of revolutionary action." Scheidemann, *Der Zusammenbruch*, p. 251, accused Barth of superimposing his interpretation upon the history of the revolution in order to make the revolution more revolutionary; one could not make a revolution nor could one make a revolution with a few cases of smuggled pistols. Most SPD writers disparaged the possible effect of these meager preparations. It is very interesting to note that even the defenders of the Dolchstoss theory did not term the revolution an armed rebellion brought about by Barth, but a collapse effected by propaganda. To Barth, no doubt, it must have been the supreme insult to be thus disregarded even by those who were frantically looking for an alibi for the causes of the revolution. See also *Der Zusammenbruch der Kriegspolitik und die Novemberrepublik*, a USPD pamphlet of 1919; the speech by Ledebour before the Congress of Councils on December 17, 1918, quoted by *Deutscher Geschichtskalender, Die Deutsche Revolution*, I, 216-18. Also speech of Wels, *Protokoll des Parteitags 1919*, pp. 152 ff.; *Vorwaerts*, November 15, 1918; Noske, *Von Kiel bis Kapp*, p. 59.

preparations had been made. At Kiel, where the revolution began, the absence of all leadership before Noske's arrival was its most striking characteristic. These two facts suffice for the conclusion that the revolution of November 9, was, in all basic respects, spontaneous. The actual revolution therefore fell short of the expectations of many people, and this circumstance became one of the main causes for the conflict between the USPD and the SPD after November, 1918.

d. CONCLUSIONS ABOUT THE USPD

The controversies of the SPD and USPD after 1916 emphasized their divergent tendencies rather than their common elements. In 1914, the differences between the SPD and the incipient minority probably was limited to the question of how the war had begun. In 1914, none among the SPD argued that socialists must support their country in an aggressive war, and few among the Independent Socialists ever denied that, in a defensive war, socialists must support the national war effort. The problem, however, whether the war was defensive or not soon ceased to be the major point at issue and after 1916, the differences between the SPD and the USPD no longer hinged on the actual facts in the case.

Regardless of the real origins of the war, the demands of the Entente countries and their military power made the war a defensive one in the eyes of the SPD. Committed to the support of the war by the policy of August 4, 1914, the nationalist trends of the party gained the upper hand. The residue of Lassalleanism, the support received from non-proletarian sections of the country, the conservatism of the trade-unions, the effects of social legislation and the changing character of the state, the opportunism evident in the problem of agrarian reforms, the implications of the struggle against revisionism, the persistent assertion of nationalistic sentiments, and the sheer weight of having grown into the largest party of Germany influenced this development. In the long controversies during the war, in the criticism offered against the internal conditions and foreign relations of Germany, and in its support of the government, the SPD placed national interests above traditional socialist, economic, democratic, or moral claims. " The majority leaders continuously push to the fore the question of the fundamental attitude towards the defense of the country ... Yet these points are no longer the basis of the conflict... Rather it is the abandonment of the fundamental policy of the party as laid down by the program and by the resolutions of the party and of the international congresses, and the adoption ... of a purely opportunistic policy of adaptation towards the domestic and foreign policies of imperialism. The majority leaders have made a virtue out of a compulsion ... What ... should have been a historical episode, they used as the starting point for the re-consideration of social-democratic politics." [52]

In time, national interests replaced historical considerations in the insistent re-iteration of the SPD that Germany was engaged in fighting a war of national defense, and that desire for moderate conquests and indemnities resulted only from the legitimate claims of Germany. The question of the origins of the war ceased to be important; the SPD had given a final answer to that question by its endorsement of national objectives. What had been done under the compulsion of the situation in August, 1914, thus became a virtue. " Opinions as to what is the historic mission of the proletariat in this responsible hour are diametrically opposed. Some seek it in coming to terms with the bourgeoisie, in a change ... towards nationalist trends, in the relegation of all specifically proletarian and socialist doctrines, and in the duty of the so-called defense of the Fatherland; while the minority thinks that now more than ever before, a principally socialist, independent, proletarian policy is imperative. These are the irreconcilable conflicts which have appeared in the German SPD." [53]

52 *Vorwaerts*, June 10, 1916; also June 11, 1916.

53 *Vorwaerts*, April 6, 1916, article by Cunow.

Dr. David once declared that " what unites the minority group amounts in practice to the sacrifice of the vital interests of our own people." [54] If Dr. David had qualified this statement by the words " what I consider to be the vital interests ", he would have very nearly expressed the controversy in a form acceptable to the USPD. The USPD strenuously denied that it desired to sacrifice what *it* considered to be the vital interests of Germany. It only had a different concept of the nature of these interests and their validity. Speaking for the USPD, Dr. Cohn proclaimed: " I know no German interests that can be attained at the price of humanity and justice." [55]

For Dr. Cohn and the USPD, the concepts of humanity and justice were not pre-determined by national interests; national interests derived rather from the concepts of humanity and justice. Since the SPD refused to accept this maxim without qualifications, the USPD decided that the SPD had ceased to be a real socialist party. The USPD hence felt itself called upon to uphold a semblance of democratic and socialist ideals in Germany.[56]

The USPD attempts to win support among the broad masses in Germany and among the troops were furthered by the deterioration of the food situation, the military oppression under the state of siege, the annexationist policies which seemed to prolong the war, and the growing conviction that Germany could not win the war. In its propa-

54 *Niederrheinische Arbeiterzeitung*, April 18, 1916. Also Scheidemann in *Internationale Korrespondenz*, May 12, 1916, etc.

55 *Verhandlungen*, CCCXIII, 5838 ff., July 5, 1918.

56 One should guard against ascribing to political parties in 1917 and 1918, who correspond to present day communistic parties, the same state of mind that ruled communistic parties the world over in the 1930's and later. In 1917 and 1918, the Marxian statement that the proletarian had no fatherland had not yet been amended to read ' except Russia '. During the period under discussion, international socialists considered Germany rather than Russia as the homeland of socialism, and, prior to 1914, German socialism had been the dominant influence among the socialist parties in Europe.

ganda, the USPD used these conditions to the exclusion of all
theoretical arguments. These conditions had not been created
by USPD agitation, and it is hardly possible to say that but
for the USPD the people would have remained unaware of the
food situation, censorship, annexationism, or the stalemate at
the front. The decline of morale, in as far as it may be attributed to controllable factors within Germany, must therefore be attributed to the prevailing conditions and to the
policies and actions which were so deeply and generally resented.

By making the German war effort dependent upon the success of the submarine, the High Command had admitted that
unless the submarine succeeded, Germany had lost the war.
And the defeat of the submarine was evident to those who met
American troops in ever increasing numbers on the battle-
field.[57] To the soldier at the front, the superiority of enemy
resources was more convincing than the influence of USPD
agitators who should never have been drafted into the army as
punishment for agitation at home. If USPD propaganda contributed to the breakdown of the morale at home and at the
front, it was because of prevailing conditions not of its own
making, and the success of USPD propaganda was hence at-
tributable to those who were responsible for the prevalent
conditions.

There is abundant opinion to challenge these conclusions.
From 1918 onward, the rightist parties and those who supported the policies of the High Command sought to deny that
conditions in Germany spontaneously produced a breakdown
of morale and of the war effort. They argued that the collapse
of Germany resulted from the vicious and insidious propaganda of the USPD (and of the SPD), who were in the pay
of foreigners (and Jews), and who wrested certain victory out
of the hands of the triumphant German army.[58] This argument

57 Bernstein, *Deutsche Revolution*, pp. 9-11.

58 For example Breithaupt, *op. cit.*

was motivated not by the analysis of actual conditions, but by the desire to free the German leaders of responsibility for the defeat.

On the other hand, the USPD asserted that the revolution of November, 1918, was the result of its own year-long preparation and plans.[59] This interpretation of the pre-revolutionary period was advanced to justify the claim of the USPD that it deserved sole control over post-1918 Germany. The SPD dominated the new body politic and endeavored to form it into a democratic republic; for the defense of its different social and economic ambitions, the USPD could not point to the support of the majority of German proletarians; it could only claim that it had ' made ' the revolution and that in consequence it should be entrusted with the future destiny of Germany. These USPD arguments, too, were not due to a correct appraisal of the facts in the case, but to political considerations, and are therefore no more acceptable than the claims of the right.[60]

59 For example Barth, *op. cit.*, p. 160.

60 *Cf. infra*, appendix 1.

CHAPTER VII

THE CAUSES OF THE GERMAN REVOLUTION

a. THE ARMISTICE OFFER

DURING the first World War, all German political parties engaged in criticism of certain domestic and foreign policies, which have been discussed in previous chapters. The policies and the dissatisfaction caused by them would probably not have affected the position of the German regime if Germany had won a decisive military victory. Military defeat ranked obviously foremost among the causes of the German revolution.

The Allied superiority in man-power, raw materials and industrial resources pre-determined a German defeat, provided the war lasted long enough. By desperate efforts, Germany repeatedly sought to avert defeat. But eventually, the consequences of the superiority of her enemies had to be faced.[1]

After the failure of the 1918 offensives and the successes of the Allies in July and August, 1918, peace overtures could no longer be evaded. At a crown council in Spa on August 14, Hindenburg still hoped that continued resistance might yet force the enemy to accept German peace terms,[2] and it was therefore decided to delay diplomatic negotiations until a more

---

1 On June 24, 1918, the German foreign minister, von Kuehlmann, told the Reichstag that "an absolute end to the war through a purely military decision without any diplomatic negotiations can hardly be expected"; *Verhandlungen*, CCCXIII, 5607 ff. As a result of this statement, Kuehlmann was dismissed from office upon the pressure of the Supreme Command. Yet Kuehlmann had voiced only the views which the Supreme Command, on June 17, had confided to him and to others; Helfferich, *op. cit.*, III, 417-418.

2 *Vorgeschichte des Waffenstillstandes*, Berlin, 1918, no. 1, pp. 13-15. Falkenhayn had already in 1915 concluded that Germany could no longer do more than try to convince the enemy of the impossibility of defeating and conquering Germany; Falkenhayn, *Die oberste Heeresleitung*, pp. 241-46.

favorable moment. But these hopes for a more favorable moment proved to be unfounded. The reverses on the Western front continued, and Germany's allies collapsed completely.[3]

As a result of the Austrian peace offer of September 14, "the tension ... [in Germany] had become unbearable. We stood helplessly before the culminating disaster of the nation ... You woke up each morning worrying: what had happened? and breathed freely at night because front and alliances have held fast." [4]

The unexpected collapse of the military and diplomatic position of Germany in the autumn of 1918 added to the misgivings aroused among the majority parties by the inability of Chancellor Hertling to resist the encroachments of the Supreme Command, and by the lack of progress in Prussian reforms or the clarification of German peace terms. The Reichstag was in recess during August and September, 1918, but the government had already anticipated sharp attacks by the leaders of the majority parties at the September 14 meeting of the Main Committee of the Reichstag, the Hauptausschuss.[5]

On September 24, Hertling faced the Main Committee to defend the Austrian peace move. Both Groeber, the leader of Hertling's own party, and Scheidemann attacked Hertling for

3 In a report of April 12, 1917, Count Czernin and Emperor Charles had warned that war, hunger and revolution chased each other in the Dual-Monarchy, and that Austria could not continue fighting beyond the autumn of 1917. (The treaties of Brest-Litovsk and Bucharest furnished her with a respite.) Erzberger, op. cit., pp. 116-22. Erzberger possessed a copy of this report, and so did many others. It soon became public, and Erzberger was widely accused with responsibility for its publication. Helfferich made himself the spokesman of Erzberger's accusers, although he agreed that Erzberger had received his copy of the report from Emperor Charles without instructions regarding its use; Helfferich, op. cit., III, 579-89. Helfferich concluded that its publication destroyed the readiness of the Entente to accede favorably to the Papal peace move.

4 Prinz Max von Baden, Erinnerungen und Dokumente, p. 317.

5 Payer, op. cit., pp. 71-78. Payer was Vice Chancellor under Hertling and Max.

his failure on domestic problems.[6] On the following day, Groeber again attacked Hertling, but in much sharper terms and with growing support. Hertling refused for a time to believe that his dismissal was being insisted upon,[7] but this illusion was destroyed when the leaders of the majority agreed, on September 28, not to participate in any government unless members of the Reichstag would be allowed to join without losing their seats in the Reichstag. To this and other constitutional changes Hertling refused to agree.[8] Thus a full grown cabinet crisis had developed whose solution was complicated by the political necessity of securing SPD co-operation.[9]

On September 23, the SPD had published a list of conditions under which it might consider joining a new cabinet. They included a repeal of paragraph nine of the constitution barring members of the government from sitting and voting in the Reichstag, equal suffrage in all German states, the clarification of the Belgian problem, autonomy for Alsace-Lorraine, and provisions regarding excessive censorship and

6 Payer, *op. cit.*, pp. 78-82, stated that the SPD points of September 23 had received a cool reception by the committee on that day. Hertling, *op. cit.*, p. 171, denied that the SPD points had been available to the chancellor or to the parties before the meeting, but he was usually unreliable in his dates.

7 Payer, *ibid.*; Helfferich, *op. cit.*, III, 520, thought that the 'system' was being made a scapegoat by the majority, and its change advocated as a nostrum.

8 Hertling, *op. cit.*, pp. 172-73, was grateful to Groeber for having spared his father the anguish of conducting the armistice negotiations and of presiding over the outbreak of the revolution.

9 Payer thought a SPD chancellor likely as early as September; *ibid.* Some months before the July, 1917, crisis, the SPD, the Center and the Progressive party had formed an 'interfraktioneller Ausschuss' to which at various times the National-Liberal Party adhered. Common steps of the majority parties were prepared and undertaken by this body. It had played a leading role in the peace resolution of 1917 and in the dismissal of Michaelis. It played a dominant role during the Hertling crisis. Opinions attributed to the leaders of the majority should properly be credited to this body.

interference with the freedom of speech and assembly. These points aggravated the ~cute cabinet crisis by making a satisfactory solution impossible, unless the government were to yield to the majority on the issue of parliamentarization.

The cabinet crisis was solved in an unexpected manner. The last days of September had not only brought the resolution of the majority of the Reichstag to insist on certain constitutional modifications, they also brought a new attack on the Western front, the collapse of the Macedonian front, and the Bulgarian armistice. The German foreign minister, Admiral von Hintze, had thereupon suggested that Hertling should be allowed to resign, that " a new government on broadest basis, on the free initiative of His Majesty," be formed, and that the new government should at the opportune moment ask for a peace of conciliation and possibly an armistice.[10]

This idea was taken up by the Supreme Army Command, which, unknown to the government in Berlin, had suddenly decided to ask for an immediate armistice and for peace negotiations on the basis of Wilson's fourteen points. The Bulgarian armistice, the exhaustion of Germany, and the absence of any built-out positions to the rear of the Western front line had motivated the armistice offer. The suggestion of Hintze was taken up in order to make the offer more palatable to the German public and to induce Wilson to grant such a request. Thus the majority of the Reichstag suddenly had the support of the Supreme Command for its program of democratic reforms.[11]

Hertling, who had gone to Spa and offered his resignation in order to receive the support of the Emperor in the cabinet crisis, therefore found that his resignation had been accepted. An imperial decree informed the people of the step, and asked that " men borne by the confidence of the people participate

10 Payer, *op. cit.*, pp. 82-85. *Vorgeschichte*, no. 12, pp. 29-30. This idea was later referred to as the ' revolution from above.'

11 Helfferich, *op. cit.*, III, 526.

... in the rights and duties of government." On the same day the allies of Germany were informed of the democratization of the government and the decision to seek an immediate armistice.[12]

During the Hertling crisis, the majority parties had envisaged only an inconclusive step towards peace, the clarification of the Belgian situation or the like. The demand for an immediate armistice came as a complete surprise.[13] Prince Max, the chancellor-designate, wanted the Supreme Army Command to commit itself irrevocably to the armistice offer before dispatching the offer. In reply to his queries about the true nature of the military situation, Hindenburg informed him on October 3, that the situation was hopeless because of German losses and the collapse of the Macedonian front. " The German army still stands firm and resists all attacks victoriously. But the situation becomes daily graver and may force the Supreme Army Command to serious decisions ... Every day costs the lives of thousands of brave soldiers." [14] On October 9, Ludendorff told Prince Max that " yesterday it hung on a thread whether a break-through would succeed ... Step towards peace is absolutely needed, towards armistice even more so." And two days later, he told Max that the danger point would be passed only if the Allies were to stop their large scale attacks.[15]

On the basis of these opinions, Prince Max had to comply with the request for an armistice; his attempts to delay it were cut short by the Emperor with these words: " You did not come here to make difficulties for the Supreme Army Command." [16] He remained unconvinced, however, that the mili-

12 *Vorgeschichte*, no. 14, pp. 30-31. Bulgaria was not informed until the next day; *ibid.*, no. 15, p. 31.

13 *Vorgeschichte*, nos. 21, 22, 23, 26, 27, pp. 34-36, furnished the documents illustrating the pressure of the High Command.

14 *Ibid.*, nos. 32, 33; pp. 40-41.

15 *Ibid.*, nos. 36, 38, 41, 42, pp. 42-54. Max, *op. cit.*, pp. 387-90.

16 *Ibid.*, p. 346.

tary situation necessitated such urgency, and many in Germany thought likewise.

For indeed, if the Supreme Command had allowed such a calamity to develop, its present judgment would necessarily also be suspect, warned Helfferich.[17] Payer wondered in despair whence the army and people should get the energy to resume fighting, if acceptable peace terms proved unattainable; the contemplated peace step would surely destroy all willingness of the Entente to grant a reasonable peace. Had not somebody lost his nerve? he wondered.[18] Walter Rathenau in fact asked publicly whether the peace move had not been precipitated because somebody had lost his nerve, and suggested a levée en masse to save Germany.[19] Even Ludendorff eventually thought that the German army could yet fight another winter.[20]

17 Helfferich, *op. cit.*, III, 535.

18 Payer, *op. cit.*, pp. 87-96.

19 In his article " Ein dunkler Tag," *Vossische Zeitung*, October 6, 1918. Ludendorff had rejected a levée en masse, because it would play havoc with the economic and military organization and yet not raise enough additional men; *Vorgeschichte*, no. 38, pp. 44 ff. It is interesting to note that Lersner, the agent of the foreign office at Spa, suggested in a note added to one of Ludendorff's missiles that he may have lost his nerve; *ibid.*, no. 21, p. 34; also no. 23, pp. 34-35. He suggested that, should there be a need to retract the offer, one could excuse the haste with the Bulgarian armistice.

20 Max originally assumed that Germany could still exhaust the ability of England and France to continue the war; Max, *op. cit.*, pp. 331 ff. Cf. H. Rudin, *Armistice 1918*, an authoritative study of the armistice negotiations and related problems. It is extremely doubtful whether a delayed armistice offer or a better prepared offer would have essentially modified the final armistice terms. The only certain results of the continuation of the war would seemingly have been continued German losses and the probable establishment of a new front in South-Eastern Germany. One of the foremost critics of the war concluded that even without a revolution, Germany would have had to accept, before the summer of 1919, essentially the same terms which she had received in November, 1918, because the 1918 offensives had deprived Germany of all alternatives to defeat; Moser, *Ernsthafte Plaudereien*, p. 379. Delbrueck fully supported this conclusion; see his brochure *Ludendorff's Selbstportraet*, p. 62. In his article

No doubt the Supreme Army Command was acting in dead earnest when it urged immediate negotiations for an armistice. Unconvinced of the imminence of defeat, Prince Max, however, had had serious reservations about concluding an armistice, the urgency of which was widely denied by influential civilians. He realized that the acceptance of Wilson's peace program would amount to the loss of Alsace-Lorraine, Posen, some of the German colonies and the imposition of huge reparations. He thought that if Germany were to fight for a few more months, the Allies might become convinced that it was impossible to compel Germany to accept the fourteen points. When he was to face the Reichstag on October 5, he drafted a " speech which will wipe out our humiliation . . . . and show the enemy that we still breathe." He prepared to discuss the severity of the fourteen points in order to dispel any illusions about them. Because this speech might endanger the armistice, he was, however, persuaded to substitute another one, but even then he talked of the redoubled German efforts in fighting for the life of the nation that would follow if the peace terms proved to be other than honorable.[21]

" Falkenhayn und Ludendorff ", *Preussische Jahrbuecher*, CLXXX, 249-81, Delbrueck came to a different conclusion. " Indeed it was only the revolution which made us fully defenseless and gave the enemy his chance to lead Germany into slavery; but . . . whoever accuses the revolution, must first accuse the leaders of the army who prepared the revolution by expecting the masses to fight for war aims whose contrariness and impossibility they perceived."

21 Max, *op. cit.*, pp. 353-70. *Verhandlungen*, CCCXIV, 6150 ff. The Emperor's order of the day on October 5, had stated that whether peace would come was still uncertain, but until it came all resources must continue to be used; Germany was still strong enough to defend her homeland; she would accept only an honorable peace; Wolff's Telegraphen Bureau (WTB), October 5, 1918. It is interesting that prior to the receipt of the second note of Lansing, nobody had suggested that the armistice offer had been caused by an internal collapse at the homefront, or by insidious propaganda. The *Korrespondenzblatt der Generalkommission*, the official organ of the SPD trade-unions, wrote on October 8: " The national defense must be pursued with greatest energy, and the new attacks of the enemy brought to a halt. Abroad, too, there must not arise any doubts that

He continued his search for a cause strong enough to rouse the German people to resume fighting with the spirit of desperation. However, the first two notes of Lansing did not in his opinion suffice to impress the public. And by the middle of October, Max was sufficiently well informed of the military situation to conclude that no change for the better was possible, and that continued fighting would only expose the Ruhr district to artillery fire.[22]

Yet at exactly this moment the Supreme Army Command decided to break off the armistice negotiations.[23] Although the Supreme Command was overruled and Ludendorff dismissed from his post, the military authorities would not accept the decision as final. The navy thought that the termination of the submarine campaign had restored its freedom of action and began preparing for a large scale fleet operation,[24] while the Army Command in an order of the day to the troops on October 24, termed Wilson's demands as equal to unconditional surrender and called upon the soldiers to resist them with all their strength.[25]

---

the German people thinks not for a second of allowing itself to be overwhelmed by the enemy. With the assumption of government by the majority parties of the Reichstag and the prompt realization of internal reforms connected with it, we hope to win such a considerable increment in power that the bravado of the enemy must subside."

22 On the basis of the October 17, cabinet meeting; Max, *ibid.*, pp. 445-48; *Vorgeschichte*, no. 57, pp. 67-86.

23 *Ibid.*; also no. 63, pp. 90-91. Max did not think that abandoning the submarine campaign was important enough an issue; *op. cit.*, pp. 414.

24 See Levetzov's article in *Sueddeutsche Monatshefte*, April, 1924. Max was not informed of these preparations. Noske, *Von Kiel bis Kapp*, Berlin, 1920, p. 9, stated that up to the time of his writings he had not been able to confirm the truth of the projected plans of operations. Vidil, *op. cit.*, pp. 147 ff., thought that these plans were tactically and strategically sound. See also the testimony of Trotha, Heinrichs, Roeder, at the Dolchstoss-trial; Beckmann, *op. cit., passim.*

25 Max, *op. cit.*, pp. 500-1. The order was suppressed but not until after it had been handed to the press and made public to some of the troops.

Thus important departments of the German government in the first three weeks of October were unwilling to accept the idea that the war was to end in a matter of weeks. They refused to acknowledge that Germany could no longer appeal to armed force; they refused to view Germany as beaten. They never stopped to ask how the period from August, 1914, until September, 1918, ought to be viewed, if the problem of national defense requiring the last ounce of strength had been ushered in only in October, 1918, or how Germany could achieve in October, 1918, what she had failed to achieve since August 1914.

During these weeks, the sentiments of the public moved in a radically different direction. Unaware of the fact that the Supreme Command had initiated the armistice offer over the opposition of the civilian government,[26] the public was confronted with the Bulgarian armistice, the parliamentarization of Germany, the evacuation of Lille, Douai and Ostend, and the manifesto of Emperor Charles of October 16 which changed the Dual Monarchy into a federal state. Above all, the notes received from Washington during October, 1918, illustrated beyond misunderstanding what demands the Allies intended to impose upon Germany. The public did not agree that the acceptance of the fourteen points was a shame deserved only by a conquered country lying prostrate, and that the enemy must be prevented from imposing such a peace on Germany.[27] The people rather clung to Wilson like a drowning person, ready to do everything to placate him.[28] The armistice offer signified that "the military collapse of the German Empire had been officially postulated," [29] and this admission removed

26 On October 9, the German press was instructed not to discuss the responsibility for the armistice offer; on October 23, it was told not to mention that the Supreme Command had wanted the peace move or approved of the evacuation of the occupied areas; Muehsam, *op. cit.*, pp. 123 ff.

27 Max thought so; *op. cit.*, pp. 353, 360 ff.

28 *Ibid.*, p. 410.

29 Payer, *op. cit.*, p. 112.

the only reason which had made Germany bear the unavoidable burdens of the war and tolerate its sufferings. The revelations about the situation which were being heaped upon each other created a panic among the public.[30] " The length of the war fatigues the people, and in addition the disappointments. The submarine war has disappointed, and so has the technical superiority of the enemy, the loss of the allies or their complete bankruptcy; in addition the increasing needs at home. Now you have the reaction to this," [31] and the reaction consisted of unconditional desire for peace. At least in this, no new disappointments would be acceptable. Every day, from the Bulgarian armistice to the Austrian armistice, brought fresh confirmation that victory was beyond hope; there was but a resolute determination not to return once more " into hopelessness, since peace had seemed near enough to be grasped." [32]

30 Because of this, the leaders of the army and especially Ludendorff were sharply attacked from the right; for there could not be any doubt that they had initiated the offer, nor that the offer had produced a reaction making any further resistance illusionary. It was largely to refute these statements that Ludendorff published his memoirs in which he stated that the pressure of the Supreme Command was intended to lead, not to an armistice, but to a new government in Berlin, and that the armistice offer had not really been honest, but had only tried to reveal the true objectives of the Allied Powers; he had only wanted to provide motives for continued national defense and for a new popular government to head it. (The formation of the new government had been delayed because of the hesitancy of the political parties to enter a government burdened with the need for dispatching an armistice offer.) Although the evidence contradicted Ludendorff in every respect, his explanation brought to an abrupt end the rightist criticism directed against him. In their eyes he was completely exonerated and became henceforth their hero. Helfferich, *op. cit.*, III, 524, accepted that explanation and thought that the Supreme Command had twice before stressed the need for negotiations; in June and in August, 1918.

31 Scheidemann at the cabinet meeting of October 17; *Vorgeschichte*, no. 57, pp. 67-86.

32 Max, *op. cit.*, p. 524.

b. The Abdication Crisis

The public and sections of the government thus disagreed radically whether the pending negotiations should lead to a truce at the earliest moment. Yet they agreed that the terms to be attained must be the best possible. It was partly because of this consideration that the ' revolution from above ' had been introduced. This step had failed to convince the public of the genuine willingness of the government to conclude peace, or of its sincerity in introducing the promised constitutional reforms.[33] It also had failed to satisfy Wilson; thus Germans interpreted almost unanimously the queries of Wilson about the true nature of the German government, about the authority behind the armistice offer and its possible enforcement, and above all his warnings that " if [the Entente] must deal with the military masters and the monarchial autocrats of Germany ... it must demand not peace negotiations but surrender." [34]

According to the accepted German interpretation of these statements, Wilson demanded the abdication of William II. The government could not evade Wilson's demand, for " if we proclaimed the fight of desperation and the masses answered: the terms are bad because the Emperor does not abdicate—then the backbone of national defense would have been broken." [35]

---

33 Autonomy for Alsace-Lorraine, one of the main conditions to which Max had pledged himself, was not effected until after the revolution. Prussia also retained her three-class suffrage until after the revolution; in fact the only progress that Max was able to make consisted of the promise that equal suffrage would be written into the multiple suffrage bill pending before the Prussian House of Peers, when it would meet again on November 15. Amelioration of censorship and of the state of siege were main points in the revolutionary program of the SPD in November, which showed how little was really effected by Max even here.

34 *Vorgeschichte*, no. 76, pp. 98-99; Lansing's third note. German diplomats from neutral countries and other 'informed and reliable' sources insisted that Wilson was calling for the abdication of William II. Cf. ibid., no. 49, p. 59, report from The Hague of October 15; no. 59, pp. 88-89, report from Brussels, October 17; and the report from Bern on October 25.

35 Max, *op. cit.*, p. 525.

On the other hand, the abdication of the Emperor would be tantamount to a revolution, even though it occurred out of considerations regarding foreign policies, and not because of pressures arising from domestic problems.[36]

Prince Max saw the solution of the dilemma in voluntary abdication effected before either Wilson or the German public openly demanded it.[37] Voluntary abdication might strengthen Wilson in his opposition to Entente chauvinists and lead to acceptable peace terms; it might also win the support of the masses for a program of national defense.[38] But above all the abdication must be a voluntary act; otherwise it would not be part of the 'revolution from above', but of a 'revolution from below', overthrowing not only William II, but the monarchial principle as well.[39]

Max, an heir to a throne himself, could perhaps not be expected to succeed to persuade William II to abdicate; he agreed later that he began arguing it too late and too tactfully to be successful.[40] On October 29, 1918, the Emperor went to Spa on some pretext, in order to escape the growing pressure in favor of abdication.[41]

But the journey of the Emperor to Spa only seemed to associate him with the idea of a last ditch fight attributed to the Supreme Command, and this possibility was given credence by the renewed mobilization of civilians late in October, 1918.

As a result, the public became obsessed with the thought

36 *Ibid.*, p. 523.

37 *Ibid.*, pp. 453, 537-40.

38 *Ibid.*, pp. 511 ff., 536-40, 550-59.

39 *Ibid.*, p. 511.

40 *Ibid.*, pp. 511 ff., 527.

41 *Ibid.*, pp. 527-30. Max thought that this trip had been due to a plot of his entourage. The pretext was the inauguration of General Groener as Ludendorff's successor. On November 1, Max went into an uninterrupted sleep of thirty-six hours because of an overdose of sedatives which his physician had administered to him, and was thus incapacitated on some of the crucial days.

" that ... certain circles in the army command might succeed in arresting the endeavors for peace which had been under way." [42] The abdication ceased to be demanded mainly as a means of insuring better peace terms; the abdication of the Emperor began to be demanded as a means to insure any peace terms at all. And public pressure for abdication rapidly outdistanced the endeavors of Prince Max. The *Frankfurter Zeitung* called for the abdication on October 25, and on the same day the USPD asked for it in the Reichstag.

The demand to bring any sacrifices in return for better terms, or for an ultimate end of the war throve on the danger that parts of German territory might become the arena of war. This was particularly true in Bavaria which, after the Austrian armistice, was threatened by an invasion both from the West and from the Southeast. By the end of October, pamphlets were circulating in Munich calling for separate peace within three days, or the establishment of a people's government to spare Bavaria from invasion.[43] In fact, the seriousness of the situation prompted the Bavarian government to dispatch troops to occupy Tyrol, if need be, by armed force.[44] Rightists and monarchists as well as leftists favored abdication and an immediate armistice for these reasons; by November 2, the Bavarian rightist and later Prime Minister Held was reported to have come out for a separate peace.[45]

This pressure manifested itself in mass meetings, newspaper articles, and pamphlets. Because the SPD did not join wholeheartedly in the campaign, the control over it passed to the

---

42 *Protokoll des Parteitags 1919*, part 1, p. 9.

43 *Muenchener Post*, October 31, 1918, warned against these; quoted by E. Buchner, *Revolutionsdokumente*, vol. I, no. 5, p. 15. There is no evidence that these leaflets emanated from leftist sources.

44 *Arbeiter Zeitung*, Vienna, November 7, 1918; cited *ibid.*, no. 88, pp. 89-90.

45 Max, *op. cit.*, p. 570, denied that Held made such a statement, although he agreed that other rightists did.

USPD.[46] In Munich, Kurt Eisner, just released from prison, provided the driving personality. In Berlin, Karl Liebknecht, just freed by the amnesty of Prince Max, gave full reign to his love for demonstrations and political harangues. On October 26 multiple USPD mass meetings in Berlin called for the abdication. Pointing to the defection of Germany's allies and to the threats to the Southeastern border, a USPD manifesto of November 4 warned that the government's attitude on peace was not clear, that the new inductions indicated the desire of the army to continue fighting, and that the workers must be ready to interfere.[47]

The pressure for abdication reflected the determination for peace. It also reflected the indignation and despair which the war-time policies of the government had created. In order to escape the consequences of this, a revolution from above had been decreed. That it failed to be convincing in vital points, and above all that the voluntary abdication failed to materialize, produced the acute danger of a revolution from below, a revolution whose threatening social character was one of the main reasons why Max continued to insist upon a voluntary abdication long after that act had become meaningless for the purposes of national defense or armistice terms.[48]

It is not surprising that this revolutionary pressure should be greatest where the consequences of continued fighting would be gravest, or where the evidence of preparations for continued fighting were greatest: in Munich, and in Kiel.

---

46 *Ibid.*, Max thought that the SPD began losing control over the masses as early as mid-October. See next chapter for the SPD attitudes.

47 Cited by Buchner, *ibid.*, no. 62, p. 64. E. Stadler, *Die Weltkriegs-revolution*, Leipzig, 1920, pp. 65 ff., termed Bolshevism "the spiritual grippe of the world war. It is the elementary eruption of the hate of the masses of the people against the horror of the conduct of the war, against militarism, against bloodshed; it is the elementary eruption of hate against the war economy, against usury and speculation.... Bolshevism is the physical and spiritual process of disintegration of the world war." Yet this author was an extreme nationalist who called for a 'Fuehrer' and a 'voelkische' rebirth; the National Assembly should step aside for a dictator, etc.

48 Max, *op. cit.*, pp. 557-9, 584-8.

c. The Naval Mutinies at Kiel

Unknown to the government, the naval staff had prepared plans for an extensive operation early in November, 1918. Its ultimate purpose was to engage the British fleet and thereby influence the armistice terms or at least to improve the morale of Germany. From the very beginning of the war, the idea had been advanced that the fleet must be saved for use at the very end of the war when a heroic gesture would remain the only way to modify its outcome. The naval command had assumed that the termination of the submarine campaign had restored freedom of action to the fleet, and its desire for an engagement was the greater, since in its opinion the fleet, too, should contribute her fair share to the war. Lack of action all through the war had prevented the fleet from serving the very purpose for which it had been created. This was now to be remedied. Preparations were therefore rushed so that the fleet could take to the high seas at the earliest moment.

These preparations had caused rumors claiming that the naval command desired to engage the British fleet in order to seek an honorable death for the fleet.[49] And " for such a heroic gesture which could no longer affect the outcome of the war the crews were not available . . . The many married sailors were unwilling . . . to die for a lost cause." [50] The fleet had suffered from the same discriminatory practices and social ills which contributed to the breakdown of the morale in the army.

49 Vidil, *op. cit.*, p. 147, thought there was some basis to the belief that the navy was seeking an honorable death; he saw in this the sequel to General Groener's suggestion that the Emperor seek a hero's death in the trenches.

50 Noske, *op. cit.*, p. 9; Max, *op. cit.*, pp. 572-76, denied knowing beforehand of the plans for a naval operation but agreed that he and Scheidemann tried to deceive public opinion when, having learned of such a plan at the height of the mutinies, they denied its existence. However, he favored the idea of the action planned by the navy, because it might favorably impress public opinion in England and at home. He thought that " without Kiel, no revolution; without the revolution, no capitulation on November 11."

In addition, the continued inaction of the fleet had deprived it of the benefits which accrue from continued struggle with the enemy and apparent successful defense. The low morale of the fleet and dissatisfaction with its social organization had already caused the mutinies of 1917. The desire to engage the British fleet was not nourished by confidence in the technical soundness of the German fleet constructions; the sailors had learned from the few encounters with the British fleet, from the vacillating naval policies, and from the restriction of the fleet to home ports, that the construction of the fleet had entailed the enmity of England without furnishing Germany with an instrument technically sound for its prospective task. The conviction that German naval units were too slow and under-armed and that quality had been sacrificed to quantity contributed considerably to the resistance of the sailors to seek out and engage the enemy in battle.[51]

The mutinies started at the Schillig naval yards where sailors refused to load their vessels or to obey orders. The threat of bombardment by other vessels finally subdued the

51 During the mutinies in 1918, the sailors were willing to fight if the British fleet should attack the German ports. In regard to the technical worth of the German fleet, the following should be pointed out to explain the relative German success at the battle of Jutland: the battle was fought at dusk and in fog, so that the longer range of British armament could not assert itself; and at close quarters the greater accuracy of the German aim and the better compartmentation of her naval units were a definite advantage. German ships of the line had only twenty-one or twenty-four centimeter cannon instead of thirty centimeter on comparable British units. The inferiority in speed was demonstrated by the loss of the battleship 'Bluecher' at the Doggerbank; this man o' war had been built in 1910, only to be used as an artillery training ship because of her serious construction faults. The most severe critic of the entire German naval program and policy was Captain Persius who presented various aspects of these problems in his works. There was general agreement about the justification of that criticism in the writings of most German admirals, although they used terms as severe as Persius only when speaking of rival admirals or of the Emperor. This latter criticism evoked protests even from among the ranks of the SPD. H. Ritter, op. cit., p. 66, lamented that the steel put into battleships was not used for tanks. Cf. Delbrueck, ibid.

mutineers who were placed under arrest. The seriousness of the disturbances, however, caused the admiralty to cancel its plans for a naval engagement.

Some of the mutinous units of the fleet had been ordered to Kiel. Upon arrival, the news of the events at the Schillig yards spread among other units of the fleet and throughout the city. In spite of the trouble at the Schillig yards, shore leaves were granted as before, and not even trade-union meeting places had been declared out of bounds. The sailors flocked there, listened to speeches, and deliberated on how to free their imprisoned comrades.[52] There was no advocacy of breaches of discipline, only a complete disregard of it, and the absence of order and resolution on all sides, including the admirality and the USPD.[53]

On November 2, a sailor named Artelt, who had once been in an insane asylum, harangued the crowds with some success. With more courage and self respect, he again talked to the demonstrators on the next day. There were demands for the liberation of the arrested sailors, the disarming of officers, and the abdication of William II.[54] By this time, however, the naval command had regained its courage, and the demonstrations and the attempts to liberate the arrested sailors by force resulted in further arrests and several deaths.

Indignant over the use of force by the admiralty, the sailors elected councils and demanded the abdication of the Emperor, the termination of the state of siege, the liberation of the arrested sailors and of those condemned in 1917, a political amnesty for all involved in the present troubles, and a liberal suffrage bill incorporating woman suffrage. The Governor of Kiel could not seriously resist the mass of rested and well-

[52] "A German revolution cannot be imagined without endless meetings and innumerable speeches." Noske, *op. cit.*, p. 13.

[53] Vidil, *op. cit.*, pp. 157-61.

[54] Popp and Artelt, *op. cit.*, pp. 10-14. It is interesting that at first there were no demands for the abdication of the lesser monarchs.

armed sailors without outside help; he was forced to receive the sailors' representatives and to listen to their demands. All demands except those whose fulfillment depended on Berlin were promptly granted. In addition the governor promised not to call outside troops to Kiel. On the fourth of November, the governor's office confirmed by radio that the councils had been recognized, that the arrested sailors would be freed, that no naval action outside the harbor would take place, and that those involved in killings would be punished.[55]

Meanwhile, rumors of the events in Kiel had reached Berlin, and Prince Max decided to send Noske and Haussmann to investigate. Noske arrived in Kiel on November 4, and was surprised by the confusion and lack of direction. Above all, the sailors were afraid that outside troops would be called to suppress them. There was much shooting, but "mostly by people trying to silence their fears. During the revolutionary days in Kiel, nowhere had there been any serious resistance against the revolting soldiers." [56] Haussmann returned to Berlin the following day; Noske remained, unaware at first of events in other parts of Germany because of the breakdown in communications.

In the absence of any other leadership, he took charge of the movement and proceeded on the assumption that there was not going to be any revolution and that the movement in Kiel must be reduced to order. He succeeded in winning the confidence of all parties; the sailors surrendered their arms and allowed him to choose a council of seven or nine out of sixty trustees elected by their councils, while the officers agreed to follow his instructions and remain at their posts for the sake of order. By November 8, complete order had been restored.[57]

55 *Ibid.*, pp. 16-20.

56 Noske, *op. cit.*, p. 14. Noske apparently spoke of the time after his arrival.

57 Vidil, *op. cit.*, pp. 162-69; Noske, *op. cit.*, pp. 15-29. Noske thought that the councils "lacked strong authority because they had been elected" and hence were not able to restore order or stop looting. He defended the officers as victims of the old regime.

Eventually, the USPD, too, learned of the Kiel events and on November 7, sent Haase to take over. He arrived too late to take charge and returned to Berlin, but transportation difficulties delayed him until after the revolution had been successful in Berlin, too.[58]

d. REVOLUTION OVER GERMANY

Noske had not anticipated a revolution spreading throughout all of Germany and had ridiculed the limited political demands of the sailors, which could be granted only in Berlin and as the result of a revolution. But from Kiel, rebellion spread along the coast and into the interior. By November 7, Councils had been elected as far South as Hannover and Braunschweig. The wave spreading from Kiel was soon joined by another wave coming North from Munich.

On November 3, Kurt Eisner had addressed a crowd of two thousand people on the Theresienwiese and, mindful of Bavarian fears of an invasion, called for a common Bavarian-Austrian peace treaty.[59] These demonstrations continued on the next day and in other cities in the South. By November 7, Eisner mustered 150,000 to 200,000 demonstrators on the Theresienwiese, who adopted a resolution calling for the abdication of the Emperor and of the Crown Prince; an oath by the army on the constitution; complete demobilization; acceptance of the armistice; and rejection of the idea of continued national defense. The demonstrators also demanded the eight-

58 The *Dresdener Volkszeitung*, November 7, 1918, denied that the Kiel uprisings had anything to do with Bolshevism. They were just a sailors' putsch provoked by the preference of the officers for battle instead of surrender of the fleet. Cited by Buchner, *op. cit.*, no. 42b, pp. 43-44. *Cf.* Haussmann, *op. cit.*, p. 267.

59 *Muenchener Neueste Nachrichten*, November 4, 1918, quoted by Buchner, *ibid.*, no. 40, pp. 36-37. The demonstrators also demanded in vain the liberation of the last three persons still imprisoned because of the January strikes. Their meeting ended with hurrahs for a socialist republic.

hour-day, unemployment insurance, and the like. A parade and a demonstration in front of the royal palace followed.[60]

During the night of November 7-8, Eisner proclaimed a republic in Munich. The immediate convocation of a national assembly in Bavaria and various social reforms were promised, and the civil servants were called upon to remain at their posts.[61] On November 8, Eisner presented his new cabinet to the Councils in Munich and justified the revolution by the need to prevent chaos which was sure to result from the attempt to execute the program of national defense; the notes of Wilson implied that Max would only be allowed to capitulate, while his, Eisner's regime, might be allowed to negotiate with the enemy and thus receive better terms.[62]

Munich was the first major German city to succumb completely to the revolution, but similar events occurred all over Germany. By November 6, the revolution had triumphed only in the ports of the North and Baltic seas; two days later only Berlin, Dresden, Breslau and Koenigsberg had not yet joined it.

Prince Max and the SPD had vainly tried to stem the rising tide; on November 6, they appealed to the public by disclosing that the armistice commission had already departed and warning that internal troubles would only threaten its success. Max was convinced that only the immediate abdication of the Emperor could prevent the further spread of the revolution, but the abdication did not come. Almost in despair, he issued, on November 9, an unauthorized proclamation announcing the abdication,[63] but he could no longer avert the revolution.

60 *Ibid.*, November 8, and *Muenchener Post*, same date, quoted *ibid.*, nos. 106, and 106 a and c, pp. 102-107.

61 Manifesto of Eisner, November 8, 1918; printed in Ahnert, *Die Entwicklung der deutschen Revolution ... in Leitartikeln ... Aufrufen ...*, Nuernberg, 1918, pp. 175-76.

62 *Muenchener Neueste Nachrichten*, November 9, quoted by Buchner, *ibid.*, no. 121, pp. 115-18.

63 Prince Max had been severely attacked for this step. On November 9, he had been in constant telephonic communication with Spa, and was in-

During the morning hours on November 9, 1918, the streets of Berlin began to overflow with workers and crowds, its garrisons went over to the revolutionaries one by one, and early in the afternoon, Scheidemann proclaimed the republic while Max handed over his chancellorship to Ebert.

The German revolution was notable because of the absence of central leadership, the absence of all resistance by the armed forces, and the readiness with which the civil service subordinated itself to the new regime. Professor Hobohm attributed this to the resentment against four years of blunders by the old regime: all knew too well that the state was too rotten to be saved.[64] " Had the old regime not been so completely brittle, the collapse would hardly have been as surprisingly fast and final." [65] Well did Barth lament that " the almost uncon-

---

formed, now that the decision was being taken, now that it was being formulated, now that he should be patient for just a few more hours. But the abdication formula, to which the Emperor finally consented, was one which still left him with all his prerogatives as King of Prussia. Max denied that such a solution had ever before been discussed and thought that it was unconstitutional and hence beyond his ability to anticipate; Max, *op. cit.*, pp. 630-34, 646-47. *Cf. Vorwaerts*, November 16, 1918, (evening edition) giving a proposed but undelivered speech by Max on the events leading up to his announcement; quoted by Buchner, *op. cit.*, no. 299, pp. 254-56. Also Max' response to the memo of the Generals in the *Deutsche Tageszeitung*, July 27, 1919, quoted by Marx, *Handbuch der deutschen Revolution*, I, 105-12. Max held the armistice offer responsible for the collapse, and the refusal of the Emperor to abdicate for the revolution; he accused the generals for failing to inform William II early enough of the true situation, and denied that he was ever informed of the possibility of partial abdication. This is one of the few important documents which Niemann, *Revolution von Oben*... failed to include in his list of fourteen reports by witnesses of the events of November 9 in Spa and in the Chancellory. Niemann believed that Germany lost the war because of the poisoning of the public mind from the left, but he was compelled to state that " the unbearably sudden fall from exaggerated hopes of victory created among the people, who saw itself threatened in its entirety, a despair which aired itself uncritically in the urge to find a guilty person and to sacrifice this guilty person; " *ibid.*, p. 314.

64 *Ursachen*, vol. XI, pt. 1, pp. 361 ff.

65 Noske, *op. cit.*, p. 12.

tested victory in Berlin on November 9, put the brake on socialism, meant its surrender to traitors." [66] There was, in the words of Dr. Fischer, the General Secretary of the ' parlamentarischer Untersuchungsausschuss ', no revolution, only a collapse of all power of further resistance. [67]

Thus the main causes for the German revolution may be summarized as follows: fighting a war in which its chances for success were none too good, and where the suspicions of a tainted record in regard to its outbreak were sufficient to discredit it, the German government had aggravated these difficulties by persisting in mistaken and foolhardy policies in regard to foreign and domestic affairs, in spite of increasing warnings and danger signals. These policies and failures bred considerable resentment which was the more grave because the government failed to correct these mistakes in time. The exaggerated hopes for victory had made hardships tolerable for a time, but disappointments were heaped on disappointments, and the final admission of defeat in October, 1918, produced a reaction. In this reaction, the desire to end the hopeless struggle and the useless deprivations was as strong as the willingness to bring all sacrifices on behalf of victory had previously been. The readiness of the government to fulfill this desire for peace was suspect, because its previous record on questions of peace was tainted. When the armistice proved elusive and preparations for continued fighting became known, when the consequences of further struggle became ex-

66 Barth, *op. cit.*, p. 126.

67 In his testimony at the Dolchstoss trial, Beckmann, *op. cit.*, pp. 133-37. *Cf.* Hermann Mueller, *Die November Revolution 1918*, Berlin, 1931, pp. 13-18. This volume by the republican chancellor is one of the most recommendable German accounts of the revolution down to the first Congress of Councils. Regarding the events in Spa on November 9, see Rudin, *op. cit.*, pp. 359 ff. The best known report of this day in Spa is the collective article by Hindenburg, Plessen, Hintze, Marschall and Schulenberg in *Deutsche Tageszeitung*, July 27, 1919. Niemann, *op. cit.*, listed this and thirteen other reports of the meeting in his appendix.

tremely objectionable and the limitations of the political reforms in Germany suspect of aggravating the armistice terms, a revolution ensued.[68]

" The entire sequence of events in its unexampled naturalness can be explained only by the fact that everybody ... was completely aware that the collapse of the monarchy ... was a fait accompli. The knowledge of the inevitability of these events explains ... that although everybody in Berlin knew that the revolution is now beginning, none as far as I know of the tens of thousands of men of the Court, the civil service, the ranks of the officers, and the so-called society, monarchial to the marrow, made even the least attempt to defend the Emperor or the monarchy at a risk to his own person." [69]

68 *Cf.* the report of the American minister in Switzerland, November 19, 1918: " The complete defeat of the German armies in the West and the abandonment of all hope for a victorious peace brought to the German people the disappointment of all its expectations and opened its eyes to the policy of deception and untruth of its government. A revolution in Germany was impossible as long as the military powers were in control and were able to strengthen their position by apparent military successes. As soon as these failed and as the defensive lines in the West pronounced impregnable were broken one after the other, the German people saw that their only salvation lay in taking the government into their own hands and entered upon a relatively bloodless but very complete revolution." *Foreign Relations of the United States, The Paris Peace Conference 1919,* II, 89.

69 Payer, *op. cit.,* pp. 165-166.

CHAPTER VIII

THE SPD AND THE GERMAN REVOLUTION

a. SPD VIEWS ON COALITION GOVERNMENT AND REVOLUTION

THOSE defenders of the Dolchstoss thesis whose efforts to interpret the revolution on the basis of the actual events command attention, specifically exonerated the SPD of all responsibility. Its foremost spokesman, Professor Cossmann, implicated only the USPD and the groups to the left of it. The record of the SPD during the war and the nature of its criticism of war-time policies justified no other conclusion: the party indeed had been motivated solely by considerations of the national weal; "regarding specifically national questions, including the problem of militarism, the majority socialists had approached rather close to the views of the bourgeois parties." [1]

Political circles hence were not surprised when, during the Hertling crisis in September, 1918, the SPD expressed its willingness to participate with other political groups in the formation of a new cabinet, ready at long last to effect some of the reforms which had been advocated for so long in vain. The Austrian peace offer of September 14, had thoroughly shaken the confidence of the Reichstag majority in the existing order; by September 30, the SPD had agreed with the Center, Progressive, and National-Liberal parties on a program of peace terms, parliamentarization, and Prussian reforms. Though more far-reaching than the terms ultimately adopted, the original conditions presented by the SPD on September 23, were in many respects not more radical than the views advocated by Bethmann-Hollweg as early as August, 1914. [2]

1 Bernstein, *ibid.*, p. 65.

2 Max, *op. cit.*, p. 321.

And even these relatively moderate views had been presented only because its war-time policies had destroyed SPD party unity; by joining a bourgeois coalition the SPD might lose all its future hopes, and hence rigid guaranties for the realization of the program had to be insisted upon.[3]

The terms finally accepted by the Max cabinet enjoyed the unreserved support of the Reichstag majority; nobody among them would at this late moment tolerate delay in the unconditional acceptance of the July, 1917, peace resolution, the endorsement of a league of nations, the clarification of the Belgian problem, of reparations or of the restoration of Serbia and Montenegro, or still resist the introduction of autonomy for Alsace-Lorraine, civilian administration in the occupied areas in the East, responsible government by members of the Reichstag, Prussian reforms, and modifications of the restrictions upon the freedom of the press, of assembly and the like.[4]

The negotiations between the inter-party committee of the Reichstag, the party leaders, the retiring Chancellor Count Hertling, Chancellor-designate Prince Max and Vice-Chancellor Payer had been conducted in complete ignorance of the decision of the Supreme Army Command that the first act of the new government was to be an appeal to Wilson for an armistice.[5] The party leaders had, like Prince Max, anticipated that the new government would be called upon to take a serious step towards peace within a short time, but the information supplied to them by Major von Bussche on October 2, dispelled any illusions that the new cabinet might evade or delay the onerous act demanded by the Supreme Command. For the

3 Erzberger, *op. cit.*, p. 308.

4 *Protokoll des Parteitags 1919*, pt. 1, pp. 7-8.

5 " The first really parliamentary cabinet ... was formed for the express purpose of suing for peace.... The parliamentary form of government and the coalition supporting it were thus discredited ... sealing its fate." Count Westarp, *Konservative Politik*, II, 656.

SPD, this revelation re-opened the problem whether the party should participate in the new cabinet under conditions which had thus deteriorated beyond its most pessimistic anticipations.

At the meeting of the party-chairmen on October 2, Scheidemann pleaded against "entering a totally bankrupt concern at the moment of its absolutely certain collapse." The monarchy, by its incompetence, had dug its own grave; the SPD must not now join a cabinet, headed by a Prince, and thus share responsibility in the worst crisis of the regime.[6]

But Ebert successfully over-rode the objections of Scheidemann and Landsberg. He thought that the extraordinary gravity of the situation forced the SPD to participate in the new cabinet. Otherwise the party could later be reproached for having refused to aid in preventing the collapse and be accused of not having tried to save what yet could be saved.[7] Since "Germany had completely lost the war. . . . nothing remained, after the military collapse, but to attempt to preserve . . . the Reich intact." [8]

Participation in a coalition cabinet dominated by a bourgeois majority and a princely prime minister was so radical a departure from traditional SPD views, that SPD leaders eventually went to great pains to show that the old views had always been an error. "Responsibility is a virtue which we used to neglect somewhat, when we were still an agitating, organizing party," thought Hermann Mueller.[9] "For fifty years, we were only a party of opposition and agitation, prepared solely to gain parliamentary-political influence . . . Old party members will recall the struggles . . . about whether . . .

6 Scheidemann, *Memoiren*, II, 190; *Zusammenbruch*, pp. 174-76. Max, *op. cit.*, pp. 335 ff.

7 Scheidemann, *Memoiren*, II, 190; *Zusammenbruch*, p. 176. Max, *ibid.* Scheidemann later regretted that he allowed himself to be persuaded, and that he did not insist that Ebert join the cabinet instead of himself; *Memoiren, ibid.*

8 Noske, *op. cit.*, p. 7.

9 *Protokoll des Parteitags 1919*, pt. 2, p. 133.

a socialist may become a minister in a class state ... We used to talk about Millerandism ... We can say that Millerandism was condemned most incisively in those circles of the International which in practice were most removed from [its possibilities]." The SPD had to participate in the cabinet of Prince Max, it was argued, because the SPD was needed to help conclude peace. The hopes of improving the peace terms overrode the objections towards entering a cabinet burdened by the gravity of the situation. " Not lust for office, but terrible necessity led us into the government in which we now remained, always under the pressure of this selfsame necessity ... We cannot pass over the fact that we were not yet able to conquer a majority ... by means of democracy, ... that we are today forced to co-operate with the bourgeois parties." [10]

" The question of the participation of Social Democracy in the government is one of the most important points ... Since we cannot seize power alone, and since we cannot wait until we can seize power alone ... and since in the meanwhile we cannot leave the protection of ... democracy to its opponents or dubious friends, it is our duty to win decisive influence upon the governments of Germany " with the aid of coalitions.[11] " We deal here with the transformation of our party from agitation to government ... We have learned that in view of the party divisions in Germany, we cannot think of gaining the whole power for our party so soon ... If we want to exercise power actively, the keenest opposition on our part in parliament will not do us any good. The whole system functions only if you have seized the helm with your own hands." [12]

10 *Ibid.*, pp. 140-45, speech of Otto Wels.

11 *Ibid.*, 1921, report of the party chairmanship, pp. 142-147.

12 *Ibid.*, pp. 192 ff., speech of Otto Braun. This congress, stressing that this did not represent a change from old party policies, adopted a resolution by a vote of 209 to 67, authorizing the party, as the sole proper republican party, to participate in a coalition with any other party (including the German People's Party, the DVP), which would accept a program of democratization and non-furtherance of monarchism, *ibid.*, pp. 207-08, 389.

The defense of the SPD leaders for participation in the Max
cabinet and their conversion to the principle of government by
coalition with bourgeois parties did not narrow the gulf which
separated such a policy from the Gotha program which saw in
all other political groups merely a " reactionary mass ", or
from the Erfurt program which saw society divided into two
" hostile camps ". It was significant that the SPD thus entered
the revolutionary period by rejecting one of its basic theses
regarding the nature and purposes of the political struggle in
class society.

More influential for the role of the SPD during the revolution were the changes which the events in Russia after mid-
1917 had wrought within the party. Belief in a revolution by
armed force had never been strong in the SPD. " The German
Social Democrats had always rejected the idea of a revolution
by force. The Social Democrat proudly called himself a revolutionary ... but the idea of the use of force had been rejected
and, as a means of achieving political and economic progress,
the revolutionizing of minds alone had been desired." [13]

" There are many people who believe that we are a great
revolutionary party and must push forward the great revolution. Certainly that is important, but we know that ... the
great changes which come as the consequence of great revolutions are generally nothing but the composite of a large
number of bagatelles. Great pasts cannot collapse all of a
sudden." [14]

Thus predisposed, the example of the Bolshevist revolution
in Russia produced a deep horror within the SPD. Ebert told
Max two days before the German revolution that " if the
Kaiser does not abdicate, the social revolution is unavoidable.
But I do not want it; I hate it like sin." [15] And Scheidemann

13 Noske, *op. cit.*, pp. 7-8.

14 *Protokoll des Parteitags 1921*, pp. 128 ff., speech of Molkenbuhr, reporter for the program committee.

15 Max, *op. cit.*, p. 599. Dr. David seconded Ebert's sentiments.

stressed that by ' social revolution ' Ebert meant " Russian-
Asiatic Bolshevism " which was but a " Barbarian-Asiatic
caricature of scientific socialism." [16] Indeed Max, who was
not favorably disposed towards Scheidemann, agreed that only
his fears of a possible Bolshevist revolution led Scheidemann
to oppose a program of national defense after the end of
October.[17]

It is interesting to note how SPD leaders talked about the
Bolshevist utopia: " The veil which lay over the Bolshevist
paradise has now been torn away. We know what terrible
conditions prevail there ... If the proletarians in Russia are
particularly favored in the distribution of food, and the like,
that does not prevent their being enslaved just as the slaves
of old. The main point is that Bolshevism has terminated
neither wage labor nor exploitation. Bolshevist state enterprises differ from capitalist enterprises only in that less order
prevails in them, that the interests of the workers are given less
consideration, that in addition to the hunger whip, workers
are under the compulsion of bayonettes." [18] Russia was pictured as ruled by " a handful of narrow-minded fanatics, who
imagine themselves to be particularly purposeful socialists ";
these " socialist amateurs " have only instituted a reign of
" the most conscienceless violation and pleasure in violation,
which has long ago been ready for its downfall ..." [19]

Indeed Bolshevism has rarely been condemned in harsher
terms than by the SPD in 1917-1918. Fear of the repetition
of the Russian experience in Germany and of the complete disintegration of all order and economy under ' pure communism '

---

16 Scheidemann, *Memoiren*, II, 266, 293. This was one of the rare moments
when Scheidemann felt like defending Ebert, of whom he did not think very
highly. According to Scheidemann, Ebert was extremely dictatorial and
inconsiderate.

17 Max, *op. cit.*, p. 523.

18 *Protokoll des Parteitags 1920*, pp. 29-30, report of Otto Wels, chairman.

19 Max Schippel's article, " Das bolschewistische Zerrbild des Sozialismus," *Sozialistische Monatshefte*, December 31, 1918, pp. 1183-89.

determined the steadfast resolution of the SPD to oppose it in Germany. To spare Germany, as far as possible, the experiences of the Russian revolution motivated to a large degree the policies of the party under Prince Max and after the revolution.

b. THE SPD AND THE ABDICATION CRISIS

As a government party, the SPD, in October, 1918, did not share the fears of the public that the Emperor or the circles close to him could prevent the conclusion of an armistice based on the Fourteen Points. The party realized, however, that if Wilson were to demand the abdication of the Emperor in return for an armistice, or if the public were to see in William II the main impediment to the armistice, their demands could be resisted only at the price of civil war.[20]

In view of its attitudes in regard to revolutions, the SPD had therefore little sympathy for the demands of abdication. Upon entering the Max cabinet, Scheidemann had promised to oppose the demands for abdication, a task which he considered to be easy because Wilson, in all probability, would also attempt to impose unacceptable armistice terms.[21]

As a result of the Lansing notes, the problem of abdication became a subject of public discussion in Germany in spite of SPD attempts to prevent it. However, the SPD was resolved to keep the problem of the abdication apart from the problem of monarchy. "If we succeed in fulfilling the demands of Wilson," Scheidemann told the cabinet, "he hopes to avoid the question of the Emperor. He does not desire to solve the problem of monarchy, desires to have it excluded entirely. For the Social Democracy, the external form of the state is unimportant." [22]

20 Max, *op. cit.*, pp. 346, 567. Max had uttered this warning on October 2.
21 *Ibid.*, pp. 376 ff.
22 *Ibid.*, p. 498.

" The Social Democracy is, in principle, a democratic party," wrote the *Vorwaerts* on November 5, " but since the time of Bebel, it has never placed decisive importance on the question of the form of the representative head. To fight with royalist Don Quixotes for perhaps thirty years and thereby to see the necessary domestic development interfered with is not one of the most pleasing prospects for a young republic." [23]

But neither Wilson nor the public heeded SPD preferences, and the calls for abdication became more insistent. Scheidemann warned repeatedly that a republic might result unless Max succeeded in persuading the Emperor to abdicate in time, but that, should he succeed, the SPD would be content with constitutional monarchy.[24] On October 29, Scheidemann urged Max to realize that there was no alternative to abdication except poor peace terms and the inability to proceed with a program of national defense.[25]

These warnings, however, were strictly confidential. The SPD issued them only to forestall the grave consequences which would result if the abdication were due mainly to public demands. In the endeavor to inhibit such public demands or the open pressure of the cabinet in favor of abdication, Scheidemann, until November 2, advised his party to refrain from insisting on abdication until after the armistice had been signed. But even Max realized that Scheidemann's influence over his party was not unlimited, and that revolutions are made not by the party press but by the masses.[26]

23 Quoted *ibid.*, p. 580.

24 Scheidemann, *Memoiren*, II, 261-2. He thought that it was silly to expect William II to be more resolute, when his cabinet was so weak in the question of abdication. See Max, *op. cit.*, pp. 531 ff., 538-40.

25 *Ibid.*, pp. 531-32. Max accused Scheidemann of thwarting, with this step, his policy to effect a gesture without outside pressure. His own failure and the Emperor's trip to Spa should have informed him better. Upon the request of Max, Scheidemann withdrew this letter later on. Scheidemann, *Zusammenbruch*, pp. 201 ff., erroneously gave the date of this letter as November 20.

26 Max, *op. cit.*, pp. 562-63.

All through October, the SPD was thus reluctant to assume leadership of the public pressure for abdication, or to further it. However, the public pressure grew, and almost by default, leadership fell to the USPD. The leaders of the USPD were in continuous touch with the Russian embassy in Berlin which furnished them with money and revolutionary literature; Russia seemed to be very eager to reciprocate in kind for the favor which the Supreme Army Command had bestowed upon the Kerensky government by the gift of Lenin and his staff.[27]

For the SPD and the government, this situation was rather objectionable, but diplomatic immunity of the embassy buildings and of its mails made it difficult to take any decisive measures, the more so since the distribution of subversive literature by the Russian embassy had not yet been proven. In this situation, Scheidemann was able to suggest a way out. In a cabinet meeting on October 28, he recommended that some of the diplomatic baggage arriving in Berlin be 'accidentally' broken, so that its contents could be revealed and steps be taken against Joffe, the Russian ambassador.[28]

On the 4th of November, the 'accident' took place at the

27 Bernstein, *ibid.*, pp. 22-23, stressed that there was nothing treasonable in this; Germany was at peace with Russia and the money was intended solely to influence domestic and not foreign policy. In connection with Lenin's journey to Russia in 1917, the pamphlet *The German-Bolshevist Conspiracy*, issued by the Committee on Public Information, Washington, D. C., October, 1918, explained Mr. Joffe's courtesy, since it pictured the Russian October revolution as having been engineered by the German High Command and the Reichsbank in order to betray Russia to the German agents Trotzky and Lenin. The support which Lenin received from the German government all through 1918 was frequently cited as a cause for the preservation of the Bolshevist regime in Russia, and even Helfferich saw the connection which existed between the friendship of Imperial Germany for the Bolshevist regime and Joffe's activities; Helfferich, *op. cit.*, III, 460-96. Helfferich, who in August, 1918, spent ten days in Moscow as German ambassador, considered himself an authority on Russian affairs, and thought that but for the German support, the communist regime would long since have been overthrown by the Russian people.

28 Scheidemann, *Memoiren*, II, 252; Max, *op. cit.*, pp. 323, 579-80; H. Mueller, *op. cit.*, pp. 12-13.

Anhalt station in Berlin. Among the literature found was Radek's *Zusammenbruch des Imperialismus und die Aufgabe der internationalen Arbeiterklasse.* On the following day, Germany broke diplomatic relations with Russia. The *Vorwaerts* on November 5 accused Russia of trying to sow internal discord in Germany and warned that Russian conditions, if transplanted, would be even more disastrous in Germany, because German industries were more fully developed and there was more to destroy. The SPD, declared the *Vorwaerts,* wanted no truck with ' Socialismus Asiaticus.'

But the public clamor for abdication did not abate. And SPD leaders slowly realized that unless the Emperor did abdicate voluntarily, a revolution would occur, and that the SPD would not be able to exercise any control over public sentiments unless the party placed itself at the head of the popular movement. Neither alternative pleased the leaders of the party. Anticipating the results of the public demand, Scheidemann warned Prince Max that " he must be perfectly aware that, if he wants to preserve the monarchy, he must insist that the Emperor abdicate. Nobody knows what the next day may bring. But should in consequence of the collapse at the front and of the emergency at home a great popular movement occur, there can be no doubt that not only the abdication of the Emperor but the substitution of the monarchy by a republic would be demanded." [29]

While urging Max to persuade the Emperor to abdicate, the SPD endeavored to restrain the increasing popular demand for abdication. On November 4, the government issued a manifesto, signed by its SPD members, which pointed to the democratic reforms achieved or pending, and called upon the public to preserve peace and order. It warned that fanatics were trying to drive Germany to destruction; the government desired peace but had no alternative but to fight on until the enemy offered terms. As soon as peace would be attained, the

29 Scheidemann, *Zusammenbruch,* pp. 203-04.

food situation would improve, veterans would be reemployed in their former jobs, and the like.[30] On the same day, the *Vorwaerts* appealed to the public not to strike or demonstrate during the next few days. The paper pointed to the democratic achievements of the government, SPD participation in the cabinet, and the urgent and earnest peace steps which had been taken. It acknowledged that Scheidemann had asked Max to recommend abdication. The workers should not now disturb the negotiations by demonstrations. Although the SPD itself might eventually call for demonstrations, now was the time for order and discipline. Irresponsible acts would only spell disaster and strengthen the reaction.

But such views were not popular in November, 1918. The Kiel mutinies and the demonstrations in Munich and Stuttgart indicated widespread unrest and revolt. "We made the greatest efforts to influence the masses," Scheidemann told Max on November 7; " if the masses began to stir in regard to abdication, bourgeois papers like the *Frankfurter Zeitung* are responsible in the first place. You can still keep the masses in harness by making concessions ... Almost everybody in the cabinet would have felt a load off his mind, had the Emperor done the right thing ... Events chase each other ... It is our conviction that if the Emperor does not abdicate at once, a revolutionary collapse of Germany will occur. If he does abdicate, we think we can guarantee that the development will be favorable." [31]

In order to insure such a ' favorable development ', the SPD had to abandon its opposition towards an abdication brought about by public pressure. A voluntary act by the Emperor might still appease the public; otherwise only a movement headed by the SPD might be able to protect the public from more radical leadership.

30 Cited by Ahnert, *op. cit.*, pp. 146-48.

31 Max, *op. cit.*, pp. 609-10.

But William II did not abdicate. Scheidemann finally asked his party for permission to withdraw from the cabinet unless the abdication was confirmed by November 7. " Do you not sense," he begged, " that we face the immediate collapse of the Reich? And then you talk about the collapse of the parliamentary majority!" Now the SPD should place itself at the head of the movement, lest anarchical conditions prevail within the empire. Perhaps the worst might yet be avoided if the Emperor abdicated at once. The party, however, rejected Scheidemann's application as premature.[32]

While the SPD feared for its following and the consequences of its attitude in the abdication problem, the Supreme Command was also worrying about the march of events, and General Groener, Ludendorff's successor, came to Berlin for consultations. He painted a black picture of the military situation and warned, on the 6th, that Germany could not wait for Wilson's reply longer than November 9; the Kiel mutiny, the Bavarian fears of an invasion, and recent successes of United States troops against the German sector near Verdun would by that time force the Supreme Command to surrender to Foch directly.[33]

Groener used the opportunity to confer with SPD and trade-union leaders, with whom he had been on friendly terms for over a year. Ebert pleaded for the abdication of the Emperor, whom the people—rightly or wrongly—accused of the collapse, lest they join the revolutionaries. Abdication should not come later than November 7. David and Suedekum pleaded that

32 Scheidemann, *ibid.*, pp. 204-05.

33 Max, *op. cit.*, pp. 582-84, 589-90. Wilson's last note, the pre-armistice compact, arrived on the 6th, but after the Supreme Command had decided to appeal to Foch directly. As soon as possible, the armistice commission departed from Berlin, but was delayed in Spa. On the 6th, Max issued a manifesto informing the public of the departure of the armistice commission, and warning that at this decisive hour of the war, domestic peace was paramount; every citizen must act according to his duty; cited by Buchner, *ibid.*, pp. 83-84.

they were not opponents of the monarchy and that the abdication would not endanger it. The meeting was temporarily interrupted by the news of the revolution in Hamburg and Hannover. Again David asked Groener to recommend the abdication: the time for discussion was past, the time for action had come. Ebert pleaded that although he was a republican, he would endorse a parliamentary monarchy, if the opportunity were used to save the monarchy by abdication. " With tears in his eyes," Suedekum begged Groener to recommend the abdication in order to prevent a terrible catastrophe, and Legien exerted himself similarly. But Groener saw no chance to yield; one could not deprive the army of its commander-in-chief. Things must then take their course, was all Ebert could say at the close of the meeting.[34]

c. The SPD and the Fall of the Max Cabinet

The SPD had resisted endangering the cabinet by the problem of abdication as long as possible, but public sentiment had to be recognized at last. Expressly approving the attitude of its leaders taken heretofore, the SPD bloc of the Reichstag, on November 7, presented Max with an ultimatum demanding the abdication of the Emperor by noon of the next day, or else the SPD would withdraw its members from the cabinet.[35] As bargaining points, perhaps, the ultimatum also asked for an immediate armistice, further democratization, and the like.

---

34 Max, *op. cit.*, pp. 591-93. At the Dolchstoss trial, Groener regretted not having accepted the advice of Ebert, which might have saved the monarchy; Beckmann, *op. cit.*, pp. 103-11. After this meeting, the cabinet concluded that the SPD no longer controlled the masses and that hence the revolution was unavoidable. Groener, knowing of the nearness of the revolution, but unable to advise the Emperor to abdicate, suggested that he seek a hero's death in the trenches; Max, *op. cit.*, p. 595. From this moment on, William II had become persona non grata with the SPD which henceforth would refer to him in contradistinction to the 'soldier-king' Frederic II by name of 'deserter-king.' "Napoleon III, of a considerably inferior dynasty, still surrendered his sword; William II found other ways;" *Protokoll des Parteitags 1919*, pp. 140 ff., speech of Otto Wels.

35 Scheidemann, *ibid.*, pp. 205-06.

Max commented bitterly in his memoirs that the revolution could use as its slogan: " The Emperor refuses to sacrifice himself." [36]

Before receiving the ultimatum, Max had talked with Ebert and David, " for whom, in a moment of national danger, party considerations no longer existed." They had approved his plan to go to Spa and to recommend to the Emperor that a regent be named who should call a national assembly. Max had hoped that the idea of democracy might stem the tide and win back the support of the SPD, but the ultimatum overthrew this plan, if indeed it had still been feasible.[37]

In the opinion of Max, Ebert and Scheidemann, who presented the ultimatum, had been filled with terror at their loss of control over the masses. Ebert had declared that " tonight, twenty-six large meetings are taking place in all large halls. Tonight we must announce the ultimatum from every tribune, otherwise the entire party goes over to the USPD." [38]

Because the armistice commission had been delayed in Spa for some time, the SPD finally agreed to delay its ultimatum until November 9. The manifesto announcing this decision pointed out that the government had accepted most of the SPD demands, especially in regard to equal suffrage on the basis of proportional representation in all states, the parliamentarization of Prussia, increased SPD strength in the cabinet and revocation of the new calls to the colors, but that a cabinet crisis at this time would endanger the armistice because the armistice commission had been delayed in Spa. The workers were asked to accept a few more hours of delay.[39]

36 Max, *ibid.*, pp. 596-97.

37 *Ibid.*, pp. 597-600. It was at the discussion of these plans, that Ebert remarked that he hated revolution like sin. David incidentally threw cold water over the fond hopes of Max by asking whether he expected the SPD to campaign as a monarchist party in the elections for a national assembly. But David left no doubt that he preferred a monarchy, to avoid the danger of royalist plots and putsches.

38 Max, *op. cit.*, pp. 604-06.

39 Cited by Ahnert, *op. cit.*, p. 179; Buchner, *ibid.*, no. 108, p. 110.

SPD policy during this period was best summarized by the *Norddeutsche Allgemeine Zeitung* which stated on November 9, that in its insistence on abdication, the SPD had been motivated solely by the thought that only abdication could preserve order and prevent the spread of anarchy. The SPD had acted not to further party aims, but to save the Fatherland from destruction. Although the consequences could not as yet be evaluated, the SPD had saved Germany in a critical situation; not opposition to monarchy, but the desire to save Germany from a worse fate was responsible for the SPD call of abdication.[40] Max was fully aware of this; in his estimation, Ebert " seized a revolutionary gesture to prevent the revolution " and Scheidemann's promise that his " party will take care that Germany be spared from Bolshevism . . . later came true." [41]

For Max, the fate of Germany now depended on Ebert's ability to roll back the revolution as Noske had done in Kiel. The abdication was a condition sine qua non in this situation. However, the Emperor refused to yield to Max on the 8th, too. Max had hoped in vain that a timely abdication followed by a national assembly might direct the movement into legal channels.[42]

Thus the ninth of November dawned over Berlin. The SPD had called the masses into the streets for this day, and the demonstrations had been set for nine o'clock in the morning. While Max was frantically trying to get the redeeming word from Spa, Scheidemann and the other SPD members handed in their resignations from the cabinet.[43]

40 Cited by Ahnert, *ibid.*, pp. 182-84.

41 Max, *op. cit.*, pp. 618 ff. Scheidemann made the promise at a cabinet meeting on November 8.

42 *Ibid.*, pp. 616-17, 619, 625 ff.

43 Scheidemann, *Zusammenbruch*, p. 208. At 9:15 a.m., Max was told that the Supreme Command would inform the Emperor of their decision not to march into Germany to suppress the revolution. At 11 a.m., he was told that the decision had been reached and was now being formulated; Max, *ibid.*, p. 632.

At ten a.m., the first strikes began in the city; half an hour later, 15,000 workers were demonstrating, carrying · placards calling for freedom, peace and bread; an hour later, electricity had been cut off and the trolleys stalled; at one p.m., the *Vorwaerts* belatedly called for a general strike under the joint direction of the SPD and USPD.[44] In the meantime, the police and the troop formations stationed in Berlin had joined the demonstrators, thus sealing the success of the revolution. In order to save what could yet be saved, Max conceived the idea of announcing the abdication without waiting for the authorization of the Emperor, and of naming Ebert chancellor. He thus tried to anticipate the will of the mob by a last desperate measure and, at noon, he proclaimed that the Emperor had abdicated.[45]

At about the same time, an SPD delegation called on Max. Ebert demanded that, in order to prevent bloodshed, the SPD must receive the chancellorship and the command over the province of Berlin (Marken), with the right to form a coalition with either the bourgeois parties or the USPD. Scheidemann explained that all troops in Berlin had joined the revolution. Max proposed the appointment of Ebert as chancellor and the convocation of a national assembly, and no member of his cabinet present objected to this step of dubious legality. Ebert accepted the idea of a national assembly at once; he was also ready to accept the chancellorship under the constitution, but not under the monarchial constitution, unless his · party instructed him to do so. To the suggestion of a regency, Ebert could only reply: " Too late." [46]

---

44 *Berliner Tageblatt*, November 9, 1918; *Vorwaerts Extrablatt*, same date. The SPD actions on the 9th were in part determined by the fact that the USPD (but not Barth) had called for demonstrations (but not a revolution) on the same date.

45 Max, *op. cit.*, pp. 632-35.

46 Max, *op. cit.*, pp. 635-40. Article by Haussman, in *Vossische Zeitung*, November 20, 1918, quoted by Buchner, *ibid.*, no. 253b, pp. 228-29. Max, whose memoirs have been written with the aid of a staff of trained his-

Endowed with the chancellorship by Prince Max, Ebert proceeded to form his cabinet and began consultations with the bourgeois parties and with the USPD. Scheidemann, in the meanwhile, had been called to address the crowds in front of the Reichstag. Being told that Karl Liebknecht was about to proclaim a socialist dictatorship, Scheidemann at about two p.m. proclaimed Germany a republic.[47]

The new government issued several manifestos to inform the public of what had occurred. One of them stated that Max had transferred the chancellorship to Ebert with the consent of all of his secretaries of state, and that a new people's gov-

torians, utilized every published or privately available record of the period. He must hence be considered a secondary source even for those brief parts of his work which dealt with events that Max actually had witnessed. Several of those present at this meeting have written their recollections of its events, but it is not possible to reconstruct an accurate story of what had transpired. That Ebert should have considered accepting the chancellorship under a monarchial constitution in public is extremely unlikely. Scheidemann denied this expressly; Scheidemann, *Memoiren*, II, 296 ff. Scheidemann, who wrote his memoirs after Max, made a canvass of all witnesses of the meeting still alive, and he reported that none recalled Solf's question about acceptance under the monarchial constitution, or indeed that the problem of a national assembly had been discussed. There had, however, been several secret conferences between Ebert and Max, and Scheidemann, visibly squirming, admitted that there was proof that such a meeting had taken place early in the morning of November 9. Hence what Max reported may well be the condensation of the conversation of two separate meetings. Scheidemann himself learned, as a result of the incident discussed in the next note, that Ebert was bound in his policies. On the other hand, one should bear in mind that Ebert never wrote his memoirs, and that the entire sequence of revelations regarding Ebert's intrigues and secret policies did not become public until after Ebert's death.

47 Returning to the committee room, where Ebert had been in consultation, he found that " Ebert had become dark in the face with wrath. He beat with his fists on the table and shouted: 'Is that true?...You have no right to proclaim the republic!...'" Scheidemann, *ibid.*, pp. 312-16. In his *Zusammenbruch*, p. 173, published before Ebert's death, Scheidemann only talked about his 'friend', who before November 9, had strongly reproached him for having termed the demand for abdication as something natural, and who, after his (Scheidemann's) proclamation of the republic violently attacked him for thus prejudicing the choice of the National Assembly.

ernment was being formed with the purpose of securing peace and liberty. The political revolution must not, however, endanger the food supply; production and distribution must go on unhampered. Another manifesto, also signed by ' Chancellor Ebert ', informed Germany that the new government had taken over to avoid civil war and starvation, and to realize the right to self-determination for Germany. For the sake of patriotism, all civil servants and government bureaus were called upon for co-operation. A third manifesto, signed by Ebert, Landsberg and Scheidemann, stressed that the SPD was negotiating with the USPD about participation in the government on an equal basis. The new government would hold elections for a national assembly on the basis of universal suffrage for all Germans over twenty years of age. Until the government emerging from the national assembly would take over, the present government would limit its task to securing an armistice, conducting peace negotiations, safeguarding the food supply, and demobilizing the army. It warned that life and property must be protected.[48]

The *Vorwaerts*, on November 9, joined the appeal for a national assembly, which should include Austria, and whose agenda was to consist of a peace treaty, a ' gross-deutsche ' constitution, and legislation for the economic transition to peacetime and for the protection of the food supply.[49]

Late in the afternoon of the same day, Max took leave of Ebert. Ebert had asked Max to remain as regent, the latter related, but he refused. In leaving, he said: " Mr. Ebert, I recommend the German Empire to your heart." Replied Ebert: " I have lost two sons for that Empire." [50]

---

48 Ebert, *op. cit.*, II, 193-94. Ahnert, *op. cit.*, pp. 189-90, 193-94, 197-98.

49 Cited by Buchner, *op. cit.*, no. 116, p. 112.

50 Max, *op. cit.*, p. 643.

CHAPTER IX
REVOLUTION LIMITED

a. Problems of Revolution and Democracy

THE SPD had entered the German revolution with a deep aversion to Bolshevism and ready to co-operate with any political group for the good of the nation. Only after the successful revolt in Kiel and after the revolution had triumphed all through Western and Southern Germany had the SPD agreed to demand the abdication of the Emperor by means of a 'revolution from below'. Essentially, the revolution of November 9 was, for the SPD, a sort of cabinet crisis solved by the aggressive participation of the mob; the party was motivated at every point by the desire to save what could yet be saved, to effect by the revolution not the greatest but the smallest possible change.

The SPD had no illusions about this, its real role, in the revolution. "We cannot say that we 'made' the revolution, but we were not its opponents. We do not believe that historical research will ultimately talk about the Revolution of the Ninth of November." [1] Scheidemann declared: "The conception current in leftist radical circles that we Social Democrats seized power by force is completely false ... When the historical autumn storm of 1918 swept the old powers overboard, we were fetched out because there was nobody else to take the helm ... We do not wish to allow for even a moment the growth of the idea that we seized power the way a robber grabs his loot." [2]

---

[1] Otto Wels, *Protokoll des Parteitags 1919*, p. 152.

[2] *Ibid.*, pp. 233-34. Noske, *op. cit.*, pp. 58 ff., wrote that in anticipation of the dismemberment, exhaustion and deepest humiliation, which faced Germany as a result of the war, "the majority socialists did not desire a violent revolution.... If now majority socialists, too, pretend to be successful revolutionaries, it only testifies to the ability of many to adjust themselves to the ringing slogans of the day.... Independent Social Demo-

The SPD considered itself as the trustee for the bankrupt old regime;[3] " the first government of the revolution ... never considered its purpose otherwise than to administer in trust the office that fell to it, until the people itself in orderly elections decided upon the future constitution." [4]

In view of the immediate causes of the revolution, the SPD was probably right in assuming that it had no popular mandate to act in any other way. The SPD always remained acutely aware that in November, 1918, " the masses of the people and of the retreating soldiers knew no other desire but peace ", and the desire to eliminate everything that stood in the way of peace.[5]

Considerations of principle reinforced the SPD views regarding the freedom of action which it had received as a result of the German revolution. There were no social revolutions, " only social evolutions; but there are political revolutions, without which the social evolutions could not indeed always become effective. Hence it is a priori wrong to assign to the proletarian revolution in Germany the immediate task of ' effecting socialism ' ... The immediate result of the ' revolution ' can only be perfect democracy, as that form of political order which is the prerequisite for socialism, the latter being the result of a technologic-economic evolution." [6]

crats prided themselves with having prepared the revolution, armed themselves for the struggle.... But if their agitation did not lack success, it was only because hunger, misery and death had prepared the soil among the masses. Securing a few hundred or a thousand pistols was childishness.... You could not effect anything with this against a few thousand firmly organized troops.... Berlin fell as a last overripe fruit after the revolution had run its course throughout the Reich."

3 Ebert's opening speech to the German National Assembly; *Verhandlungen*, CCCXXVI, 1 ff., February 6, 1919.

4 *Ibid.*, pp. 44 ff., declaration of policy by Chancellor Scheidemann, February 13, 1919.

5 *Protokoll des Parteitags 1920*, p. 29, report of the party chairman. Cf. *ibid.*, *1919*, pp. 217-18.

6 Hans Marckwald, "Evolution-Revolution," *Neue Zeit*, vol. XXXVII, pt. 2, no. 16, January 17, 1919, pp. 361-65.

This conviction went to the very origins of the party. Lassalle, too, had argued that revolutions were the result and not the cause of deep social changes, and that the only proper objective of socialists was political democracy, since it enabled the workers to conquer political power whenever they would be ready for it.[7] The SPD acted in the belief that " with political means, with revolutions and parliamentary revolutions you cannot advance socialism any further than the social conditions ... have developed anyway. Political actions can, essentially, only confirm an economic development." [8]

Marx had, of course, talked about the dictatorship of the proletariat. The SPD, however, denied that by ' dictatorship of the proletariat ' he had meant a dictatorship exercised by a minority. Marx, according to the SPD, stated that no regime could endure, unless both the social-economic development and the majority of the people were ready for it, for Marx saw in the political order only the reflection of the social-economic development. Hence the political conquest of power by the proletariat was not tantamount to the abolition of the class-state, and the dictatorship of the proletariat, of a minority, was not the true purpose of the revolution. The true socialist purpose of the revolution was a democratic national assembly, declared the first issue of the chief theoretical organ of the SPD, which mentioned the revolution at all.[9]

Thus political democracy was, for the SPD, the only legitimate purpose of the revolution, and political democracy meant a constitutional assembly elected by the most liberal suffrage and convened as soon as possible. Given political democracy,

7 *Cf. supra*, p. 20.

8 Artur Heichen's article "Neumarxismus," *Neue Zeit*, vol. XXXIX, pt. 2, no. 9, May 27, 1921, pp. 201-206.

9 H. Cunow's article "Die Diktatur des Proletariats," *Neue Zeit*, vol. XXXVII, pt. 1, no. 8, November 22, 1918, pp. 170-77. Neither the issue of November 8, nor of November 15, mentioned the revolution or the events leading up to it. But in October, 1918, for the first time during the war, the publication printed appeals to subscribe to the new issue of war-loan bonds which were then being floated.

all other objectives could be reached without hindrance from decadent classes whose power was merely a product of the lack of freedom; given political democracy, the government could not help being a true representative of the actual strength of the classes. Even if a revolution could achieve more than political democracy, the SPD did not need more than that. Indeed, some within the SPD asserted that in 1918 a revolution had not even been needed in order to achieve political reforms; " a generous democratization of Germany at the end of October could be viewed as inevitable. It would have occurred without revolution too." [10]

It was therefore a foregone conclusion that the SPD would not allow the revolution to become a dictatorship. A Junker or a leftist dictatorship were equally objectionable to it. Not class rule but justice for all did Ebert demand on behalf of the SPD. On December 16, 1918, he declared that the SPD would no longer suffer any rule of compulsion; " the victorious proletariat does not erect class rule." Democracy and the national assembly were the only assurance for equality; " Democracy is the rock on which alone the working class may erect the edifice of Germany's future." [11]

Neither the USPD nor the Spartacists (who became, before the end of 1918, the ' Kommunistische Partei Deutschlands ', the KPD) were less truly Marxist than the SPD. But these groups were not convinced that the conquest of political democracy was the only genuinely socialist purpose of the revolution. In fact, they did not think that the conquest of political democracy ranked among the socialist purposes of a revolution, except maybe at some future stage when all was sweetness and light. The USPD chairman of the Executive Council of the Berlin Workers' and Soldiers' Councils declared on November 19: " The question of the constituent national assembly is for us a question of the future. We do not only want a demo-

10 Noske, *op. cit.*, p. 7.

11 Quoted in *Deutscher Geschichtskalender, ibid.*, I, 153-54, 202-03.

cratic, but a socialist republic. Such a republic would be endangered by too early a convocation of the constituent. The speedy convocation would be for us a sentence of death." The calls for an early national assembly represented the attempt to rob the proletariat of the fruits of the revolution whose protection could not be left to a democratic republic.[12]

Instead of democratic parliamentarism, the USPD and the KPD recommended the council system which, under the name of 'soviet system', had proven to be an efficient tool, if not of proletarian dictatorship, at least of dictatorship in Russia. Indeed, by the end of 1918, this Russian experience provided some of the most potent arguments used by the SPD in its opposition to the councils.

In spite of its inherent weaknesses as a representative system, the council system could theoretically operate on a franchise as wide and with results as fair as any democratic system of representation. But the USPD and the KPD did not advocate the council system because in theory it might provide a fair sample of public opinion; they advocated it rather because the council system had demonstrated the facility with which it could be used to distort public opinion and to perpetuate a rule which did not rest on majority support. The system of councils was advocated by the leftists exactly because no other representative system could produce socialist majorities with equal ease and without the wide use of open disfranchisement.[13]

Yet it would be rash to assume that the USPD and the KPD favored the council system because of lust for power or office.

12 Cited from the *Vorwaerts* by Buchner, *op. cit.*, no. 362, pp. 295-98. R. Mueller, who made these remarks, declared a few weeks later that the way to the national assembly would lead over his dead body, which earned him the nickname of 'Leichenmueller' by which he was known in the literature of the period.

13 *Cf.* for example the statement of Daeumig that on the basis of all previous elections, the socialists may never expect to receive a majority, and that hence they must use the council system in order to protect the revolution; speech of December 19, 1918, at the first Congress of Councils in Berlin; cited in *Deutscher Geschichtskalender, ibid.*, pp. 237-38.

The leaders of the two parties were men of integrity, motivated only by their ideals. They wanted to disfranchise the majority of the German people and to subject that majority to the dictatorial rule of a minority only because they were fully aware of their inability to command a majority of the public in their own support. They were conscious of the blunders and errors which had precipitated the German defeat, if indeed it had not caused the war in the first place; they were acutely agitated by the compulsion to prevent the possible recurrence of similar consequences born of incompetence; and no doubt ever crossed their minds that they and they alone knew how to achieve this and that the revolution had given them a mandate to do so.

The struggle between the system of councils and a national constitutional assembly elected on the widest democratic franchise was therefore not as much an academic struggle over the comparative merits of each system, as it was, in final analysis, a struggle between two contending interpretations of the purposes of the revolution and the mandate bestowed on the revolutionary government by the events of November 9. In view of this, the nature of SPD policies was less important than the fact that they had been enunciated in opposition to those who wanted to exploit the chance of the revolution to eradicate all that was ill or reprehensible in Germany, and to rebuild German society in the image of their own conception of ideal social order and of law. Like all crusaders, the latter wanted to spread salvation; that their ambitions would violate the democratic rights of the people was, for them, regrettable but of secondary importance.[14]

14 The SPD was firmly convinced that it would receive a majority at the national elections. It has been argued, that the miscalculations of the SPD regarding its strength were responsible for the absence of the sense of urgency which marked the Provisional Government and its legislative and administrative policies. This ex post facto argument however worked both ways; secure in the knowledge of future endorsement by the majority of the public, reforms could have been undertaken with doubled vigor. Not the least among the factors which favored the council system in Germany in 1918 was the German experience with the Reichstag during the Bismarck

b. The Formation of the Provisional Government

In its organizational form, the German revolution of November 9, had been a council movement. Four distinct types of councils had sprung up during the revolution, with distinct political and economic tendencies and desires. The soldiers stationed within Germany had elected Soldiers' Councils which tended to lean towards the USPD or the KPD and were particularly intransigent on the question of the officers' corps and its power of command; the councils elected by the workers varied according to their geographic distribution: in great industrial centers they tended to support the USPD, but the SPD controlled a majority of them all over Germany; Peasants' Councils had been elected only in Bavaria, and played a dominant role there during Kurt Eisner's administration; and the soldiers at the front had elected their own Soldiers' Councils who provided the most reliable support of the SPD views regarding the revolution and its purposes.[15]

Most of these councils had sprung up spontaneously all over Germany. Frequently elected by dubious methods, they took

Empire. Although elected on a comparatively liberal and democratic franchise, this body had been condemned to impotence from its conception down to October, 1918. This experience had favored belief in the irrelevancy and impotence of democracy and parliamentarism; to inaugurate self-government, the discredited forms of the empire should be replaced by a new form of representation.

15 Cf. Denkschrift ... vom Soldatenrat der Obersten Heeresleituung, November 28, 1918, which gave the texts of all proclamations and appeals issued by this council up to the time of its publication. These proclamations usually repeated the orders of the Government or of the Army, giving them added authority in this way. In a proclamation on December 1, this council backed the idea of a national assembly and attacked the Executive Council of the Berlin Soldiers' and Sailors' Councils; it also claimed credit for the orderly retreat, and it seems that the soldiers' councils deserved more credit for this than was usually given by German historians. Cf. Bericht ... vom Vollzugsausschuss des Soldatenrats des Feldheeres, December 12, 1918, which contained the answers given by the leading SPD and USPD politicians in reply to a questionnaire. It may be pointed out that the USPD and the KPD were not slow in condemning all councils, which did not reflect their own particular views, as tools of reaction.

over the government and administration from the old regime as agents of the revolution. Where they did not take over the administration directly, they placed their trustees side by side with the old officials whose business henceforth would be conducted under their supervision and subject to their approval. To the soldiers it was particularly important that officers should exercise their power of command only subject to the consent of the soldiers' councils.

It was perhaps unavoidable that the councils should produce much incompetence and much waste, many excesses and many failures.[16] On the whole, however, the councils made valiant efforts to preserve order, prevent sabotage, and protect the food supply. Their self-assumed tasks frequently exceeded their abilities, but in conjunction with the old administration they were able to use their authority in the interests of public order and domestic peace. Most of their members quickly disappeared into the anonymity from which they had briefly emerged. Noske commented on them by saying that " depending in whose hand they came . . . [they] became the terror of the population or its most secure protection. Their human composition was not worse than our people in general." The SPD readily admitted that many councils had done important work to keep political and economic life moving, to secure domestic peace and to retire the old government without bloodshed.[17]

Thus the revolution in Germany had resulted in fact in the rule of various types of councils or combinations of them. In the formation of any new government on November 9, they

16 An incomplete report on the expenses of the Soldiers' Councils was presented by the government to the National Assembly on August 18, 1919. It placed the total costs of the Soldiers' Councils at RM. 83,699,744.56 for the army and RM. 8,301,588.05 for the navy, both covering the period up to March 31. Of these, a total of RM. 34,429,798.38 spent by the army, was charged to illegal use and sale of state property, extortion, theft, etc. *Verhandlungen*, vol. CCCXXXVIII, no. 1006, pp. 1007-13.

17 Noske, *op. cit.*, pp. 37 ff. Cf. *A.-und S. Raete; was sie koennen und was sie nicht koennen*, a Vorwaerts pamphlet, published probably by December, 1918.

had to be taken into consideration. Their protection and expansion was the chosen task of the USPD, while the SPD endeavored to suppress all political power of the councils and to convene a national assembly unprejudiced by ' faits accomplis ', by the destruction of the old administrative organs, or by radical changes in the social and economic life.

Neither the USPD nor the SPD had alone felt strong enough on November 9 to form a government. The USPD and other radical groups were quite unconvinced that their own strength allowed them to assume the government independent of other groups,[18] while the SPD viewed their strength as a serious threat to its own leadership. The SPD feared that unless it formed a coalition with the USPD, most of its members would go over to the more radical parties. As soon as Ebert had succeeded to the chancellorship, the SPD therefore sought a coalition with the USPD. Ebert was even willing to accept the collaboration of Karl Liebknecht on the day of the revolution. After some deliberation, the USPD declared in a formal letter that it would join the SPD in a Provisional Government only if the plans for a national assembly were dropped and all legislative, administrative and judicial functions transferred to the councils. At eight-thirty p.m. on November 9, the SPD replied to the USPD: the SPD must let the National Assembly decide whether Germany should become a socialist republic; the SPD must refuse the demand that all legislative, executive and judicial functions pass to a minority group opposed to the majority of the people; the USPD suggestion of the exclusion of the bourgeoisie must be rejected because of the danger to the food situation; the USPD suggestion of a coalition limited to three days must be rejected, instead the coalition must last until the convention of a constitutional assembly; but both parties agreed that departmental heads (Fachminister) were to be technical aides only, without

18 See R. Mueller, *Vom Kaiserreich zur Republik*, II, 31. R. Mueller was the chairman of the Executive Council of the Berlin Workers' and Soldiers' Councils. *Cf.* Barth, *op. cit.*, pp. 46, 57-64.

cabinet rank and without a voice in political affairs; and both
agreed on parity in the new government, although the SPD
qualified this by making it subject to the approval of the constituent assembly.

The USPD answer to this communication was received on
November 10, and formed the basis for the formation of the
Provisional Government. The USPD was ready to join the
cabinet provided only its own members and members of the
SPD enjoyed cabinet rank; each party was to furnish one
secretary of state for each ministry; no time limit was set for
the coalition, and political power was to be vested in the
councils who should be called together in a congress as soon
as possible. The question of a national assembly was to be
decided later on.[19]

19 The text of this correspondence appeared in *Protokoll des Parteitags*
1920, pt. I, pp. 11-12. The Provisional Government had the following composition: Ebert (SPD) was responsible for the ministry of the interior and
the army; Haase (USPD) for foreign and colonial affairs; Scheidemann
(SPD) for finance; Dittmann (USPD) for demobilization and health;
Landsberg (SPD) for press and news; and Barth (formally accredited by
the USPD, but supported mainly by the revolutionary foreman) was responsible for social policy. Except for the posts held by Haase, the SPD
thus controlled the crucial departments of government. The ministries were
originally divided as follows:

Office	Secretary of State	Undersecretary	Assistant
Posts	Ruedlin		
Interior	Dr. H. Preuss		
Economy	Dr. A. Mueller (SPD)	R. Schmidt (SPD)	Dr. A. Erdmann (USPD)
Nutrition	E. Wurm (USPD)		
Labor	G. Bauer (SPD)	J. Giesberts	H. Jaeckel (USPD)
Foreign Affairs	Dr. Solf	Dr. E. David (SPD)	K. Kautsky (USPD)
Navy	von Mann	E. Vogtherr (USPD)	G. Noske (SPD)
War	Scheuech	P. Goehre (SPD)	E. Daeumig (USPD)
Demobilization	Dr. Koeth	O. Schumann (SPD)	O. Buechner (USPD)
Justice	Dr. Krause		Dr. O. Cohn (USPD)
Treasury	Dr. Schiffer		E. Bernstein (USPD)

In agreeing to these terms, each party assumed that their own viewpoint had been accepted by the other. But both parties also knew that they had entered but an uneasy truce.

The first test of the coalition came on November 10, the very day when the Provisional Government was formed. The Spartacists had no confidence in a government headed by the SPD. In order to deprive the SPD of its position in the government, they had called a meeting of the Berlin councils at Circus Busch. They demanded the adoption of the following program: all police, officers and troops who disapproved of the revolution should be disarmed, but no proletarian may be disarmed; all military and civilian bureaus, all arms and all arsenals were to be taken over by councils; the councils must assume control over all communications; military jurisdiction and justice and all parliamentary bodies were to be replaced by councils; Germany was to be declared a military socialist republic and should at once resume relations with the socialists of all countries and with Russia. In their proclamation, the Spartacists sharply attacked Scheidemann and the SPD and accused them of ruling only to save the German bourgeoisie.[20]

In the nick of time, the SPD learned of this projected meeting and its " party leadership ... took the necessary precautions."[21] The danger was averted by SPD and Soldiers' Councils whom the Spartacists could not refuse to seat. In a very stormy session presided over by Barth, and frequently interrupted by demonstrations and attacks on Ebert, the 1,500 delegates present confirmed the Provisional Government and elected an Executive Council (The Executive Council of the Berlin Workers' and Soldiers' Councils) which was to be co-

---

Not all posts were initially occupied and there were many holdovers from the cabinet of Max. Erzberger enjoyed special rank as head of the armistice commission. There were very soon many changes in this cabinet, some of which will be discussed later on.

20 Proclamation in the *Rote Fahne* (formerly *Berliner Lokal Anzeiger*) November 10, 1918; quoted by Buchner, *op. cit.*, no. 140, pp. 142-43.

21 *Protokoll des Parteitags 1919*, pp. 12-13.

ordinate to the Provisional Government. The Executive Council was to consist of five USPD and five SPD members, and ten delegates of the soldiers' councils. The meeting called for the election of councils all over Germany, the socialization of all means of production and all 'mature' industries. It stressed that militarism was dead and that the Provisional Government should conclude peace; "whatever character the peace treaty were to have, it would be better than the continuation of the immense mass slaughter." [22]

The Provisional Government thus derived its authority from Prince Max, from the Berlin Councils, and from the membership of the SPD and USPD, a situation which was not conducive to internal peace. The government was never able to solve this conflict about the origin in a satisfactory manner.[23]

22 See *Leipziger Volkszeitung*, November 10, 1918, cited by Ahnert, *op. cit.*, pp. 198-200, and the *Vossische Zeitung*, November 11, 1918, cited by Buchner, *op. cit.*, no. 158, pp. 155-57, for some interesting contrasts. The SPD incidentally thought that it had received authorization for a national assembly; cf. *Protokoll des Parteitags 1919*, pp. 12-13. H. Mueller, *op. cit.*, pp. 89-104. The Executive Council soon expanded mysteriously, and eventually none knew who belonged to it. It was presided over by Richard Mueller and Captain von Beerfelde, whose pamphlet *Michel wach auf!* (Berlin, 1919) represents a ne plus ultra in confusion of ideas. Beerfelde was the person responsible for the unauthorized publication of the memoirs of Lichnowsky during the war. On November 12, he was removed from the Executive Council, and this expulsion was soon followed by that of Walz, a notorious agent provocateur, and of Colin Ross, the later intimate of Hitler. The Executive Council exhibited in the five weeks of its existence a degree of inefficiency, waste and unproductiveness, which was a tremendous aid in the growth of opposition and in winning support for the SPD.

23 The SPD eventually denied outright that the Provisional Government had been installed by the Circus Busch meeting. Stampfer, the editor of the *Vorwaerts*, termed this a legend; Ebert had been appointed by Prince Max and the Circus Busch meeting only confirmed this fait accompli. Stampfer went on to say: "After the victory of democracy in Germany, the Social Democracy has become a conservative party in regard to the constitution. . . . That is no novel phenomenon, because the Social Democracy was previously, too, conservative in regard to all existing democratic achievements." Stampfer's article in Drahn and Friedegg (ed.), *Deutscher Revolutionsalmanach 1919*, Berlin, 1919, pp. 73-84.

On November 12, the new government published its program. It decreed the termination of the state of siege and of the restrictions upon the freedom of assemblies, organizations, speech, press, and religion; granted a political amnesty; revoked the war-time compulsory labor acts and the regulations for rural workers, (Gesinde-Ordnung); re-instituted the social legislation suspended on August 4, 1914; and promised to enact an eight-hour-day before the end of the year. It promised unemployment insurance to be financed by the federal government, the states and the local communities, and the extension of sickness and accident insurance, a housing program, and an adequate food supply. Orderly production was to be safeguarded and excesses against individuals and property prevented. All elections were to be based on equal, secret, direct and general franchise for all men and women above twenty and on proportional representation. Regarding the national assembly, further information was to be issued.[24]

Many decrees were subsequently issued by the Provisional Government to enact extensive social legislation. Although they served to satisfy many, especially in the trade-unions, they did not signify Germany's socialization.[25] The struggle between the supporters of politically dominating councils and the SPD had only just been joined.

c. The SPD and the Supreme Command

Various factors aided the SPD in this struggle. It was believed that the Entente would not negotiate with the councils.[26]

---

24 Cited by Ahnert, *op. cit.*, pp. 221-22.

25 For the social legislation of the Provisional Government see: *Die Regierung der Mitte,* and the pamphlet *Nichts getan? Die Arbeit seit dem 9. Nov. 1918,* published between February and May, 1919, by the Arbeitsgemeinschaft fuer staatsbuergerliche und wirtschaftliche Bildung. The texts of the social legislation were presented to the National Assembly as Document No. 215, and appeared in vol. CCCXXXV of the *Verhandlungen,* 141 p. (between pp. 136 and 137.)

26 The Provisional Government repeatedly asked the Entente to declare that they would invade Germany unless the National Assembly were al-

Concern for the food supply and the good will of the agricultural classes restricted the role of council government, a factor which had already been exploited at the Circus Busch meeting. The frequent excesses of various councils and the formation of the Council of Deserters and Unemployed helped rally public support behind the SPD. The imperial civil service and its administrative organizations, too, zealously supported the SPD in its struggle with the USPD and KPD.

At the time of the revolution, it was widely recognized that the civil service would frequently be able to circumvent policies laid down by the cabinet and to thwart democratic and social innovations in the fields of justice, education, communal administration, and trade. Councils made a feeble attempt to guard against this by supervision or direct assumption of administrative duties. It was, however, obviously impossible to replace an organization as strong and large as the German civil service all at once.[27] It was equally impossible to preserve administrative efficiency without the good will of the civil service which was being alienated by the councils. The Executive Council acknowledged these factors by dissolving, on November 12, all temporary bureaus and administrative councils formed since the revolution.[28] Immediate, far-reaching changes in the civil service were thus ruled out. But the introduction of democratic ideas into the administration by long range processes, too, met with considerable opposition. The civil service objected to it, and the SPD, suspicious of the arguments of pro-council adherents and mindful of the preferences of the civil service, failed to advocate civil service reforms

----

lowed to meet and to establish orderly government. See note of the British Chargé to the Secretary of State, November 20, 1918, and note of the American Chargé in Denmark, November 26, 1918; cited in *Foreign Relations of the United States, Paris Peace Conference 1919*, II, 94-95, 103.

27 The SPD widely used this argument in its anti-council publications. *Cf. A.-und S. Raete . . . , passim.*

28 *Vossische Zeitung*, November 12, 1918, cited by Buchner, *op. cit.*, no. 187, p. 181.

with sufficient vigor. By refraining from interfering with the position and influence of the administrative organizations, the SPD strengthened the tendency of the civil service to prefer SPD government to USPD rule. The SPD hence enjoyed the wholehearted support of the civil service in its struggle against the USPD, but allowed the old administrative organizations to flourish under the republic essentially unimpaired.

In the struggle against the USPD, the decisive source of SPD strength was provided by the Supreme Army Command. In an order of the day, Hindenburg, on November, 11, placed himself behind the government of Ebert. In agreement with the government, the Supreme Command wished to secure public safety and domestic peace, and ordered that none might leave his regiment without permission. Obedience and discipline must continue; however, the army was not to fire on German nationals (except looters and criminals.)[29]

The desire to preserve the officers' power of command probably was the major cause for this declaration by the Supreme Army Command. Although the soldiers' councils of the field army did not challenge the power of command in purely military matters, this attitude was not to be trusted; retention of the power of command was needed for quick withdrawal and demobilization, and was therefore favored by these councils; but nobody could predict whether their influence would be effective after demobilization, and whether they could resist the demands of the workers' and soldiers' councils at home after demobilization.

On the other hand, the Provisional Government and the SPD in particular realized that without reliable troops firmly controlled by experienced officers, they could not prevent the victory of the council movement. In a proclamation to the army on November 12, the Provisional Government therefore accepted the proffered hand of the Supreme Command and declared that the government wanted the speediest possible demobilization of the troops and their return home. This could

29 Quoted by Ahnert, *op. cit.*, pp. 217-18.

only be effected in accordance with an ordered plan; unorganized reforms would only lead to chaos and hunger. The Supreme Command was therefore instructed to issue the following orders to the troops: relations between officers and men must be built on mutual trust; officers were to continue in their position as superiors; military discipline and order must be preserved; the soldiers' councils were to have only an advisory voice in questions of furloughs, food, disciplinary measures, and should endeavor to prevent disorder and mutiny; officers and men were to share equally in food, pay increases for field services, and the like; only in self-defense was the army to fire on fellow-citizens.[30]

These public orders provoked immediate opposition among various soldiers' councils at home.[31] But even though the abolition of the powers of command remained one of the foremost demands raised by all councils wherever they acquired power, the SPD leaders and the army never wavered in their mutual understanding to preserve the power of command, in return for the prevention of chaos at home and protection from the dictatorship of the councils.

When it proved to be impossible to save the imperial army from complete disintegration, a decree of December 12, 1918, signed by Ebert and Haase, provided for the formation of free-corps on the basis of unrestricted power of command. Ostensibly created for the protection of the Eastern frontier, the free-corps were kept free of republican and democratic influences.[32] The attempts of the Executive Council to form in-

30 *Berliner Tageblatt*, November 13, 1918, cited by Buchner, *op. cit.*, no. 209, p. 195.

31 *Cf. ibid.*, nos. 250 and a to c, 251, pp. 223-26.

32 *Cf.* Maercker, *op. cit.*, pp. 27-65. Maercker firmly believed that there was no relationship between conditions in pre-revolutionary Germany and the success of the leftist propaganda. But in the formation of one of the most widely used free-corps (Freiwillige Landjaegercorps, which later became Reichswehrbrigade No. 16), he carefully avoided the inherent faults of the old army; he introduced the closest possible integration between

stead a red army were quickly suppressed because the existing troop formations might resent this as an expression of distrust of their own reliability.[33]

The close harmony between the Supreme Command and the SPD was disturbed only once, when, in December, 1918, the Congress of Councils voted unanimously to vest the supreme command in the Provisional Government, to abolish rank insignia and the carrying of arms off duty, and to establish the rule that all officers were to be elected by the troops. (These were the so-called Hamburg decrees.) In a bitter protest to Ebert, Hindenburg stated that he could not enforce these decrees which were contrary to what Ebert had promised him.[34] But Ebert simply ignored the decrees and so did the army. The whole problem was finally resolved in favor of the officers by the decree of January 19, 1919, which restricted the activities of the soldiers' councils and restored the military power of command. The statute for the Provisional Reichswehr of February 25, 1919, finally secured the position of the officers' corps beyond any further attempts to tamper with it.[35]

---

artillery and infantry by way of mixed corps; even the smallest units were made self-sufficient in machine-guns, batteries, food supply, etc.; new regulations regarding salutes were introduced, and trustees of the troops supervised the food supply; *ibid.*, pp. 45-53.

33 WTB November 13, 1918, government dispatch, cited by Buchner, *op. cit.*, no. 210c, p. 196. The Executive Council had asked for two thousand trained members of the social democratic parties for a red army; *ibid.*, no. 210, p. 195.

34 Quoted in *Deutscher Geschichtskalender, ibid.*, I, 82, dated December 27, 1918.

35 Testifying at the Dolchstoss trial, and after Ebert's death, Groener declared under oath that Hindenburg, Groener and Ebert had secretly agreed to restore the power of command, to destroy the power of the councils and to elect a national assembly. *Cf.* Beckmann, *op. cit.*, pp. 103-11. Although there was no evidence to support Groener, many historians have accepted his word in this respect; among them Halperin and F. L. Neumann. It must however be pointed out that while the question of such a secret pact was of highest interest to the biographer of Ebert, and while Ebert was suspect as an intriguer from the days of Prince Max onward, the information contained in Groener's testimony would be of interest in the

d. The Conference of Prime Ministers

On the morrow of the revolution, the SPD was rather unsure of its ability to influence the fate of the revolution; prudence and caution were imposed by the lack of armed strength which, it was hoped, the return of the field army would remedy. However, early conflicts between the Executive Council and the Provisional Government about their respective jurisdiction arose whenever a new appointment had to be made, or whenever the national assembly was mentioned. They soon ended with the complete success of the Executive Council. The Provisional Government had to agree that, for the present, all power rested with the Workers' and Soldiers' Councils, and that the Provisional Government held office subject to the pleasure of the Executive Council.[36]

---

study of the revolution only, if one assumed that Ebert had the power to sway his party unreservedly to his own liking, and if the history of the revolution would not in itself throw any light on the situation. That there was agreement between Ebert and the Supreme Command about purposes and aims had always been a matter of public record. Their decrees and the events following the adoption of the Hamburg decrees were never secret. If it can be shown that, during the course of the revolution, the two cooperated in conformity with such an agreement, the knowledge about the existence of such an agreement would not materially alter any appraisal of the situation. And if there was no realization of such program or no attempt to realize it, the interpretation of the revolution would also remain unaffected by the revelation of such a pact. Now, as a matter of public record, Hindenburg and Ebert had agreed about co-operation on certain objectives, and these objectives had been achieved to a remarkable degree. Since the daily contacts between Ebert and Hindenberg or Groener were maintained over a secret telephone wire, it is possible that Groener only jumped to the conclusion that their objectives had also been the result of a secret intrigue. A. Rosenberg, *A History of the German Republic*, pp. 324-26, pointed out other inconsistencies in Groener's testimony; he may have been mistaken about the mode of this agreement as well. H. Mueller, *op. cit.*, pp. 75-76, 172, was probably right that no pact was needed since there was evident agreement between the two to prevent disorder and to elect a national assembly, an agreement which had always been open and public.

36 Official text of this agreement was published in *Deutsche Allgemeine Zeitung*, November 23, 1918, cited by Buchner, *op. cit.*, no. 393, pp. 319-20.

However, the assumption of dictatorial powers by the Berlin Councils was not approved outside of Berlin. The revolutionary governments which had sprung up in the various German states were not prepared to entrust their own powers to Berlin; particularism had only been strengthened by the revolution and by the ideological differences between the various local governments. Munich, Darmstadt, Karlsruhe, Stuttgart, and other cities, protested against the Executive Council, and Bavaria and Wuerttemberg threatened to oppose the Berlin councils at the cost of secession, if need be. Unless the central government in Berlin was strong enough to enforce the principles of a federated democracy and of a national assembly, they threatened to secede from the Reich.[37]

Thus, although its immediate struggle for power with the Executive Council resulted in a set-back for the Provisional Government, it found an early and unsuspected ally in the revolutionary governments of the German states. Federalism could thrive only under democracy.

In order to clarify the future relationship between the central government and the states and to establish a common basis for action, a conference of the prime ministers of the various states had been called to Berlin for November 25. In his opening address to the prime ministers, Ebert declared that the socialist republic had succeeded the monarchy; the Provisional Government held the executive power, but the councils wielded political power. It was now necessary to establish a provisional relationship between the states and the central government which was to last until the convocation of the national assembly.[38] Ebert won the support of the prime ministers of

37 *Muenchener Neueste Nachrichten*, November 20; *Vossische Zeitung*, same date; *Deutsche Allgemeine Zeitung*, November 24; *Vorwaerts*, November 23; all cited by Buchner, *op. cit.*, nos. 362 b to d, pp. 299-302. These comments were also directed against a speech by R. Mueller to the Executive Council, held on November 20, *ibid.*, pp. 295-98.

38 Ebert, *op. cit.*, II, 112-20.

Wuerttemberg, Baden, Hamburg and Braunschweig for an immediate national assembly. Barth wanted an assembly only after a congress of councils had decided on the problem, and Haase and Eisner favored delay. The conference adopted no formal resolutions, but in his closing address Ebert, applauded by his listeners, declared that as a result of the conference all German 'tribes' now supported the new German republic, that German unity had been accepted as paramount and that the states would not foster separatism; the national assembly would be convened as early as possible, but until then the councils were to continue to represent the popular will.[39]

The Conference of Prime Ministers meant a decisive advance for the cause of the national assembly, even though its deliberations resulted in an informal agreement to preserve the federal character of Germany and to sacrifice the hope of a unitary state as the crowning achievement of German unification.

The repercussions of this change in the fortunes of the SPD were soon evident. In a stormy session of the Executive Council on November 28, which featured repeated physical attacks on speakers and at times resulted in complete bedlam, Molkenbuhr pleaded that the Executive Council had been formed in complete ignorance of the extremely chaotic conditions in regard to the food supply, raw materials, and military affairs; the Executive Council was only a trustee acting until the convention of a national assembly. But other members launched a sharp attack on that body for usurping the rights to supervise the government, and for bringing distrust and ill-fame upon the councils and upon Berlin. After a hand to hand

39 See *Deutsche Allgemeine Zeitung*, November 26 and *Berliner Tageblatt*, November 25, both quoted by Buchner, *op. cit.*, nos. 418 and a to b, pp. 339-344. At this meeting Eisner had sharply attacked Solf and Erzberger, and within a few days, Solf was sacrificed to Eisner's will. He was succeeded by Count Brockdorff-Rantzau. Various councils and the Executive Council added their voice to that of Eisner who thought that the Entente would be antagonized, if forced to negotiate with men, discredited by their participation in the old regime. See *ibid.*, nos. 447, 447 d and e, pp. 364-65.

scuffle, Scheidemann took the floor and gloatingly told the Council that Hindenburg and Groener had assured him only on the day before that they would support the Provisional Government. The meeting finally appointed a committee to examine the charges brought against it, to restore the confidence of the Southern states, and to counteract the deterioration of public esteem for the council system to which the Executive Council had contributed so much.[40]

e. The Congress of Councils

At the time of the formation of a provisional government and at the conference of the prime ministers, it had been suggested to call a congress of all councils which should thrash out the problems that agitated the various political parties. This (first) Congress of Councils met in Berlin from December 16 to 24, 1918. The elections to this congress resulted in a complete SPD victory.[41]

Ebert opened the Congress with a flaming defense of democracy and an incisive attack upon class rule and restricted franchise. Richard Mueller defended the Executive Council which was being attacked only because it represented those who since 1916 had prepared the revolution. The Executive Council, he said, has so far remained the only concrete result of the revolution. He agreed that the revolution had anticipated the revolutionary preparations, but defended fervently the rule of the councils because they alone could prevent a counter-revolution. Kautsky supported Ebert's plan of a national assembly because no government could long rule in opposition to the majority of the people.

40 *Berliner Tageblatt*, November 29, cited by Buchner, *op. cit.*, no. 466, pp. 380-97.

41 Its chairmen were: Leinert (SPD); Seeger (USPD); and Gromolka (Front-Soldier). For the proceedings, see Leinert (ed.), *Allgemeiner Kongress der Arbeiter und Soldatenraete 16. bis 24. December 1918. Stenographische Berichte.* 442 delegates were finally seated at the Congress, but at times more than this number actually cast votes.

The idea of a national assembly was supported by Dittmann, who declared that it was needed in order to embody in a constitution the revolutionary changes so far effected. " We must act in accord with conditions as they happen to be and not as we would like them to be," he declared. " The leaders must be tools of the masses. They certainly have the right to win the masses of the people to their own opinions, but a policy in opposition to the will of the masses is impossible." These opening skirmishes resulted in the complete defeat of the supporters of the Executive Council. Only twenty members of the Congress voted in favor of a motion accusing the Provisional Government of undermining the council system. Instead, the Congress vested all powers in the Provisional Government under the supervision of a Central Council.

On December 19, the issue of the national assembly versus the Council system was finally debated. Cohen declared that the National Assembly was needed to end disorganization and to raise production. The councils could never express public opinion as a whole and Marx never had advocated a Bolshevist dictatorship. Socialism could not be decreed by force or in opposition to the bourgeoisie which could cripple Germany by strikes. The allies had refused to negotiate with the councils, but their good will was needed to supply Germany with food, raw materials, and the like. Daeumig strongly opposed the views of Cohen. He pleaded that a dictatorship has nothing to do with a police state, nor did council rule have to imitate the Russian example. He asked that the congress declare itself a national assembly. The old powers still ruled Germany as officials, and a national assembly would only perpetuate the rule of the capitalist minority. Haase tried to reconcile the two viewpoints; the Provisional Government had already agreed to the national assembly, only the date was still subject to controversy. He asked for a late date, so that German soldiers could be demobilized and the new frontiers of Germany first be determined. Haase also expressed the thought that a national assembly and the council system were not two mutually exclusive concepts. Scheidemann strongly attacked the councils; to retain them would be to ruin German industry and trade, the Reich and the people.

By a vote of 400 to 50, the Congress decided to hold elections for a National Assembly on January 19, 1919. An all SPD Central Council of twenty-seven members was appointed to assist the Provisional Government, but a vote of 290 to 115 deprived it of the right to pass on every individual measure of the Provisional Government. A vote of 344 to 98 rejected the suggestion that the National Assembly should make the council system the constitutional basis of Germany. Thus, from the ranks of the councils themselves, the policies of the SPD had been approved; a democratically elected National Assembly was to be entrusted with Germany's future.[42]

f. The Disruption of the Coalition between the SPD and USPD

In spite of the Congress of Councils, the Spartacists resolved to oppose the elections to the National Assembly. Among the USPD too, many of the members, and particularly the revolutionary foremen—who considered themselves the pioneers of the revolution—preferred council government. Opposition to SPD policies had been stimulated among the left by many factors such as the reactionary putsch of December 6 which culminated in proclaiming Ebert as president; the bloody clash of rival demonstrators on that day; the oath taken by all troops to support the Provisional Government of Ebert; the restoration of the military power of command; the return of large bodies of armed soldiers to Berlin; the pro-SPD propaganda spread among them and Ebert's ill-chosen words addressed to them; [43] the formation of the free-corps; and the

42 See *Deutscher Geschichtskalender, ibid.*, I, 202-47, for the essential parts of the proceedings.

43 See Ebert, *op. cit.*, II, 127-30. Ebert had told them on December 20, 1918, that "no enemy has vanquished you.... Never have men achieved or suffered more." In regard to SPD propaganda among the troops, the

restrictions imposed upon the functions of the councils. On the other hand, the excesses of the leftists and the councils, their confiscation of bourgeois and SPD newspapers; unauthorized arrests like that of Stinnes and Thyssen in Muehlheim on December 8, 1918; the wild newspaper campaign against the National Assembly and the SPD; the distribution of arms among the civilian population; the general insecurity which made even members of the government quasi prisoners; the presence of criminal elements, who had escaped from prisons during the revolutionary upheaval, within the revolutionary Sicherheitswehr and the People's Marine Division, could not be tolerated much longer. Due to these conditions, Berlin had become a " seething overflowing witches cauldron ". The government had sunk so low that it had to accept private money gifts in order to provide even a minimum of protection for its citizens.[44]

---

following pamphlets and leaflets are of interest: *Die Augen Auf!* wherein the SPD claimed credit for the revolution and asked the returning soldiers to support the government and the National Assembly in opposition to the leftists and their rule of force; *Willkommen Daheim!* addressed to returning prisoners of war, probably an official publication issued in 1919; it stressed that the National Assembly was the main demand of the revolution and that it had now been achieved; *Deutschland als freie Volksrepublik*, published by the SPD and addressed to the troops; it justified the overthrow of the monarchy with the usual grievances of the soldiers; it promised an extensive program of social reform and asked them to join the party; the pamphlet *Was ist in Deutschland geschehen?*, distributed by the Zentralstelle fuer Kriegs und Zivilgefangene, was later made 'the subject of an interpellation in the National Assembly for improper political propaganda by the government; see *Verhandlungen*, CCCXXX, 2875 ff.

44 Anton Fischer, *Die Revolutionskommandantur Berlin*, pp. 4-10. Fischer, a former Franciscan friar and professor of theology, was the successor of Otto Wels as military commander of Berlin during the Spartacist riots. The main sources for the period from the Volksmarineaufstand to the Spartacist riots inclusive are, in addition to Fischer, R. Mueller, *Der Buergerkrieg in Deutschland*, and *Vom Kaiserreich zur Republik*; Barth, *op. cit.*; Emil Eichhorn, *Eichhorn ueber die Januar Ereignisse*; Bernstein, *Revolution*; and in particular the *Bericht des Untersuchungsausschusses der verfassungsgebenden Preussischen Landesversammlung ueber die Januar Un-*

The attempts to restore order had been delayed because of the absence of reliable troops. The establishment of the Sicherheitswehr, the Republikanische Soldatenwehr, and of the Volksmarinedivision in Berlin had failed to provide the needed instrument for order, in spite of the efforts of Wels and Eichhorn, the military commander and the chief of police in Berlin after November 9. But after the middle of December, reliable formations of the old army were stationed near Berlin, and towards the end of December, the first free-corps were expected to be ready and at the disposition of the government.

After the middle of December, the willingness of the government to tolerate these conditions was therefore bound to diminish. And first among the steps to be taken was the dissolution of the revolutionary corps favorable to the extreme left.

Among these, the Volksmarine Division had provided considerable trouble for some time. It had been formed to protect the government, but although prompt in its collection of pay, it failed to provide the support needed by the government in the struggle of rival factions. From a very small force, it had rapidly expanded, because it was able to provide food, quarters and pay to all comers. This division had been stationed in adjuncts to the Royal Palace in Berlin, but it had lately fallen down on its job of guarding the palace.[45]

---

ruhen 1919 in Berlin; Verfassungsgebende Preussische Landesversammlung; Sammlung der Drucksachen, vol. XV, no. 4121 a to d, pp. 7669-8191. *Cf.* Noske, *op. cit.,* and Maercker, *op. cit.*

45 *Bericht des Untersuchungsausschusses* . . . , no. 4121a, pp. 7669 ff., accused them of looting the castle. But the press repeatedly brought reports of arrests of looters by the division; for example *Berliner Lokal Anzeiger,* November 14, cited by Buchner, *op. cit.,* no. 239, p. 216. While the responsibility of the Division was thus doubtful, conditions in the castle were intolerable. Three commanders sometimes succeeded each other in one day, in order to give everybody a chance to loot. Kurt Heinig, *Hohenzollern; Wilhelm II und sein Haus,* pp. 64-67, denied that there had been any wilfull destruction in the castle before the suppression of the Division on December 24. Neither the food supply, nor the wine-cellar, nor the linen chambers had ever been raided and it was probable that the vandalism was just due to

There had been some trouble with the Division over pay as early as December 18, but an agreement had been reached that the People's Marine Division should reduce its strength to 600 men by January 1, and that it should receive its back pay upon delivering the keys of the castle to the military commander of Berlin, Otto Wels. On the December 23, a delegation of the Marine Division called at the offices of Barth carrying a heavy case of keys. Barth telephoned to Wels and instructed him to pay the salaries. But Wels refused unless the delegation reported to his office in accordance with the letter of the agreement; otherwise, he would pay the money (RM. 80,000) only upon receiving instructions from Ebert himself.[46]

The delegation then proceeded to look for Ebert whom they could not find, although he had been in the chancellery all day. They therefore occupied the chancellery, cut off telephone communications, and waited. They also sent some of their members to Wels' office, but on the way, two of them were shot and killed. Rather enraged by now, they took their money by force, arrested Wels, and took him to their quarters.[47]

At nine o'clock in the evening, Ebert telephoned General Groener over a secret wire and asked to be liberated by what-

---

playful or vengeful visitors. It was quite possible that the actual charges levied against the Division were incorrect; the SPD was never choosy in its pretexts to fight the left. This would also explain the impatience and resistance of the Division to subordinate itself to the government.

46 Barth, *op. cit.*, pp. 98-107. Barth gave the text of his telephone conversation with Wels, but is so obviously unconvincing, that one cannot follow the practice of most historians and accept it as genuine. Like Fischer and other writers of USPD and SPD, Barth was obviously trying to write the way he imagined a well educated and experienced statesman might, trying to be very polite and persuasive. He endeavored to reveal in every word how bored he was with the stupidity of the reader which necessitated the discussion of such self-evident things. Although the content of the conversation given by Barth may be correct, it formed obviously an unsuccessful attempt of re-styling for his own purposes.

47 Barth, *ibid.*, thought they arrested Wels so that he could prove his innocence in the shooting.

ever troops were available.[48] In the next few hours, the chancellery and the palace, already occupied by the rebellious Marine Division, were surrounded by government troops. Barth learned of these measures and made strenuous efforts to cancel them. He succeeded in having the chancellery cleared of both parties, but Wels was still a prisoner in the quarters of the Division and was thought to be in danger of his life. Ebert tried to prevent an assault by the troops upon the castle,[49] but he was amenable to Groener's argument that the morale of the troops required action and that the sincerity of the government in suppressing the leftists must be demonstrated.[50]

On the morning of December 24, the troops opened artillery fire upon the castle. As a result Wels was freed and the Marine Division agreed to abide by the terms of its erstwhile agreement. But the government was unable to suppress the division completely because, as a military action, the operation proved to be a failure. The noise attracted crowds who intermingled freely with the soldiers. Many of them simply went home and a sort of public truce was concluded. The government could only bow gracefully before it had lost the last soldier who could obey the cease-fire order. The net result of this operation was the complete disintegration of the last military formations presently at the disposal of the government and increased Spartacist and leftist opposition. If the leftist did not attempt to overthrow the government before the arrival of the free-corps a week later, it was because, in the opinion of General Groener,

48 Groener's testimony at the Dolchstoss trial; Beckmann, *op. cit.*, pp. 103 ff.

49 *Ibid.*; Barth, *ibid.*, thought that the war ministry refused to heed Ebert's order and insisted on a cabinet order instead.

50 After the fighting, the war ministry and the government accused each other of responsibility; it is however probable, that the counter-orders of Ebert came too late to be communicated to the commanders on the scene of the struggle. See Eichhorn, *op. cit.*, pp. 46-55; R. Mueller, *Buergerkrieg*, p. 8.

the Christmas spirit which had caused the government's troops to evaporate in front of the castle affected the leftists too.[51]

No doubt the Provisional Government had bungled the entire affair, but it was clear that no government could allow itself to be imprisoned by its own troops because of a financial squabble. The Central Council therefore exonerated the government, after Wels had resigned his post in favor of Fischer. The USPD, however, objected strenuously to the decision of the Central Council. The USPD decided that, in view of the attitude of the SPD since the day of the revolution, it could no longer co-operate with the SPD in the government, and its members resigned. The resulting vacancies were filled by SPD members. A government unencumbered by the USPD thus appeared, and this new government, freed of the influence of pro-council members, was able to concentrate on the second phase of the struggle against the councils: the destruction of their political strongholds within the provincial and city governments throughout Germany.

51 Groener's testimony, Beckmann, *ibid.*; Fischer, *op. cit.*, pp. 41-48.

CHAPTER X

CIVIL WAR

a. THE MILITARY CAMPAIGN AGAINST THE LEFT

THE resignation of the USPD members from the cabinet, the verdict of public opinion rendered by the elections to the first Congress of Councils, and the arrival in Berlin of the first free-corps strong enough to bar the successful introduction of the council system enabled the government to proceed against the leftists with relative freedom. At the same time, the leftists had been freed of the restraints which participation in the government and political responsibility had imposed on them.

The result was " a mad, criminal, internecine war causing the most severe political and economic damage to the empire and the people, and undermining confidence in the working class and its political organizations. In Germany's hour of fate, a large section of the social-democratically minded proletariat and its leaders failed ... Lack of economic insight, political narrow-mindedness, and the commonplace triumphed over the vital political and economic necessities of the people ... A mad mangling took place." [1]

A few days after the USPD had withdrawn from the Provisional Government, the first test of strength between the two groups occurred.

The incident was provided by the USPD chief of police in Berlin, Emil Eichhorn. Upon instructions of his party he had failed to resign from his post when all other USPD members had left the government. Immediately pressure was exerted to remove him from office, and he was publicly accused of maladministration of funds and of illegally arming the workers from the police arsenal.[2] Eichhorn, however, refused to resign.

---

[1] Noske, *op. cit.*, pp. 59-60.

[2] *Bericht des Untersuchungsausschusses.* The pertinent documents regarding the Spartacist riot of January, 1919, are in this collection and in R. Mueller, *op. cit.* This commission was forced to conclude that Eichhorn was personally scrupulously honest. Fischer, *op. cit.*, pp. 54 ff., thought very highly of Eichhorn, but agreed that he should have resigned.

Therefore, on January 4, 1919, the Prussian government dismissed him.

Eichhorn, however, thought that before accepting dismissal, he ought to consult the leaders of the revolutionary proletariat and the revolutionary foremen who had appointed him to office.[3]

In the discussion of the Eichhorn case, the USPD and the KPD at first refused to exploit the incident by calling for a revolution; they feared that they would not be able to hold on to the government after conquering it.[4] But they were loath to allow the incident to pass without protest. And in order to express their protest against the dismissal of Eichhorn, they called upon the population to demonstrate in the streets of Berlin on January 5.

The mobs thus called into the streets were under the influence of criminal elements and adventurers [5] who occupied police headquarters and newspaper buildings throughout Berlin. Encouraged by these demonstrations of the 'popular will' and by rumors of troops in Spandau joining the fresh revolt, the leaders of the USPD, the KPD and of the foremen approved, by a vote of seventy-two to six, the immediate declaration of war against the Ebert regime to the bitter end. They elected a revolutionary committee of fifty-two; Ledebour, Liebknecht and Scholze were elected chairmen.[6] But the demonstrations of

3 Eichhorn, *op. cit.*, pp. 67 ff.

4 R. Mueller, *Buergerkrieg*, pp. 25-31.

5 *Bericht des Untersuchungsausschusses, ibid.* It is perhaps of interest to note how Fischer, *op. cit.*, p. 3, described the role of the mob in the revolution of November 9: "Thus a new age came, covered and burdened with the curse and the backwash of the old era, dirty and unimpressive like a premature birth; too weak to live, too strong to die. The Berliners, anxious for sensations, had a sensation for their over-sensitized war nerves, joined it, admired it, only to turn within a few weeks back to the new sensation of the reawakening military and police state."

6 R. Mueller, *ibid.*, pp. 32-35, opposed these decisions. He claimed that the newspaper buildings had been occupied by agents-provocateur, and that it only indicated the willingness of the government to enter a head-on struggle. Therefore, not radical, but moderate demands should be made. Eichhorn, *ibid.*, pp. 67-84, supported this appraisal.

January 5 and the following day ended peacefully. The radical leaders showed little initiative and resolution in utilizing the masses. They restricted themselves to demonstrations and to harangues to the crowds.[7]

In the meantime, Noske had assumed the Supreme Military Command.[8] Convinced that only well-disciplined troops could score any successes against armed masses, he proceeded to apply this strategy on a large scale. Some time was allowed to pass in negotiation, before Noske struck. With heavy artillery, one building after the other in Berlin was reconquered; laws were invoked which the government had long since abrogated; the KPD was forced to withdraw from the struggle by January 10, and three days later, the USPD called off its general strike. On the night of January 11, amidst the applause of the population, the free-corps occupied Berlin.[9]

The January riots had demonstrated the strength of the government and its willingness to use it. Some of the ablest leaders of the left were killed in the struggle; notable among them were Liebknecht and Luxemburg. The struggle broke the back of the power of the Spartacists in Berlin, and they made no subsequent attempt to interfere with the elections to the National Assembly on January 19.[10]

Outside of Berlin, however, dissatisfaction with the meager results of the revolution was still increasing. The assassination

7 Noske, *op. cit.*, pp. 69-70, agreed that only the inability of the Spartacist leaders to exploit the situation and to use the desperate masses of armed proletarians insured the success of the government.

8 *Ibid.*, pp. 65-68. *Protokoll des Parteitags 1919*, p. 203: "Somebody had to do the job and I understood perfectly well that it will mean for me that I must go through the German revolution as a bloodhound." It was a popular saying among the leftists that there were "Schweinehunde, Bluthunde und Noskehunde."

9 Maercker, *op. cit.*, pp. 65 ff. R. Mueller, *ibid.*, pp. 85 ff., bitterly lamented the putschist tendencies of the Spartacists who numbered only 1000 intellectuals out of touch with the masses, but who discredited everything the leftists stood for.

10 H. Mueller, *op. cit.*, pp. 246, 270.

of Liebknecht and Luxemburg, the decree of January 19, restoring the power of command to the officers' corps, and the rigorous measures taken by the government to dissolve soldiers' councils evoked strong displeasure in leftist circles. Many among them thought that the gains of the revolution would be small indeed, if the old administration were left intact, the economic interests of workers advanced no further than had happened so far, and the bourgeois parties permitted again to play a leading role in the government. The SPD government championed in particular the preservation of the old administration and the restoration of the power of command to the officers, while the soldiers' councils resisted these policies in many parts of Germany. Strikes followed each other as a means to coerce the central government, and the political demands of the strikers included the dissolution of the free-corps, recognition of the councils, the formation of a republican army, and the grant of an amnesty. It was perhaps fortunate for the central government that there was no united movement of resistance; the center of rebellion shifted constantly, and no attempt at coordinated or common action was made.

All through the first half of 1919, in Saxony, in the Ruhr, at the coast, in Berlin, Central Germany, and Bavaria, the attempt was made to extend the revolutionary gains. And all through the first half of 1919, the government suppressed these attempts with armed force. One city after another was taken from USPD control: Erfurt, Gotha, Halle an der Saale, Merseburg, Zeitz, Magdeburg, Braunschweig, Dresden, Leipzig, Munich, Bremen, Berlin, Hamburg, Baden, Eisenach, and others. In these measures, the government of Scheidemann enjoyed the full support of the civil service, the administration, the courts and of the National Assembly.

In this campaign, extensive use was made of the free-corps, whose only political dogma was, supposedly, anti-Bolshevism. But all officers, who declared themselves to be republican in sentiment, were weeded out by these corps because either they had always been republican and therefore had practiced deceit in the old army, or they had formerly been monarchists and had then changed their conviction faster than good character would allow.[11] The conduct of these free-corps was frequently extremely objectionable.[12] They exceeded in brutality and license anything that local USPD or communist councils were to commit even under severe pressure. The President of Oldenburg felt constrained to write about the behaviour of their officers: " The old professional generals were brutal, but they had tradition and that gave them a certain reserve and moderation; but the new parvenu generals only aped them in clearing their throats and spitting, and inherited only their brutality and not their reserve." [13]

b. The Propaganda Campaign Against the Left

But the military power of the free-corps was insufficient to proceed simultaneously to all various parts of Germany where USPD or council government had taken hold. Economic sanctions—for example, cutting off the food supply—were used, and an extensive propaganda campaign was conducted against the USPD, the KPD and against the councils.

The government and the SPD exploited the policies and the excesses of the leftists to play upon the fears of the public, and

11 Maercker, *op. cit.*, pp. 50, 65. The appeals to enlist in these free-corps declared, for instance, that "within our body politic, too, the Bolshevist movement makes further progress. Disregarding the nameless misery which Bolshevism has brought upon the Russian people, certain conscienceless elements prepare anew the bloody struggle against the government and the convening National Assembly.... If a terrorist minority succeeds in seizing power by force...the fate of our people will be hunger, enslavement, lack of right and work;" Appeal of Noske and the Central Council, cited by *Deutscher Geschichtskalender, ibid.*, I, 421-22.

12 Maercker, *op. cit.*, pp. 91 ff. Maercker stressed that the frequently objectionable searching of passengers and trains was purely bluff; no effective control of the entire civilian population could possibly have been effected. In Berlin, the measures of preparedness included anti-aircraft defenses and pursuit planes. Measures like these contributed of course to stirring up suspicions and rumors. Noske, *op. cit.*, pp. 91, 169 ff., agreed that the behavior of the troops was such that their mere appearance would produce protests.

13 Quoted by R. Mueller, *ibid.*, pp. 107-108.

the leftists provided them with more than enough cause to arouse the public. The leftists diligently searched for the choicest bits of Marxian terminology to hurl at the SPD and at the government; the campaigns waged by the USPD *Freiheit* and the KPD *Die Rote Fahne* exceeded anything that had heretofore been witnessed in Germany. Strikes, particularly in the mining districts and on the railroads, demonstrations, revolutionary attempts, and the confiscation of newspapers were employed without discrimination by the left, and provoked the opposition of many who would otherwise have favored USPD objectives. " Where the USPD ruled," the minister of war Noske told a SPD party congress, " only their will was valid. In dozens of cases they declared a state of siege, took hostages, stole from us one paper after another, in dozens of cases suppressed bourgeois papers. These selfsame people cry murder, when in the defense, we were occasionally a little rough on them ". (. . . wenn es ihnen an den Kragen geht.)[14]

Since the left, by preference, resorted to political strikes in order to win concessions, the SPD made strenuous efforts to demonstrate that political strikes were self-defeating to the highest degree.

" Shall Germany become a mad house? " asked a *Vorwaerts* pamphlet in 1919, and warned the workers that strikes would only destroy their own wealth. The KPD sponsored the repudiation of the war debts but, warned the SPD, this would affect the workers most, because it was their savings that would be wiped out. In addition it would destroy the financial foundation of all social security institutions.[15] Strikes were a crime

---

14 Speech of Noske, *Protokoll des Parteitags 1919*, pp. 200 ff. Among the causes which motivated some of these strikes, one may be recorded. A strike in the ' Oberschlesischer Berg und Huettenmaennischer Verein', which had just been settled by negotiation, was reopened when the published text of the agreement negotiated was found to contain a printer's error. The second strike proved to be rather difficult to settle. *Berliner Tageblatt*, November 27, 1918, cited by Buchner, *op. cit.*, no. 442, p. 357.

15 *Soll Deutschland ein Tollhaus werden?*, Vorwaerts, no date.

against all socialist hopes; to consider wage demands as superior to all other interests was to degrade the revolution, declared another pamphlet in 1918.[16] " A word to Germany's grave diggers " warned in 1918, that the conditions in Russia were not due to the war, but to Bolshevist rule, and that similar consequences would result in Germany unless the entire people co-operated on a democratic basis.[17] Rudolf Wissell, who had joined the Provisional Government after the resignation of the USPD, warned that strikes would only undermine the ability of Germany to pay for her food imports. Only work could prevent the inevitable economic collapse, only more and cheaper work would restore German prosperity.[18] " You would not kill the hen that lays the golden egg. That means: you must not paralyze the activities of industry and agriculture, trade and the professions, by making demands that no capitalist can fulfill," declared a *Vorwaerts* pamphlet. Buildings did not build themselves, bread did not bake itself; only hard work could restore prosperity.[19] Another *Vorwaerts* pamphlet told the pro-letariat that class-struggle presented a statement of an eco-nomic fact and not an invitation to use arms and fists. The un-Marxian conditions of general strike would only produce a " non-socialist, undemocratic dictatorship of the councils on the basis of the Russian example, a threat to the republic and productive of the greatest misery." Socialism could not pro-duce a Schlaraffia; only energetic, purposeful and productive work, only labor could produce wealth and prevent misery.[20]

" In political strikes, a worker's duty does not lie with his fellow worker, but rather, as a party member, his duty lies

16 *Sozialismus ist Arbeit. Ein Aufruf der Regierung.* No date.

17 Quotation is the subtitle of *Gedeih oder Verderb?* written by a ' Social Democrat', probably in 1918.

18 *Sollen wir zugrunde gehen?*, January, 1919(?).

19 *Allgemeine Arbeitspflicht*, 1918 (?). The USPD proposal for a six-hour work day to provide jobs for the returning veterans was referred to by the *Vorwaerts* as the "no-hour-day." *Vorwaerts*, November 21, 1918.

20 *Generalstreik und sozialdemokratische Arbeit*, 1919.

with his fellow party member. He therefore has to ask solely: what position does my party take in the problem raised by the strike? And thus, and thus alone, should he determine his attitude. In such cases the principle of general solidarity of the workers is hence excluded. Party solidarity alone is to be considered ... In political strikes directed against one's own government, the striker is a traitor to this his own party ... To prevent them, he is duty-bound by honor." [21] And Eduard David agreed that "we now live in an exceptional situation of the most terrible sort, and no analogy with previous conditions is possible. What could ... be considered a justified means of struggle in peace-time, cannot now, when our people stands at the rim of an abyss and when this means will so terribly increase the danger of falling into this abyss [speaker was interrupted at this point]. No, you have to consider this. The right to strike ... is limited by the vital rights of the people. When the strike turns against the life of the community ... it would be a crime to make use of that means." [22]

Scheidemann declared at the height of the strikes in the Ruhr basin, in February 1919: "Today I wish to reveal to you the grave danger from within. I want to tell you quite frankly that the young republic, perhaps already in a very short time, will face the most serious disturbances, if not collapse. The Reich, its food supply, its productive capacity are all most seriously threatened, not by unyielding enemies, but by fellow citizens, by Germans who now, after the termination of the war, wish to complete what fate has fortunately spared our country ... We wish to state quite openly, the Reich will collapse within perhaps a very short time, if we do not succeed resolutely to put a stop to craze and crime in the Ruhr basin. In the first months of the revolution, excesses were excusable

21 H. Mueller, "Die Beteiligung an politischen Streiks," *Neue Zeit*, vol. XXXVII, pt. 2, no. 1, April 4, 1919, pp. 6-10.

22 *Verhandlungen*, CCCXXVI, 648-49, March 10, 1919. *Cf.* A. Franke, *Nach Eden oder Golgotha?*, Berlin, (1919 ?).

... I do not think of condemning ... the workers' and soldiers' councils ... and to hold them responsible for all evil that has occurred in our country; on the contrary, I wish to state explicitly that much good and useful work has been done by the workers' and soldiers' councils ... Today, I only wish to touch upon a category of transgressions, which run like a red thread through the months of the revolution and ... make one blush for shame ... I mean ... the violations of the freedom of the press ... the robbery of papers of various opinions, their transformation or suppression in order to censor the political ideas of some opposing point of view. Bolshevism is possible only in a nation which has been debarred from access to different opinions by force and which has been exposed without interference to forceful indoctrination in the gospel of terror. And, only in a nation whose information is thus one-sided, may such an inconceivable confusion of ideas occur that people can believe a new world will arise if you simply demolish the old one, and that an old world-wide system of economy can be replaced by a new one by a handful of confused fanatics and dreamers, whose only proof of ability consists in the theft of as many machine guns as possible. That to me seems to be the most detestable point of Bolshevism; its cowardice. It is cowardly, for it will not place itself in an open intellectual struggle, it feels secure only if by treacherous putsch it has acquired all opposing press organs ... Let me say, all of you ought to send this government to the devil if it did not place resolute and strong force against force and if it would not mobilize everything to save the last piteous remnant of German national wealth from disruption and destruction ... We go before you with clean hands and with the firm decision to end the sufferings of our people, to protect it against the Spartacist terror." [23]

It must, however, be pointed out that this SPD propaganda campaign which attributed the strike psychosis in Ger-

[23] Speech of February 21, 1919, *Verhandlungen*, CCCXXVI, 253-56.

many to the USPD, and expected to restore willingness to work by the destruction of the political strength of the left, based on the same fallacies that had prompted the old regime to hold the USPD responsible for the discontent which had spread through Germany during the war. " The economic position of the worker, the civil servant, and the petty bourgeois middle strata deteriorated with every additional year of warfare. This was responsible to a considerable degree for the political and military collapse of 1918. After the collapse, economic conditions became only worse ... The fall of the old governmental power, the new ' freedom ', the psychological results of the revolution gave the movement a wild, unfettered and confused character ... Marooned in deepest economic misery, the hungry proletariat could not be sated with the political liberties which the revolution offered. They would fill neither a growling stomach nor cover a freezing body. They had to attempt to improve their economic position. And ... the closest means at hand was the strike." [24]

c. Character of the Campaign Against the Left

As if the actual record of the USPD and the KPD did not provide adequate cause for action against them, pretexts were frequently used by the SPD. The government operation against Saxony and the occupation of Dresden and Leipzig by government troops in May, 1919, for example, had been preceded by wildest rumors about public riots and the hardships of the USPD dictatorship in these cities. Yet even Noske had to admit that everything was quite peaceful there, that there had

---

24 R. Mueller, *Buergerkrieg*, pp. 124-28. *Cf.* speech of SPD minister of labor Schlicke, *Verhandlungen*, CCCXXX, 3247 ff., October 18, 1919. It is interesting to note that Noske, *op. cit.*, pp. 186-87, agreed that the continued unrest was due to the failure of the government to improve the standard of living after the revolution and the peace treaty. But Noske was probably right that no ready solution was possible at all, and that hence the government could proceed against this unrest only by armed force and applying the state of siege.

been no disturbances, and that the occupation could not be ascribed in riotous conditions.[25]

The most flagrant example of the use of trumped-up charges was probably the release of the news that fifty policemen had been murdered in cold blood by the leftists in Lichtenberge. Duly spread by the press, this report was made the excuse for the introduction of an unprecedented state of martial law: suspicion of anti-government action was sufficient for summary execution. The application of this degree cost 1,200 people their lives in Berlin alone during the first ten days of March, 1919, but the news proved to be completely wrong and the press eventually corrected it.[26]

The frequently false reports spread by the government regarding the actions of the USPD and KPD, and its predictions of the dire consequences of political strikes and council government did not contribute to calm public sentiments or to insure to known leftists even their most elementary right, the right to live.[27]

The Munich soviet government had cost the lives of only twelve persons, most of whom had been arrested as notorious plotters of a secret rightist organization during an actual state

25 Noske, *op. cit.*, pp. 144-46. Maercker, *op. cit.*, pp. 180-220, agreed that in addition this interference in the states lacked all legal basis.

26 E.. J. Gumbel, *Vier Jahre politischer Mord* (5th ed.), pp. 15-17. Noske refrained from mentioning the incident in his memoirs.

27 *Cf.* O. Kilian (ed.), *Der weisse Schrecken in Mitteldeutschland; die Wahrheit ueber die Maerzkaempfe. Stenographischer Bericht des Untersuchungsausschusses des Preussischen Landtags 27. und 28. Oktober 1921.* (Published by the KPD.) Had this or other material not been indubitably published so far back, one might be tempted to assume that it represented a reprojection into the past of methods not generally used until a much more recent date by a German government. *Cf. Die Enthuellungen zu den Maerzkaempfen,* a KPD defense against the newspaper campaign and the government propaganda regarding their presumed plots, etc. For a USPD view of the Munich soviet republic, the Freiheit publication *Die Muenchener Tragoedie,* Berlin, 1919, is of interest. Eugen Prager's *Geschichte der USPD,* also a USPD publication, provided many of the leaflets, proclamations and communications of the party during the period here covered.

of war. But the March, 1919, struggles in Berlin cost about 1,200 lives, and the suppression of the Munich soviet republic in April and May, 1919, cost well over 700 lives, of which 457 were not lost until after the re-conquest of Munich itself. In conjunction with the government operations against them, this campaign of murder hit the leftists at their most vulnerable spot, their leadership. Liebknecht, Luxemburg, Eisner, Haase, Landauer, and many others who never attained national prominence were thus eliminated.

Disregarding cases of actual or pretended self-defense, cases which occurred at the scene of public riots, and summary trials which had a pretext of legality (for example the 186 executions of the Bavarian 'Volksgerichte'), a German statistician enumerated a total of 354 political assassinations committed by the right against the left, and only twenty-two such cases committed by the left.[28]

If the rampage of political murder and its accompanying horrors were astonishing, the fate of its perpetrators at the hands of the police and the courts was even more so. Of the 354 cases of murder committed by the rightists, 326 remained completely unpunished, and twenty-three culprits were freed even though they pleaded guilty in open court. Not one was executed; and the twenty-four persons condemned at all received a total of ninety years, two months in prison in addition to one life term and RM. 730 in fines. The twenty-eight

---

[28] E. J. Gumbel, *Vier Jahre politischer Mord*. The author considered each case from all its angles, used court records wherever possible, and furnished a detailed account on each individual case. This publication caused repeated interpellations in the Reichstag, as a result of which the government promised to investigate Gumbel's data. After several years, a report from the various state governments confirmed Gumbel's data in all essentials. The government refused to publish it, but a private copy of it got into the possession of Gumbel and he published it at his own expense. Gumbel (ed.), *Denkschrift des Reichsjustizministers zu "Vier Jahre Politischer Mord"*, Berlin, 1924, thus provided an invaluable check on Gumbel's original statements. On the activities of the secret rightist organizations, see Gumbel, *Verschwoerer*, Wien, 1924.

cases for which some punishment was imposed at all included the assassination of twenty-one Catholic youths in Munich who had been mistaken for Communists.[29] On the other hand, the twenty-two leftist murders were followed by trial and sentences in seventeen cases. The courts imposed ten sentences of death, and a total of 248 years, nine months in prison in addition to three life terms. But the courts meted out punishments for other political crimes besides murder, too; up to February 20, 1920, 5,233 leftists were brought to trial in Bavaria alone and of these 2,209 were sentenced.[30]

Thus a journalist by the name of Fechenbach was sentenced to ten years in prison for republishing a once secret letter of the Bavarian ambassador at the Vatican, which dated back to July, 1914. Yet the publication of such documents had been made mandatory upon Germany by the treaty of Versailles and hence by public law; press delicts could not be prosecuted after more than six months from the time they occurred; and a different court had found Fechenbach not guilty of violating any press laws, because this particular document had been published before in Eisner's collection of war guilt documents.

The complaints of some SPD members about these conditions were drowned out in the general political struggle. It was in vain, that the SPD delegate Radbruch criticized this double-faced justice and its administration, and denied that " this and much else is only slander. It is a matter of fact ", he

29 Cf. Gumbel, *Vier Jahre politischer Mord*, pp. 78-81; *Denkschrift* . . . , pp. 118-130. The Bavarian minister of justice reported that, of 193 cases of assassination from the right, none except those of the Catholic youths had led to a conviction. From the left, the minister confirmed that there had been only twelve cases.

30 This record becomes the more appalling if one remembers that after the Kapp putsch, only one person was sentenced, although officially 705 persons had been listed as involved. Of the additional 755 officers involved none was brought to trial, and only forty-eight were removed from active service. At the time of the Kapp putsch, Chancellor Bauer had promised " severest punishment " for the rebels; *Verhandlungen*, CCCXXXII, 4901 ff., March 18, 1920.

declared, " that in almost all politically tainted trials our justice has failed terribly." [31]

d. Conclusions: The Political Views of the SPD

The SPD and its government could indeed not be expected to change basically the composition and the views of the highly praised German administration.[32] The suppression of the poli-

---

31 *Protokoll des Parteitags 1921*, pp. 227 ff. *Cf.* Curt Rosenberg, " Schutz der republikanischen Staatsverfassung," in *Sozialistische Monatshefte,* October 31, 1921, pp. 944-48. A notable exception to this general picture was furnished by the trial of Ledebour who had been indicted for high treason because of his role in the January riots, but who had been freed. One must also mention that the government of Scheidemann sought a pardon for Leviné who, as president of the Munich soviet republic, had been condemned to death, but the Bavarian authorities cut these endeavors short by executing him the day after his sentence. Of interest is the case of the USPD member of the National Assembly, Brass, who in the aftermath of the Kapp putsch had been accused of informing the Allied High Commission of the Rhineland that not eight thousand but eighty thousand German troops had been sent into the demilitarized zone of the Ruhr basin, and who was charged with having furnished documentary proof that these troops went there not to suppress but to extend the Kappist adventure. Brass denied ever having named any number or furnished documents which had not been made public before, but the government wanted to prosecute him for treason. Both the minister of war and the minister of justice recommended that the Assembly waive his status of immunity. The matter came to a vote twice; however the absence of a quorum made any decision impossible. Since the National Assembly was not formally dissolved until after the elections to the next Reichstag, which sat from 1920 to 1924, Brass continued to be protected by immunity. *Cf. Verhandlungen,* CCCXXXIII, 5130-34, 5142-46, 5147-51, 5713 ff.

32 Michaelis, a scion of a family long in the civil service, furnished in his memoirs a picture of the training and upbringing of German political leaders which may well explain why this system of government produced more pride than ability, more promise than fulfillment, and more failure than success. For his poor showing upon graduation from high school, Michaelis accused an educational system which placed more emphasis on concrete knowledge than on innate ability; he almost failed in German. He studied in Wuerzburg to prepare himself for the civil service but he hardly knew where the university was. Upon his appointment to the judicial branch of the civil service, he himself had qualms about being excused thrice a week from his duties to go hunting. He barely passed his examination as an 'Gerichtsassessor'. When in need of a Ph.D. degree for a semi-official position

tical power of the left—which meant council control of the administration on the local level,—was the foremost objective of the SPD in its fight for democracy and against the councils; by destroying the power of the old administration, the party would have fulfilled one of the main demands of the USPD.

General Maercker, whom Noske called his 'Staedteerobe-rer', declared: "The struggle of the federal government was exclusively for the retention of political power . . . The weakness of the government, however, did not allow this to be stated openly. It feared to reveal its colors and to declare that the free-corps served to remove council government where it still existed . . . It avoided this by using the military state of affairs as an excuse for interference. But the labor leaders recognized at once that this was only an excuse, that the execution of the degree regarding the power of command was basically more of political than military importance." Maercker would much have preferred to tell the leftists openly: "My presence signifies the struggle against the council government to which you aspire, and against the government of compulsion by the armed proletariat." [33]

Richard Mueller, in commenting on the revolution, wrote: "The historic mistake of the proletariat consisted in believing itself to be in the possession of governmental power, in per-

---

in Japan, some friends of his arranged an examination whose professors were prejudiced by the promise of the publication of their works. And this man reached the highest ranks of the administration and became war-time chancellor; *op. cit.*, pp. 41-60. The Swiss historian Zurlinden, in *Der Weltkrieg*, I, 141 ff., commented already during the war on "the principle of authority which founds on the false premise of a degree of wisdom and prudence in the governing classes exceeding the average. . . . The result of this system is the ruin of Europe." The SPD of course never had any doubts about the merits of the German civil service. At the party congress in 1919, Steinkopf made it a special point to laud the professional civil service, without which the revolution would not have been as smooth and bloodless as it was, and which would be needed even in the future socialist state. *Protokoll des Parteitags 1919*, pp. 393 ff.

33 Maercker, *ibid.*, pp. 161 ff. Noske, *ibid.*, pp. 93-95, agreed to this analysis.

severing in this illusion in spite of all warnings, and in not
conquering power in reality, which means seizing the state
apparatus of the bourgeoisie, breaking it up and building it
anew ... Upon the bourgeoisie rested the moral and political
responsibility for the war ... The sudden fall from the illusion
of victory into terrible defeat robbed it of the belief in its own
might ... It stood compromised and trembling ... Immediately after the war, the proletariat could have seized power,
if its battle-trained, experienced, and politically trained sector
had recognized the need to do so, provided that a political
party with a clear program, with revolutionary experience and
with resolution had stood by its side. That was missing. The
Social Democracy, the strongest political party, had not wished
the revolution ... It violated its democratic sentiments to hold
fast to this gift of nature." But Mueller agreed reluctantly
that "those masses which were ready to put themselves behind the revolutionaries were repulsed and driven into the
arms of the opposition ... If you view the total result of the
elections as a gauge for the political desires of the people, then
indeed every attempt to overthrow the government would
have been a hopeless undertaking." [34]

And the elections to the National Assembly were indeed
the crux of the matter. In the 1912 Reichstag, the SPD occupied 110 out of 397 seats or 27.5 percent; in the National
Assembly, it gained 165 out of 423 seats or thirty-nine percent;
but in the elections to the Reichstag in 1920, it won only 113
out of 466 seats or about twenty-four percent; and in 1924,
with part of the USPD joining its ranks, it received only one
hundred seats out of 472, or a meager 21.2 percent. In 1919,
the USPD won twenty-two seats or 5.2 percent and in 1920,
eighty-one seats or 17.4 percent. If the two KPD seats of the
1920 Reichstag were added to this, the total vote of the leftists
was still less than eighteen percent. In 1919, when SPD
strength was the greatest ever recorded by the party, the right-

[34] R. Mueller, *ibid.*, pp. 203-07.

ist parties were completely disorganized by the revolution, and many had voted for the SPD in full knowledge of that party's opposition to the councils, and of its strict democratic views. These factors lead to the conclusion that the overwhelming majority of the German people resisted the council system as a future form of government.

One may well ask how in view of the verdict of public opinion and the overwhelming rejection of socialism, the SPD, as a party confessing the strongest faith in political democracy from its very beginnings, could have acted differently or could have resisted executing the will of the majority of the population against the revolutionary leftists who had rather wanted to impose their own will on the majority.

The origins of the party provided the answer to this question. From its beginnings until the turn of the century, public opinion had rejected the SPD quite as decisively as it rejected the USPD and the KPD after the revolution; until the elections of 1887, the SPD never polled more than ten percent of the popular vote. But this overwhelming opposition had not caused the SPD to abandon its revolutionary tendencies or to place itself in the vanguard of those who executed the popular will of the masses of those days. The SPD insisted upon its own points of views and program because it held that democracy means not alone the execution of the will of the majority but that democracy also means leadership with the aim to win the hostile majority for its own camp. In 1918 and 1919 too, the idea of democracy did not force the SPD to adopt and to execute the will of the majority unless the will of the majority and the will of the SPD were, practically, identical.

During the revolution, the SPD's assumption of leadership in the execution of the will of the majority could hence indicate only one of two things: that the SPD had (in a mistaken interpretation of democracy) sacrificed its minority views and embraced the opinions of the majority of the public, that it had deteriorated from a party of democratic leadership to one leaning towards demagogy; [35] or that the SPD doubted its own program and its ability to win the support of the majority and to provide the democratic leadership needed to effect its own ideas with the consent of the public.[36]

The failure of the SPD to provide this democratic leadership was perhaps the more important factor. The election results, including those of the Congress of Councils and of various local elections in November and December, 1918, fail to provide an adequate picture of the trends of public opinion. The public could choose only between the various programs offered by the political parties. The SPD, anxious to prevent the success of the USPD and the KPD, had erased all characteristics which clearly distinguished between the SPD and the other parties of the Weimar coalition. The elections were therefore not able to record more than public opposition towards the leftists. One must assume, that if, between November, 1918, and the elections to the National Assembly, the SPD had made an attempt to enact its traditional program, a considerable sector of the public would have supported the SPD.[37]

[35] The report of the party chairmanship of the SPD at the party congress declared in 1921: "We must excise from the program everything which...cannot be attained except by compromise with the bourgeois parties.... To state this is a priori a demand of sincerity towards the proletariat and of necessity for the party, so that we can prevent. hopes... which can never be fulfilled;" *Protokoll des Parteitags 1921*, p. 149.

[36] It is hardly necessary to point out that, by 1918, the German public had not come to embrace the SPD program of 1891 or the original SPD concept of democracy.

[37] "We have to confess it frankly: the German Social Democracy has not so far shown itself able to meet the tasks posed by the collapse of Germany and by the German revolution. The masses have failed and the leaders no less. The main responsibility falls upon the leaders. Had they had a clear program of construction, had they followed an idea,...had they but felt the duty for socialist action alone, the masses would have supported them." H. Peus, "Wie wird das neue Deutschland?", *Sozialistische Monatshefte*, February 9, 1920, pp. 73-77.

But the record of the party during the abdication crisis revealed that the SPD was no longer able to provide the challenge of political leadership, and that it preferred to follow a confused public which had been deprived of its full range of choices by the timidity of SPD leaders.

The willingness of the SPD to make this unguided and hence static will of the public the test of its program and to enforce this will of the public against the leftist, if need be, with armed force, represented a change within the SPD whose effects could be traced in every aspect of its political activities. That the most pronounced democratic party in Germany should thus devaluate the concept of democracy at the very moment when democracy became the chosen form of the German polity could not but influence deeply the fate of democracy in post-1918 Germany.

CHAPTER XI

SOCIALISM RECONSIDERED

a. The Introduction of the Economic Councils

DURING the revolutionary period, the SPD had opposed the political power of the soldiers' councils with all its authority and force.[1] In suppressing the political power of the councils, no regard was paid to their actual performance in individual cases or to any other factors in addition to the factor of principle.

However, opposition to SPD policies helped swell the ranks of the supporters of the council system among whom many were motivated less by the example of Russia, than by the need to insure a firm basis for German democracy by the selection of a new medium of democratic expression. In view of the increasing strength of the council adherents, the SPD thought it wise to compensate for the suppression of the political power of the councils by a significant concession in some other field.

The concession made by the SPD consisted of the introduction of the council system as a means of economic control by the worker. An elaborate system was developed which allowed delegates of the workers in each industrial concern to determine, in co-operation with employers, the economic and humanitarian conditions of work; larger bodies were provided to help determine production, marketing and employment

---

1 Dr. H. Lauffenberg, *Zwischen der ersten und zweiten Revolution,* Hamburg, 1919. Lauffenberg thought that the ability of the old powers to resume control after the revolution was due to their alliance with the SPD in the latter's fight against the leftist and the council government. Hence the SPD could no longer ally itself with the left and lost the ability to resist the bourgeoisie too. This was a persuasive argument adopted by many, but it presumed that the SPD had a choice between the left and the right. A decent regard for democracy did not allow such a choice; the SPD could choose only between the right and a third alternative. Not its rejection of the left, but its rejection of the third alternative deserved attention.

policies of entire branches of industry; and a supreme economic council was envisaged to make recommendations regarding national economic policies as such. All political power of these three types of councils was excluded. They had only advisory rights in matters of legislation, and the representation of the workers in them was held equal to that of their employers.[2]

It was evident that these councils would rival the activities of the trade-unions, and the trade-unions were none too happy about their introduction.[3] However, the advantage of the trade-unions and their opinions of the subject were over-ruled: only the promise of the introduction of the economic councils provided the government with a means to settle the March, 1919, strikes which had paralyzed the Ruhr basin and Central Germany. In fact, the government could settle these strikes only by yielding on this point in a formal agreement with the strikers.[4]

2 Although these provisions had been embodied into the German constitution, legislation was passed only in reference to the lowest type of organization, the work councils, which enjoyed a peaceful and uneventful history under the republic.

4 Bromme argued at the Party Congress in 1919 that the trade-unions made councils of this type superfluous and that they had been introduced only to appease the public and to draw strength from the USPD. Kahmann charged that they had been introduced only to compensate the public for the disappointments of the peace treaty; *Protokoll des Parteitags 1919*, pp. 439-440. Legislation for these councils provided of course that they should not rival the trade-unions where the latter were the recognized agents for the employees.

4 *Die gesetzliche Verankerung der Arbeiterraete,* Vorwaerts Verlag, Berlin, 1919, pp. 5 ff. The agreement was concluded on March 15, 1919, at Weimar and provided for the following points: (1) to give constitutional sanction to workers' councils as representing the economic interests of the workers in determining conditions of work, in forming co-operate organizations of administration in all industrial branches with power to regulate production and distribution, and in establishing provincial and central councils to aid in the socialization of enterprises and their control; (2) to adopt a uniform labor law; (3) (to liberate all political prisoners, a demand rejected by the government as impossible); (4) crimes committed by government troops should be tried in civil courts; (5) diplomatic relations should be reestablished with all states including Russia; and (6) the program of socialization should be extended.

In view of the intransigence of the SPD on the question of political councils, in view of the fact that this concession was wrested from the SPD by one of the most violent and widespread strikes in Germany, and in view of the fact that the SPD might be hatching a serious rival to the trade-unions,[5] the SPD played the role of a champion for the economic councils with rather good grace.

The defense of the economic councils was the task of Dr. Sinzheimer, who represented the official views of the party in regard to the council problem. Dr. Sinzheimer denied that the council movement had been motivated solely by the desire to imitate the Russian example, or that it was an artificial movement. In his opinion it had been caused by a certain sense of disappointment which had gripped the masses after the attainment of full democracy. "A new political democracy had been erected. But the masses felt that in spite of this change in political respects their social content of life had not been changed. The old social system had remained the same." The worker longed to evade the disastrous consequences of war and unemployment. "He felt inwardly that he possessed an indestructible purpose in itself, that the objective factors of life should not dominate him, on the contrary that he was rather called upon to rule them according to the laws of reason ... To seize and to guide the forces determining the fate of life ... is the deepest desire inspiring a large part of the masses following the idea of councils." Dr. Sinzheimer rejected the idea of the dictatorship of the councils; "political revolutions may be effected by force, but not a social revolution ... New economic methods depend not only on laws which may be changed, but upon economic activities which must be developed ... Force may tear down

---

5 Since, however, the trade-unions had not been established universally in Germany, the work councils provided a means of extending trade-union tactics into every factory. It need not be stressed that the trade-unions were also conciliated by the hopes that they might dominate the economic councils.

an old economic system, not build a new one ... [However], pure political democracy can influence social conditions only by legislation and governmental action. Both are insufficient to assist the social development to the degree which we, as social democrats, must desire. The entire nature of social life, and especially of economic life eludes purely governmental action ... which in its essence is too schematic, bureaucratic, general, and rigid. . ." An independent economic constitution was needed which, on the basis of constitutional principles, could solve the problems of economic organization. " Parliament is and must remain the organ of political democracy ... The councils are the organ of economic democracy." Only such an organization could mobilize production beyond the limits of the free rule of the profit motive, and yet give free play to private initiative and enterprise. But "the economic constitution cannot change economic law itself. Its change is the task of political democracy." [6]

On July 21, 1919, Dr. Sinzheimer told the National Assembly: " There is a need for organizing economic life. The state alone cannot satisfy the need for organization and regulation ... It is necessary that the economic forces themselves provide the regulations and norms needed ... The council movement therefore intends to erect an ... industrial constitution, whose task it is to solve the question of industrial organization by utilizing the forces of economy themselves." He explained in detail why these councils could not become organs of socialization which could proceed only from the state. He argued trenchantly against all dictatorship of the councils, and then he turned to the suggestion that the councils might provide a third chamber on the example of the medieval estates: " The committee on the constitution has rejected this idea mainly because, if the economic interests would ... in a separate chamber find ... expression equal in regard to the political parliament, politics would be subordi-

6 *Protokoll des Parteitags 1919*, pp. 406-418.

nated to an economic point of view. This would cause politics, even cultural policies, to be dominated by materialism, which is not in the interests of an ideal polity." Councils should have some influence, but no power in politics. "The basic idea of the councils ... aims to liberate economy from politics, to emancipate the economic system, to free the state of the task of industrial organization, and to found, besides the political constitution, an economic constitution with its own and independent field, with its own sphere of influence." [7]

b. The Problem of Socialization

Just as the political role of the councils was advocated as a means of attaining the greatest possible political change from the revolution, so the economic role of the councils was advanced by the leftists as a means of achieving the greatest possible economic results from the revolution, as a means of introducing the socialist utopia. [8]

It was indeed not possible to read into the German revolution a mandate to introduce the socialist order, and the SPD had not sponsored the economic councils as a means of socializing production, but in order to remove discontent among the workers. Yet, the imperative need for a successful transition from war-time economy to peace-time production, the prospect of huge reparation demands from the Allies, and the decay of the German economy as a result of the abuse of German industrial resources and the lack of replacements during the war forced all German political parties to examine very closely whether the existing economic order was best fitted to German needs or whether farreaching innovations should not be introduced into the future economy of Germany. [9]

7 *Verhandlungen*, CCCXXVIII, 1748-52, 1790 ff.

8 For example, Richard Mueller, *Was die Arbeiterraete wollen und sollen,* published probably in 1919. All the previously cited SPD pamphlets took issue with the projected role of the councils in socializing industry.

9 See *Verhandlungen*, CCCXXVII, 798-802, speech of Wissell summarizing the influence of the factors mentioned upon the German economy. It is

The disruption of German economic life appeared to many radical leftists as the best opportunity to reap the benefits of socialism. However, the SPD and the responsible leaders of the USPD arrived at the conclusion that socialism could not provide the solution which the economic problems of Germany so deeply craved.

Well in advance of the German revolution and of the end of the war, Karl Kautsky had warned that, after the war, all belligerents would be so impoverished that the workers could not simply take over the existing organs of production. Should socialism come to power in the period of transition after the war, it would be handicapped by the absence of its basic requirement: abundance of capital. " No socialist regime can lift the misery which is due to general want in society. It can only lift the misery of want amidst abundance." The material prerequisites for socialism would be extremely restricted in the transition period, and socialists should not then desire to attain political power.[10]

Eisner was another prominent USPD leader who had warned that at a time when the productive resources of the country have nearly been exhausted, it did not seem possible to transfer industries to public ownership; " you cannot socialize where there is hardly anything left to socialize ".[11] Hilferding,

---

interesting to note that Helfferich, too, condemned the Hindenburg program because of its effects upon the German economy during the war and after. Helfferich accused the Hindenburg program of responsibility for inflationary war-time expenses and declared: "With quiet deliberation of the needs and expert examination of the possible, one should have avoided to invest masses of precious materials and even more precious manpower into industrial ruins which, because of the lack of men and coal, were never finished or fully utilized. With less manpower and materials, considerably more could have been done for the armament of the army, and yet our economy saved from disturbances and interferences which finally attacked the root of the power of the people to resist." Helfferich, *op. cit.*, II, 282.

10 K. Kautsky, *Sozialdemokratische Bemerkungen zur Uebergangswirtschaft*, Leipzig, 1918, pp. 157-66. This volume was written in the first half of 1918, but was not published until after the revolution.

11 From Eisner's program of November 15, 1918, printed in the *Muen-*

the leading USPD economist, too, held that socialization must be a slow and tedious process. The first task was to get the economy going and in order to do so, vast sections of industry, agriculture and export industries had to be left alone.[12]

These attitudes of the USPD leaders on socialization surprised even the SPD. " Many will be confounded by the most recent experience. For until now, socialization, state ownership, nationalization of production (or whatever the more or less debatable expression for the abolition of the conflict between the dominant possession of the means of production and the executing labor may be) seemed to be the immediate basic demand of every purposeful class movement of the workers, the irreducible essential of socialism as such. But now we have ... the socialist republic ... And the first serious and impressive manifestation of some of our most renowned party theoreticians and practicioners ... consists in warning circumspectly against all complete and sudden nationalization." [13]

However, these statements by USPD leaders unloosed an avalanche of argument and reason from within the SPD examining the idea of socialization in its relation to problems of (1) international exchange; (2) economic crises; (3) co-operative ownership; and (4) state ownership.[14]

1. Many SPD leaders argued that socialism, being more beneficial to the worker than capitalism, was too expensive a form of production. The need to export in a world dominated by the cheaper, capitalist mode of production restricted socialism to rather narrow fields. " Where production for world

chener Post, November 16, and cited by Buchner, op. cit., no. 296, pp. 251-53.

12 Speech of December 20, 1918, before the Congress of Councils; quoted by Deutscher Geschichtskalender, ibid., I, 248-50.

13 Max Schippel's article " Sofort Verstaatlichen?," Sozialistiche Monatshefte, December 10, 1918, pp. 1123-28.

14 One may perhaps dismiss the statement that " we have no interest in now organizing large industrial branches, so that Germany's enemies may quite comfortably put their hands on them." Verhandlungen, CCCXXVI, 72 ff., speech of SPD representative Keil, February 14, 1919.

markets begins, the possibility to socialize economic life ends
... The unavoidable need to produce goods for the world markets [to pay] for our imports from abroad draws limits to the
socialist mode of production, which no power on earth, not
even the dictatorship of the proletariat, could remove." [15]

2. Full socialization was thus ruled out because of the consequences of socialism upon the international exchange of
manufactured goods in return for foods and raw materials.
In addition, socialism, the SPD concluded, could not be recommended for crisis times like those which Germany faced in
1919. "Karl Marx had assumed that at the time of the socialization of the means of production, capitalist economy would
have attained its highest level, whereas we have to liquidate an
economy which has been brought to the rim of the abyss by
the unholy war ... Karl Marx never thought that his party
would be forced to realize socialism after a war which even the
most fertile mind could not have imagined as possible." [16]

"We are, as has been frequently expressed in the National
Assembly, a poor people, and therefore we cannot afford expensive experiments. Such experiments might probably have
been undertaken in Germany before the war, although even
then they would have constituted a crime against the national
wealth. But today, we must decidedly reject such plans ... We
know that the many-branched blood vessels of the German
economy are extremely sensitive ... For that reason it is in
our opinion not possible to interfere with economic life with
too rough a hand ... We have had enough experience with the
Russian example." [17]

3. But the examination of the concept of socialism by the
SPD was not restricted to a discussion of foreign and internal

15 Dr. L. Quessel, *Der moderne Sozialismus*, Berlin, 1919, pp. 207, 222,
etc. The author frequently contributed to the *Sozialistische Monatshefte* as
editor for foreign affairs.

16 *Verhandlungen*, CCCXXVI, 718 ff., March 12, 1919, speech of Dr.
Braun.

17 *Ibid.*, CCCXXIX, 2273 ff., August 9, 1919, speech of Dr. Kahmann.

economic conditions. The discussion went much deeper and the reasons marshalled for the rejection of socialism became more trenchant.[18]

Traditionally, the co-operative ownership of a factory by its workers had been considered as socialism par excellence.[19] But " the method imported from the East ... that the workers simply acquire possession of the means of production, of landed estates, factories, machines and tools, and distribute among themselves the profits realized ... would in practice mean only that a majority of capitalists replace the few previous ones." [20] " This sort of socialization which consists in taking the salaries and dividends of the Directors General and the dividends of the capitalists in order to raise with them wages and the like, this insane method of socialization which haunts the minds of intelligent workers, we wish to fight." [21]

4. The SPD thus denied that socialism meant the acquisition of ownership by the workers, that it was a process originating in the smallest economic cell, the productive unit in the factory and in the shop. But the SPD also denied that the state could provide for socialism.

" The state is not a fit bearer of the economy ... Within the framework of those necessities which the interests of the population impose, it should leave business activities to those who (thanks to their membership in a branch of industry con-

18 Laufkoetter in the discussion of the party program, and without protest from any other SPD delegate, called socialization a " meaningless " concept; *Protokoll des Parteitags 1920*, p. 211.

19 H. Cunow's article " Verstaatlichung," *Neue Zeit*, vol. XXXVII, pt. 1, no. 10, December 6, 1919, pp. 217-23. Cunow insisted that Marx had never recognized any other form of socialism, since the state would no longer exist in classless society and hence could not own or operate property.

20 *Verhandlungen*, CCCXXVI, 458-66, March 3, 1919, speech of Vogel.

21 *Ibid.*, pp. 591-94, March 8, 1919, Giesberts, the speaker for the government, pointed out that this type of program had it strongest support in areas where foreign (Polish, Italian) workers were most numerous, and where 'yellow' unions had predominated before the war; trained trade-unionists did not become Bolshevists.

cerned) possess a knowledge of its needs, and whose sense of responsibility for the prosperity of this branch of industry has been sharpened by its connection with their own interests." [22] " Economic life is simply too complicated to be regulated in detail by laws and edicts. You cannot shackle this living, highly over-sensitive organism. Economic life is too liquid to be poured into fixed forms." [23] " The economic organism cannot at this time bear any miracle cures . . . We must attempt to solve the problems facing the ministry of economy from the point of view of rapid and useful reconstruction, and we must probably not tie ourselves too closely to a general, definite program . . . We cannot tolerate the continued grievances of industry . . . because, to a considerable degree, they are justified. For it is unavoidable that the bureaucratic conduct . . . offers handicaps, delays . . . which must be avoided." [24]

Government control over industry was not only considered to be harmful to industry; government control was undesirable for the workers too. " Concerns that are transferred into public ownership are managed by representatives of the public and not by the representatives of the workers of those concerns . . . In a government enterprise, the influence of the workers should not be different from private ownership; on the contrary, in a private concern it should be greater than in a concern owned by the public." [25]

Thus the SPD concluded that socialization of one country in the midst of a capitalist world was limited by international trade, that socialization was not possible in times of crisis, and that socialization meant neither state control—because of the

22 *Ibid.*, pp. 541-47, March 7, 1919, speech of Wissell, SPD minister of economy.

23 *Protokoll des Parteitags 1919*, pp. 363-70, speech of Wissell.

24 *Verhandlungen*, CCCXXVIII, 1866 ff., July 24, 1919, speech of Robert Schmidt, Wissell's successor as SPD minister of economy.

25 *Protokoll des Parteitags 1920*, pp. 152 ff., speech of Gustav Bauer.

unfitness of the state—nor co-operative control because this would continue a type of capitalist control which differed only quantitatively from the old system. Scheidemann indeed arrived at the conclusion that " Socialism ... is nothing but the application of scientific knowledge to the economy for the purpose of the direct good of the working community." [26] " Socialism is not a purpose in itself, but it should be a means to aid suffering mankind." [27]

However, the economic position of Germany after the war called loudly for decisive remedial measures, and the SPD had to heed the call. But instead of socialism, the SPD was interested exclusively in the increase of production, and, in the opinion of the SPD, this could best be obtained by a system of ' laissez-faire.' Indeed the need for production was one of the main economic causes for the SPD opposition to council government and the economic control of council dictatorship, whose economic and political demands had closed too many factories by strikes or by the sheer impossibility of fulfilling them.[28]

26 *Verhandlungen*, CCCXXX, 2886-92, October 7, 1919. These SPD views on socialization were quickly taken up by the bourgeois parties. For a discussion of the problem from the viewpoints of the Democratic party (which was probably even more representative of the Weimar republic than the SPD) see Dr. Otto Neurath and W. Schumann, *Koennen wir heute sozialisieren?*, Leipzig, 1919. These two authors together with the SPD writer Kranold were responsible for the Saxonian socialization act of 1919. *Cf.* the pamphlets of A. Feiler and E. Kahn in the series *Flugschriften der Frankfurter Zeitung.*

27 *Protokoll des Parteitags 1919*, pp. 233 ff., speech of Scheidemann.

28 See *Soll Deutschland ein Tollhaus werden?*; *Sozialismus ist Arbeit!*; *Gedeih oder Verderb?*; *A.-und S. Raete*; *Sollen wir zugrunde gehen?*; *Allgemeine Arbeitspflicht*; *Generalstreik und sozialdemokratische Arbeit*; *Sozialismus und Bolschewismus in Stimmen der fuehrenden Maenner*, Berlin, probably in 1919. Two of these may perhaps be paraphrased here in part, to indicate the opinions which they advocated. *A.-und S. Raete* considered the councils as unfit to effect socialization; their expropriations would at best lead only to the substitution of a different kind of capitalism for private capital, and at worst to economic chaos and anarchy; councils were inherently incapable of administering or advancing industrial enterprises.

In its desire to stimulate production, the SPD rejected economic strikes as decisively as political strikes: " The masses which are now striking are not engaged in class-struggle, but are raging against themselves," declared the SPD representative Sollmann.[29] Robert Schmidt, the German SPD food minister, declared: " Every strike in the transportation industry, in the railroad shops, in mining, means the demolition of the last remnants of our national economy." [30] " Strikes are a crime against the German nation, insane, . . . an excess committed against oneself," proclaimed Scheidemann.[31]

In the search for increased production, unsuspected virtues were suddenly discovered by the SPD in capitalism. Molkenbuhr, one of the more prominent SPD members of the National Assembly, declared: " Nobody in Germany intends to proceed in the way in which for instance the Bolshevists in Russia proceeded, [where they] destroyed capitalism . . . We cannot avoid stating it; the capitalist evolution must proceed." [32] " After the experience of the years since the revolution, it seems to be recognized that capitalism . . . is still developing upward . . . Capitalism has shown a vitality and perserverance which bars the conclusion that it will soon disappear." [33]

Socialism did not mean the distribution of existing wealth, which would not amount to much for each worker; socialism only meant increasing production with decreasing use of labor. *Sollen wir zugrunde gehen?*, expounded the view that Germany could recover only by creating new values through labor. Strikes and unemployment—with compensations too high to leave an incentive to work—hurt the workers most of all. Only work could prevent the complete economic collapse. To regain prosperity, more and cheaper work was needed.

29 *Verhandlungen*, CCCXXVI, 657 ff., March 10, 1919.

30 *Ibid.*, pp. 625 ff., March 10, 1919.

31 *Ibid.*, pp. 576 ff., March 8, 1919.

32 *Ibid.*, pp. 578 ff., March 8, 1919.

33 A. Heichen, " Hat der Kapitalismus abgewirtschaftet? " *Neue Zeit*, vol. XXXIX, pt. 2, no. 23, September 2, 1921, pp. 529-32.

Indeed, Dr. David, in an address at the SPD party congress in 1919, advocated capitalism in terms difficult to surpass: " It has been pointed out that only dutiful work can save our people ... And what was the answer? A strike psychosis! a further disruption of economic life, because large sections of the working people saw in the revolution only a large wage movement ... Nobody thought ... of working more intensely or conscientiously than before, because everybody only thought of driving money wages up as fast as possible, cutting work time even more, and, what is worst, to produce in a given working time not more intensely and conscientiously, but worse and less ... The capitalist system possessed the great mainspring which drove production to an immense level in the interests of the individual, of the capitalist enterpreneur, but also in the interests of the worker who was eventually hit by the hunger whip if he did not work enough ... Socialism wants to put in a different mainspring, namely social consciousness of duty. But this mainspring is not yet there. That is the main point of the whole difficulty in which we find ourselves ... We must guard against viewing things as possible, which are impossible as long as this new mainspring does not operate with sufficient force." [34]

Cunow aptly summarized these considerations: " Revolutionary parties yearning to reform the political or social order have at all times shown a strong inclination towards utopian constructions of the future and illusory self-deception in respect to their existence, their progress, and their victory. Filled by their ideal, they almost always misjudged the resistance and handicaps opposing their realization, underestimated the evolutionary potentialities, and judged these according to the desires and hopes activating the hearts of their impatient followers ... Away with these illusions! ... This continued new hatching of various impossible, impracticable plans is a serious danger to our future political development ... It is inevitable

[34] *Protokoll des Parteitags 1919,* pp. 374 ff.

that the demands and hopes raised by such projects change into accusations against the party and against the government if they remain unfulfilled ... We must pursue 'Realpolitik' ... We cannot conserve old party views and illusions." [35]

The SPD had never before been called upon to effect its traditional economic program; this probably explains why the rejection of the intrinsically socialist aspects of that program had not occurred before 1918. That the party should, at the very time when it came into power, reject in addition to a more advanced concept of democracy the essence of its socialist economic ideas, that the party should at that moment discard all its revolutionary aspects and prevent the realization of any but the most formal changes in the old social order would indeed be sufficient to explain, even in the absence of all other factors, why the expected fruits of the revolution, why democracy could not take root and mature, if indeed it might otherwise have done so.

c. The Socialization Acts and Trade Union Gains

It was to be expected that policies like these would neither satisfy the expectations raised by the republic nor alleviate unrest and discontent. The election results in 1919 and 1920 indicated this in clear terms:

	1919 votes cast	percent	1920 votes cast	percent
KPD			441,995	1.7
USPD	2,317,290	7.6	4,895,317	18.8
SPD	11,509,048	37.9	5,614,456	21.6
German People's Party	1,345,638	4.4	3,606,316	13.9
Weimar Coalition [36]	23,131,089	76.1	11,357,620	43.7

35 Article, "Weg mit der Illusionspolitik," *Neue Zeit*, vol. XXXVIII, pt. 1, no. 5, October 31, 1919, pp. 97-104.

36 The Nationalists increased their strength between 1919 and 1920 from 3,121,479 to 3,736,778; the Democratic party was another big loser, decreasing from 5,641,825 to 2,202,334. For an example of the USPD election arguments used in 1920, see *Was hat die Nat. Vers. geleistet?*

From the very start, the SPD was aware that the failure to attain the socialist utopia might have such a result. "We cannot expect our people to suffer for forty years in a desert, in order to reach the promised land. Surely we have had desert enough behind us. The people long to attain an immediate improvement of its position," declared Scheidemann.[37]

The widespread demand for socialization had to be given some consideration regardless of the theoretical possibilities of socialization. In anticipation of such demands, the Provisional Government created a Commission on Socialization composed of the leading economists of all parties of the left and center. "And what has this commission on socialization done so far?" asked Landsberg in the National Assembly. "The only thing that the commission on socialization has so far recommended, was to declare mineral resources to be national property, and it commented that such a declaration would of course be nothing but a gesture." [38]

However, the commission had done more. It had recommended the nationalization of those branches of industry which had attained a monopolistic character, which needed neither new markets nor new sources of raw materials, which had exhausted all possibilities of further development, and which needed not enterprising management but only efficient routine administration. (They were called 'mature' industries.) If the few industries, which were thus singled out, were reduced by those where the costs of production were limited by consideration of the needs for export, little indeed was left to socialize in order to appease public desires.[39]

With due consideration of the demand of the masses and of the USPD, the SPD took up the suggestions of the

37 *Verhandlungen*, CCCXXX, 2886-92, October 7, 1919.

38 *Ibid.*, CCCXXVI, 442 ff., March 1, 1919.

39 It must be pointed out that from 1919 onward, all political parties in Germany favored the nationalization of mature industries for the national good, and that the SPD, in supporting this program, was not advancing any specifically socialist demands.

Socialization Commission and sponsored constitutional provisions for the socialization of 'mature' industries. The SPD also introduced legislation for the socialization of the coal and potash industries and of the production of electric power.[40]

Upon presenting the bill to nationalize the coal mines, Wissell declared: "The government considers it a duty to attempt through legislation to assign to the socialist tendencies a legal field of activities, to guide the mighty stream of desire for socialization into a regulated system." [41]

But the measures finally enacted had, (in a country long practicing public ownership of utilities and of various industries), little to do with socialization. Electric power production was nationalized by the cabinet of Fehrenbach, which included no SPD members. No nationalization of the mining industries was ever effected; all that was done was to enlarge the syndicate, formed before the war with government support, into a 'Reichs-Kohlenrat' which had supreme direction over policies affecting the industry and enjoyed an undisturbed and fruitful career, until the Allies occupied Germany in 1945. At the second reading of the socialization act, the SPD representative, Dr. Braun, indeed asked: "What has this law to do with the logic of Karl Marx? This law has to do with the war ... and the terrible destruction of uncounted assets." [42]

40 *Protokoll des Parteitags 1919*, pp. 363 ff., speech of Wissell, who saw in the fear of the masses the main cause for the introduction of these bills. Scheidemann denied vigorously that such considerations played any role, but his very vigor made him unconvincing; *Verhandlungen*, CCCXXVI, 576-8, March 8, 1919.

41 *Ibid.*, pp. 541 ff., March 7, 1919. When the bill for the nationalization of the production of electric energy was presented, SPD representative Kahmann declared: "A pleasing consequence of enacting this bill into law will show itself in again eliminating the dissatisfaction of the working classes." *Ibid.*, CCCXXIX, 2273 ff., August 9, 1919.

42 *Ibid.*, CCCXXVI, 718 ff., March 12, 1919. At various times, the National Assembly had received petitions to nationalize the outdoor advertising industry, pharmacies, information bureaus, Spas and Mineral Watering places, building and construction, fisheries, plate glass industries, mortgages, employment agencies, insurance, Mitropa Sleeping Car Service, etc. but no action was ever taken, and no bill introduced.

Since the SPD considered socialization impossible, it was not surprising that even public pressure could not produce a single act of socialization beyond a meaningless constitutional provision. One may perhaps apply to these constitutional provisions the characterization which the SPD spokesman on constitutional affairs, Katzenstein, had applied to the constitutional bill of rights: " It is conceded that paragraph 107 has more of an instructive than legal character, for immediate consequences in law are not to be derived from it . . . While every other article of the first part of the constitution has a definite legal consequence, the basic rights often postulate only a principle." [43]

After the acceptance of the treaty of Versailles, the SPD was wont to ascribe the inability to effect the socialist ideas to the hardships imposed by that treaty. Indeed the party argued occasionally that the sole purpose of the treaty was to prevent the populations of the allied countries from learning how well socialism could work under normal conditions.[44]

But the reasons for the SPD rejection of socialization have been outlined in the words of its own leaders; that Germany was a state within a capitalist world was not a result of the peace treaty, that socialism could not work in crisis times was not a result of the peace treaty, that the state was not capable of administrating as sensitive an organism as a national economy was not due to the peace treaty, and that co-operative ownership was essentially capitalist was also not due to the peace treaty.[45]

43 *Ibid.*, CCCXXIX, 1558, July 15, 1919. In its second reading, paragraph 107 had been assigned to the bill of rights of the German constitution.

44 For example, *ibid.*

45 After his dismissal from office, Wissell became almost the sole advocate of the idea that the treaty of Versailles had nothing to do with the economic position of Germany and that those who accused the treaty for the German economic crisis only " devolve our own weakness upon enemy superiority. If we have retained relative freedom in any area, then in the field of internal economic policy . . . " Wissell accused sharply the economic

Nor was this rejection of socialism due to SPD co-operation with bourgeois parties after the elections to the National Assembly. Dr. David testified that "it is false to consider the coalition government as the main brake. That is not so. I state here in public that from the membership of the non-socialist members of the cabinet, no difficulties in this field have been raised." [46]

Thus by contact with reality, all cherished SPD ideas crumbled into dust. But there was one large area of SPD economic endeavors, where the traditional SPD objectives attained complete realization to the satisfaction of all concerned. It was perhaps significant that this sole realization of SPD aspirations came in an area outside of government control, and without the participation of the SPD as a political party.

On November 15, 1918, the four large German trade-unions (the Free Trade-Unions, the Hirsch-Duncker Unions, the Christian Unions, and the Polish Union) concluded an agreement with twenty-one industrial associations, which contained the following provisions: the unions were recognized as the agents of the employees; all restrictions on the formation of unions were abolished; all company unions were dissolved; veterans would be re-employed in their former positions; employment offices were to be jointly administered by the associations and the unions; conditions of work were to be determined in joint conferences; all firms employing more than fifty workers would elect workers' committees; a board of arbitration was to be established and to be recognized in all contracts; both parties would be represented equally on it; a central committee equally representing both groups was to protect the pertinent interests of the industry, and to decide

---

policies of the government which were responsible for the decline of the value of the Reichsmark and for the shortage of goods. *Protokoll des Parteitags 1920*, pp. 120 ff.

46 *Ibid.*, *1919*, pp. 374 ff.

all questions affecting more than one interest group; and, finally, the eight-hour-day would be introduced.[47]

For industry, such an agreement immediately after the revolution was highly desirable; co-operation with trade-unions was preferable to bureaucratic control, because trade-unions at least knew something about the needs and requirements of their industries. Also, an industrial system which granted such sweeping concessions to the trade-unions might win their invaluable support in resisting government control and expropriation, and at the same time also eliminate the worst grievances brought against the existing economic order. For the unions, too, negotiating with private concerns was always preferable to dealing with the government as owner. Immediate concessions of this nature were better than waiting for the actions of a government as insecure in its political control as the Provisional Government in November, 1918. Max Schippel indeed commented, in an argument against socialization, that " trade-union successes . . . include in fact much more socialism than the rattling and fire-cracker-like policy of expropriation by an immature, self-satisfied, superficial, verbal radicalism." [48]

d. SPD Criticism of Official Party Policies

The advent of the socialist government in Germany had thus resulted in significant trade-union gains, (which presupposed continued capitalist modes of ownership and production,) the rejection of socialization as a practicable form of economic organization, the adoption of a meaningless constitutional provision for socialization, and the establishment of a system of

47 The agreement was initially limited to three months. Its text and an able discussion of it was furnished by Paul Umbreit in his article " Die Arbeitsgemeinschaft zwischen Arbeitgeberverbaenden und Gewerkschaften," *Neue Zeit*, vol. XXXVII, pt. I, no. 14, pp. 313-20, January 3, 1919. Umbreit stressed that this agreement grew out of the co-operation of the two groups in the economic crisis following the outbreak of the war, and their practice to co-ordinate their activities in preventing the complete disruption of industry because of the Hindenburg program.

48 *Sozialistische Monatshefte*, December 10, 1918, pp. 1123-28.

economic councils which largely imitated trade-union practices. The most revolutionary of these measures, the constitutional protection of economic councils, was effected only
under the pressure of a restless and dissatisfied public. The
reasons for the meagerness of these results were well founded
in the SPD conceptions of the causes and purposes of the revolution, and in its reconsideration of the idea of socialization.
The very strength of SPD reasoning condemned to sterility
all criticism, levied from within the ranks of the party against
these meager achievements.

Nevertheless not all SPD members could agree that the re-
appraisal of the idea of socialization left the party with no other
alternative but to return, essentially, to the pre-war economy.
In view of the economic consequences of the war, and the
urgency of restoring normal levels of production, they refused to subscribe to the idea that this was the opportune
moment " to free the state of its task of industrial organization."

Rudolf Wissell was probably the most notable SPD leader
who thought that, the idea of socialization having proven to
be impractical, if not impossible, the government had assumed
a greater obligation to intervene constructively in the economic
life of the nation. As minister of economy in the Scheidemann
cabinet, he was much concerned with the future economy of
Germany, and consequently, in May, 1919, he presented to the
government a detailed program for the economic future of
Germany, based on the idea of a thoroughly planned and integrated system of economy, and culminating in a number
of legislative proposals.[49]

Wissell's memorandum attacked the government for its do-
nothing policies in the face of the economic difficulties of

49 The memorandum was dated May 7, and had been drawn up by the
undersecretary of state Moellendorff. Through indiscretion, it was published
in the *Vossische Zeitung* on May 24, 1919, evening edition. *Cf. ibid.*, May
16, 1919; *Frankfurter Zeitung*, May 25, 1919; Wissell, *Praktische Wirtschaftspolitik*, Berlin, 1919; and *Protokoll des Parteitags 1919*.

Germany. Although the government had at its disposal a multiplicity of bureaus and ministries charged with various economic tasks, none bore a clear responsibility for planning. Yet the mobilization of the industrial resources of the country was demanded in order to meet German obligations, reparations, and the costs of imports. In the absence of a completely reorganized, uniform economy, many Germans would have no other recourse left but emigration. The absence of resolution within the government only contributed to confusion and conflicting economic demands. What was needed was leadership. "We need a firm and clear economic program so that everybody can take into consideration what the immediate future may bring . . . A socialist government may not watch carelessly while, because of some excesses, prejudiced groups poison public opinion against an obligatory, planned economy."

Wissell proposed among other things that a labor peace should be proclaimed in all industries affecting the supply of fuel, food, and clothing and in transportation. Strikes were to be permitted only after compulsory arbitration had failed and after a strike-vote, supported by at least ninety percent of the workers concerned, be taken. Government funds were to be appropriated to insure increasing production in certain fields; and the utilization of the power of taxation to influence production was envisaged. Workers, employers, merchants, and consumers were to organize 'Fachliche Wirtschaftsgruppen' on various levels. These autonomous bodies were to be charged with creating a new planned economy. Their political activity might be restricted, but whatever their actual form or scope, a compulsory plan of economic life had to be imposed and duty and discipline had to become the principle of the new life.

"The government ought to introduce into Germany not only a new political order, but also a social-economic order which allows each individual to participate organically in the formation of the will of the community . . . It must be expressed in clear and lucid terms that in the future, social and economic life shall be possible only in the spirit of subordinating the individual to the community. The people miss the spirit of social justice, the planned integration of each individual into the whole ... Economic life must not be permitted to receive its impetus only from the desire of individuals for profit, but must be subordinated to the duties of moral law." [50]

It was perhaps inauspicious that Wissell should have presented his proposals just a few days before the attention of the government was distracted by the increasing agitation over the Treaty of Versailles. The cabinet failed to act on Wissell's proposals for several months and finally rejected his proposals outright. Nor was Wissell able to rally the support of the party congress in his favor. As a result, Wissell resigned from his ministerial post.

Although Wissell's proposals exercised no noticeable result upon the doctrines and policies of the party, dissatisfaction and criticism of official SPD policies were only stimulated by this experience.

Wissell provided a keynote for this criticism when he declared that " in spite of the revolution, the people sees itself deceived in its hopes. What the people expected of the government had not taken place. We have further expanded formal democracy, certainly! But we have not done anything else but continue the program already inaugurated by Prince Max of Baden ... We could not satisfy the dark grumbling of the masses ... We lacked the spirit and the ideas, with which we could have awakened the heart and soul of the people. Essentially, we governed according to the old political forms of our body politic. We could infuse no new spirit into these forms. Nor could we influence the revolution so that Germany should seem to be filled by a new spirit. The inner essence of German culture, of social life, seems little altered ... The people be-

50 *Ibid.*, pp. 363 ff. It is interesting to note that in this speech Wissell warned against the nationalization of industries because the government would have to compensate the owners in inflated marks and thus grant them an exorbitant profit, for the Mark would surely be stabilized at its old value in the near future.

lieve that the conquests of the revolution bear merely a negative character, that the place of the old militaristic and bureaucratic rulers has only been taken by someone else and that the principle of government does not essentially differ from that of the old regime ... I believe that history will render a harsh and bitter judgment regarding the National Assembly and the government ... We have failed to satisfy the need of the masses for a deeper sense in life." [51]

Dr. Behne, a member of the staff of the *Sozialistische Monatshefte,* wrote: " We look upon the achievements of our revolution with sentiments of sorrow and shame ... What has happened within the ten weeks of the revolutionary period? Censorship has been lifted and so has the state of siege ... But except for this, after the few short days of the first enthusiasm, the spirit of the old regime has returned. Many would like best to get the old machine going again, with only its face lifted a little. You cannot achieve the impossible within ten weeks. But if you recall what was achieved within the ten weeks after the outbreak of the war, does not that which the new regime has achieved seem a little meager? One thing should at least have been demanded from it: proof that a new era had really begun, a clean, unequivocal break with the past, the resolution to make a fresh start, an open and honest condemnation of past events, not by phrases but by deeds ... It is comfortable to unload the responsibility upon the old regime, to use it as a scapegoat. But it is dishonest. For the break has nowhere been effected." [52] " That this did not take place," Max Cohen declared, " could not surprise those who knew the development

51 *Ibid.* Robert Schmidt, Wissell's successor, acknowledged that " the party members who were in the government are agreed that the SPD program has not been fulfilled by the government"; *ibid., 1920,* pp. 132 ff.

52 Article, " Unsere moralische Krise," *Sozialistische Monatshefte,* January 20, 1919, pp. 34-38. *Cf.* the articles of Wally Zepler, " Zur deutschen Nationalversammlung," *ibid.,* February 10, 1919, pp. 65-74; and Hans Brinckmann, " Staats-Neubau," *Neue Zeit,* XXXVII, pt. 1, no. 17, January 24, 1919, pp. 385-89.

of our party and hence never anticipated with all too great confidence the day which would give the direction of the body politic to Social Democracy." [53]

It is interesting, however, that not all of the critics placed the blame for these failures entirely upon the SPD. Wally Zepler, another sharp critic of official SPD policies serving on the staff of the *Sozialistische Monatshefte,* pointed out that " Germany has not yet ceased to be a land without political freedom and independence; there has not yet been nor is there now a revolution of the spirit; we have not yet learned that objectivity and striving after truth are the basic prerequisites of political morals and hence of political action as well. Nothing essential has changed .... The German army is still thought to be invincible, the German people the chosen vessel for singular spiritual grace but, with its unsophisticated noble spirit, the victim of enemy evil ... But of what use is a revolution if it does not recreate man, or a democratic constitution without social consciousness of community permeating all members of society? ... We still wait in vain for the fruits of the German revolution of 1918." [54]

The SPD had indeed been restricted in its policies by the various factors which Wally Zepler enumerated. These factors did not, however, excuse the failures of which these critics accused the party. The rejection of the proposals of Wissell, and the indifference of the party to alternative proposals signified not only a failure to solve the economic problem of Germany or to abide—in as far as was possible—by the party program of 1891; it signified the inability of the SPD to provide political initiative.

53 "Am Beginn des Friedens ", *Sozialistische Monatshefte,* January 26, 1920, pp. 7-12.

54 " Das geistige Ergebnis eines Revolutionsjahres," *ibid.,* pp. 18-27.

CHAPTER XII

THE SPD AND THE PEACE SETTLEMENT

a. The SPD and the Armistice Terms

THE Supreme Army Command had urged immediate armistice negotiations in order to end the war before Germany's collapse had become evident to the Entente leaders. "Today the army still stands, but at any moment a breakthrough may occur, and then our offer would come at the most inopportune moment," Ludendorff had warned on October 1, 1918.[1]

To insure the success of the appeal to Wilson, a 'revolution from above' had been introduced. Because there had been some doubts whether this 'revolution from above' went far enough to please Wilson, and because it had failed to forestall a reaction against the discontent bred by the war, the 'revolution from below' superceded it. Thus it was that the 'revolution from above', and the democratic and republican regime in Germany had all been introduced in order to evade the full consequences of the military defeat of Germany.

The terms which Germany accepted were based on Lansing's note of October 5, 1918, which accepted the fourteen points of Wilson with the exception of the clause about the freedom of the seas, and which stipulated "that reparations will be made by Germany for all damage done to the civilian population of

---

1 *Vorgeschichte*, no. 23, pp. 34-35. Many Allied military leaders in October, 1918, had seriously doubted whether Germany had suffered a military defeat already, and went ahead with their plans for continued warfare. The adherents of the Dolchstoss theory frequently cited this fact as proof that in the opinion of the Entente Germany had not been defeated. But the Supreme Army Command had hoped that the Entente leaders would have some illusions about the remaining German strength, and made its decisions in spite of Allied doubts about a German defeat. That the Supreme Command proved correct in its assumptions about the Allied estimate of the German position cannot therefore be cited as proof that the judgment of the German military leaders had been faulty.

the Allies and their property ... by land, by sea, and from the air." [2]

Except for the time limits imposed, the armistice terms accepted by Germany on November 11, 1918,[3] were on the whole moderate and possible of fulfillment; Erzberger was justly proud of the significant improvements which he had won.[4]

Nevertheless, Hindenburg, in his note of November 10, 1918, had advised that unless further significant concessions could be wrested from the Entente, the terms should be signed only after flaming protest and appeal to Wilson.[5] In accord with these instructions, Erzberger warned the Allied armistice commission that Germany would, without fault of her own, be unable to fulfill the terms on time, that the attempt to enforce the terms would lead to anarchy and famine, and that " a nation of seventy millions may suffer but will not die." [6]

Erzberger thus started an avalanche of protests, demonstrations, warnings and threats against the terms imposed upon Germany which got under way well before the final signature of the armistice agreement and the publication of its final terms and which enjoyed the full support not only of the government but also of the SPD.

2 *Vorgeschichte*, no. 101, p. 124.

3 *Der Waffenstillstand 1918-1919*, I, 22-57, listed in four parallel columns the original terms presented by Foch, the German objections to them, the Allied replies to the German objections, and the terms finally accepted.

4 Erzberger, *op. cit.*, pp. 340 ff. He stated that the Supreme Command was pleasantly surprised by these modifications.

5 *Vorgeschichte*, no. 107, p. 128.

6 Protocol of the final session of the armistice commissions at Compiègne; *Der Waffenstillstand*, I, 61-73. On January 10, 1920, according to a protocol signed by Germany, Germany still had not fulfilled the original armistice conditions in the following respects: 42 locomotives and 4460 railroad cars were as yet undelivered; the withdrawal of her troops from the East to her pre-war boundaries had not yet been effected; Germany had not yet stopped her requisitions in the East; she had not returned the specie, shares, stocks, and currency taken from the occupied areas; and not all submarines had been delivered. The protocol appears as No. 1, pp. 6-8, in *Protocols and Correspondence between the Supreme Council...and the German Government...Between January 10, 1920 and July 17, 1920*, CMD 1325.

On November 10, 1918, Solf warned Lansing that the present terms and the continuation of the blockade, the cession of rolling stock and the imposition of the costs of Allied occupation would lead to starvation and breed an atmosphere unfavorable to order and peace.[7] The *Vorwaerts* termed the armistice conditions " truly terrible." [8] Kurt Eisner warned the Entente that the news about the armistice terms dashed all hopes placed on the success of the revolution. " If these terrible terms are unalterable, the new republic will within a short time be a desert and a chaos ... If these demands are insisted upon, we approach conditions which no human fancy can imagine." German democracy must not be destroyed by the lack of mercy shown by the victors.[9] In a joint appeal to Branting, Stauning, and Troelstra, the socialist leaders of Sweden, Denmark, and Holland, the USPD and the SPD called attention to the continuation of the blockade and the " policy of starvation ". Germany could not be supplied with food, if the blockade continued and if German shipping was barred from the high seas, if railroad material was to be ceded and foreign occupation troops fed. Because these terms hit the German revolutionary masses hardest, the socialists of the neutral countries were asked to use their endeavors in the interest of modification.[10]

On November 15, 1918, the Executive Council declared that the restoration of the economic life of Germany and her salvation from misery and starvation were impossible, if the Entente imposed unbearably severe armistice and peace terms.

7 Cited by Ahnert, *op. cit.*, pp. 207-08.

8 Cited by Buchner, *op. cit.*, no. 155d, pp. 152-53. Wrote the *Leipziger Volksstimme* on November 11: " The armistice terms are of a severity which makes the treaty of Brest-Litovsk look like child's play, a severity which can be explained only by the bottomless hate and deeply rooted fear, which the damnable militarism ... has provoked all through the world; " *ibid.*, no. 155e, p. 153.

9 Appeal of Eisner of November 10, 1918, cited *ibid.*, no. 180, pp. 177-78.

10 Cited *ibid.*, no. 181, p. 178.

Germany offered the hand of a brother, it was said, to the peoples of the Entente and asked them to influence their governments so as not to condemn Germany to political impotence and starvation. True to the reiteration of Entente leaders, the Entente should help attain true peace and brotherly understanding between nations, without conquests or oppression. The Entente should provide for the free development and self-determination of all peoples, and should not condemn Germany to enslavement.[11]

The continuation of the blockade in particular proved a convenient pretext for attacking the armistice terms. These protests ignored the fact that the armistice terms, Wilson's address to Congress on November 11, and Lansing's note to the German government on November 15, had all promised to supply Germany with food, provided that German shipping could be used and an equitable distribution be assured. The government, however, attacked the 'continuation' of the blockade as being responsible for the German infant mortality which was placed at thirty to fifty percent.[12] And these pro-

11 *Vorwaerts*, November 15, 1918. Prince Lichnowsky in the same paper and on the same date pleaded that the armistice terms breathed a spirit of revenge, which would result in anarchy and chaos, misery, starvation and Bolshevism in Germany. " Must I point out that a peace of compulsion under the cruel exploitation of our present situation would endanger the ideal of a league of nations, of future world peace; that a peace leading to our financial and economic ruin, that the dismemberment of the Fatherland, the separation of geographically and economically vital areas, which owe their prosperity to German administration, German order, would mean the destruction of the labor of many generations and the cession of compact German national areas? "; the restoration of German economy was vital to England, etc.

12 *Deutsche Allgemeine Zeitung*, November 16, cited by Buchner, *op. cit.*, no. 281, pp. 241-42. *Cf. The Starving of Germany*, papers read at the extraordinary meeting of the United Medical Societies in Berlin, December 18, 1918. After the prolongation of the armistice on December 13, 1918, the provisioning of Germany depended on her readiness to supply 2,500,000 tons of shipping to the Allied shipping pool. The argumentation used by the Germans in regard to the blockade was of the same type that was furnished by an exchange of telegrams between Hindenburg and Foch,

tests continued until at long last Germany was ready to put the required shipping at the disposal of the Entente and to make arrangements for the payment of food imports. As late as March 1, 1919, the National Assembly adopted a unanimous resolution calling for an end of the blockade.[13]

The blockade was not the only point of the armistice terms which the government and the SPD consistently opposed. Noske witnessed the sailing of the fleet to its internment at Scapa Flow with feelings of sorrow and of shame.[14] And rather than surrender the fleet to the Allies, its commander ordered the fleet to be scuttled.[15] The deliveries in kind, agreed upon by the armistice terms, fell hopelessly behind. There was continued opposition against the evacuation of territories in the West and to the inclusion of German areas in the same

---

published by the *Vorwaerts*, on November 17, 1918. Foch had charged the German troops with continued looting and destruction in Belgium; Hindenburg answered that the responsibility for this rested with the Entente whose time limits for evacuation precluded an orderly retreat, the methods of the Entente made the protection of German and Allied populations impossible, and in addition, not German soldiers, but Belgian civilians had committed these acts.

13 *Verhandlungen*, vol. CCCXXXV, no. 30, pp. 34-35; CCCXXVI, 410 ff. Edler von Braun, the undersecretary of state for food, presented in his report to the National Assembly a summary of the negotiations regarding this; *ibid.*, pp. 632 ff. The texts of the negotiations etc. will be found in *Der Waffenstillstand, passim.* R. B. Mowat, *A History of European Diplomacy*, London, 1927, argued in his Chapter VII, that the immediate lifting of the blockade would have had no effect on the food situation. S. M. Bouton, *And the Kaiser Abdicates*, New Haven, 1920, *passim*, also thought that the reports which reached the Allied world about the German food situation were biased and colored. For an example of such a report see *Further Reports of British Officers on the Economic Conditions Prevailing in Germany*, CMD 208, March and April, 1919. *Cf.* Bane and Lutz, *The Blockade of Germany*, Stanford, 1942.

14 Noske, *op. cit.*, pp. 39 ff.

15 Admiral Reuter, *Scapa Flow*, Leipzig, 1921, pp. 84 ff. Reuter assumed that Germany would refuse to sign the peace treaty, and hence acted to prevent the acquisition of the fleet by the Entente while hostilities were being reopened.

evacuation zone as Entente provinces.[16] The financial clauses of the armistice terms remained unfulfilled until 1920. There were sharp protests against the threat of the annexation of the German colonies,[17] and above all, against the evacuation of the Eastern territories occupied by Germany under the treaty of Brest-Litovsk and the cession of German areas to Poland.[18]

After a return from an official visit to the Eastern areas, Under-Secretary for foreign affairs, von Gerlach, had declared that there was no danger of disturbances in these regions. The food supply from Posen was secure, and the recent Polish elections intended only to legalize the Polish People's Councils which were ready to function within the boundaries of Ger-

16 Note of Solf, November 25, 1918: "It does not seem impossible that this was done in order to add these areas to Alsace-Lorraine, respectively Luxemburg.... The German government... most solemnly objects." Cited by Buchner, *op. cit.*, no. 395, p. 320.

17 On March 1, 1918, the National Assembly adopted a resolution supported by all parties except the USPD, calling for the restitution of German colonies as League of Nations' mandates; *Verhandlungen*, vol. CCCXXXV, no. 96, p. 72; CCCXXVI, 411 ff. Dr. Bell, Germany's minister for colonies, declared: "Germany's demand for the restitution of her colonial possessions is unyielding and not expendable. Free of lust for conquest or annexationist imperialism, we demand our own colonial possessions, because we consider it to be a vital necessity for a people of seventy millions to take part in the spread of culture and civilization, and to mobilize our entire ability for the spiritual and economic advancement of the natives.... An arbitrary exclusion of Germany from this colonial cooperation would mean an unbearable moral degradation of Germany, an evil as unpardonable and as disastrous as the throttling of the economic sinews of our . . . slowly recovering economy by cutting off our vital colonial trade;" *ibid.*, pp. 411-14. The entire trade of all of the German colonies in 1912 was only two and one-half percent of the entire German foreign trade.

18 The Statistisches Amt, in a pamphlet entitled *Are the Eastern Provinces of Germany indisputably Polish territories?* pointed out that, although sixty-one and two-tenths percent of the population of the province of Posen were Polish, the German minorities in Polish districts were twice as large as the Polish minorities in the districts with German majorities; Germans owned a larger share of the homes, of private properties, of factories and paid a large share of taxes; hence the region could not be considered as Polish.

many and which did not intend to confront the peace conference with a fait accompli.[19] Yet in spite of this report, the press flooded Germany with reports of Polish expansion into 'German' areas, and the Government eventually broke off relations with Poland.[20] SPD representative Schulz declared before the National Assembly on March 5, 1919: "The Poles cannot show that they were in any way provoked ... by the Germans"; even the treatment accorded to these provinces during the war would not excuse the Polish annexations of these regions.[21]

The formation of the free-corps had been excused by the need to defend the Eastern regions against Polish aggression.

19 *Deutsche Allgemeine Zeitung*, November 22, 1918, cited by Buchner, *ibid.*, no. 396a, pp. 321-22.

20 A Polish ultimatum of December 24, 1918, had demanded that the retreating German soldiers surrender a certain amount of their arms when returning to Germany. As a result, the Provisional Government on December 26, 1918, discussed a declaration of war against Poland, but the motion to declare war failed. See Barth, *op. cit.*, pp. 108-119. For an example of the press campaign see *Hannoverische Kurier*, November 23, 1918: "It is probably no longer necessary to point out in detail how perniciously this action is directed against international conciliation in general and against the program of Wilson in particular. The prerequisite for the fulfillment of Polish desires in Posen would be first their indubitable Polish population and secondly ... clearly defined national demands.... Within the province of Posen, there are 806,000 Germans among 2,000,000 inhabitants; of the total real estate, 1,124,000 hectars are in Polish compared with 1,618,680 hectars in German hands. These figures tell all. In their light the Polish uprisings in Posen appear as ... a cowardly assault upon their German fellow citizens." One SPD spokesman talked about the German population of these areas as being handed over, by their cession to Poland, to 'Unkultur'; *Protokoll des Parteitags 1919*, pp. 259-60. Another SPD spokesman declared in the National Assembly: "Immediately after taking over the areas, which had been torn from us without plebiscite, Poland began to sabotage the peace treaty. Visas and passports are required for transit, two Polish and two German controls must be passed, and the Polish soldiers today use towards us the tone, which previously, while in German uniforms, they used ... towards other inhabitants of this area;" *Verhandlungen,* CCCXXXIII, 5284-5; April 21, 1920. A similar campaign, incidentally, directed itself against Danish desires in Schleswig-Holstein. *Cf.* the pamphlet *Up ewich ungedelt!* (1919?).

21 *Verhandlungen*, CCCXXVI, 511 ff.

A special division ' Heimatschutz Ost ' had been created and
Noske warned that " the terrible danger threatening our homeland in the East increases daïly. Russians, Poles, and Czechs
stretch out their hands for German possessions. Already the
armies of the Bolshevists stand before the gates of East-Prus-
sia, and the Poles stand deep in old German territory." [22] The
creation of the temporary Reichswehr in February, 1919, too,
had largely been motivated by these Eastern conditions. Erzberger declared on March 5, 1919: " It is the duty of the German people to oppose in the strongest possible manner the expansion of the Poles. The Assembly has done its duty by
creating ... the Reichswehr. It is now the duty of our youth
of military age, particularly of the youth in the East, to defend their homeland with all resolutions.[23]

These attacks launched upon individual provisions of the
armistice terms were out of all proportions to their actual
consequences or hardships, and the vehemence and the intransigence of these attacks made it seem doubtful that factual
considerations were their sole cause. But the attacks directed
against the armistice terms as a whole went even further.

Paul Lensch, for example, wrote in the *Neue Zeit*: " Germany ... has fulfilled the most brutal armistice terms with a
promptness and exactness which should have won recognition
of even the toughest opponent, if this opponent really cared
about peace and its security. But he does not, as is known, care
for that, but for the economic and political strangulation of
Germany ... Germany is as defenseless now as she was in the
sixteenth and seventeenth centuries. But far from bringing
about peace, this condition has only encouraged the enemy ...
Heretofore, Negro potentates hardly ever were treated in the

22 Quoted in *Deutscher Geschichtskalender, ibid.,* I, 421-22.

23 *Verhandlungen,* CCCXXVI, 507 ff. There was a great deal of pamphlet
literature inciting the population by the threat of the repetition of the
' terrible atrocities' committed by the Russians in 1914; *Cf.* Heimatschutz
Ost, *Ostpreussen wacht auf!*; Reichsverband Ost, *Die Polnische Schmach,*
etc.

manner in which the spokesmen of the French bourgeoisie dare treat the German socialist republic. Does the revolutionary government not have threefold reason and cause to brand the foreheads of this gang of slavers, to denounce them as traitors to liberty and democracy, as mortal enemies of the peace of nations and the league of nations? . . . A people which in fifty months of world war achieved such superhuman tasks, which has starved and bled, conquered and fought, has the right to demand that in the end it be not dishonored too." [24]

Noske wrote about the armistice terms in the following vein: " More brutal armistice terms than those imposed upon the German people . . . could not have been dictated . . . An icy fear should have gripped the body of the last German; only one thought should have filled the entire population: How to preserve the Reich from the destruction which was obviously being prepared . . . Instead, one section wanted to drive the revolution further and threw the country into serious internal disturbances . . . In the streets of Germany flowed the blood of citizens because of the horrible internecine war, and in the National Assembly one debate of fight and scandal followed another . . . Meanwhile, month after month, men sat in Paris, their heads filled partly by glowing desire for revenge, partly by coolest aspiration for power, and hatched out what later came to be known as the peace treaty. If in these months the Allied and Associated [Powers] took notice of Germany, it was only to exact new extortions and deeper humiliations . . . Hate, paired with the avarice of the victors led . . . to a result, than which none more conniving and cruel could have been designed . . . To the dismemberment of the Reich and the economic strangulation had been added the attempt at dishonoring . . . They did not spare the tortured German people the last dregs of the cunningly designed malice, but forced it pitilessly through the Caudinian yoke." [25]

24 Article, " Die Waffenstillstandsverhandlungen und die Haltung der Partei," *Neue Zeit*, vol. XXXVII, pt. 1, no. 18, January 31, 1919, pp. 415 ff.

25 Noske, *op. cit.*, pp. 147-53.

In a note to the German government on November 20, 1918, Hindenburg declared that the enemy, by insisting on impossible armistice terms, was only trying to find a legal basis for the resumption of hostilities, while the German army, due to the armistice terms and conditions at home, was in no position to resume fighting.[26]

Solf, in a note to the enemy governments, developed the argument that although Germany had asked for an armistice on the basis of the fourteen points, she had in fact received an armistice of violation and annihilation, precluding any future international conciliation. The armistice represented nothing but the continuation of warfare with different means. It aimed to make domestic peace and orderly demobilization impossible, and to deliver Germany to anarchy and chaos. The German government saw " in the imposition of the severe conditions an attack upon the principles of civilization, and must conclude that the governments of the Allied countries seek nothing but the violation and annihilation of the German people ... The German people begins to wonder whether behind the delay of the peace there does not lurk the intent of the enemies to put into the wrong the hunted and tired German troops through non-fulfillment of impossible armistice conditions, and thus to create for the Allies a cause for the continuation of war. If the peace is to be concluded as a peace of justice, one must not anticipate the decisions of the peace conference in matters of controversial legality ... In conflict with these principles enunciated by the President, ... the measures taken by the French government in Alsace-Lorraine and the actions of the

26 WTB, November 22, 1918, quoted by Buchner, *op. cit.*, no. 391, pp. 319. Continued Hindenburg: " I consider it my duty to emphasize this also, because ... the enemy governments will conclude a peace treaty only with a German government, based on a majority of the German people." *Cf.* report of the *Hamburger Echo*, November 23, that the Entente would abrogate the armistice terms, if the disturbances in Berlin continued or if diplomatic relations with Russia were resumed; the Entente would deal only with a government which had been confirmed by a plebiscite in Germany; *ibid.*, no. 400, p. 324.

Poles in the Eastern borderlands of Germany ... are nothing but attempts to anticipate by force the decisions of the peace conference." [27]

The Provisional Government and the government of Scheidemann repeatedly presented what *they* considered to be acceptable peace terms. Scheidemann's foreign minister, Count Brockdorff-Rantzau, declared before the National Assembly on February 14, 1919, that Germany must not be treated as a people of secondary rank to be quarantined. Germany was willing to agree to disarmament and the arbitration of international disputes, if her neighbors agreed too. Germany must be given a clear title to her colonies, her merchant marine, Alsace-Lorraine, Austria, the Sudeten area, and the territories seized by Poland—at least until a final determination of their ethnic character had been made. In return for these concessions, Germany would grant to Poland the right of free transit through West Prussia to the Baltic sea.[28]

On April 10, 1919, the National Assembly, with the support of all parties except the USPD, resolved to support only those peace terms which effected the fourteen points, self-determination, national and political freedom, the liberation of the prisoners of war, lifting of the blockade, and the evacuation of the areas occupied by the Entente, and to reject a territorial settlement in contradiction to these terms. The government was instructed to refuse any treaty which sacrificed present and future German interests.[29]

27 Note of November 23, 1918, cited by Buchner, *ibid.*, no. 401, pp. 324-25. In its desire to evade the armistice terms, the Provisional Government even offered, on December 12, 1918, to march together with the Entente against Russia and to help avert the danger of Bolshevism from Europe, in return for the right to arm soldiers and ships; see *Verhandlungen*, CCCXXVI, 196-98, February 19, 1919.

28 *Ibid.*, pp. 66-70.

29 *Ibid.*, CCCXXVII, 961.

b. THE SPD AND THE PEACE TREATY

The frenzy of protest and indignation that greeted the peace treaty of Versailles was comparable only to the reception which had been accorded to the Armistice terms in Germany.

As early as March 26, 1919, Scheidemann had pointed out that according to semi-official sources, the peace treaty would impose upon Germany "unheard-of sums for reparations," the cession of "large stretches of purely German soil," and "strangling limitations upon our financial and military affairs." While these exorbitant demands had been permitted to leak out in order to accustom Germany to the idea of a peace of violation, "the whole of Germany is an appeal [sic], not of chauvinist character, but an appeal from torture and despair, an appeal ... to the conscience of mankind ... We protest against the attempt of our enemies to garrot us." [30]

On May 12, 1919, the text of the treaty was presented to a special session of the National Assembly. Talking about the territorial cessions, Scheidemann declared: " He who tries to separate us, cuts with a murderous knife the living body of the German people." He referred to the treaty as the " most horrible and murderous ' Hexenhammer ' with which a great people shall be forced to confess their own worthlessness, agreement to merciless dismemberment, and accord to enslavement and helotism ... This book must not become the law of the future." He termed it " the strangling hand at our throat "; a comparison of its terms to the fourteen points would be " blasphemy "; it put a people of sixty million behind barbed wire as forced laborers. What " hand must not wither, which puts itself and us into such fetters? " `All these measures of " shackling and humbling and plundering " meant, in fact, " the miserable enslavement of child and grandchild ... This treaty

30 *Ibid.*, pp. 807-09.

is, in the opinion of the Reich government, unacceptable. Away with this blueprint for murder!" [31]

In the debate over this declaration, the SPD representative Mueller agreed that the treaty sacrificed Germany's right to a peace based on justice, that it continued the war but with other means. The treaty meant the abandonment of the ideals for which the Entente professedly had fought the war; it was inherently unfit to usher in the promised era of eternal peace. Its economic burdens were such that they could not be fulfilled " even if you take the last shirt off the back of the last German ... This proposed treaty is unbearable and impossible of fulfillment, and therefore it is, in its present form, unacceptable. I am making this statement in the name of the [SPD] faction." [32] Other SPD speakers in the same debate expressed similar sentiments. [33]

Similar protest meetings were held all over Germany. Ebert termed the provisions unbearable and impossible; the treaty sought to destroy German industry and economy, and must be opposed for the sake of honor. " I can assure you in the name

31 *Ibid.*, pp. 1082-84. On this occasion, the National Assembly met at the University of Berlin, probably to symbolize that the present plight of Germany should be compared to that of 1810 when the university was founded.

32 *Ibid.*, pp. 1085-86. The speaker went on to say that the treaty terms obviously meant the termination of all present social security schemes, that it would lead to unemployment and disorder, and create a threat to the neighbors of Germany. " In German socialism, the Entente capitalists basically wish to hit [the idea of] socialism in all countries."

33 *Ibid.*, pp. 1089-90, 1106. During this debate, all parties rivalled each other in the search for words strong enough to condemn the treaty. Yet none of the speakers of the day, except Scheidemann, knew the text of the treaty. None of them could possibly have read it, since its text had not yet been published and had not been distributed to the members of the National Assembly until immediately before this session opened; according to Groeber, the Centrist speaker for the day; *ibid.*, pp. 1087 ff. In closing the session, its president, the later chancellor, Fehrenbach, declared that the popular reaction would convince the Entente of Germany's resolution to reject the treaty. He termned Germany the " most peace-loving people in the world"; *ibid.*, pp. 1110-11.

of the government: we cannot and will not sign this peace."
" A people of seventy million will never submit to such shame-
ful terms. The German government will never accept these
terms. We reject them come what may." [34]

The government of Scheidemann was thus earnestly resolved
not to sign the peace treaty, unless significant and far-reaching
changes were embodied in it. In her note to the Allied and
Associated Powers, Germany therefore asked for a thorough
revision of the peace terms. But although the Allies agreed to
some basic changes, notably in respect to Danzig and Upper
Silesia, they remained adamant. " If these things are hardships for Germany, they are hardships which Germany has
brought upon herself. Somebody must suffer for the consequences of the war. Is it to be Germany, or the peoples she has
wronged? " [35]

This attitude ruled out the possibility of a major revision of
the treaty by way of negotiations. In order to appraise the
military prospects for renewed resistance against the demands
of the Allies, the government consulted the leaders of the
army. On June, 19, 1919, Noske, Groener, Maercker, and
others conferred in Weimar on the possibilities of reopening
hostilities. They concluded that Germany was able to maintain
public order with the forces at her disposal in such a contingency. If Poland were the only enemy to face Germany,
Germany could probably conquer her. But if Germany were to
face the armies of the Western Powers too, all her western
provinces would have to be evacuated as far east as the Elbe,
and even at the banks of the Elbe a successful stand against
the Western Powers was out of the question.[36] On June 20,
1919, Hindenburg confirmed this estimate of the military

34 Ebert, *op. cit.*, II, 165-68.

35 For the text of the German note, see *Foreign Relations of the United
States, 1919; the Paris Peace Conference*, VI, 795 ff., XIII, 39 ff. For the
reply to this note, see *ibid.*, VI, 926 ff., XIII, 44 ff.

36 Maercker, *op. cit.*, pp. 286 ff.

situation, but advised—as other generals had done—that honor demanded even suicidal action.[37]

The hope of avoiding the signature of the treaty either by negotiations or by resuming hostilities was thus in vain. Indeed the desire of the German government and of all political parties (except the USPD) to do so had been quite unrealistic from the very beginning.[38] It was Erzberger who insisted on discussing not only the consequences of acceptance, but the consequences of the rejection of the treaty as well. In a detailed memorandum, he compared the probable results of either alternative; and by June 19, he had won half of the cabinet to the view that the consequences of acceptance were preferable to the consequences of non-acceptance, since the treaty could be enforced by the Entente in any case.[39] In the resulting cabinet crisis, the government of Scheidemann was replaced by a cabinet headed by Gustav Bauer, with Hermann Mueller as minister of foreign affairs.

37 Text of note cited by Horkenbach, *Das Deutsche Reich von 1918 bis heute*, Berlin, 1930, I, 78. Originally, the officers' corps had wanted to make Noske a dictator with the purpose of heading resistance, but Noske refused; Maercker, *ibid.* The lingering hopes for resistance were finally suppressed by Groener. As an alternative, many officers had decided to resign. Most were finally persuaded to stay on; Noske, *op. cit.*, pp. 151 ff.; Hindenburg, however, did resign. The idea of resistance was so strong that the interned German battle fleet was scuttled in preparation of renewed warfare, and the conquered French battle flags of 1870 burned. Erzberger, *op. cit.*, pp. 380, thought that because of this action, the Entente refused to accept the signature of the treaty with reservations about paragraphs 227-231, which provided for extradiction of war criminals, etc.

38 Scheidemann, *Zusammenbruch*, pp. 240-41, declared that he rejected the treaty only because of the pressure of his cabinet. But, in the absence of any support for that statement, and in view of his entire attitude during the crisis, one may perhaps doubt this.

39 Erzberger, *op. cit.*, pp. 371-73, gave the text of this memorandum. He had arrived at this conclusion by the end of May. Cf. *ibid.*, pp. 365 ff.; Scheidemann, *ibid.*, pp. 243 ff. The hostility of the right towards Erzberger was probably caused by this stand on the treaty more than by his role in the armistice commission.

On June 22, 1919, Bauer presented his cabinet to the National Assembly and asked for powers to sign the treaty with reservations regarding the war criminal clauses. He declared that the refusal to sign the treaty would not delay its execution for more than a few hours, because Germany was unable to prevent its execution; but if accepted, "the treaty itself offers a lever, of which we cannot allow ourselves to be deprived," namely the promise of periodical revision. He would sign the treaty yielding to force only and without inner conviction; "we raise [our] protest for all future and we swear that no signature shall weaken it." [40]

Loebe declared on behalf of the SPD that the party advocated acceptance of the treaty "only because we anticipate even more terrible things in case we reject it ... We lack all power of resistance against this peace treaty; this is why we must bear it. We also know that with the best will and most zealous efforts to execute the conditions of the enemy, we and the enemy, too, will eventually learn that many conditions of the treaty cannot be fulfilled .... even after our signature ... The more deeply the German nation is humbled, the more faithfully will the German workers support it ... [and] in spite of the unheard of conditions ... do their all for the re-birth of the German people." [41]

The Allies, however, refused to accept a conditional signature of the treaty, and on June 23, 1919, Bauer went to the National Assembly for further authorization, because "in addition to enslavement, the enemy wants to burden us with

40 *Verhandlungen*, CCCXXVII, 1113-15.

41 *Ibid.*, pp. 1115-17. He expressed his hopes for the dawn of a happier era, when the Sudeten area, Austria, Tyrol, and certain parts of Hungary would become parts of Germany; *ibid.* Haase, *ibid.*, pp. 1125-29, accused the government of duplicity; it should have known full well that it would have to sign in the end, and therefore its propaganda in opposition to the treaty served only to raise the nationalist sentiments of the people to a fever pitch. The vote on the acceptance of the treaty was 237 to 138 with five abstentions. Stresemann, because of sickness, was not present at any of these debates and votes.

shame as well ... A defeated people is being violated body and soul as no other people ever before." Bauer accepted the supreme insult, which the rightist parties tendered him by affirming that his cabinet had been guided by patriotic sentiments alone in recommending the acceptance of the treaty of Versailles.[42]

The SPD henceforward defended the *signature* of the treaty staunchly and ably. The German rightist groups had asked " what would have happened, had our national representation opposed a rigid no? In the worst case, a few more villages would have been burned, perhaps we would have had a little less bread; but we would have preserved our national honor, and shouldered the terrible ill-fortune with dignity. Then we would have worn the enemy's chains in honor." [43] In a sharp polemic against this argument, the SPD representative Kraetzig declared: " We hence should have increased the immense ill-fortune, and having done so, we would have shouldered the ill-fortune with dignity. I cannot agree that, if somebody is forced to something, he will appear in special dignity if he has to be beaten to comply with his task. For such insane concepts of honor and dignity we have no understanding ... I point to another officer, who also occupied himself with that question. He wrote: '... I believe that the preservation of our honor will not be assured if we allow ourselves to be fettered completely by the enemy invading the country, but only if we mobilize all our energies and strive to

42 *Ibid.*, pp. 1139-41. The refusal of the Entente to accept conditional signature had produced a cabinet crisis. Bauer wanted to resign, and the rightist parties were thrown into turmoil since they would have had to accept the chancellorship and agree to the signature of the treaty. When Bauer therefore asked that the rightist parties confirm in open session that he was acting for the national good, they jumped at this opportunity. On June 23, there was no roll call, and it has later been charged that even members of the rightist parties voted in favor of the treaty to insure its passage, but the evidence is doubtful.

43 Richard Henn, *Betrachtungen und Rueckschluesse zur Unterzeichnung des Friedens.*

prove to the world that we still are the efficient German nation which others urgently need for their own prosperity.' The preservation of national honor consists of this action and not in heroic gestures and phrases." [44]

In a vehement (tax) debate, provoked by the statement of Hugenberg that the enemy " had better occupy the entire Ruhr basin at once," [45] the SPD representative, Dr. Braun, declared: " I cannot conceive of a graver anti-nationalism than that which makes it impossible for us to recover, to reconstruct, and again lead an economic life ... What does it mean ... to refuse the means needed to recover and to grant to the Entente that which, on the basis of the peace treaty of Versailles, we must grant it, even with a heavy heart and grinding of teeth? But does it not mean solely that we will become an English or French colony, to give up our entire Fatherland, to let it become an object for Entente exploitation? That is the nationalism of those men! The only consequence would be that there would no longer be any Germany but only a colony of the Entente ... But we wish to let Germany continue to exist, we wish to protect Germany ... we wish to secure for us the sovereignty of our country, we do not wish that the Ruhr basin be occupied, we do not want Germany to become a colony. ... We could well understand that instead of paying taxes, he [Hugenberg] advocates granting the Reich loans at interest. But this speech . . . was an uninterrupted vilification of what Germany suffers and fights for today." [46]

But this defense of the acceptance of the treaty by the SPD and the government did not mean that the SPD had agreed to

44 *Verhandlungen*, CCCXXVIII, 1876 ff., July 24, 1919.

45 *Ibid.*, CCCXXXI, 3932 ff., December 9, 1919. This was one of the many scandalous debates attacking Erzberger, and Hugenberg was orating against the latter's tax proposals.

46 *Ibid.*, pp. 3949 ff., December 10, 1919. Erzberger's refutation of Hugenberg, *ibid.*, pp. 3940 ff., was one of his most uncompromising attacks upon the right in an ever increasingly violent series of debates; his oratory even swayed the president of the National Assembly to call Hugenberg to order for his " crude impertinence "; *ibid.*, pp. 3947-48.

observe the treaty. There was no compromise or acquiescence with the treaty proper. From the day of the signature until the outbreak of war in 1939, and in regard to every provision of the treaty requiring the co-operation or good will of Germany, the record was one of unparalleled obstruction, evasion and negation up to the very limits which military inferiority after 1918 had imposed.[47]

The SPD declared: " We vow today that we shall never abandon our compatriots who have been torn from us ... Unbreakable is the bond which ties us to the Germans in Bohemia, Moravia, and Silesia, in Tyrol, Carinthia, and Styria. In all of us lives the hope that all Germans ... will soon be united ... We protest against the taking away of our colonies ... The day will come when this unheard-of injustice will be repaired ... We shall not rest in our zealous task to create ... the power ... to renounce this treaty." [48]

Upon the ratification of the treaty, Hermann Mueller declared: " Today and for ever, we maintain our unanimous protest against this violation-become-treaty ... Our entire people faces today a forty years' march through the desert ... We will have a dismembered Germany, of which parts have been torn away whose population according to language and custom is German ... We do not have the power to prevent this disaster. But we wish to assure these Germans that we shall not forget them ... until ... in the not too distant future ... all controversial national issues will find their just solution." [49]

47 An SPD delegate to the 1921 party congress declared that " the great historical task which this republic must solve is to remove the dictate of peace, to overcome the consequences of the destructive war;" *Protokoll des Parteitags 1921*, p. 291. *The Foreign Relations of the United States, 1919; The Paris Peace Conference*, XIII, provides an indispensable reference work for the history of later modifications, etc., of each clause of the treaty of Versailles. It is unfortunate that this work fails to live up to its own standards of complete and exhaustive coverage for the period prior to 1921.

48 *Verhandlungen*, CCCXXVII, 1408-09, July 9, 1919.

49 *Ibid.*, p. 1408. The SPD speaker Eisenbarth declared at the party congress in 1920: " We now have the opportunity to estimate the con-

The SPD representative Winnig assured the National Assembly that the Eastern settlement did not provide fair plebiscites and " hence the German character of these areas could
never be affected by the results of such a vote ... The day
will come when the victory of justice will repair the injustice
of Versailles." [50]. Nor was the SPD foreign minister of the
Hermann Mueller cabinet, Dr. Koester, less outspoken on this
matter. " I affirm here that we, the German people, and particularly the people within our borders can never recognize
these plebiscites and their results ... that we may perhaps
recognize the results with our heads and brains, but never
with our hearts." [51]

In an article entitled " *Dennoch!* " the SPD minister of
education in Prussia, Konrad Haenisch, wrote: " Never did
my friends and I believe in the pretty illusion of a ' peace of
understanding ', ... in the illusion of a peace ' without victors
and vanquished '. ... That which now has become a terrible
reality ... was the horror of our days ... In these days of the
most terrible collapse, ... piteous [individuals] of all sorts
seemingly cannot get enough of masochistic spitting upon
themselves and beating themselves. They shout daily into the
ears of the whole world their hysterical bellows of self-indict-

---

sequences of the peace treaty of Versailles. We must credit to the account
of the treaty all the misery which came upon us and under which the proletariat suffers most.... We must undermine and abolish this treaty sys-
tematically.... This treaty is a threat to our life; it seizes the German
people at the throat, and we must destroy it with all the moral means which
[alone] are at our disposal"; *Protokoll des Parteitags 1920*, pp. 67-68.
Wissell was almost the sole SPD party member who objected against the
indiscriminate use of the Versailles treaty as a scapegoat for all Germans
ills.

50 *Verhandlungen*, CCCXXVII, 1413 ff. This session ratified the treaty by
a vote of 209 to 116.

51 *Ibid.*, CCCXXXIII, 5255-60. Koester argued that the plebiscites asked
for a vote not only between two nationalities, but also between victor and
vanquished, high and low taxes, hunger and plenty; he thought that the
1815 settlement of Eupen and Malmedy was an injustice only because
Prussia had not also acquired their hinterland at the time.

ment for the 'sole criminal guilt of Germany for the World War.' But in these days especially we need a confession in favor of national dignity and self-respect ... This termination of the war, this peace of shame ... which represents the t e m p o r a r y victory of Entente c a p i t a l i s m over German s o c i a l i s m   i s   n o t   y e t   t h e   l a s t   w o r d ... In the end the 'ideas of 1914'. . . will yet carry the victory over the military and political successes of the Western Powers and over the ideas of 1789, which now seemingly are victorious ... The peace of dishonor of Versailles will ultimately mean nothing more than 'a scrap of paper '." [52]

c. SPD OPPOSITION TO THE OCCUPATION OF THE RHINELAND

Among the most deep-felt grievances of the German government and of the SPD was the loss of Alsace-Lorraine, of Eupen and Malmedy, and the Allied occupation of the Rhineland.[53]

The French use of colonial troops in the Rhineland in particular enraged the German public and the SPD. France had been persuaded to use colored troops because of the breakdown of discipline among her white troops. Dr. Koester, the SPD foreign minister, commented on this point: " If we should further suffer by the occupation, we will accept this inferior discipline which you state to exist among your white troops if you will only rid us as fast as possible of this black plague." [54] " Senegalese Negroes," lamented Hermann Mueller, the SPD chancellor, " occupy the university of Frankfurt and guard the Goethe House." [55]

52 The article was printed as the introduction to Haenisch, *op. cit.*, pp. 1-8. Spacings in the original.

53 Since the reparations problem did not become acute until 1921 and the problem of the war criminals had been successfully sabotaged, the occupation of the Rhineland provided the main grievance in the interim period.

54 *Verhandlungen*, CCCXXXIII, 5692-93, May 20, 1920.

55 *Ibid.*, pp. 5048-53, April 12, 1920.

During a discussion on the use of colored troops in the Rhineland, Mrs. Roehl, the SPD spokesman, declared that their presence among the occupation forces was a humiliation of German womanhood. Their use was insulting and revolting; it only increased inter-national hate. Their actions were so repugnant, declared Mrs. Roehl, that only with reluctance did one make public the known cases of rape committed. The use of these colored troops exposed young girls and defenseless women to the most grievous moral dangers; whole classes of girls and their teachers sometimes had to flee from them. There was a difference in the moral standard of colored troops and Westerners, and hence it did not represent racial discrimination, if she was calling upon the women of all nations to oppose the continuation of this shame in the Rhineland.[56]

The German SPD foreign minister, Dr. Koester, told the National Assembly in May, 1920, that France still had twenty regiments of colored soldiers in the Rhineland; if he objected to their use, he did so not because he wanted to stir up race hatred or because of his antipathy for colored people, but because the utilization of 50,000 colored soldiers in the heart of

---

[56] *Ibid.*, pp. 5690-92, May 20, 1920. The German pamphlet literature showed none of the reluctance of which Mrs. Roehl spoke. Works like *Farbige Franzosen am Rhein; Ein Notschrei deutscher Frauen*, Berlin, 1920 (2nd ed.), or *Schwarze am Rhein; Ein Weltproblem*, 1921, etc. tried to stir up public opinion by reciting the ten or fifteen cases which had occurred, and which had been prosecuted by the French army, and by conveying the impression that no one in the Rhineland was safe anymore. A similar but even more violent campaign was waged after the occupation of the Ruhr; it is odd that works like *So sieht es in der Ruhr aus*, or *Die Greueltaten der Franzosen in Dortmund am 9. und 10. Juni*, or the April, 1923, issue of *Sueddeutsche Monatshefte* under the title *The French Terror* repeated almost word for word the cases reported in 1920. Wrote a certain R. Einhacker in an opus entitled: *Hass, Antwort deutscher Dichter auf Versailles*, Muenchen, 1921: "German authors: become aware that today, more is expected of you than sweet reveries and dainty artistry. ...As long as your people is as yet shackled, forget in no work of yours the shame of Versailles." He cited a number of authors who had in their novels and poetry admirably stirred up all passions against the Entente and against the use of colored troops.

Europe represented an offense against all of Europe. During the war, their use had been a dangerous experiment; now it was a crime. It was a " psychological kick " to place a hungry and miserable population under the rule of " blacks." Their use endangered public hygiene throughout all of Europe. " The continuation of their acts of force, the assassination of harmless citizens, the rape of women, girls and boys, the tremendous increase in prostitution, the establishment of numerous brothels in even the smallest town as well as the rapid spread of venereal diseases ... can be termed only the continuation of warfare by all means in the midst of peace-time ... and leads to the permanent degeneration of the German national body at its western fringes." He regretted that Germany did not have the armed force to prevent the use of colored troops in the West.[57]

There were some objections raised against such attacks upon the treaty within the party but they only served to emphasize how isolated the critics were.

57 *Verhandlungen*, CCCXXXIII, 5692-93. In a country with a system of legalized prostitution and an illegitimate birth-rate of over ten percent already before the war, a breakdown in public morals was perhaps inevitable after a lost war. A veritable uproar resulted in the National Assembly, when the USPD representative, Mrs. Zietz, made the following statement: Of course, she condemned rapes and crimes, but only as such and not because they were committed by colored people. Sex crimes would always occur where there was a large accumulation of men in one place, who were under the brutalizing influence of militarism and war. Germany could effect the withdrawal of all occupation forces just as easily as she effected the annulment of the provisions regarding the extradiction of war criminals, the only prerequisite being honest demilitarization and respect of the neutralized zone. She chided those who now protested, for their silence when such acts were committed by German troops and by the free-corps in Germany proper during the recent civil war, or in Belgium, in France, and during the China war. In the face of a public uproar in the Assembly, she insisted that truth demanded this to be stated. She termed the speech of the minister an incitement to race hatred in a country already over-burdened with another 'Kulturschande', namely anti-semitism. (The president of the Assembly thereupon forbade her to touch upon anti-semitism.) Mrs. Zietz concluded by saying that if Germany observed the terms of the treaty to the letter, especially in regard to its military clauses, the occupation would end; *ibid.*, pp. 5694-96.

At the party congress in 1919, Eduard Bernstein, who had but recently returned to the party fold, had been asked to report on foreign affairs. He told an unwilling audience: " Comrades! The peace conditions imposed upon us by the Allies are hard, very hard, and in part ... simply impossible ... But ... we recognize the necessity of a large part of them. (Lively opposition.) Nine-tenths of them are undeniable necessities. (Strong continuous opposition and great unrest. Calls: Scandal!)." Even the German counter proposals had accepted most treaty conditions. The reconstruction of Poland within the boundaries of 1772 had been demanded by Lassalle, Marx and Engels; and the demarcation lines of 1919 corresponded roughly to the ethnic borders. Was the German case so weak, asked Bernstein, that Germany could not face the truth? The SPD should accept the post-1919 borders with Poland as a basis for a friendly understanding. It should not oppose the confession that Germany had committed some wrongs, but should make an honest acknowledgment of them. The attempt of the SPD to justify all pre-1918 foreign policies in the face of the Entente must end; in 1914 both England and France had peaceful governments.[58]

A storm of indignation greeted this speech. One SPD delegate after the other took the floor to denounce the views of Bernstein. Bernstein ultimately had to apologize for his views; he had only wanted to say that the terms were unavoidable, that they coincided with the fourteen points, that even the German counter proposals were quite unacceptable. In regard to 1914, " if I say that the German government of that time was responsible, I do not say that the German people is guilty, least of all the German working class. On the contrary, I free them of responsibility. I only regret ... that I stand here almost alone." [59]

---

58 *Protokoll des Parteitags 1919*, pp. 240-49.

59 *Ibid.*, pp. 277 ff. Among those who took the floor against Bernstein were Otto Braun, Adolf Braun, Hermann Mueller, Max Cohen, Dr. David, Keil, Scheidemann; he was termed a pervert, stabbing Germany in

A similar fate befell Cohen who, at the party congress in 1920, stated: " While I think that the peace treaty of Versailles can never literally be fulfilled, I must openly state that the largest part of its material content must be fulfilled because it simply corresponds to the destruction caused by the war. . ." And Cohen attacked sharply the campaign of hate being waged in the press—including the SPD press— against France with all its widespread use of lies, misinformation, and deceit. Cohen stressed in particular that French troops in the occupied zones were behaving just as well as German troops ever did.[60] Bernstein nodded only partial agreement to the remarks of Cohen and added that France knew more militarism than Germany did. Scheidemann expressed the hope that none in the party shared Cohen's views. Indeed both debates only indicated how isolated such views were within the ranks of the party.[61]

---

her back, an irresponsible dreamer, etc. He was called up to show instead that the treaty did not conform to the fourteen points. One of the critics pointed out that it is silly to reject the treaty at all, if nine-tenths of it were necessary; the other tenth did not justify the opposition to it. Only one speaker, Hoch, defended Bernstein by stating that Bernstein's views might be a good influence in winning the support of socialists outside of Germany, but that in reality Bernstein thought both the treaty and the fourteen points unbearable; *ibid.*, pp. 250-81.

60 *Ibid., 1920*, pp. 56-58. In 1919, during the Bernstein debate, Cohen had joined Bernstein's opponent and declared, in reference to Bernstein's remarks on Poland: " The only possible form of independence for smaller nations lies within the frame of an inter-national economic area. When we have on the map an abundance of small, completely independent states, this independence is a sham only, for they are dependent upon the nearest strong neighbor.... With our objective of a socialized economy, we cannot wish for a multi-colored map of all possible, small, completely independent states, but we must tell them: you may have cultural autonomy in a large measure, then you will possess all that is possible for you in the way of independence. Formal independence is only a deceit; " *ibid. 1919*, pp. 260 ff. *Cf.* L. Quessel' article " Eduard David und der bolschewistische Separatismus," *Sozialistische Monatshefte*, September 3, 1918, pp. 826-32.

61 *Protokoll des Parteitags 1920*, pp. 58-86. In 1921, a delegate from the occupied zone lamented the rapes committed by colored troops, the beatings of crippled war veterans, and the huge fines imposed by the occupation authorities upon clubs and organizations for the minutest violation of the rules of the occupying forces. At the very end of the congress, he again

d. THE SPD AND THE REVISION OF THE PEACE TREATY

Propaganda, non-co-operation, delays, and passive resistance provided means for the SPD and for the government in their struggle against the treaty, and in their attempt to make it ineffective. But in addition to these the SPD and, to some extent, the government leaned heavily on other means.

One of these was the utilization of the reviving International. At the party congress in 1920, which was attended for the first time since the war by foreign socialists, Hermann Mueller told the SPD: "We can only state that, disregarding individuals, only the socialist trained working class is prepared to contribute to the moderation and revocation of those parts of this peace treaty which we have always considered impossible of fulfillment and unbearable... We wish to lighten the task of our friends abroad, who work for the revision of the unbearable conditions of this peace of violation, by making it indubitable that we on our side wish to do everything to restitute what, beyond the necessities of war, has been ruined in the former enemy countries. But ... we can make restitution only if we ourselves regain faith in the possibility of a better future ... We have no reason to despair of the successful co-operation of the International in this field." [62]

---

took the floor to state that no invalids had ever been beaten; he knew of only one case of a veteran, not wounded in any way, who ever was beaten; and during the last four months not RM. 800,000 but only RM. 8,000 had been levied in his home town as fines for violations of the rules regarding organizations. Lest a rash listener might jump to the conclusion that a decent regard for truth prompted this dementi, he stressed that he corrected himself, because otherwise he might be prosecuted for slander upon his return; *ibid. 1921*, pp. 287 ff., 325. The delegate in question was Lewerentz. The party indeed considered it as intolerable that the enforcement of the laws of libel sometimes prevented the blackening of the record of the occupation armies in the Rhineland. In connection with Cohen's remarks in 1920 about the comparative behavior of the present occupation forces and the German troops in France in 1871, Scheidemann regretfully stated that libel laws prevented the delegates of the occupied zones from openly refuting Cohen; *ibid. 1920*, p. 70.

62 *Protokoll des Parteitags 1920*, pp. 10-12. In September 1923, the German foreign office published a white paper containing the texts of *Die den*

Indeed, the conference of the International at Lucerne, in August, 1919, adopted a majority report favoring the revision of the treaty of Versailles, and advocating the immediate admission of Germany to the League of Nations.[63] There was a marked cordiality in the relations of the German and French delegates at the congress held in Geneva in 1920, and resolutions were adopted condemning the treaty of Versailles as preserving Europe in a state of insecurity and dismemberment. The treaty was termed a document permeated by the spirit of imperialism which imposed intolerable burdens on the vanquished; the military occupation of the Rhineland, undiminished re-armament, and the provisions of the League of Nations statute permitting warfare in certain circumstances, (the " damnable " paragraph twelve) were strongly attacked.[64]

However, the SPD had to earn such resolutions by declaring that Germany had severely shaken the peace of the world by the settlement of the Franco-Prussian war, that Alsace-Lorraine should no longer be a problem of German concern,

---

Allierten seit Waffenstillstand uebermittelten deutschen Angebote und Vorschlaege zur Loesung der Reparations — und Wiederaufbaufrage, 138 pp., printed as Document No. 6138 between pages 7422 and 7423 in *Verhandlungen*, CCCLXXIX. The German proposals are perhaps best characterized by the fact that at no time between 1919 and 1932 did Germany ever transfer to the reparations account values even remotely approximating the most modest burdens which she herself had declared acceptable and possible. In 1920, the party chairman Wels told the SPD congress about SPD proposals for reparation: " The demand for reparation is justified ..." he stated, but he warned that on the mode of its solution depended " whether the reparations question will become an element of expedient compromise or the seed for new conflicts. On the basis of this ... we must warn urgently against the stipulation of definite sums of indebtedness payable annually. One look ... shows that we could never keep them up.... Similarly it is in regard to the attempt to put main emphasis on deliveries in kind ... because in their production, too many imponderable factors play a role. Therefore they cannot form the main substance of reparations..." *Protokoll des Parteitags 1920*, pp. 24 ff.

63 Quoted in the *Bericht des Parteivorstandes, ibid.*, pp. 53-63. There was a minority report attacking the treaty in even sharper terms.

64 *Ibid.*, pp. 64-68.

that the invasion of Belgium in 1914 had been a crime, that republican Germany accepted the obligation to repair the consequences of the war, and that the responsibility for the outbreak of the war "in its immediate causes, mainly if not exclusively rests with the heedlessness and lack of responsibility ... of the German and Austrian rulers who have since been deposed." [65]

It is true that this declaration was coupled with another one, which stated that "the German Social Democracy at present is still of the conviction that the principle of its attitude [of August 4, 1914] had been prescribed by the events themselves, and at present it cannot reproach itself for having striven to avert the victory of an inimical imperialism over its people." [66]

But neither the need for making a statement on the war guilt problem, nor the nature of that statement, nor indeed the impotence of the International in influencing the policy of the home governments of its members pleased the SPD. Meerfeld, the SPD reporter to the party congress on the conferences of the International declared appeasingly: "The text of the resolution did not please any of us completely, but we yielded in the interests of a higher aim." [67]

Although the SPD continued to make verbal concessions to the International, and although the latter continued to pass resolutions attacking the settlement of Versailles, the SPD

---

65 *Ibid.*

66 *Ibid., Protokoll,* p. 175.

67 *Ibid.* In the ensuing debate, various speakers deplored that the promises of the International did not find the desired echo abroad. The workers of the Entente countries too readily accepted the anti-German sentiments of their chauvinist leaders. French workers should refrain from protesting against reductions in the shipment of Ruhr coal, but should not refuse to load ships with food for Germany. English workers should protest when —as had happened recently—an English judge trying a German smuggler remarked that relations with such inferior persons should be broken off; *ibid.,* pp. 179-85.

soon ceased to place much confidence in the ability of the International to achieve any amelioration of the conditions established by the treaty of Versailles." [68]

The Wilsonian idea of democracy in international affairs appealed to the party much more and was successfully exploited for the actual, if not the formal, revision of the treaty with striking success. After 1918, Germany was inferior to the Entente powers only in military force, but Germany could quickly regain her position of equality with the victors, if the latter agreed that in international disputes power should be ruled out as an instrument of policy. By negating the validity of the concept of power as a determinant for international affairs, the lack of power could be turned into a virtue and the idealistic nature of the German republic emphasized. Indeed Hermann Mueller stated: " As a result of the war, we wish to declare that in the future the German sword will no longer count as an aid in the art of diplomacy ... The more we emphasize the holy zeal of the German people for the idea of peace ... the easier we make it for the Germans torn away from our national body ... Germany can expect the re-establishment of her rank among the great people only from the progress of the democratic idea among us and among the other nations." [69]

The *Sozialistische Monatshefte* declared in July, 1919: " Among the so-called civilized powers before the war, politics meant striving after the greatest possible power for oneself without recognizing a superior interest of mankind. With such views, the relations between the various states could in the most favorable case only result in a sort of armistice ... In last analysis, such a policy led to the domination of the stronger and the subjection and exploitation of the weaker nation ...

[68] It is interesting that the Dawes plan, which temporarily settled the reparations problem on a basis agreeable to Germany—allowing her to borrow twice as much abroad as she paid back in reparations—was accepted at a time when both France and England had socialist ministries.

[69] *Verhandlungen*, CCCXXVIII, 1852-59, July 23, 1919; *Cf.* speech of Scheidemann, *ibid.*, CCCXXX, pp. 2886-92, October 7, 1919.

Within the foreseeable future, we will not be able to oppose Anglo-American imperialism with force. We cannot emphasize too strongly that we have been defeated and that every thought of military counter-measures as an aid is sheer insanity ... A policy of desperation would only increase the catastrophe. Our future policy can be built only on the recognition that power will not help us any more. We have no other choice but to prepare, by conscious choice of new points of view, a new era when right and not might, community and not opposition shall rule." [70]

German diplomacy thus strove to reconstruct inter-national relations on a basis which disregarded the concepts of power almost completely. That the League of Nations and many European statesmen favored this policy, made it easy for Germany to exploit this policy for her own purposes. The removal of German disabilities resulting from the war by this changed approach to the problems of international relations was most successfully undertaken by Gustav Stresemann, who—after a change of heart which Scheidemann termed "unusually great and pleasing"—proceeded on the assumption that by outlawing force as a means of policy, Germany could become the equal of all other European nations, and that the treaty of Versailles could thereby be effectively annulled.

The uncompromising SPD policies towards the armistice and the treaty of Versailles were criticized both within the SPD and from the USPD and KPD. The latter two groups argued that Germany should effect a genuine socialist revolution and entrust all powers to political councils. The inevitable result of such a course would be similar revolutions in London and Paris. The victorious proletariat in these countries would thereupon break the fetters of the treaty of Versailles and embrace Germany as a lost brother in a new universal era of happiness and joy.[71] They argued that a genuine Bolshevist

70 Th. Steltzer, "Die Ueberwindung der Gewaltpolitik," *Sozialistische Monatshefte*, July 7, 1919, pp. 616-20.

71 Upon the outbreak of the German revolution and during the weeks following, there were persistent newspaper reports in the German press

revolution in Germany would have made impossible the imposition of terms as disastrous as those actually imposed at Versailles and pointed out that thus a united sphere of interest would be created between Russia and Germany which could have effected the Anschluss at once and could have opposed to the Entente an invincible bloc of Central and Eastern European powers.[72]

However, the SPD could never be expected to agree to the Bolshevization of Germany and the hopes for similar revolutions in the Entente countries were so utopian that they hardly deserved discussion. In 1919, the strength of Russia was potential and not actual strength; Russia could hardly have been expected to protect Germany from the Entente whose opposition to a Communist Germany would have been even more uncompromising.[73]

More important than the suggestions offered by the USPD, but of no greater effect upon the official SPD policy, was the steady criticism which emanated from a section of the staff and of the regular contributors of the *Sozialistische Monatshefte*. Max Cohen, Ludwig Quessel, Hermann Kranold, Wally Zepler, Victor Eschbach, and a few others formed a group which Otto Wels, the party chairman, accused of advocating an opinion not shared or approved by the party " with a tenacity which would do credit to a better cause." [74]

The *Sozialistische Monatsheft* between 1916 and 1922 argued as follows: The main enemies of Germany were England and the United States; the most severe terms of the treaty, the loss of colonies, of the fleet, and the intolerable economic

---

that Foch had been assassinated, King George V abdicated, Clemenceau deposed, and Wilson in open rebellion against the armistice terms. For example *Weserzeitung*, November 12, 1918, cited by Buchner, *ibid.*, no. 177, p. 170.

72 For example Lauffenberg, *op. cit., passim*.

73 See *A.-und S. Raete*; also speech of Scheidemann, *Verhandlungen*, CCCXXVII, 914.

74 *Protokoll des Parteitags 1920*, p. 81.

burdens, were due to them, and the benefits of these clauses accrued only to these two states. In France, there was a definite willingness to bury the past and to accept Germany as an equal, provided only that Germany honestly abstained from her desires in Alsace-Lorraine, a region which according to all considerations properly belonged to France and which desired nothing but union with France.[75]

Similarly, Germany should compose her differences with Russia. It had been wrong to antagonize her by the mistaken policy which led to her dismemberment at Brest-Litovsk. There were no basic, unbridgeable conflicts between Germany and France, or between Germany and Russia, but there existed a natural conflict between all three of them and the Anglo-Saxon powers. France expected from Germany only the well deserved restoration of her devastated areas; the past military rivalry of those two countries had been motivated only by the Alsatian problem. A settlement of these two questions in favor of France would open the way for a grand ' continental system '

[75] The overwhelming public manifestations of joy, evidenced in Alsace after their return to France, astounded the German public and press. But they were quick to ascribe this to the results of German policy towards the Reichslande during the war, and to their hopes to evade the consequences of the German defeat by union with France. See *Vossische Zeitung*, November 21, *Weserzeitung*, November 30, and December 11, 1918, quoted by Buchner, *ibid.*, pp. 304 ff. The *Sozialistische Monatshefte* printed a series of articles by Victor Eschbach on "Deutschland und das Elsass," August 25, 1919, pp. 791-803; "Das Elsass und Frankreich," September 29, 1919, pp. 887-98; and "Die Volksabstimmung in Elsass-Lothringen," January 26, 1920, pp. 35-44, which provided one of the finest analyses of the problem ever written in Germany, and which were a credit to the SPD and to the magazine. Eschbach argued that the concept of "Der Raub des Elsass" always had been completely unknown in the province, that according to every possible test and argument, the provinces had always been French in sentiment and always preferred union with France, and that the French elections of November 16, 1919, disproved all claims that there existed any significant minority preferring union with Germany. The author contrasted the reaction of the provinces to their acquisition by Germany in 1871 with their reaction in 1919 or under Louis XIV and concluded that there was not a shred of evidence to show that the provinces were German in nationality, sentiment, or culture, or that they wanted to belong to Germany.

which could successfully oppose the Anglo-Saxon powers, and in which Germany would find the needed salvation for her present ailments and a remedy for the treaty of Versailles.[76]

The desires of the *Sozialistische Monatshefte* for a ' continental system' remained unfulfilled. Nor did the castigations, heaped upon the actual policies of the party by this paper, find the desired echo. Wally Zepler wrote on February 10, 1919: "The behavior of our negotiators vis à vis the leaders of the enemy armistice commission completely lacked the quiet objectivity which alone can now regain for Germany political confidence abroad. In the daily press, in the social democratic press, too, the very same agitation against ' the enemy' rages [as before 1918], an agitation now even more senseless than then. But today France is the 'Main Enemy' against whom sentiments of hate and revenge are provoked by one lie after the other ... The sense that you must pursue not a clever, but an honest policy is as yet nowhere present." [77]

" Our old attitude was nationalistic deceit, ... each one's fear of his responsibility, ... neglect of all political motivations, lack of consideration in economic affairs, and a certain indolence towards moral demands of the public ... I do not believe that the German people are more evil than any other. But it almost seems that in no other people are the sources of originality buried so deep. ... We saw the revolution start

76 See the following articles: L. Quessel, " Eduard David · und der bolschewistische Separatismus," *Sozialistische Monatshefte*, September 3, 1918, pp. 826-32; Max Cohen, " Der Weg der Aussenpolitik fuer das neue Deutschland," *ibid.*, February 10, 1919, pp. 79-84; Max Schippel, " Die Schicksalsstunde der deutschen Kolonien," *ibid.*, March 3, 1919, pp. 137-43; and Max Cohen, " Vor der letzten Entscheidung," *ibid.*; March 24, 1919, pp. 222-28. L. Quessel, " Der angelsaechsische Friede," *ibid.*, May 19, 1919, pp. 432-36, argued that " every line of the peace treaty of Versailles shows who really is the master over Europe," and called: " Peoples of all European countries: Unite! " *Cf.* Max Cohen, " Was sollen wir also tun," *ibid.*, pp. 425-32; and " Die deutsche Politik und Frankreich," *ibid.*, May 3, 1920, pp. 313-27. Also *Protokoll des Parteitags 1920*, pp. 56-58, etc.

77 Article, " Zur deutschen Nationalversammlung," *Sozialistische Monatshefte*, pp. 65-74.

with enthusiastic hopes. Was not the horror of the old regime so terribly great? . . . A break with militarism, a break with dishonesty, the beginnings of public humanity, this we had to, this we could expect. But none of this has happened . . . Without doubt, the first period of the revolution had had a moral character. Hence we could hope for a world-historical moral crisis in Germany . . . But it did not come to that . . . Therefore it is so important that we oppose with closed ranks every attempt to heroize war . . . that we see to it that this true picture of war never be polished up." [78]

Criticism like this fell on deaf ears within the SPD. The party tolerated no compromise in regard to its irreconcilable opposition to the treaty of Versailles and its supporters. Following so close upon the war-time policies of the party, the objectives of SPD foreign policy after 1918 and the nature of their discussions within the ranks of the party left no doubt that, regardless of all consequences, the party had transformed itself into a party of pronounced nationalistic tendencies, with all the concomitants which such a policy implied in post-1918 Germany. If discussions about the treaty of Versailles still reverberated throughout the republic, they were discussions about means and not about ultimate objectives. In ultimate objectives, the gap between the SPD and the parties to the right of it, so wide in 1870, had finally been closed.

[78] Adolf Behne's article, "Unsere moralische Krise," *Sozialistische Monatshefte*, January 20, 1919, pp. 34-38.

CHAPTER XIII
THE PROGRAM OF GOERLITZ

In the years following 1914, the SPD had thus been changed into a nationalistic party, ready to co-operate with any other political group on a democratic basis, opposed to proletarian dictatorship, and resisting all practical steps toward the socialization of the means of production. However, such changes were only sporadically reflected in increasing criticism of orthodox Marxism and of the Erfurt program.

When Heinrich Cunow took over the editorship of the *Neue Zeit* from Karl Kautsky in 1917, he declared that the new editors were Marxists in their historical and social interpretation, but would keep themselves free of the spirit which " sees in cleaving to Marxian phrases the mark of true Marxism . . . Social theories, even if postulated by Marx, are determined by time and are of necessity subject . . . to change. Marx' theories may be deemed valid only in as far as they will time and again be confirmed by the facts of social life. This question will always remain open: from which experimental facts did Marx start? . . . In how far has the social process of life changed? All dogmatism, socialist dogmatism included, retards the progress of knowledge." [1]

Max Schippel wrote that the war has shown that social and economic class conflict was not the only basic social conflict. It was now recognized that various stages of economic development might co-exist peacefully. The whole economy of no country or society moved uniformly. This affected the entire interpretation of class-struggle in society. As compared to the socialists, all other classes were not capitalistic in their inter-

---

[1] *Neue Zeit*, vol. XXXVII, pt. 1, no. 1, October 5, 1917, declaration by the new editors. See also Bernstein's remarks about a ' Marx scholasticism'; Marx, he declared, had never decided any problem with finality, and just as he himself did in his later writings, socialists now too must give a decisive role to later experience; *Protokoll des Parteitags 1920*, pp. 216 ff.

relation with each other, and socialists could not be dominated by a uniform interpretation of all other classes. Even capitalism still represented a revolutionary advance over other co-existing social-economic forms, and in relation to these socialism must support capitalism as a trail-blazer. Society must be viewed as being divided not into two classes, but into many groups, and the proletariat must sometimes co-operate with this group and sometimes with that.[2]

With these changes in the traditional ideas of the nature of the division of society into classes, the attitude of the party towards the state changed too. " The party, which for half a century had been attacked as inimical to the state, which had been put into juxtaposition with the so-called state-preserving parties, proved to be the most state-preserving party, after the state had been led to the rim of the abyss." [3]

Arno Franke argued in the following way: The SPD used to exaggerate the strength of the factors able to paralyze the state. But the sacrifices of the people during the war proved the vitality of the idea of the state and confirmed that the individual was more than ever dependent upon the state. It must now be admitted that the concept of the state had a superior meaning. The SPD, as the strongest party, must hence approach the concept of the state differently. However, there were two rival concepts of its function: the conservative interpretation saw in the state an instrument for the preservation of historical rights and privileges, with a corresponding differentiation in the role of the various classes in its preservation, and the identification of one single class with its interests and well-being; while the liberal interpretation viewed the state as an institution of the totality of all its members, composed of individuals all equally important for its preservation. The war had vindicated the latter concept. It was only between

2 Article, " 30 Jahre Erfurter Programm," *Sozialistische Monatshefte*, September 19, 1921, pp. 788-92.

3 *Verhandlungen*, CCCXXVI, 72 ff., speech of Keil, February 14, 1919.

these two interpretations that any conflict was yet possible. The theoretical negation of the state by the SPD could no longer be condoned; the party must align itself squarely behind the democratic interpretation of the state.[4] " Is the state really only an organization of domination, an instrument of class rule, or does it not float as an independent patron above the classes, an honest broker and arbiter? " asked Arthur Heichen.[5]

But on the whole, the criticism of Marxism was implied in the changed party policies. There was no systematic attempt to build a new theory by consistent criticism or to justify the changed policy by a new idea. Wally Zepler complained that " the creative source has dried up in [the party] ranks, the inner vitality is lacking ... The clearest proof of this is the stagnation of the theoretical development within its ranks ... Thus there grew eventually an unordered agglomeration of radical and reformist, elementary and advanced, socialist and orthodox-liberal views, which progressively lost their uniform basic idea of support." [6] " The party rejects the theoretical continuation of Marxism, as it had been begun by revisionism, and it still drapes its bourgeois thought with seemingly revolutionary terminology. Since it no longer has a [clear] program

4 Article, " Der Kampf um den Staat," *Neue Zeit,* vol. XXXVI, pt. 2, no. 7, May 17, 1918, pp. 156-60. " Socialism is not the abolition, but the ennoblement of the state. The closer the worker approaches socialism, the closer he comes to the state; " H. Heller, *Sozialismus und Nation,* Berlin, 1931, p. 71. (1st ed. 1925.)

5 Article, " Neumarxismus," *Neue Zeit,* vol. XXXIX, pt. 2, no. 9, May 27, 1921, pp. 201-06. Fr. Stampfer declared: one could not favor one particular type of state, if one rejected the whole idea of the state as such. The endorsement of the republic by the SPD was tantamount to an endorsement of the state as an idea. " We need no longer bother about the old theoretical state, or whether the ultimate objective of socialism is the socialized state or the stateless socialized society"; *Protokoll des Parteitags 1921,* pp. 302-07. In fact, this was the only statement about the state made, although this congress discussed and adopted the new party program.

6 Article, " Zur deutschen Nationalversammlung," *Sozialistische Monatshefte,* February 10, 1919, pp. 65-74.

of its own, and yet cannot bring itself to confess the historical
revisionism born of the socialist spirit, it has nothing left but
to navigate from case to case without belief, as it has now
been doing for six years." [7] Cunow thought that " the retention of old views and formulas outdated by social evolution
has contributed to the decline of our party. All too many members have left the old theoretical basis, without as yet having
found a new one." [8]

At the turn of the century, even Bebel ceased to believe in
the crisis theory and in the idea of pauperization, but the un-
related attempts of the few anti-revisionist party thinkers to
formulate a new integrated theory remained essentially sterile
rationalizations.[9] No improved theory emerged.

Yet the conviction spread that the Erfurt program could no
longer be maintained. Organizational considerations kept alive
the desire to change the program in spite of the inability to replace it. Thirty years of economic evolution could not pass
without leaving a mark. The party had ceased to appeal to the
worker alone; it now appealed to the entire population and to
all classes of society. Revisionism and SPD attitudes toward
it, the war and the policies of the SPD during the revolution
all equally imposed the urgent need to re-establish a degree of
harmony between the program of the party and its policies.

It was widely recognized that the advantages of the Erfurt
program, with its calm confidence, seductive phrasing, and
fervent hopes, had been mainly propagandist.[10] Such a program,

7 Article, " Nach den Sozialistischen Parteitagen," *ibid.*, November 4,
1920, pp. 921-29.

8 Articles, " Die Notwendigkeit des Umlernens," *Neue Zeit*, vol.
XXXVIII, pt. 2, no. 13, May 25, 1920, pp. 289-93; " Zur Kritik des
Erfurter Parteiprogrammes," *ibid.*, no. 16, June 16, 1920, pp. 361-68.

9 Adolf Braun told the party congress in 1921 that not a single member
still believed in the theories of crisis, pauperization and catastrophe;
Protokoll des Parteitags 1921, pp. 311 ff.

10 Wally Zepler, " Sozialistische Bewegung," *Sozialistische Monatshefte*, September 19, 1921, pp. 820 ff., termed the essence of the Erfurt
program its ' religious ' faith in the coming of the new society, a faith
which was now practically dead within the party.

however, was not wholly acceptable to a party actively participating in government. The gap between the promises of the program and the actions of the government was too wide. Cunow warned that "the cause of the insecurity evident at present in party life is due to the fact that before the war our party became increasingly a machine for agitation and voting, a mechanism serving almost exclusively agitation and the winning of new votes ... If the crisis within the party is to be overcome, the party must cease to be a mere agitatory group.[11]

The traditional preference of the party for agitation was thus inhibited and the difference between the mere opposition possible before the war and the present degree of responsibility weighed heavily upon the party and its programmatic discussion.[12]

But if agitation was no longer adequate, and if the theories of the 1891 program had been discredited by the war and by the revolution, if the 'unmistakable' trends recorded in the Erfurt program had been disproven or had been reversed, then, SPD authors stated, it was no longer possible to define a socialist program that would be a valid declaration of enduring principles, it was no longer possible to make an economic prognosis on the basis of socialist thought.[13] Cunow held that all possible prognoses like those of the Erfurt program were hypothetical, since experience could not be projected into the future. But, he added, it was immaterial whether or not a program took cognizance of that; the SPD had ceased to be a

11 Article, "Heraus aus dem Turm!" *Neue Zeit*, vol. XXXVII, pt. 2, no. 10, June 6, 1919, pp. 219-24.

12 Conrad Schmidt's article "Die Programme der deutschen Sozialdemokratie," *Sozialistische Monatshefte*, August 1, 1921, pp. 641-47; *Protokoll des Parteitags 1920*, pp. 187 ff., speech of A. Braun; *ibid.*, pp. 128 ff., speech of Molkenbuhr; *ibid.*, pp. 296 ff., speech of Loebe.

13 *Cf.* Cunow's article, "Zur Kritik des Erfurter Programmes," *Neue Zeit*, vol. XXXVIII, pt. 2, no. 16, pp. 361-68, June 16, 1920. Cunow stressed that for example the present dearth of goods disproved the prognosis that production would increase beyond the ability to consume.

class party and its program would not affect the actual policies of the SPD.[14] Programs were only the product of time and did not embody the pure essence of truth.[15]

Thus the new program could not be expected to reflect an integrated confession of zealous faith. Instead of the former ' materialistic socialism ', a ' cultural socialism ' was expected to dominate.[16] The difference between socialist and social behavior had been " wiped out," [17] and the only foundation left for a program was the vague belief in an " upward development rooted in the firm, earthly basis of economy." [18]

There was, however, one factor which influenced the program in a different direction. The desire for reunion with the USPD had been strong in the SPD, especially after the formation of the KPD. The split of the party had seriously weakened the power of the SPD, and the armed conflict precipitated by the two groups had gravely prejudiced the recovery of Germany. It was thought desirable to frame a program, which would not radically repel the USPD or prevent their return to the party fold.

The product of these theoretical, tactical and political considerations, which had agitated the SPD since 1914, was the Program of Goerlitz which, in 1921, was adopted by the party against only five dissenting votes. Its substance stated:

---

14 Article, " Zur Kritik des Programmentwurfes," *ibid.*, vol. XXXIX, pt. 2, no. 21, August 19, 1921, pp. 481-88. It was pointed out that the SPD never believed in the Erfurt program and its theory of pauperization; trade-unionism was incompatible with such a theory and the party had emphasized trade-unionism most strongly.

15 Article, " Zur Kritik des Erfurter Programmes," *ibid.*, vol. XXXVIII, pt. 2, no. 16, June 16, 1920, pp. 361-68.

16 *Protokoll des Parteitags 1920*, pp. 211 ff.

17 *Ibid., 1921*, pp. 318 ff, speech of Dr. David.

18 Schmidt's article, " Die Programme der deutschen Sozialdemokratie," *Sozialistische Monatshefte*, August 1, 1921, pp. 641-47. The first draft of the new program did not even contain the word " class-struggle."

The Social Democratic Party of Germany is the party of the urban and rural working class. It strives for the co-ordination ... of all physically and mentally creative persons, who depend upon the earnings of their work.

Capitalism has brought the essential part of the means of production ... under the domination of a relatively small number of large proprietors; it has separated the large masses of the workers from the means of production and transformed them into proletarians without possessions. It has increased economic inequality and engendered, in opposition to a small minority living in surplus, wide masses who degenerate in need and misery. Thus it has made the class-struggle for the liberation of the proletariat a historical necessity and a moral duty.

The world war and the dictatorial peace aggravated this process. ... The evolutionary trend towards high capitalism increased the endeavors to dominate world economy by imperialistic expansion of power. . . . Comparable to its unsatisfactory solution of national and international economic problems by the peace treaties in force, it has created the danger of new bloody conflicts threatening to bring about the collapse of human culture.

At the same time the world war has swept away withered systems of domination. Political revolutions have given to the masses the rights of democracy needed for their social advance. ... Mightier than ever rises the resolution to overcome the capitalist system and, by international co-ordination of the proletariat, by the creation of an international order of law, by a true league of nations with equal rights, to protect mankind from new annihilation, due to war.

To show the way to this solution ... is the task of the Social Democratic Party.

The Social Democratic Party ... considers the democratic republic as a form of state ordained irrevocably by historical development.

It fights for the domination of the will of the people, organized in the free state of the people ... for the renewal of society in a social spirit of community.

It fights not for new privileges of classes and advantages, but for the abolition of class rule and of the classes themselves.

The program advocated that real estate, mineral wealth, and natural sources of power should be removed from capitalist exploitation and transferred to the service of the community. Government enterprise should progressively be extended, but, at the same time, bureaucracy should be avoided. Non-profit co-operatives should be favored. So should the role of the economic councils for the protection of the social and economic interests of the workers. The party advocated a uniform labor law, protection for the right to organize, a legal eight hour day, utmost restriction of night work and its complete prohibition for women, a complete ban on the labor of children of school age, an uninterrupted weekly rest period of at least forty-two hours, annual paid vacations, and the abolition of the domestic system. Income, profit and inheritance taxes should be extended and strengthened. The state should receive a share of all estates, varying according to the numbers and the degree of relationship of the natural heirs. All government institutions should be democratized. The courts should interpret law not from the point of view of private property, but from a social point of view. Property rights were to be subordinated to the rights of persons and of the social community. Legal language should be made comprehensible to the general public. The death penalty was to be abolished. Penalties should be preventive rather than punitive in nature. Elected judges should function side by side with professional judges. State and church should be separated; instruction, the means of instruction and board in schools should be free. The party recommended co-education, and advocated compulsory international arbitration, self-determination for all peoples according to the same rules, international disarmament and the placing of all colonies under the League of Nations. The final article of the program demanded the " revision of the treaty of Versailles so as to ease the economic burdens and recognize national rights to exist." [19]

Cunow noted that the Erfurt program had brought to the fore the Marxist interpretation of historical evolution, which had become dominant within the party under the anti-socialist legislation of Bismarck. Goerlitz, too, he commented approvingly, was introducing a new historical era. "German Social Democracy is finally willing to accept the political lessons of the world war and the following period of the revolution, to leave behind the out-dated traditions and party formulas, to re-align itself politically and to enter new paths of development ... This process ... of liberating itself from traditional narrowness deserves recognition," the more so since there had been extremely little opposition to it.[20]

19 *Protokoll des Parteitags 1921*, pp. III-IV.

20 Article, " Die geschichtliche Bedeutung des Erfurter Parteitags " (*sic.* should be " Goerlitzer Parteitag," as in index), *Neue Zeit*, vol. XL, pt. 1, no. 2, October 7, 1921, pp. 25-30.

CHAPTER XIV

CONCLUSIONS[1]

THE SPD had been the product of the fusion of two minor rival groups, organized to meet the needs created by the rapid industrialization of Germany in the 1860's, and by the conflicts regarding the mode and purposes of German unification.

One of these groups, with its romantic nationalism, its democratic faith, its confidence in the power of the state to protect the worker from social and economic disabilities, and its economic misconceptions, had hardly left the stage of utopian socialism. As long as the state refused to champion social legislation, the unification of Germany, and the principle of universal, equal suffrage, the effectiveness and popularity of Lassalleanism were limited. But as soon as the social functions of the state began to expand, the influence of Lassalle began to grow. Lassalle had taught that political revolutions were unable to do more than sanction changes which have already taken place in society prior to the revolutionary event, that a democratic franchise was the sole instrument of political power needed to give the workers proper influence in society, and that the state was the only organ capable of protecting the worker and of insuring his fullest development. These ideas impressed themselves deeply upon the SPD and helped to determine, to a large extent, the policies of the party even after the German revolution.

The other group, which had emerged in the 1860's, had embraced the conclusions of Karl Marx, interpreting a passing phase of the social, political and economic evolution as the normal behavior pattern of modern society. This group was characterized by its religious zeal, its confidence in success, and its belief in the soundness of its analysis. However, many points of its program were demolished by later developments

1 *Cf. supra*, pp. 67-69, 135-37, 168-70, 255-60.

and by criticism based on a more complete interpretation of social and economic processes. Within the SPD, this ultimately led to the eclipse of Marxian views by Lassallean ideas; only a small minority preferred to follow the example of Lenin.

The fusion of these two socialist groups and the temporary subordination of Lassalleanism had been prompted by the increasing hostility of the state towards socialism. The anti-socialist legislation of 1878 in particular entailed the temporary ascendancy of the radical tendencies of the SPD which culminated in the ringing Marxist phrases of the Erfurt program.

But the anti-socialist legislation had been accompanied by social legislation and, eventually, the rise in the standard of living which marks expanding, capitalist industry. These two developments above all revealed that the assumptions of Karl Marx were true only for certain periods of time and under certain economic conditions. It became evident that the worker had ultimately much more to lose than mere chains: he had acquired a fatherland. Trade-unions sensed this earlier than other political groups, and built their program accordingly. Trade-union experience showed that even under the unfavorable political conditions prevailing in Germany the proletarian could advance his standard: he was not condemned to linger at the edge of destitution, not even under high capitalism. Nor did capitalism show any signs of its predicted senility.

Revisionism made the attempt to restore harmony between the doctrine of Karl Marx and the more recent political-economic trends. Eduard Bernstein, who formulated revisionism in its most complete form, re-examined the evolution of capitalism during the nineteenth century and concluded that the doctrines of the concentration of the means of production, the accumulation of capital, the pauperization of the masses, the cycle of crisis, and the imminence of an ultimate catastrophe were not fully supported by historical developments and of only uncertain value. The victory of the proletariat, in the opinion of Bernstein, would not be the result of a revolution provoked by intolerable exploitation, but of increasing advances of the workers in many diverse social and economic fields.

The SPD, however, rejected revisionism. In doing so, the party ignored the true implications of Bernstein's observations, and denounced revisionism as a tactical aberration and mistake. This line of argument constituted a tacit admission that tactics might, under certain circumstances, warrant a revision of party theories no less radical than that proposed by Bernstein. And indeed, the pre-eminence accorded to tactics eventually led to such a result.

This failure to make the necessary adjustment in party theories and the rejection of revisionism were motivated in part by the surprising success of the SPD as a vote-getting organization. This success at the polls helped diminish the importance ascribed to theories and to discredit the demands for a change in the program. Furthermore, the theoretical part of the Erfurt program, which Bernstein had proposed to change, was largely responsible for the propagandistic successes of the party. The Erfurt program exercised a very strong appeal upon the most diverse sections of the German public. The theoretical theses of the program breathed a sense of serenity, of assurance, and a hope, whose persuasive character was little affected by the fact that belief in their practical value was waning. The confidence with which the program charted the future history of the workers only dulled the sense of urgency in regard to political action, enhancing the propagandistic appeal of the program, and justifying a concentration upon organizational tasks. The SPD thus could consider it a major achievement that, from 1881 until 1919, the popular vote of the SPD increased in every national election, in spite of the fact that, as a result, the class-character of the SPD became questionable and the policies of the party became entangled in compromise, opportunism and circumspection, which alone could preserve the harmony of all the divergent interests among its voters. The party became the largest political party in Germany, but it ceased to be unified

in its desire to exchange the existing order for one whose theoretical foundations, in spite of their propagandistic value, had
become subject to serious doubt.

The emphasis on tactics and the advance in the numerical
strength of the party went hand in hand. Through the process
of growth, the party became ever more a true sample of public
opinion, reflecting in its aggregate the political whims, prejudices and pride of the Wilhelminian era. At the same time,
there was an imperceptible change from a party spear-heading
public opinion to one following public opinion, from a purely
idealistic party to one subordinating its idea to the reality of
success at the polls. The outbreak of the war in 1914 revealed
how far this process had advanced.

The war proved to be extremely popular in Germany. Germans, including SPD members and SPD Reichstag representatives, rushed to the colors full of enthusiasm, and local
SPD and trade-union chapters played a leading role in helping
their communities to meet the problems posed by mobilization,
unemployment, and emergency legislation. The war provided
a release for long pent-up energies and desires, and many,
even in the SPD, expected it to sweep away much that was
rotten and decayed, bringing in its stead more wholesome and
desirable trends to fruition. All too many considered the war
as the supreme test of the German Empire, and the readiness
with which Germany rose to meet the test left little room for
doubt about its eventual outcome or about its causes and
origins.

The SPD, on August 3, 1914, was firmly convinced that
Germany had been the victim of an unprovoked enemy attack,
and that opposition to the war effort would have entailed the
dissolution of the party. Inclination and duty thus seemed to
combine and compel the SPD to support the war. The sense
of responsibility weighed, no doubt, heavily upon the largest
German party. But few party leaders stopped to consider
whether a doctrinaire political party—unlike a government—
did not owe first responsibility to its idea above all.

And few leaders considered whether or not a radical departure from orthodox party doctrines was less radical a departure, because it could be capably defended, or because public opinion, in the first onrush of events and emotions, approved of this.[2]

The vote on August 4, as such did not at the time constitute an irreparable breach with the Erfurt program. It was taken under circumstances which made a sober evaluation of the situation difficult, and many, like Karl Liebknecht, were able to retrace their steps at the first opportunity. The irreparable breach of the SPD with the Erfurt program was rather the result of many different acts and policies which were championed by the SPD during the war and which can be demonstrated only on the basis of a composite evaluation of SPD policies and the SPD defense of such policies in many different fields.

In defense of the vote on August 4, and of the subsequent SPD policies, SPD writers rewrote party history in order to emphasize the heritage of nationalism and anti-Tsarism, active within the party since its founding. Some SPD writers concluded outright that Germany in 1914 represented *Progress* while Germany's enemies represented only retrogressive forces. The close co-operation between the government and the SPD on many domestic economic and social problems represented the virtual suspension of class-struggle during the war. In its war aims, the SPD wished to safeguard " the territorial integrity of the state, its political independence, and its free economic development." The party rejected annexationism because annexationism, in its view, was productive only of increasing hostility towards Germany abroad. But the SPD strongly objected also to any implementation of the principle of national self-determination beyond a point where it might threaten the retention of Alsace-Lorraine or Posen by Germany.

In its criticism of the food situation, of political conditions within Germany, of the state of siege, and of the treatment of

2 " The party only wanted to continue to be," wrote Wally Zepler in *Sozialistische Monatshefte*, February 10, 1919, pp. 65-74.

soldiers and of ethnic minorities, the SPD during the war ceased to utilize reprehensible conditions in order to justify its class opposition to the government. Instead, the SPD sought to prevent the untoward consequences which might flow from such conditions and urged the government to remove their causes. In fact, in all its varied aspects during the war years, SPD policy furthered those purposes to which the German state had been dedicated, ignoring the gulf which, according to official party theory, separated the state and the SPD.

The course upon which the SPD embarked on August 4, 1914, proved, however, to be controversial within the ranks of the party. Not only the radical wing—whose separation, in Cunow's opinion, became inevitable as soon as historical events had by-passed political dreams and illusions,[3]—but many others, who resisted this departure from orthodox tradition, eventually separated from the SPD. The resulting division of the party allowed the SPD to reveal in the defense of its policy and in its criticism of the domestic and foreign policies of the Empire a nationalistic fervor and holy zeal which was incompatible with the erstwhile party of ' vaterlandslose Gesellen '.

The war had revealed the patriotism of the public. It had also disproved the most cherished Marxian expectations regarding the consequences of war upon modern capitalist society. The SPD was resolved to abide by these two decisions above all.

However, the war did not progress favorably for Germany. Military censorship for a time had lulled the country into a false sense of imminent victory, but the armistice offer of October, 1918 shattered this illusion and a panic ensued. The revelation of the certainty of defeat produced a mad scramble to save what could yet be saved, and to terminate the war as fast as possible.

3 "Nach der Wuerzburger Tagung," *Neue Zeit*, vol. XXXVI, pt. 1, no. 4, October 26, 1917, pp. 75 ff.

In this situation, the government considered it imperative to win the good-will of Wilson whose fourteen points were widely thought to promise to Germany the restoration of the status quo ante bellum. But the government considered it equally imperative to secure the good-will of the masses in Germany, for the latter had borne many of the hardships of the war only in the hope of victory, and might, in a rising wave of disappointment and indignation, threaten the powers-that-be. The strategy of a ' revolution from above ' was chosen in the hope that it might placate both Wilson and the German public.

The SPD was pleased by the political reforms introduced under Prince Max of Baden, although some SPD leaders had reservations about the sagacity of entering a cabinet burdened with the heavy responsibility of liquidating the war. Wilson, however, did not seem to have been pleased by the limited reforms of Prince Max, as was shown by the first indications of the severity of the armistice terms and by his warnings that Germany would not receive any consideration unless she first rid herself of her military masters.

In view of Wilson's attitude, some influential circles in Germany proposed that Germany should continue to fight, thus forcing the Allies to grant more acceptable armistice terms. Others advocated a political revolution in order to obtain those mild peace terms which the enemy was thought to have promised, and which the sacrifices and deprivations of fifty months of warfare were deemed to have warranted.

The proposal that the Emperor should abdicate won growing support among the German public for several reasons. It might satisfy the discontent bred by the conduct, loss, and hardships of the war; it might satisfy Wilson, thus assuring better terms without the need of fighting for them; and it might silence those who still advocated a desperate last ditch stand of the German armies.

The SPD, however, showed little sympathy with these ideas. The SPD agreed with Prince Max that a voluntary act of abdication by the Emperor might satisfy Wilson and those in

Germany who advocated it, without incurring the consequences of a political revolution which, to the SPD, seemed extremely objectionable. But rather than incur the consequences of a forced abdication, brought about by public pressure, the SPD preferred the continuation of the monarchy.

The hostility of the SPD towards a violent revolution coming as the result of a great popular movement may be attributed to various factors. The SPD had inherited from Lassalle the belief that political revolutions did not modify social or economic conditions; they only bestowed legal sanction on economic changes which have taken place in society without the benefit of revolution. Under Prince Max, Germany had been assured universal and equal suffrage, parliamentary government and constitutional limitations on the powers of the monarch; traditionally nothing more had been demanded by the SPD in order to assure its victory. From 1871 onward, the record of the SPD had been peaceful and non-violent; the lessons taught by the success of peaceful methods during half a century could not suddenly be unlearned. The SPD had grown into a cumbersome organization with major stakes in the existing order and did not now readily tolerate the change of a system which had permitted the party to attain its present influential position. In October, 1918, the SPD was a government party and as such it opposed any changes of the government suggested by outsiders. But above all, the experiences of Russia in 1917 and 1918 imbued the SPD with a deep horror of revolution. Russia, in the opinion of the SPD, had shown that even a relatively peaceful, democratic revolution may end in Bolshevism, the destruction of the state, dismemberment, the ravages of civil war and of foreign mercenaries, the disintegration of its productive resources, and the complete disruption of order. To court such a fate in Germany by advocating the abdication of the Emperor or by forcing the Emperor to abdicate was unthinkable for the SPD. It objected to this with all the means at its disposal. If the party favored a voluntary act of abdication, it was solely because such an act would remove the threat of revolution.

But the SPD was unable either to check the growth of public sentiment in favor of abdication or to persuade the Emperor to abdicate voluntarily. In fact, the refusal of the Emperor to abdicate helped considerably to inflame public sentiment, and his escape to Spa convinced many that rather than sacrifice himself for the good of the nation, he was only preparing to sacrifice the nation in continued warfare.

Resistance to such a course of action was strongest where its consequences would be gravest, or its likelihood most evident: in Bavaria and in Kiel. In both these centers of revolution, the desire was uppermost to terminate further bloodshed, to bring all sacrifices to induce the enemy to grant the best possible terms, and to save Germany from invasion.

The imminence of revolution forced the SPD to reconsider its erstwhile attitude in regard to the question of abdication. Having failed to avert the revolution by its refusal to countenance it, the SPD might yet be able to spare Germany the fate of Russia by placing itself at the head of the revolution.

In consequence, the SPD, after due warning to Prince Max, withdrew from the cabinet, called the people of Berlin into the streets on November 9, and assumed the leadership of Germany. Its horror of revolution, and its opposition to Leninism were, however, not diminished by this experience. Nor did the SPD ignore the fact that the revolution was, basically, only the attempt to liquidate the war in the best possible way and did not imply the authorization to enact far-reaching social and economic changes; public demonstrations, local elections in November and December, 1918, the elections to the Congress of Councils and to the National Assembly, and SPD preferences regarding the purposes of the revolution combined to deprive the revolution of any other meaning.

SPD preferences were a factor of prime importance in determining the purposes of the revolution. The SPD was the most important new group brought to the helm of Germany by the revolution; it depended in large part upon the SPD whether the public would demand and endorse changes more incisive than those already effected in mid-November by the introduction of a republican, parliamentary regime. Important though the constitutional provisions of Weimar were, they could not by themselves guarantee that in the future the army, the civil administration, the judiciary, the foreign office, or public sentiment would be ruled firmly by democratic, republican principles. In order to flourish, democracy must be implanted not only in formal, legal provisions—and even this was not fully accomplished in Germany, for constitutional provisions were not deemed by the SPD to warrant corresponding changes of the Civil Code—but in the hearts of each individual citizen, and in the practices of each department of the government and its many bureaus. That the SPD should provide the leadership towards such a 'revolution of the spirit' was, however, incompatible with the policies of the party prior to November 7.

Instead, the SPD endeavored to preserve as much of the spirit and organization of the Empire as was possible. It allied itself with the old powers in the army and in the administration in order to prevent the success of those ambitious to secure from the revolution more than just unavoidable changes. Only those changes were approved and enacted by the SPD, which had long since been advocated by the majority of the bourgeois parties too; in every sphere where the SPD differed from the bourgeois parties, the SPD itself prevented any modification of the existing order by armed force, and marshalled the most trenchant arguments to support resistance to everything not sanctioned by the majority of the political parties.

The soldiers' councils made an attempt to curb the power of the officers' corps, but wherever they raised their head, the SPD suppressed them. The workers' councils made attempts to moderate the conservative and anti-republican spirit of the German administration and higher civil service, but the SPD persuaded them to vote themselves out of office. The council movement made a feeble attempt to replace the system of

representation which had been discredited by the impotence
of the Reichstag during the period of the Empire, but the SPD
rigorously opposed all these attempts. The SPD, under pressure of a restless public, consented to the introduction of economic councils, but they were never permitted to function.

Nor did the SPD consider the revolution and its own
acquisition of governmental powers as sufficient reason to
initiate those changes in the economic system which its own
program and a large body of liberal opinion had long since
urged. The agrarian problem had always been a stepchild
within the party, and the SPD made little more than feeble
and ineffective gestures towards its solution. The party was
unable to deal with the problem of war profits which had been
left intact because of the absence of war taxes in the years
1914-1918. It ignored all proposals for a planned economy
and, in spite of the emergency during 1919, removed economic
controls and favored a system of ' laissez-faire ' in internal economics and in international trade. Above all, it disassociated
itself from Marxism: of the economic program of 1891 nothing
remained; socialization was now considered by the SPD as a
meaningless phrase, impossible of realization both because of
its alleged wastefulness and because of human nature.

Indeed, the ideals expressed at Erfurt and the expectations
based upon the revolution could not have been disavowed more
decisively than by the zeal of the successful revolutionaries to
resist the enactment of their own traditional program. It is true
that the Provisional Government and the SPD had not received,
on November 9, 1918, a mandate to enact the Erfurt program,
but it must be assumed that large sections of the public would
have followed the SPD, if it had made the attempt to do so.
The meagerness of the results of SPD rule and of the revolution was due, to a certain degree, to the prevailing hostility
between the SPD and the groups to its left; by advocating
more far-reaching changes in the political and economic structure of Germany, the SPD would frequently have approached
rather close to the objectives of the USPD and KPD. Yet, the

failure to enact its own program at a favorable moment, and the rejection of the most significant parts of its program— those dealing with the ownership of the means of production —signified in conjunction with its policies during the war and especially during the political crisis in October, 1918, the repudiation of the cardinal points of its own program by the SPD.

The change in the character of the SPD became most obvious in regard to the policies adopted by the party towards the treaty of Versailles. The 'revolution from above', the abdication, and the actual revolution had been conceived largely as a means to advert the consequences of the German defeat, and the republic emerging from the revolution could hardly be dedicated to a different objective. Regardless of the merits of individual clauses of the peace settlement or its own traditional views on many of the points, the SPD and the republic, within the limits imposed upon Germany by her military disabilities, strove, by every means available, to escape the consequences of the defeat and to evade the conditions imposed by the treaty of Versailles. There is no way to decide whether the vehemence of the SPD in this campaign or its dishonesty, whether its intransigence or its opportunism, whether its pretense or its demagogic-chauvinistic character deserved most attention.

With the functions of the republic thus defined, with the victorious party of the revolution thus dedicated, there was left little hope that democracy might take firm root, and that the success of the republic would not be measured by its citizens solely by its ability to break the fetters of Versailles. That any other purpose of the republic might take a firm hold on public opinion lacked in fact all necessary prerequisites, and the SPD refrained from providing them.

Rejecting its distinctive qualities at the very moment of its political success, the SPD was left with a rudimentary program identical in all essentials with the programs of the old bourgeois parties. The victory of the SPD thus failed to achieve a clear break with the economic, social and foreign aspirations of the German Empire and its bourgeois supporters.

In consequence, the SPD was unable to provide a third way out of the unhappy alternative between the old powers and the extreme left which faced Germany after 1918. That the party, instead of showing this third way out of the dilemma, rejected the essential points of its traditional program and failed to provide the needed political leadership, signified the failure of the SPD; it prejudiced the subsequent history of the German republic.

APPENDIX

1. Note on the Dolchstoss Theory

The extent to which the Dolchstoss thesis dominated German historiography is surprising indeed. The vast majority of German historians, politicians and actors in the period under discussion accepted it in a more or less qualified form. The classical statement of the thesis was made by Professor Cossmann, the editor of the *Sueddeutsche Monatshefte*, in the April and May, 1924, issues of that publication. Among the contributors to these two numbers, General von Kuhl and Admiral Levetzow were foremost in its endorsement. In order to support the thesis in the face of the conditions which have been discussed previously A. Niemann in *Kaiser und Revolution* and in *Revolution von Oben—Umsturz von Unten* denied that revolutions ever grow out of the prevailing social conditions. E. O. Volkmann in *Der Marxismus und das deutsche Heer im Weltkriege* and in *Revolution ueber Deutschland* recognized many of the faults inherent in the old regime and in annexationism, but he saw in the war a dual struggle against the external enemy and against Marxism which undermined the morale and led to the defeat of the national idea. Needless to say that Maercker, Ludendorff, Hindenburg, Tirpitz, Scheer, Capelle, Michaelis, Hertling, all supported the Dolchstoss thesis. General von Wrisberg, *Der Weg zur Revolution 1914-1918* and in the following two volumes of his memoirs provided a modification of the thesis, to wit: there was no stab in the back but only a slow process of poisoning which ultimately led to defeat. *Cf.* Breithaupt, *op. cit.* General Stein, *Erlebnisse und Betrachtungen aus der Zeit des Weltkrieges*, p. 159, declared that " treason within our country cut the veins of the army." Works of the nature of F. Bley, *Am Grabe des deutschen Volkes* may perhaps be disregarded in a historical study. Colonel W. Nicolai discussed the various counter-measures of the government against the seditious propaganda in his *Nachrichtendienst, Presse und Volksstimmung im Weltkriege*. Dr. Hans Thimme, *Weltkrieg ohne Waffen*, concentrated on the role played by enemy peace propaganda. There was a further modification of the thesis stating that while the armistice offer had not been caused by the Dolchstoss, the Dolchstoss had prevented Germany from resisting the terms imposed at Compiègne after the offer had been made. Prince Max was an adherent of this thesis. Moser in his *Ernsthafte Plaudereien ueber den Weltkrieg*, in *Das militaerisch und politisch Wichtigste vom Weltkriege*, and in *Die obersten Gewalten im Weltkrieg* also argued that the Dolchstoss had not caused the German defeat but had only contributed to the severity of the armistice terms. It is interesting that Ebert contributed to the spread of the thesis by telling the returning soldiers on December 10, 1918, that " no enemy has vanquished you; " Ebert, *Schriften, Aufzeichnungen und Reden*, II, 127-30. For a full discussion of the thesis and the objections to it see, *Der Dolchstossprozess von Muenchen 1925* (published by Birk); Ewald Beckmann, *Der Dolchstossprozess in Muenchen vom 19. Oktober bis 20. November 1925*; and *Ursachen*. . . . Dr. Kurt Muehsam reversed the thesis and held the disillusionment caused by the armistice offer responsible for the panic which forced Germany to accept the armistice terms in 1918; he thought that such a result had been made certain by wartime censorship. Among those who objected to the Dolchstoss thesis, *Die Regierung der Mitte* presented the best statement in its class; its weakness consisted in its neglect of the domestic situation. Georg Gotheim, *Warum verloren wir den Krieg?*; Hermann Kranold, *Deutsche Generale und Admirale in Kriegsfuehrung und Politik*; the anonymous pamphlet *Der " Dolchstoss ". Warum das deutsche Heer zusammenbrach*; Hans Delbrueck, *Ludendorff's Selbstportraet*; and his articles " Lüdendorff " in the *Preussische Jahrbuecher*, CLXXVIII, 83-101, and " Ludendorff und Falkenhayn," *ibid.*, CLXXX, 249-281; Captain Persius, *Die Tirpitz Legende*, confidentially printed in 1918, in *Warum die Flotte versagte*, and in *Der Seekrieg*; and Admiral Galster, *England, deutsche Flotte und der Weltkrieg*, all denied the Dolchstoss thesis more or less decisively. Dr. Menke-Glueckert, *Die November Revolution 1918*, provided a recommendable study presenting a discussion of the causes of the defeat and of the revolution from the point of view of the Democratic camp. The following articles by SPD authors gave the SPD view on the subject: H. Kranold, " Was uns an den Abgrund fuehrte," *Sozialistische Monatshefte*, March 24, 1919, pp. 83-101; H. Schuetzinger, " Die erdolchte Front," *ibid.*, February 14, 1921, pp. 121-25; L. Quessel, " Die militaerische Leistung des deutschen Generalstabs," *ibid.*, February 9, 1920, pp. 88-95; Kranold, " Das deutsche Militaersystem im Weltkrieg," *ibid.*, April 12, 1920, pp. 230-40; and C. Herkeler, "Wie kam es zum Zusammenbruch unserer Marine?", *ibid.*, January 20, 1919, pp. 30-33. *Cf.* B. Guttmann and R. Kirchert, *Bethmann-Tirpitz-Ludendorff*, one of the notable *Flugschriften der Frankfurter Zeitung*; and Herm. Mueller, *Von der Marne bis zur Marne*.

The imposing array of German authors supporting the Dolch- stoss thesis necessitates an appraisal of their arguments and of the role played by social and political conditions in Germany and by USPD propaganda. Many of the authors cited disparaged these conditions and consequently denied that they played a de- cisive role in determining the outcome of the war. But even if these conditions were essentially atypical border-line cases, as alleged by most supporters of the Dolchstoss thesis, it would not necessarily diminish their efficacy. Belief in the prevalence of certain conditions may be quite as consequential as their actual prevalence. Indeed if these conditions were atypical as alleged, the mere failure to remedy them would cause them to be accepted as typical by the German public, and aggravate their consequences. The efficacy of these conditions does not therefore depend solely on a quantitative analysis; all that is needed is to determine whether sufficient attention was paid to them by the German public, and whether the actions of the government were such as to create widespread belief in their prevalence.

Nor is it possible to ignore these conditions or to assert that they would not have played as decisive a role as they did, had it not been for the USPD propaganda campaign. The propaganda campaign of the USPD was not the only campaign waged in Germany at that time. The rival pro-annexationist campaign, which has been discussed previously, was so much superior in every factor under the control of the propagandists that one cannot avoid asking why the annexationist campaign failed and why the comparatively amateurish USPD campaign, waged under the most adverse conditions, was successful. It is not enough to say that annexationism failed because the German people refused to have the war of national defense perverted into a war of conquest; one cannot explain a failure by the failure itself. This relative success of the two propaganda campaigns can be explained only by reference to inherent social factors; the responsibility for these social ills was hence identical with responsibility for the success of the leftist propaganda campaign. Indeed one cannot avoid this conclusion because all the events which marked German history from mid-1918 until the revolution could be fully accounted for without reference to propaganda or sedition.

The ready acceptance of the Dolchstoss theory must be ascribed to war-time censorship and the deception practised in order to preserve the morale of the public and to prevent a reaction against the conditions prejudicial to a German success. Under the pretensions of war-time security needs, censorship was extended to every field of public interest; the submarine campaign, the battle of the Marne, British labor troubles (lest Great Britain learn how to cope with them) and the advertisements of lonely soldiers seeking the acquaintance of girls for the purpose of matrimony were all equally barred from the press. Even high ranking personalities in public life were completely uninformed about the true military situation and about the domestic problems. When the armistice offer was finally made public, disbelief greeted it. How could a nation be so deceived?, how could a government be so incompetent? Few could force themselves to agree with Stresemann that " the system failed even where it ought to have had its main support ... in military technics, ... that we had to allow ourselves to be beaten in technics' by amateurs ... We ... believed that if we accept a small degree of ' unfreedom ', we could rely on being the great teachers of the world in this field ... One must indeed ask if one can still defend a system which failed ... where it should have had its strongest support—in its military-technical capabilities." (*Verhandlungen,* · CCCXIV, 6172 ff., October 22, 1918.) The search for a scapegoat, the concept of the Dolchstoss, was the ultimate result of censorship, making it possible to ignore that the superiority of the allies and the record of the German war-time governments in all fields of policy were quite sufficient to account for the German defeat.

The German story of the origins of the war provided the counterpart of the alibi furnished by the Dolchstoss theory for the failure of Germany's war effort. The old regime could be defended only if the internal disintegration of Germany during the war years was not due to inherent weaknesses, and if the war was not due to factors under the control of the German government. The unfavorable position of Germany in the war created—almost as a measure of self defense—the argument that, on August 1, 1914, Germany had been the innocent victim of an unprovoked and unjustified attack, powerless to escape the evil and aggressive intentions of the Entente. Any compromise on this interpretation would settle the old powers with responsibility for having contributed to the doom of Germany from the outset. Hence the truly treasonable character of asserting German war guilt—even in a conditional form—for it indicted the old regime for contributing to the genesis of a war which was beyond its power to successfully terminate. The conventional theory of the Dolchstoss became necessary, because it proved to be impossible to substantiate the claim that Germany could not under any circumstances have averted the war. In addition, the idea of even an excusable failure was incompatible with the admiration and adulation demanded for the Wilhelminian era. There existed a strong correlation between belief that Germany was a victim of a base attack by the Entente and support of the policies of the Supreme Command, and between the rejection of these policies and the rejection of the Dolchstoss theory. The record of the old regime in the first world war could be defended only if the failure was due to sedition, and if Germany did not have any choice about participation in the war because of the evil intentions of the Entente.

2. Note on Antisemitism within the SPD during the Revolutionary Period

After the war, even anti-semitism raised its head within the party in an extremely disquieting way. It was however directed not against German Jewry, but against the Jews from Poland and Russia, who had during the war followed the invitation of the German Government and come to Germany as laborers, or who were fleeing the pogroms following in the wake of the white Russian armies in the Ukraine. Scheidemann, *Memoiren*, I, 418-19, was one of the few who cited the text of Ludendorff's proclamation "Zu die Jidden in Paulen." (sic.) Theodor Mueller,

"Die Einwanderung der Ostjuden," *Neue Zeit*, vol. XXXIX, pt. 2, nos. 13 and 14, June 24, and July 1, 1921, pp. 293-98, and 325-30, wrote: "The Eastern Jews are in their majority a proletarian group, sunk into uncleanliness, poverty, and the lowest level of business morale. . . . They are unable to industrialize themselves, in addition to the fact that in general they are, because of their physical constitution, little fit for industrial and agricultural work. Most of them lack all sense of order and cleanliness; thus their clothes are full of holes and dirt, thus their homes are of incredible dirtiness. . . . For our soldiers, its remembrance will most likely be one of their most disgusting war memories." Yet in spite of their unfitness for work, he concluded that their immigration must stop, because they competed unfairly with organized workers for jobs. During a debate on the decontrol of shoes and leather and their resulting rapid advance in prices, Becker, an SPD member of the National Assembly, made the following remarks: "You can imagine with what desires Polish smugglers across the border looked forward to decontrol. . . . Hardly had it taken place, when they inundated Germany with their masses. The Warschowsky, Auerbach, and Sickmann from Lodz, and the Stachowsky and Alexandrowitsch from Warsaw busy themselves in masses in Breslau and Berlin. With faked or expired passports they come across the borders. . . . Proudly they loaf in their most typical form in the first class compartments of our express trains. . . . This gang really does not deserve to continue to exist in this world, these parasites . . . must be put out of this world." *Verhandlungen*, CCCXXX, 3054-9, October 13, 1919. Indeed even the SPD government joined in these sentiments and acted. On March 27, 1920, there took place a raid on the Jewish quarter of Berlin, motivated ostensibly by the search for smugglers and Bolshevist agents. About one thousand Jews were arrested. Of these, about three hundred were kept all day without food or water, and then transported to a concentration camp (they already existed in 1919) at Wimsdorf, near Zossen, through a jeering and insulting mob, and under the supervision of former Baltic free-corps members, armed with grenades, machine guns, etc. No legal pretext for these arrests was ever offered, yet the death penalty had been decreed for resisting orders, approaching the barbed wire, leaving the barracks after seven p. m., or talking to the guards. Wrote

Maximilian Harden in an article " Die Sturmglocke ruft," in *Die Zukunft*, vol. CIX, April 17, 1920, pp. 31-58: " Fifteen hours before, these people had been taken from their apartments, their beds, their synagogues, stores; stood till six p. m.; truck; train; not a bite, not a drop; fear, terror, threats of death; torturing imagination of the orthodox not to be able to observe the religious duties on the approaching Passover.... Into the barracks. No chair or stool, no straw or blanket." There was a complete lack of sanitary facilities, of heat, light, and of hospitals for the sick. There were the now familiar insults of drunken officers, shootings, intimidations, and thefts. On the day after their arrest, food was distributed for the first time: seven hundred grams of bread, and some soup. Except for the fact that this action ended with the release of all arrested persons, it differed little from more recent acts of this nature in Germany. There was no action taken against any of those responsible, but there was an attempt to keep it out of the press. Maximilian Harden was one of the very few who protested against conditions like these. It is interesting that Dr. Friedrich Thimme, who was readily accepted in SPD circles, and whom Carl Legien, the trade-union leader, chose as co-editor of the previously cited *Die Arbeitsgemeinschaft im neuen Deutschland*, should write in regard to Harden: " The German people has a triple duty to reject this leper. German people ... you cannot sink so deep as to suffer any community with this Judas-Ischarioth; German people, do your duty !"; Thimme, *Maximilian Harden am Pranger*, Berlin, 1919. Even Fr. W. Foerster, in *Mein Kampf gegen das militaristische und nationalistische Deutschland*, Stuttgart, 1920, p. 35, could write about the " very special world-historical marriage of the Jewish soul with money." True to their general opposition to official party policies, the *Sozialistische Monatshefte* attacked the SPD campaign against the Eastern Jews and the above mentioned raid on the Jews of Berlin. See Ernst Hamburger, "Antisemitismus und Sozialdemokratie" in *Sozialistische Monatshefte*, May 17, 1920, pp. 393-401.

3. SPD Votes Cast in the Elections to the Reichstag 1871 – 1920

Year	SPD votes	Percent of total	Mandates
1871	113,048	2.91	2
1874	350,861	6.76	10
1877	493,258	9.13	12
1878	437,158	7.59	9
1881	311,961	6.12	13
1884	549,990	9.71	25
1887	763,128	10.12	11
1890	1,427,298	19.75	36
1893	1,780,989	23.21	48
1898	2,113,073	27.23	56
1903	3,010,472	24.0	81
1907	3,259,020	24.4	43
1912	4,250,329	34.7	110
1919	11,509,048	37.9	165
1920	5,614,456	21.6	113

SPD Membership 1906 – 1921

March 31	Members
1906	384,327
1907	530,446
1908	587,336
1909	633,309
1910	720,038
1911	836,562
1912	970,112
1913	982,850
1914	1,085,905
1915	515,898
1916	432,618
1917	243,061
1918	249,411
1919	1,012,299
1920	1,180,208
1921	1,221,059

BIBLIOGRAPHY

I

NEWSPAPERS AND PERIODICALS

a. BIBLIOGRAPHIES OF THE GERMAN PRESS

Bibliographie der deutschen Zeitschriftenliteratur, F. Dietrich, Leipzig, 1896–
Mueller, *Zeitschriften und Zeitungsadressbuch*, C. F. Mueller, Leipzig, 1909–

b. NEWSPAPERS AND PERIODICALS

Acht Uhr Abendblatt, 1918-1919.
Berliner Lokalanzeiger, 1918-1919.
Berliner Tageblatt, 1916-1919.
Deutsche Allgemeine Zeitung, 1918-1919.
Frankfurter Zeitung, 1915-1921.
Die Freiheit, 1918-1919. (USPD)
Der Kampf, 1907-1921. (SPD)
Die Neue Zeit, 1883-1922. (SPD, USPD 1915-1917)
Preussische Jahrbuecher, 1918-1920.
Die Rote Fahne, 1918-1919. (KPD)
Sozialistische Monatshefte, 1897-1922. (SPD)
Sueddeutsche Monatshefte, 1918-1924.
Taegliche Rundschau, 1918-1919.
Vossische Zeitung, 1916-1919.
Die Welt am Montag, 1918-1919.
Der Vorwaerts, 1883-1922. (SPD, USPD 1914-1917.)
Die Zukunft, 1920.

II

PROCEEDINGS

Allgemeiner Deutscher Arbeiterverein, *Protokoll der Generalversammlung.*
   With minor variations in the title, this series was published annually
   from 1863 until 1874, except for 1866 and 1867, when two congresses
   had met.
Die ersten deutschen Sozialistenkongresse, 1863-1875, Frankfurter Volks-
   stimme, Franfurt a. M., 1906.
Kommunistische Partei Deutschlands, *Bericht ueber den...Parteitag der
   Kommunistischen Partei Deutschlands (Spartakus-Bund)*. This series
   covers the founding congress of the KPD in 1918, the congress in 1919,
   the three congresses meeting in 1920 and the joint meeting of the KPD
   and the left-wing USPD in 1920.
Kommunistische Partei Deutschlands, *Bericht ueber die Verhandlungen des
   ...Parteitags der Kommunistischen Partei Deutschlands (Sektion der
   Kommunistischen Internationale)*. The first volume of this series rep-

resents the last item of the previous series listed. KPD congresses met irregularly from 1921 onward.

R. Leinert, ed., *Allgemeiner Kongress der Arbeiter und Soldatenraete, 16. bis 24. Dezember 1918. Stenographische Berichte*, Berlin, 1919.

W. Schroeder, ed., *Handbuch der sozialdemokratischen Parteitage 1863-1909*, Birk, Munich, 1910.

Sozialdemokratische Partei Deutschlands, *Protokoll ueber die Verhandlungen des Parteitags der Sozialdemokratischen Partei Deutschlands*, Vorwaerts Verlag, Berlin. With minor variations in the title, these proceedings were published for the following years: 1875, 1876, 1877, 1880, 1883, 1887, annually from 1890 until 1913, 1916, 1917, 1919, 1920, 1921, 1922, and from 1924 onward. The meeting of 1916, however, had the status of a conference and not of a congress.

Sozialdemokratische Partei Deutschlands (Eisenach group), *Protokoll ueber den...Kongress der Sozialdemokratischen Arbeiterpartei*. With minor variations in the title, this series was published annually from 1869 until 1874, with two congresses covered in 1870.

Unabhaengige Sozialdemokratische Partei Deutschlands, *Protokoll ueber die Verhandlungen des...Parteitags*. With minor variations in the title, this series was published to cover the founding congress in 1917, the two congresses in 1919, the two congresses in 1920, and the last congress of the party in 1922. The series was published by Freiheit, Berlin, except for the volume covering the congress of 1917, which was published by A. Seehof, Berlin, 1921.

Verfassungsgebende Preussische Landesversammlung, *Sitzungsberichte der Verfassungsgebenden Preussischen Landesversammlung 1919-1921*, 12 vols., and *Sammlung der Drucksachen der Verfassungsgebenden Preussischen Landesversammlung*, 15 vols., Preussische Verlagsanstalt, Berlin, 1920-21.

Verhandlungen des Deutschen Reichstags. This series includes both the stenographic reports and the collection of documents. Vols. I-XVIII cover the period of the Norddeutscher Bund, vols. XIX-CCCXXV cover the Imperial Reichstag, vols. CCCXXVI-CCCXLIII cover the National Assembly at Weimar, and vol. CCCXLIV onward cover the German republic.

III

Collections of Documents

K. Ahnert, *Die Entwicklung der deutschen Revolution und das Kriegsende in der Zeit vom 1. Oktober bis 30. November 1918 in Leitartikeln, Extrablaettern, Telegrammen, Aufrufen und Verordnungen nach den fuehrenden deutschen Zeitungen*, Burgverlag, Nuremberg, 1918.

E. Buchner, *Revolutionsdokumente. Die deutsche Revolution in der Darstellung der zeitgenoessischen Presse*, 6 vols., Deutsche Verlagsgesellschaft fuer Politik und Geschichte, vol. I, Berlin, 1921.

E. Drahn und S. Leonhard, *Unterirdische Literatur im revolutionaeren Deutschland waehrend des Weltkrieges*, Verlag Gesellschaft und Erziehung, Berlin, 1920.

The Foreign Relations of the United States, 1919. The Paris Peace Conference, 13 vols., Edited by the Department of State, GPO, Washington, D. C., 1942-47.

J. Hohlfeld, ed., *Deutsche Reichsgeschichte in Dokumenten*, 2 vols., Deutsche Verlagsgesellschaft fuer Politik und Geschichte, Berlin, 1927.

H. Marx, *Handbuch der deutschen Revolution*, A. Groebel, Berlin, vol. I, 1919.

Materalien betreffend die Friedensverhandlungen. Im Auftrage des Auswaertigen Amtes, Deutsche Verlagsgesellschaft fuer Politik und Geschichte, Berlin, 1920.

Materalien betreffend die Waffenstillstandsverhandlungen. Im Auftrage der Waffenstillstandskommission, Deutsche Verlagsgesellschaft fuer Politik und Geschichte, Berlin, 1920.

E. Meyer, *Spartakus im Kriege*, Vereinigung Internationaler Verlagsanstalten, Berlin, 1927.

Protocols and Correspondence between the Supreme Council and the Conference of Ambassadors and the German Government and the German Peace Delegation between January 10, 1920, and July 17, 1920, respecting the Execution of the Treaty of Versailles of June 28, 1919, CMD 1325, HMSO, London, 1921.

F. Salomon, *Die deutschen Parteiprogramme*, 3 vols., G. B. Teubner, Leipzig, vols. I and II, 1912, vol. III, 1922.

Vorgeschichte des Waffenstillstandes. Amtliche Urkunden herausgegeben im Auftrage des Reichsministeriums des Innern, Hobbing, Berlin, 1919.

Der Waffenstillstand 1918-1919. Das Dokumentenmaterial der Waffenstillstandsverhandlungen von Compiègne, Spa, Trier und Bruessel, 3 vols., Deutsche Verlagsgesellschaft fuer Politik und Geschichte, Berlin, 1928.

IV

OTHER PRIMARY SOURCES

A., *Friedrich der Vorlaeufige*, Taegliche Rundschau, Berlin, 1920.

Emil Barth, *Aus der Werkstatt der Revolution*, Hoffmann, Berlin, 1919.

A. Bebel, *Aus meinem Leben*, 3 vols., Dietz, Stuttgart, 1910-14.

——, *Die parlamentarische Taetigkeit des deutschen Reichstags und der Landtage und die Sozialdemokratie*. This series covers the period of 1871 until 1893. Allgemeine deutsche Associations—Buchhandlung, Leipzig, 1876-1893.

E. Beckmann, *Der Dolchstossprozess in Muenchen vom 19. Oktober bis 20. November 1925*, Verlag der Sueddeutschen Monatshefte, Munich, 1925.

Bericht: den Abgeordneten des Feldheeres auf der Tagung aller A.-und S. Raete am 16. Dezember 1918 ueberreicht vom Vollzugsausschuss des

Soldatenrates bei der obersten Heeresleitung, Wilhelmshoehe bei Kassel, December 12, 1918.

E. Bernstein, *Aus den Jahren meines Exils,* 2 vols., Reiss, Berlin, 1918.

——, *Die heutige Sozialdemokratie in Theorie und Praxis,* Munich, 1906.

——, *Der Revisionismus in der Sozialdemokratie,* M. G. Cohen, Amsterdam, 1909.

——, *Sozialdemokratische Voelkerpolitik,* Grubel, Leipzig, 1917.

——, *Voelkerrecht und Voelkerpolitik,* Cassirer, Berlin, 1919.

——, *Die Voraussetzungen des Sozialismus und die Aufgaben der Sozialdemokratie,* Dietz, Stuttgart, 1899.

E. Bernstein, ed., *Der Briefwechsel zwischen Friedrich Engels und Karl Marx,* 4 vols., Dietz, Stuttgart, 1921.

——, *F. Lassalles Reden und Schriften,* 3 vols., Vorwaerts, Berlin, n. d.

Th. von Bethmann-Hollweg, *Betrachtungen zum Weltkriege,* 2 vols., Hobbing, Berlin, 1919-21.

Wilhelm Blos, *Von der Monarchie zum Volksstaat,* 2 vols., Stuttgart, 1922-23.

Karl Buecher, *Die Sozialisierung,* Laupp, Tuebingen, 1919.

E. David, *Die Sozialdemokratie im Weltkrieg,* Vorwaerts, Berlin, 1915.

Klemens von Delbrueck, *Die wirtschaftliche Mobilmachung in Deutschland 1914,* Muenchen, 1924.

Denkschrift den Vertreter der Soldatenraete des Feldheeres am 1. Dezember 1918 in Bad Ems ueberreicht vom Soldatenrat der Obersten Heeresleitung, Wilhelmshoehe bei Kassel, November 28, 1918.

Der Dolchstossprozess in Muenchen, Birk, Munich, 1925.

E. Drahn and E. Friedegg, eds., *Deutscher Revolutionsalmanach 1919,* Hoffmann and Campe, Hamburg and Berlin, 1919.

F. Ebert, *Schriften, Aufzeichnungen, Reden,* 2 vols., Reissner, Berlin, 1926.

E. Eichhorn, *Eichhorn ueber die Januarereignisse. Meine Taetigkeit im Berliner Polizeipraesidium und mein Anteil an den Januar Ereignissen,* Freiheit, Berlin, 1919.

K. Eisner, *Gesammelte Schriften,* 2 vols., Cassirer, Berlin, 1919.

P. Eltzbacher, ed., *Die deutsche Volksernaehrung und der englische Aushungerungsplan,* Braunschweig, 1914.

M. Erzberger, *Erlebnisse im Weltkriege,* Deutsche Verlagsanstalt, Stuttgart, 1920.

E. von Falkenhayn, *Die Oberste Heeresleitung 1914-1916,* E. S. Mittler, Berlin, 1920.

A. Fischer, *Die Revolutionskommandantur Berlin,* Berlin, 1922.

Further Reports by British Officers on the Economic Conditions Prevailing in Germany, CMD 261, HMSO, London, 1919.

W. Goeth, ed., *Deutschland und der Friede,* Teubner, Leipzig, 1918.

E. J. Gumbel, ed., *Denkschrift des Reichsjustizministers zu "Vier Jahre Politischer Mord",* Malik Verlag, Berlin, 1924.

J. Gumpertz, ed., *Karl Liebknecht; Reden und Aufsaetze,* Verlag der kommunistischen Internationale, Hamburg, 1921.

K. Haenisch, *Die deutsche Sozialdemokratie in und nach dem Weltkrieg,* C. A. Schwetschke, Berlin, 1919, 2nd edition.

von Hausen, *Erinnerungen an den Marnefeldzug 1914*, K. F. Koehler, Leipzig, 1920.

C. Haussmann, *Schlaglichter*, Frankfurter Societaetsdruckerei, Frankfurt a. M., 1924.

C. Haussmann, ed, *Geheimbericht Nummer 7 vom Februar 1917*, Deutsche Verlagsgesellschaft fuer Politik und Geschichte, Berlin, 1921.

E. Heilfron, ed., *Die deutsche National—Versammlung im Jahre 1919-1920 in ihrer Arbeit*, 9 vols., Norddeutsche Buchdruckerei, Berlin, 1919-20.

W. Heine, *Zu Deutschlands Erneuerung*, E. Diederich, Jena, 1916.

K. Helfferich, *Der Weltkrieg*, 3 vols., Ullstein, Berlin, 1919.

G. von Hertling, *Erinnerungen aus meinem Leben*, 3 vols., J. Kresel, Kempten-Muenchen, 1919.

K. von Hertling, *Ein Jahr in der Reichskanzlei*, Herder, Freiburg, 1919.

J. Jastrow, *Im Kriegszustande*, G. Reimer, Berlin, 1915, 2nd edition.

K. Juenger, ed., *Vom kommenden Weltfrieden*, Montanus Vérlag, Siegen, 1918.

K. Kautsky, *Bernstein und das sozialdemokratische Programm*, Stuttgart, 1899 (no publisher, probably Dietz.)

——, *Das Erfurter Programm*, Dietz, Stuttgart, 1892.

——, *Ethik und materialistische Geschichtsauffassung*, Dietz, Stuttgart, 1906.

——, *Sozialdemokratische Bemerkungen zur Uebergangswirtschaft*, Leipziger Buchdruckerei, Leipzig, 1918.

K. Kautsky und B. Schoenlank, *Grundsaetze und Forderungen der Sozialdemokratie*, (no publisher), Berlin, 1899.

O. Killian, ed., *Der weisse Schrecken in Mitteldeutschland. Die Wahrheit ueber die Maerzkaempfe. Stenographische Berichte ueber die Verhandlungen des Untersuchungsausschusses des Preussischen Landstages 27. und 28. Oktober 1921*, Kommunistische Partei Deutschlands, Halle-Merseburg (1922?).

R. Kittel, *Leipziger Akademische Reden zum Kriegsende*, A. Lorentz, Leipzig, 1919.

Kommunistische Partei Deutschlands, Zentrale der, *Die Enthuellungen zu den Maerzkaempfen*, Produktiv-Genossenschaft Halle-Merseburg, 1922.

H. von Kuhl, *Der Marnefeldzug 1914*, E. S. Mittler, Berlin, 1921.

G. Ledebour, *Der Ledebour Prozess*, Freiheit, Berlin, 1919.

P. Lensch, *Die deutsche Sozialdemokratie und der Weltkrieg*, Vorwaerts, Berlin, 1915, 2nd edit.

——, *Drei Jahre Weltrevolution*, S. Fischer, Berlin, 1918.

L. Maercker, *Vom Kaiserheer zur Reichswehr*, Koehler, Leipzig, 1921.

Prinz Max von Baden, *Erinnerungen und Dokumente*, Deutsche Verlagsanstalt, Stuttgart, 1921.

——, *Die moralische Offensive*, Deutsche Verlagsanstalt, Stuttgart, 1921.

F. Mehring, ed., *Politische Aufsaetze und Reden von J. B. von Schweitzer*, Vorwaerts, Berlin, 1912.

G. Michaelis, *Fuer Volk und Staat*, Furche Verlag, Berlin, 1922.

K. Muehsam, *Wie wir belogen wurden*, A. Langen, Munich, 1918.

R. Mueller, *Der Buergerkrieg in Deutschland*, Phoebus, Berlin, 1925.

——, *Vom Kaiserreich zur Republik*, 2 vols., Malik Verlag, Vienna, 1924-25.

W. Nicolai, *Geheime Maechte*, Koehler, Leipzig, 1924.

——, *Nachrichtendienst, Presse und Volksstimmung im Weltkrieg*, E. S. Mittler, Berlin, 1920.

A. Niemann, *Kaiser und Revolution*, Scherl, Berlin, 1922.

G. Noske, *Von Kiel bis Kapp*, Verlag fuer Politik und Wirtschaft, Berlin, 1920.

F. Payer, *Von Bethmann-Hollweg bis Ebert*, Frankfurter Societaetsdrukkerei, Frankfurt a.M., 1923.

R. Poincaré, *Messages, lettres et discours de M. R. Poincaré, 1914-1918*, Bloud, Paris, 1919.

L. Popp unter Mitarbeit von K. Artelt, *Ursprung und Entwicklung der November Revolution 1918*, A. Hoffmann, Berlin, 1918.

F. Purlitz, ed., *Deutscher Geschichtskalender*, F. Meiner, Leipzig.

L. Quessel, *Der moderne Sozialismus*, Ullstein, Berlin, 1919.

W. Rathenau, *Kritik der dreifachen Revolution*, Fischer, Berlin, 1919.

von Reuter, *Scapa Flow*, Koehler, Leipzig, 1921.

Ph. Scheidemann, *Memoiren eines Sozialdemokraten*, 2 vols., Reissner, Dresden, 1928.

——, *Der Zusammenbruch*, Verlag fuer Sozialwissenschaft, Berlin, 1921.

M. Schippel, ed., *Berliner Arbeiterbibliothek*, 3 vols., Vorwaerts, vols. I and II, 1894, vol. III, 1891.

Sozialdemokratische Partei Deutschlands, Vorstand der, *Handbuch fuer sozialdemokratische Waehler*, Vorwaerts, Berlin, published irregularly. This series covers the activities of the party and of the German Reichstag from 1893 onward.

The Starving of Germany. Papers read at the Extraordinary Meeting of United Medical Societies held at Headquarters of the Berlin Medical Society, December 18th, 1918, L. Schumacher, Berlin, 1919.

von Stein, *Erlebnisse und Betrachtungen aus der Zeit des Weltkrieges*, Koehler, Leipzig, 1919.

Fr. Thimme and K. Legiens, eds., *Die Arbeitsgemeinschaft im neuen Deutschland*, S. Hirzel, Leipzig, 1915.

E. Troeltsch, *Spektator Briefe. Aufsaetze ueber die deutsche Revolution und die Weltpolitik 1918-1922*, Tuebingen, 1924.

Graf Westarp, *Konservative Politik im letzten Jahrzehnt des Kaiserreiches*, 2 vols., Deutsche Verlagsanstalt, Berlin, 1935.

R. Wissell, *Praktische Wirtschaftspolitik*, Verlag Gesellschaft und Erziehung, Berlin, 1919.

Th. Wolff, *Vollendete Tatsachen, 1914-1917*, Kronen Verlag, Berlin, 1918.

E. von Wrisberg, *Erinnerungen aus dem Kgl. Preussischen Kriegsministerium*, 3 vols., Koehler, Leipzig, 1921-22.

Zentrale fuer Heimatdienst, *Der Geist der neuen Volksgemeinschaft*, S. Fischer, Berlin, 1920.

V

PAMPHLETS

Allgemeine Arbeitspflicht, Vorwaerts, Flugschriften zur Revolution, Berlin (1918?).

An alle Lehrer und Lehrerinnen, (No author, no publisher, no date.)

A.- und S. Raete. Was sie koennen und was sie nicht koennen, Vorwaerts, Berlin (December, 1918?).

W. Bacmeister, *Der U. Boot Krieg als Weg zum Endziel*, Duncker, Weimar, 1917.

Oberst Bauer, *Der 13. Maerz 1920*, (no publisher, no date).

A. Bebel, *Gewerkschafts-Bewegung und politische Parteien*, Dietz, Stuttgart, 1900.

——, *Nicht stehendes Heer sondern Volkswehr!*, Dietz, Stuttgart, 1898.

——, *Unsere Ziele*, Leipzig, 1874.

A. Bebel und G. von Vollmar, *Die Frage der Taktik*, Birk, Munich (1903?).

H. G. von Beerfelde, *Michel wach auf*, Neues Vaterland, Berlin, 1919.

F. Behrens, *Was der deutsche Arbeiter vom Frieden erwartet*, Rippel, Hagen, 1917.

E. Bernstein, *Die Wahrheit ueber die Einkreisung*, Neues Vaterland, Berlin, 1919.

Beschwerden gegen die Zentral—Einkaufs—Gesellschaft in Berlin, Hammerverlag, Leipzig, 1916.

S. M. Bouton, *Chiefly Concerning Garet Garret*, privately printed, Berlin, 1923.

H. Class, *Zum deutschen Kriegsziel*, J. F. Lehmann, Munich, 1917.

Committee on Public Information, *The German-Bolshevist Conspiracy*, Washington, D. C., 1918.

H. Cunow, *Parteizusammenbruch? Ein offenes Wort zum inneren Parteistreit*, Vorwaerts, Berlin, 1915.

E. Daeumig, *Der erste Akt der deutschen Revolution!*, Neumann, Berlin, 1918.

Der Dolchstoss; Warum das deutsche Heer zusammenbrach, Zentralverlag, Berlin, 1920.

Ritter von Eberlein, ed., *Schwarze am Rhein; Ein Weltproblem*, Schroeder, Heidelberg, 1921.

Farbige Franzosen am Rhein. Ein Notschrei deutscher Frauen, Engelmann, Berlin, 1920, 2nd edit.

A. Feiler, *Der Ruf nach den Raeten*, Flugschriften der Frankfurter Zeitung, Frankfurt a.M., 1919.

——, *Der Staat des sozialen Rechtes*, Flugschriften der Frankfurter Zeitung, Frankfurt a.M., 1919.

——, *Vor der Uebergangswirtschaft*, Flugschriften der Frankfurter Zeitung, Frankfurt a.M., 1918.

W. Foerster, *Hans Delbrueck—Ein Portraetmaler?*, Mittler, Berlin, 1922.

Gedeih oder Verderb? Ein Wort an Deutschlands Totengraeber, by a 'social democrat', printed by H. Doormayer, Berlin (1918?).

Der Geiselmord in Muenchen, Hochschul Verlag, Munich, 1919.

Generalstreik und sozialdemokratische Arbeit, Vorwaerts, Berlin, 1919.

Die gesetzliche Verankerung der Arbeiterraete, Vorwaerts, Berlin, 1919.

J. Giesberts, *Neudeutscher Parlamentarismus*, Arbeitsgemeinschaft fuer staatsbuergerliche und wirtschaftliche Bildung, Berlin, 1918.

G. Gotheim, *Warum verloren wir den Krieg?*, Deutsche Verlagsanstalt, Berlin, 1919.

Die Greueltaten der Franzosen in Dortmund am 9. & 10. Juni. (No author, no publisher, no date, no place.) (1923?)

B. Guttmann und R. Kircher, *Bethmann-Tirpitz-Ludendorff*, Flugschriften der Frankfurter Zeitung, Frankfurt a.M., 1919.

R. Henn, *Betrachtungen und Rueckschluesse zur Unterzeichnung des Friedens*, 1919.

E. Kahn, *Zwischen Waffenstillstand und Frieden*, Flugschriften der Frankfurter Zeitung, Frankfurt a.M., 1919.

W. Kapp, *Die Maindenkschrift aus dem Jahre 1916*, 'Das groessere Deutschland,' Dresden, 1917.

K. Kautsky, *Soziale Revolution und Am Tage der sozialen Revolution*, Berlin, 1907.

J. Keller, *Franzoesische Menschlichkeit!*, Kiepenheuer, Weimar, 1916.

H. Kranold, *Deutsche Generale und Admirale in Kriegsfuehrung und Kriegspolitik*, Bremer Volkszeitung, Bremen, 1924.

Kriegspresseamt, *Das Kriegsziel der Entente. Dargestellt auf Grund der Veroeffentlichungen der russischen Geheimdiplomatie*, Berlin, 1918.

——, *Vortrag von Major Hosse im Generalstab, Oktober, 1917; Das Eingreifen der Vereinigten Staaten in den Weltkrieg und seine Bedeutung fuer die militaerische Lage*, Berlin, 1917.

——, *Wirkungen der Kriegsziele unserer Gegner auf die Arbeitsloehne in Deutschland*, Berlin (1916?).

——, *Wirkungen und Aussichten des Ubootkrieges. Vortrag gehalten im Auftrage des Chefs des Admiralstabs der Marine*, Berlin (1917?).

——, *Zum Jahrestag unseres Friedensangebots*, Berlin, 1917.

H. Lauffenberg, *Zwischen der ersten und der zweiten Revolution*, Willaschek (C. Hoyen), Hamburg, 1919.

K. Liebknecht, R. Luxemburg and F. Mehring, *The Crisis in the German Social Democracy*, Socialist Publication Society, New York, 1918.

W. Liebknecht, *Die politische Stellung der Sozialdemokratischen Partei*, London, 1889.

——, *Was die Sozialdemokraten sind und was sie wollen*, Chemnitz, 1874.

E. von Mach, *The Horror on the Rhine*, Steuben Society, New York, 1921.

R. Mueller, *Was die Arbeiterraete sind und was sie sollen*, 'Der Arbeiterrat', Berlin, 1919.

Die Muenchener Tragoedie. Entstehung, Verlauf und Zusammenbruch der Raete Republik Muenchen, Freiheit, Berlin, 1919.

O. Neurath und W. Schumann, *Koennen wir heute sozialisieren?*, Klinkhardt, Leipzig, 1919.

Nichts getan? Die Arbeit seit dem 9. Nov. 1918, Arbeitsgemeinschaft fuer staatsbuergerliche und wirtschaftliche Bildung, Berlin, (February-March 1919?).

F. Oels, *An meine lieben Deutsche: Allen Heervolk und Heimligen im deutschen Heimbereich: Ein Sendschreiben Lutheri wider Peter Peterlein*, Diesdorf (1917?).

H. Oncken, E. Meyer, E. Brandenburg, H. Ueberberger, K. Rathgen, und R. Stammler, *Die Macht—und Wirtschaftsziele der Deutschland feindlichen Staaten*, Heymann, Berlin, 1918.

Ostdeutscher Heimatdienst, *Ostpreussen wacht auf!* (1919?).

Reichsverband Ostschutz, *Die Polnische Schmach. Was wuerde der Verlust der Ostprovinzen fuer Deutschland bedeuten*, Berlin, 1919.

A. Penck, *Wie wir im Kriege leben*, Engelhorn, Stuttgart, 1916.

E. Pistor, *Die entscheidende Wirkung des Uboot Krieges*, Unabhaengiger Ausschuss fuer einen deutschen Frieden, Berlin, 1918.

Pressestelle Ruhr—Rhein, *So sieht es in der Ruhr aus*, Bielefeld (1923?).

K. Radek, *In den Reihen der Revolution 1909-1919*, Wolff, Munich, 1921.

Die Regierung der Mitte. Ihre Taten und Aufgaben, Zentralverlag, Berlin. (1920? Probably a government publication prior to the election.)

F. Runkel, *Werberede auf der 1st. Vollversammlung der gross-Berliner Einwohnerwehren im Zirkus Busch am 15. Juni 1919.*

Ph. Scheidemann, *Die deutsche Sozialdemokratie und der Weltkrieg*, Breslauer Volkswacht, Breslau, 1916.

——, *Es lebe der Frieden!*, Vorwaerts, Berlin, 1916.

Schiffer, *Von der Nationalversammlung zum Reichstag*, Demokratischer Verlag, Berlin, 1920.

H. Schuetzinger, *Zusammenbruch*, Oldenburg, Leipzig, 1919.

Dr. Silbergleit, *Are the Eastern Provinces of Germany indisputably Polish territories?*, Statistisches Amt, Berlin, 1919.

Soll Deutschland ein Tollhaus werden?, Vorwaerts, Berlin (1918?).

Sozialdemokratische Partei Deutschlands, *Die Augen auf* (1918?).

——, Vorstand der, *Die deutsche Sozialdemokratie im Krieg und Frieden*, 2 vols., Confidentially printed, Berlin, 1916-17.

——, Vorstand der, *Deutschland als freie Volksrepublik*, November, 1918.

——, Vorstand der, *Sozialdemokratie und nationale Verteidigung*, Vorwaerts, Berlin, 1916.

Sozialismus ist Arbeit, Ein Aufruf der Regierung (1918?).

Sozialismus und Bolschewismus in Stimmen der fuehrenden Maenner, Printed by S. H. Hermann, Berlin (1919?).

F. Stampfer, *Sozialdemokratie und Kriegskredite*, Vorwaerts, Berlin, 1915.

G. Stresemann, *Michel horch, der Seewind pfeift ... !*, Kalkoff, Berlin, 1917.

F. Thimme, *Maximilian Harden am Pranger*, Neue Woche, Berlin, 1919.

Die Tragoedie von Spaa. Des Kaisers Enthronung nach autentischen Berichten des Generalfeldmarschalls von Hindenburg, Generaloberst von Plessen, Staatssekretaer von Hintze, General Freiherr von Marschall und General Graf von Schulenberg in der Deutschen Zeitung vom 27. Juli 1919, K. Rohm, Lorch, Wuerttemberg, 1919.

Unabhaengige Sozialistische Partei Deutschlands, Bezirksverband Berlin, *Was hat die National-Versammlung geleistet?* (1920?).

Up ewich ungedelt!, Arbeitsgemeinschaft fuer staatsbuergerliche und wirtschaftliche Bildung, Berlin (1919?).

G. von Vollmar, *Die innerpolitischen Zustaende des deutschen Reiches und die Sozialdemokratie*, Munich (1903?).

——, *Lehren und Folgen der letzten Reichstagswahlen*, Munich, 1903.

——, *Die Sozialpolitik in Deutschland und Frankreich*, Dresden, 1901.

W. E. Walling, ed., *The German Socialists. Do they stand for a democratic Peace?*, (No publisher, no place.) March, 1918.

Was ist in Deutschland geschehen? Eine Uebersicht ueber die Rev. Ereignisse. Von der Reichszentrale fuer Kriegs — und Zivilgefangene den heimkehrenden Kriegsgefangenen, (1919?).

Willkommen, Daheim!, Printed by W. Buexenstein (1919? no author or editor).

R. Wissell, *Sollen wir zugrunde gehen?*, (probably January-February, 1919).

Der Zusammenbruch der Kriegspolitik und die Novemberrevolution, Freiheit, Berlin, 1919.

VI

SECONDARY WORKS

F. Aereboe, *Der Einfluss des Krieges auf die landwirtschaftliche Produktion in Deutschland*, Deutsche Verlagsanstalt, Stuttgart, 1927.

G. Adler, *Die Geschichte der ersten sozialpolitischen Arbeiterbewegung in Deutschland*, Trewendt, Breslau, 1885.

Ch. Andler, *La décomposition politique du socialisme allemand, 1914-1918*, Bossard, Paris, 1919.

S. L. Bane and R. H. Lutz, *The Blockade of Germany after the Armistice 1918-1919*, Stanford University Press, 1942.

M. Baumont, *The Fall of the Kaiser*, London, 1931.

R. Berger, *Fraktionsspaltung und Parteikrise in der deutschen Sozialdemokratie*, Volksverein Verlag, M. Gladbach, 1916.

L. Bergstraesser, *Geschichte der politischen Parteien in Deutschland*, Bensheimer, Berlin, 1924.

E. Bernstein, *Die Arbeiterbewegung*, Ruettgen und Loening, Frankfurt, 1910.

——, *Die deutsche Revolution*, Verlag fuer Gesellschaft und Erziehung, Berlin, 1921.

——, *Von der Sekte zur Partei*, Diederich, Jena, 1911.

E. Bevan, *German Social Democracy during the War*, Allen and Unwin, London, 1918.

F. Bley, *Am Grabe des deutschen Volkes. Zur Vorgeschichte der Revolution*, Scherl, Berlin, 1919.

H. Blum, *Die Luegen unserer Sozialdemokratie*, Wismar, 1891.

Th. Brauer, *Der moderne deutsche Sozialismus*, Herder, Freiburg, 1929.

W. Breithaupt, *Volksvergiftung 1914-1918*, Koehler, Berlin, 1925.

R. Brunhuber, *Die heutige Sozialdemokratie*, Fischer, Jena, 1906.

F. Bumm, ed., *Deutschlands Gesundheitsverhaeltnisse unter dem Einfluss des Weltkrieges*, 2 vols., Deutsche Verlagsanstalt, Stuttgart, 1928.

R. Calwer, *Das sozialdemokratische Programm*, Diederich, Jena, 1914.

R. T. Clark, *The Fall of the German Republic*, Allen and Unwin, London, 1935.

J. F. Coar, *The Old and the New Germany*, Knopf, New York, 1924.

H. Cunow, *Allgemeine Wirtschaftsgeschichte*, 4 vols., Dietz, Stuttgart, 1926-31.

——, *Die Marxsche Geschichts—Gesellschafts—und Staatstheorie*, 2 vols., Vorwaerts, Berlin, 1921.

H. G. Daniels, *The Rise of the German Republic*, Scribner, New York, 1928.

H. Delbrueck, *Ludendorffs Selbstportraet*, Verlag fuer Politik und Wirtschaft, Berlin, 1922.

E. Direnberger, *Die Beziehungen zwischen Oberster Heeresleitung und Reichsleitung von 1914-1918*, Junker und Dimmhaupt, Berlin, 1936.

W. Dittmann, *Die Marinejustizmorde von 1917 und die Admiralitaets-Rebellion von 1918*, Dietz, Berlin, 1926.

E. Drahn, *Fuehrer durch das Schrifttum des deutschen Sozialismus*, 2nd edit., 1920.

R. Einhacker, ed., *Hass: Antwort deutscher Dichter auf Versailles*, Universal Verlag, Munich, 1921.

K. Erdmann, *Der Missbrauch der Revolution*, Der Firn, Berlin, 1919.

B. S. Fay, *The Origins of the World War*, Macmillan, New York, one volume edition, 1943.

R. Fester, *Die politischen Kaempfe um den Frieden (1916-1918) und das Deutschtum*, Lehmann, Munich, 1938.

J. Fischart (pseudonym for E. Dombrowski), *Das Alte und das Neue System*, 4 vols., Oesterheld, Berlin, 1918-25.

Marschall Foch, *Zur Steuer der Wahrheit*, Helmrich, Berlin, 1919.

Fr. W. Foerster, *Mein Kampf gegen das militaristische und nationalistische Deutschland*, Verlag "Friede durch Recht", Stuttgart, 1921.

W. Foerster, *Graf Schlieffen und der Weltkrieg*, Mittler, Berlin, 1921.

A. Franke, *Nach Eden oder Golgotha*, Der Firn, Berlin, 1919.

A. Freymuth, *Das Fechenbach Urteil*, Verlag der Neuen Gesellschaft, Berlin.

K. Galster, *England, deutsche Flotte und der Weltkrieg*, Scheible, Kiel, 1925.

O. Goebel, *Deutsche Rohstoffwirtschaft im Weltkriege*, Deutsche Verlagsanstalt, Stuttgart, 1930.

B. Goldenberg, *Beitraege zur Soziologie der deutschen Vorkriegssozialdemokratie*, Berlin, n. d.

J. P. Gooch, *Germany*, Scribner, New York, 1925.

Gradnauer and Schmidt, *Die deutsche Volkswirtschaft*, Berlin, 1921.

R. Grelling (published anonymously) *I Accuse*, G. H. Doran, New York, 1915.

——, (published anonymously) *Das Verbrechen*, 3 vols., Payot, Lausanne, 1917-18.

S. Grumbach, *Das annexionistische Deutschland*, Payot, Lausanne, 1917.

E. Guenther, *Die revisionistische Bewegung in der deutschen Sozial-demokratie*, Duncker and Humblot, Leipzig, 1905.

C. W. Guillebaud, *The Works Council. A German Experiment in Industrial Democracy*, Cambridge, 1928.

E. J. Gumbel, *Verschwoerer*, Malik Verlag, Vienna, 1924.

——, *Vier Jahre politischer Mord*. Verlag der Neuen Gesellschaft, Berlin, 5th ed., 1925.

S. W. Halperin, *Germany Tried Democracy*, Crowell, New York, 1946.

K. Heinig, *Hohenzollern; Wilhelm II und sein Haus. Der Kampf um den Kronbesitz*, Verlag fuer Sozialwissenschaft, Berlin, 1921.

H. Heller, *Sozialismus und Nation*, Rowohlt, Berlin, 1931, 2nd ed.

K. Hesse, *Das Marnedrama des 15. Juli 1918*, Mittler, Berlin, 1920.

M. Hobohm and P. Rohrbach, *Die Alldeutschen*, Engelmann, Berlin, 1919.

J. Hohlfeld, *Der Kampf um den Frieden 1914-19*, Bibliographisches In-stitut, Leipzig, 1919.

C. Horkenbach, *Das deutsche Reich von 1918 bis heute*, 4 vols., Verlag Presse, Wirtschaft, und Politik, Berlin, 1930.

O. Hué, *Die Sozialisierung der deutschen Kohlenwirtschaft*, Berlin, 1921.

L. Kantorowicz, *Die sozialdemokratische Presse Deutschlands*, Tuebingen, 1922.

H. Koenig, *Das neue Deutschland und der borussische Sozialismus*, Baedecker, Essen, 1924.

E. G. Kolbenheyer, *Wem bleibt der Sieg?*, Kloeres, Tuebingen, 1919.

F. Lentz, *Staat und Marxismus. Die deutsche Sozialdemokratie*, 2 vols., Berlin, 1922-24.

H. Lichtenberger, *Relations between Germany and France*, Carnegie En-dowment for International Peace, Washington, D. C., 1923.

E. Loeb, *Wirtschaftliche Vorgaenge, Erfahrungen und Lehren im Europae-ischen Krieg*, 2 vols., Fischer, Jena, 1918-19.

W. Lotz, *Die deutsche Staatsfinanzwirtschaft in Kriege*, Deutsche Verlags-anstalt, Stuttgart, 1927.

R. H. Lutz, *The German Revolution, 1918-1919*, Stanford University Press, 1922.

S. Marck, *Reformismus und Radikalismus in der deutschen Sozial-demokratie*, Berlin, 1927.

F. Mehring, *Die Geschichte der deutschen Sozialdemokratie*, 4 vols., Dietz, Stuttgart, 1919.

——, *Zur Geschichte der deutschen Sozialdemokratie*, Faber, Madgeburg, 1877.

E. Mencke-Glueckert, *Die Novemberrevolution 1918*, Klinkhardt, Leipzig, 1919.

A. Mendelsohn-Bartholdy, *The War and German Society*, Carnegie En-dowment for International Peace, New Haven, 1938.

O. von Moser, *Ernsthafte Plaudereien ueber den Weltkrieg*, Belser, Stutt-gart, 1925.

——, *Das militaerisch und politisch Wichtigste vom Weltkrieg*, Belser, Stuttgart, 1926.

——, *Die obersten Gewalten im Weltkrieg*, Belser, Stuttgart, 1931.

R. B. Mowat, *A History of European Diplomacy*, Arnold, London, 1927.

H. Mueller (Brandenburg), *Von der Marne bis zur Marne*, Verlag fuer Sozialwissenschaft, Berlin, 1919.

H. Mueller (Franken), *Die November Revolution*, 'Der Buecherkreis', Berlin, 1931.

O. Nanck, *Der Militarismus Deutschlands und der Entente*, Spamer, Leipzig, 1918.

F. L. Neumann, *Behemoth*, Oxford University Press, New York, 1942.

A. Neumann-Hofer, *Die Entwicklung der Sozialdemokratie bei den Wahlen zum deutschen Reichstag*, Skopnik, Berlin, 1898.

A. Niemann, *Revolution von Oben — Umsturz von · Unten*, Verlag fuer Kulturpolitik, Berlin, 1928.

L. R. O'Boyle, *The Ideology of the German Social Democrats during the first World War*, doctoral dissertation, Harvard, 1948.

L. Persius, *Der Seekrieg*, Die Weltbuehne, Berlin, 1919.

——, *Die Tirpitz Legende*, secretly printed, Berlin, 1918.

——, *Warum die Flotte versagte*, Oldenburg, Leipzig, 1925.

J. Plenge, *Die Revolutionierung der Revolutionaere*, Der Neue Geist, Leipzig, 1918.

H. Pol, *The Hidden Enemy*, Meissner, New York, 1943.

E. Prager, *Geschichte der U. S. P. D.*, Freiheit, Berlin, 1922.

H. Preuss, *Das deutsche Volk und die Politik*, Diederich, Jena, 1919.

H. Quigley and R. T. Clark, *Republican Germany*, Dodd, Mead and Co., New York, 1928.

H. Ritter (published anonymously), *Kritik am Weltkrieg*, Koehler, Leipzig, 2nd ed., 1921.

W. Roemer, *Die Entwicklung des Raetegedankens in Deutschland*, Berlin, 1921.

H. O. von Rohr, *Der Einfluss der deutschen Laender auf die Gestaltung der Reichsverfassung von 1919*, Goettingen, 1931.

A. Rosenberg, *The Birth of the German Republic*, Morrow, New York, 1931.

——, *A History of the German Republic*, Methuen, London, 1936.

R. Rotheit, *Kernworte des Weltkrieges*, Ullstein, Berlin, 1916.

H. R. Rudin, *Armistice 1918*, Yale University Press, 1944.

F. Runkel, *Die deutsche Revolution*, Grunow, Leipzig, 1919.

C. Schoen, *Der Vorwaerts und die Kriegserklaerung*, Buexenstein, Berlin, 1926.

A. Skalweit, *Die deutsche Kriegsernaehrungswirtschaft*, Deutsche Verlagsanstalt, Stuttgart, 1927.

E. Stadler, *Die Weltkriegsrevolution*, Koehler, Leipzig, 1926.

J. Stammhammer, *Bibliographie des Sozialismus und Kommunismus*, 3 vols., Jena, 1900-09.

H. Stroebel, *The German Revolution and After*, Jarrolds, London, n. d.

O. von Stuelpnagel, *Die Wahrheit ueber die deutschen Kriegsverbrecher*, Staatspolitischer Verlag, Berlin, 1921.

H. Thimme, *Weltkrieg ohne Waffen*, Cotta, Stuttgart, 1932.

P. Umbreit and O. Lorenz, *Der Krieg und die Arbeitsverhaeltnisse*, Deutsche Verlagsanstalt, Stuttgart, 1928.

Ch. Vidil, *Les mutineries de la marine allemande 1917-1919*, Payot, Paris, 1931.

E. O. Volkmann, *Der Marxismus und das deutsche Heer im Weltkriege*, Hobbing, Berlin, 1925.

——, *Revolution ueber Deutschland*, Stalling, Oldenburg, 1930.

A. Weber, *In Defense of Capitalism*, Allen, London, 1930.

P. Weidmann, *Die Programme der Sozialdemokratischen Partei Deutschlands von Gotha bis Goerlitz*, Kellinghusen, Hay, 1926.

Das Werk des Untersuchungsausschusses der verfassungsgebenden Deutschen Nationalversammlung und des Deutschen Reichstags 1919-1930. (Vierte Reihe.) Die Ursachen des deutschen Zusammenbruches im Jahre 1918. (Zweite Abteilung.) Der Innere Zusammenbruch, 12 vols., Deutsche Verlagsgesellschaft fuer Politik und Geschichte, Berlin.

S. Zurlinden, *Der Weltkrieg*, 4 vols., Orell Fuessli, Zuerich, 1917 ff.

INDEX

In addition to KPD, SPD and USPD, the following abbreviations will be used in the index:

G.	German
imp.	imperial
min.	minister
MNA.	Member of the National Assembly
MR.	Member of the Reichstag
PrGv.	Provisional Government
ScSt.	secretary of state

SPD, 136 f., 156; USPD interpretation of, 156 f.
National-Liberal Party, 55, 122, 152, 175, 196
Naval Mutinies, of 1917, 117 f., 162 ff., 188; of 1918, 167 f., 187 ff., 206, 336; causes of, 187 ff.
Near East, 80
Neue Zeit, 56 f., 60, 146 f., 216, 292 f., 319
Niemann, A., German officer and historian, 193 f., 341
Norddeutsche Allgemeine Zeitung, 210
Norddeutscher Bund, 18
Norddeutscher Reichstag, 24, 33
Noske, Gustav, SPD MR., MNA., editor, assumed command in Kiel after outbreak of 1918 mutinies, member of PrGv., min. of defense 1919-20, 72, 107, 116, 121, 123, 164, 168, 198, 200, 210, 214 f., 217, 221, 246 f., 251, 256, 288, 292, 298 f.; on armistice terms, 293; assumes military command, 243 ff.; during Kiel mutinies, 187, 190 f.

O

Occupied territories, by Germany during the war, 104, 106 ff., 130, 150, 152, 197, 286, 290
Oldenburg-Januschau, Count E. von, conservative MR., 93
Officers' Corps, 100 ff., 228 ff., 245 f., 299, 337
Oldenburg, 246
'Open Door', 81, 123
Ottoman Empire, 80 f., 123, 155

P

Pan-Germanism, 72, 82, 85, 97, 110 f., 117 f., 120 f., 124, 126 ff., 163
Pannekoek, Anton, Dutch astronomer and socialist, served with the SPD 1906-14, 89
Papal Peace Endeavors, 133, 151, 174
Paris Commune, 1871, 39
Parvus (Alexander Helphand), Russian writer and revolutionary, influential in the SPD, 64, 66
Payer, Friedrich von, Democratic politician, vice-chancellor 1917-18, MR., 174 f., 177, 195, 197
Peace Conference 1919 at Paris, 290, 293 ff., 298
Peace Resolution of July, 1917, 111, 117, 129, 132 f., 150 f., 175, 197
'Peace without annexations', 99, 122, 129, 132, 135, 164

Persius, Captain Ludwig, G. naval officer and writer, 188
Peus, Heinrich, SPD MR., writer and editor, 62f.
Poincaré, Raymond, French statesman, 74, 84
Poland, 104, 107, 120, 124, 137, 138, 151, 156, 290 ff., 295, 298, 308 ff., 345 f.; Polish councils, 290; Polish trade-unions in Germany, 278
Politische Briefe, 143, 157
Popp, Lothar, G. sailor, leading revolutionary agitator, 164
Posen, 179, 290 f, 332
Preuss, Hugo, Democratic politician, MR., MNA., min. of interior 1919-20, author of G. draft constitution, 223
Preussen der Welt voran, 159
Progressive Party, 122, 175, 196
Progroms, 345
Proportional Representation, 44, 114, 117, 119, 209, 226
Prostitution, 307
Protective custody, 104, 109, 158, 161
Provisional Government, 219, 234 f., 248, 275, 279, 291, 295, 338; breakup of SPD-USPD coalition, 241; formation of, 222 ff., and the Executive Council, 224 f., 231 ff.; program of, 226, 230
Prussia, 18 f., 24 f., 33, 102, 108, 112, 115, 292, 304; electoral reform, 70, 114 ff., 159, 161 f., 174, 183, 196 f., 209; war with Austria, 25
Prussian diet, 70, 112, 115 f., 117 f.

Q

Quessel, Ludwig, SPD writer on staff of *Sozialistische Monatshefte*, 315

R

Radbruch, Professor Gustav, G. jurist, SPD MR., repeatedly min., 254 f.
Radek, Karl, Communist politician, organizer of KPD, 89, 143, 205
Radloff, L., SPD writer, 78
Reichslande, see Alsace-Lorraine
Rathenau, Walter, G. industrialist, Democratic politician, MR., MNA., foreign min. 1922, 178
Reichs-Kohlenrat, 276
Reichstag, 31 f., 33, 49, 52, 62 f., 65, 70, 74 f., 79, 92, 96 ff., 100, 103, 105, 109 f., 114 ff., 117, 121, 123, 127, 131 ff., 139, 143 ff., 151 ff., 154, 157, 163 f., 174 ff., 179, 185, 196 f., 219 f., 257, 331

of the revolution, 256 f.; assumes popular leadership during
abdication crisis, 185 f., 204 f.;
causes of the success of its propaganda, 159 f., 166 f., 204; coalition
with the SPD, 213 f.; and the
council system, 218 ff., 236 ff.; criticism of G. war-time policies,
148 ff.; defense of its policies as
patriotic, 154 f.; early opposition
to SPD policies, 138 ff., 333; formation of the party, 146 f.; genesis
of the 'group of twenty', 143 ff.;
its leadership in war-time strikes,
160 ff.; and mutinies of 1917,
162 ff.; and mutinies of 1918, 189,
191; opposition to war credits,
154; pamphlets issued by USPD,
139-43, 157 ff.; propaganda campaign, 157 ff., 343 f.; purposes of
the revolution, 217 ff.; resignation
from PrGv., 241, 242, 248; revolutionary preparations, 162 f., 165 f.;
role in January 1919 riots, 243 f.;
role played in revolution, 166 ff.,
211, 214, 343 ff.; and socialization,
265 ff.; strength of party during
the war, 147; and the treaty of
Versailles, 295, 300, 314 f.; and
its war aims, 155 ff.
United States of America, 68, 96,
115, 125, 131, 315 f.
University of Berlin, 297
University of Frankfurt, 305
Unterschriften Flugblatt, 141
Die Ursachen des Weltkrieges, 159

V

Vandervelde, Emile, Belgian social-
ist, repeatedly min. after 1914, 84
Vaterlandspartei, 127 ff.
Vatican, 254
Verband der deutschen Arbeiter-
vereine, 27 f.
Versailles, treaty of, 254, 277, 282,
289, 291, 296 ff., 308 ff., 310 ff.,
314 f., 317 f., 325, 327, 339
Vogtherr, E., USPD member of
PrGv., 223
Volkmann, E. O., G. historian,
Reichsarchivar, 102, 125, 341
Volksgerichte, 253 f.
Volksmarinedivision, 237 f.; riots
of, 239 ff.
Vollmar, Georg von, Bavarian SPD
leader, 50, 52, 56, 146
Der Vorbote, 146
Vorwaerts, 70, 144, 147, 203, 205 f.,
211, 213, 287; pamphlets opposing
political strikes, 242 ff.

Vossische Zeitung, 73

W

Walz, Oberleutnant, 225
War criminals, 153, 299 f., 305, 307
Wels, Otto, Chairman of SPD, MR.,
MNA., 199, 207 f., 214, 237 ff., 241,
311, 315
Die Welt speit Blut, 159 f.
Wendel, SPD MR., 105
*Weniger Brot, keine Rechte, neue
Steuern*, 159
Wer hat die Schuld am Kriege?, 159
Westarp, Kuno Count von, con-
servative MR., 105, 152 ff., 197
William I, G. Emperor, 39
William II, G. Emperor, 40, 70, 74,
110, 116 f., 128, 176 f., 179, 183 ff.,
189, 191 ff., 202 f., 207 f., 334 f.
'Willy-Nicky' correspondence, 115
Wilson, Woodrow, President of US.,
175, 179 ff., 181, 183 f., 192, 197,
202 f., 207, 285 f., 288, 291, 294,
313, 315, 334 f
Winnig, August, SPD writer, 78,
304
Wissell, Rudolf, SPD MR., MNA.,
min. of economy 1919, 248, 265 f.,
270, 276 ff., 284, 304; his economic
program, 280 ff., 338
World War I, referred to as the
War in this monograph, 65 f.,
armistice offer, 173 ff; outbreak
of, 69 f., 312, 344 f.; SPD views
on its causes, 72, 80 ff.; SPD war
aims, 120 ff.
Wrisberg, Colonel E. von, ScSt. in
min. of war, 103, 341
Wuerttemberg, 53, 139, 232
Wupper-Rhine district, 17
Wurm, Emanuel, USPD member
of PrGv., 223

Y

'Young-Ones', 40 ff., 46, 49, 55, 58

Z

Zabern' Affair, 70, 104
Zepler, Wally, SPD writer on staff
of *Sozialistische Monatshefte*, 284,
315, 317, 321 f., 332
Zietz, Luise, USPD MNA., MR.,
307
Zimmermann Note, 115
Zimmermann, W., SPD writer, 78
Zollverein, 17
Zur Deutschlands Erneuerung, 127
*Der Zusammenbruch des Imperia-
lismus und die Aufgabe der inter-
nationalen Arbeiterklasse*, 205